Horace H. Moore

A Classified Catalogue of the Mercantile Library of San Francisco

Horace H. Moore

A Classified Catalogue of the Mercantile Library of San Francisco

ISBN/EAN: 9783337177928

Printed in Europe, USA, Canada, Australia, Japan

Cover: Foto ©Andreas Hilbeck / pixelio.de

More available books at **www.hansebooks.com**

A

CLASSIFIED CATALOGUE

OF THE

MERCANTILE LIBRARY

OF

SAN FRANCISCO;

WITH AN

INDEX OF AUTHORS AND SUBJECTS;

CONSISTING OF

ABOUT FOURTEEN THOUSAND VOLUMES.

MADE BY THE LIBRARIAN,
JANUARY, 1861.

SAN FRANCISCO:
PUBLISHED BY THE ASSOCIATION.
1861.

PREFACE.

EITHER of the names, Index, or List, rather than Catalogue, would perhaps have been a more correct title for this work; for, although the names and authors of all the books in the Library are given, the sizes, places of publication, and dates, are in most cases omitted.

The list of Novels is a duplicate one, the first of which is arranged by the names of authors, and the second by the running titles of the works; while in all the other classes, books of a two-fold character, or those of which the classification is doubtful, are included in each of the departments to which they may appertain.

A Table of Contents is placed at the beginning, and an Index arranged alphabetically by the names of authors, and including the titles of anonymous works, will be found at the end.

Although classifying and indexing a library, while it is being continually borrowed from, is a work requiring much care and labor, the compiler of this might receive more credit from some than would be justly due to him, by omitting to acknowledge his indebtedness for the use of the first Catalogue of the Library, made by Mr. Horace Davis, in 1854; the accuracy and good judgment displayed in the classification of which, was of material assistance in the compilation of this.

For its prompt publication, after its completion, the Association is under obligations to Mr. WM. H. STEVENS, their President; Mr. J. W. J. PIERSON, of the Printing Committee, and to the other members of the Board of Directors of 1860, for their zealous and active exertions to that end.

HORACE H. MOORE,

Librarian.

SAN FRANCISCO, January 21st, 1861.

REGULATIONS OF THE LIBRARY.

[NOTE. — For convenience in returning and taking out Books, each member is requested to apply for a Card of the number of the folio assigned to him in the Register.]

THE Library shall be open every day throughout the year, from nine o'clock, A. M., to ten o'clock, P. M., excepting Sundays, the Fourth of July, Thanksgiving Day, Christmas, and New Year.

A member may receive, applying personally, or by his WRITTEN ORDER, one volume, if it be a folio or quarto, and two, if an octavo or duodecimo, or volume of less size.

Every member may detain each book or set delivered as aforesaid, if it be a folio or quarto, four weeks; an octavo, three weeks; or a book or set of less size, two weeks : except new publications, which, until they have been in the Library two months, shall not be detained, an octavo longer than two weeks, and books of less size one week, and which shall not be renewed. No book shall be reserved by the Librarian for any director or member.

Any member who shall detain a book or set longer than the time above limited, respectively, shall forfeit and pay to the Librarian for every day a volume is so detained, if it be a folio, twenty cents ; a quarto, fifteen cents ; an octavo, ten cents ; if it be a duodecimo, or smaller volume, or pamphlet, five cents.

If any member lose or injure a book, he shall make the same good to the Librarian ; and if the book lost or injured be one of a set, he shall pay to the Librarian, for the use of the Association, the full value of said set, and may thereupon receive the remaining volumes as his property.

No member shall be permitted to receive a book from the Library until he shall have paid all sums due from him to the Association, and made good all damages and losses which he may have occasioned.

Books of Reference, and such others as may from time to time be specially designated by the Board, shall not be taken from the Library, except by special permission of a member of the Board of Directors ; provided, however, that Newspapers, Encyclopædias, Cyclopædias, Dictionaries, and Atlases, shall in no case be taken from the Library Rooms.

Any member wishing to withdraw from the Association, must inform the Librarian of it, see that his resignation is registered, and pay up his dues and fees, else he will be considered as continuing a member, and charged accordingly, unless otherwise ordered by the Board of Directors.

REGULATIONS OF THE READING-ROOM.

SECTION 1. The Reading Room shall be open every day throughout the year, from eight o'clock, A. M., to eleven o'clock, P. M.

SEC. 2. No member shall assume the liberty of arranging the books of the Library, or periodicals on the tables, or of performing any of the duties that devolve upon the Librarian.

SEC. 3. None but members shall be allowed the privilege of the Reading Room, unless introduced by a member of the Association.

SEC. 4. Any member may have the privilege of introducing a friend not a resident of the city, whose name shall be registered by the Librarian in a book kept for that purpose, and who shall receive a ticket of admission to the Reading Room for the term of four weeks.

SEC. 5. No member shall be allowed the privilege of the Reading Room, unless all dues and forfeitures incurred are liquidated.

SEC. 6. No member shall. be allowed to remove papers from the files, or books, plates, or periodicals, from the Reading Room.

SEC. 7. Any member who shall mutilate the periodicals or papers placed on the files or tables in the Reading Room, or remove them therefrom, shall be liable to fine and expulsion.

SEC. 8. Should a member transgress any article in these Regulations, he shall be reported to the Board of Directors, who may take such measures thereon as they may deem expedient.

SEC. 9. The Regulations of the Library and Reading Room shall not be altered, amended, or suspended, unless by the votes of seven members of the Board of Directors present at a stated meeting, notice being given for that purpose.

TABULAR STATISTICS,

Showing the progress of the Mercantile Library Association, from its organization in January, 1853, to January, 1861.

FINANCES.

Year			Expenditures	
1853.	Receipts	$10,858 50	Expenditures	$10,726 51
1854.	do.	13,387 30	do.	11,838 02
1855.	do.	9,015 85	do.	8,747 96
1856.	do.	10,300 00	do.	8,989 27
1857.	do.	11,777 87	do.	12,474 73
1858.	do.	12,089 15	do.	11,704 09
1859.	do.	16,854 82	do.	19,045 16
1860.	do.	16,513 00	do.	16,470 00

GROWTH OF THE LIBRARY.

1853.	Number of Volumes at commencement of the year,				 1,500
1854.	do.	do.	do.	do.	 2,705
1855.	do.	do.	do.	do.	···· 3,315
1856.	do.	do.	do.	do.	 3,833
1857.	do.	do.	do.	do.	 6,135
1858.	do.	do.	do.	do.	 8,447
1859.	do.	do.	do.	do.	10,066
1860.	do.	do.	do.	do.	11,485
1861.	do.	do.	do.	do.	13,821

INCREASE OF MEMBERS.

1854.	Number of Members at commencement of the year				 392
1855.	do.	do.	do.	do.	 552
1856.	do.	do.	do.	do.	 550
1857.	do.	do.	do.	do.	 1,250
1858.	do.	do.	do.	do.	 1,176
1859.	do.	do.	do.	do.	 1,319
1860.	do.	do.	do.	do.	 1,817
1861.	do.	do.	do.	do.	 1,694

OPERATIONS OF THE LIBRARY.

1854.	Number of Volumes taken out,		3,371
1855.	do.	do.	8,367
1856.	do.	do.	10,466
1857.	do.	do.	17,528
1858.	do.	do.	17,321
1859.	do.	do.	21,903
1860.	do.	do.	25,757

The terms of Membership in the Association are, for a Subscribing Member, an initiation fee of $2, and quarterly dues of $3, payable in advance. Shares of $25 subject to the same assessments as Subscribing Memberships. Life Memberships, $100, without further assessments.

LIST OF OFFICERS OF THE ASSOCIATION.

FOR 1860-61.

WM. H. STEVENS, ...President.
WM. R. GARRISON, ...Vice President.
J. G. KELLOGG, ...Treasurer.
EDW. HUNT, ...Recording Secretary.
R. B. SWAIN, ...Corresponding   "
CHAS. WOLCOTT BROOKS,
FRANK BAKER,
D. P. BELKNAP,
WILLIAM NORRIS,
JAMES W. J. PIERSON,   } ... Directors.
JOHN SHAW,
H. C. MACY,
CHARLES R. BOND,
THOMAS BENNETT, M.D.
H. H. MOORE, ...Librarian.
D. E. WEBB, } Librarian's Assistants.
J. J. TAYKER, }

FOR 1861-2.

JAMES W. WHITE, ...President.
THOMAS J. LAMB, ...Vice President.
BENJAMIN SMITH, ...Treasurer.
E. H. JACQUELIN, ...Recording Secretary.
WALTER MARTINEAU, Corresponding   "
MAJ. H. LEONARD, U.S.A.
A. L. EDWARDS,
JOHN S. DAVIES,
J. P. NOURSE,
R. C. ROGERS,   } ......Directors.
J. LAWRENCE POOL,
J. M. STROBRIDGE,
J. C. JOHNSON,   •
J. M. McNULTY, M.D.,
H. H. MOORE, ...Librarian.
D. E. WEBB, } Librarian's Assistants.
J. J. TAYKER, }

SYNOPSIS

OF THE

CLASSES COMPOSING THE ANALYTICAL CATALOGUE.

CLASS I.

Page

PART I.—NOVELS AND ROMANCES, BY AUTHORS,.................................... 1
PART II.—NOVELS AND ROMANCES, BY TITLES,............................ 14

CLASS II.

RELIGION,.. 26

CLASS III.

JURISPRUDENCE AND GOVERNMENT,.. 31
 SECTION I.—Law of Nations, Treaties, and Diplomacy,........................... 31
  " II.—Statute Law,.. 31
  " III.—Common, Chancery and Miscellaneous Law, State Trials, etc. 31
  " IV.—Government and Politics,.. 33
  " V.—Political Economy, Finance, Money and Commerce,............ 34

CLASS IV.

PHILOSOPHY, SCIENCE, AND THE ARTS,.. 36
 SECTION I.—*Philosophy*, ... 36
   1. Metaphysics,.. 36
   2. Moral, Social, and Ethical,... 36
   3. Logic and Oratory,.. 37
   4. General and Miscellaneous Works,................................. 37
  " II.—*Sciences and the Arts*,... 38
   1. Mathematics, ... 38
   2. Physics,... 38
    (A) Astronomy,.. 38
    (B) Mechanics,... 38
    (C) Chemistry, Electricity, Galvanism and Mechanism, 39
    (D) General and Miscellaneous Works,..................... 40
   3. Natural History,... 40
    (A) Geology, Mineralogy, Metallurgy and Mining...... 40
    (B) Botany, Agriculture and Horticulture,.............. 41
    (c) Zoology, ... 42
    (D) Anthropology and Ethnology,.......................... 43
    (E) Miscellaneous Works,.. 44
   4. Medicine, Physiology, Phrenology and Physiognomy,... 45
   5. Fine Arts, Sports and Amusements,................................. 45
   6. Useful Arts, Architecture, Manufacturing, and Civil
    Engineering, ... 47
   7. Cookery and Domestic Economy,.................................. 48
   8. Military and Naval Works,.. 49
   9. Alchemy, Magic, etc.,... 49

CLASS V.

VOYAGES, TRAVELS, AND PERSONAL ADVENTURES,........:................. 50
Section I.—In America,.......... 50
"   II.—Europe, the Levant, and Egypt,..................................... 54
"   III.—Asia, Africa, Australia, and Oceanica,............................... 57
"   IV.—Voyages around the World,. Miscellaneous Collections, and
Personal Narratives,................................... 59
"   V.—Geographical and Topographical Works, Atlases, Guide
Books, and Statistics,... 61

CLASS VI.

HISTORY,........ 63
Section I.—European History,... 63
"   II.—Asiatic History,.. 66
"   III.—African History,................... 67
"   IV.—American History,.. 67
"   V.—Special History, ... 71
"   VI.—General History and Chronology,..................................... 72
"   VII.—Biography,.. 73

CLASS VII.

MISCELLANEOUS,.. 87
Section I.—Ancient Literature, Antiquities, and Mythology,.................. 87
"   II.—Poetry,... 89
"   III.—Drama,.. 92
"   IV.—Education, and Elementary Works,..................................... 92
"   V.—Philology, Technology and Names,..................................... 93
"   VI.—Heraldry and Genealogy, ... 93
"   VII.—Numismatics,.. 94
"   VIII.—Dresses and Costumes,... 94
"   IX.—Free Masonry,... 94
"   X.—Criticism, Essays, and Letters,.. 94

CLASS VIII.

MISCELLANEOUS WORKS OF AUTHORS, COLLECTED INTO VOLUMES
AND SETS,... 99
Section I.—Works,... 99
"   II.—Orations and Speeches,............................ 100
"   III.—Proverbs, Epitaphs and Quotations,.....................................100
"   IV.—Wit, Humor, and Anecdotes,..100
"   V.—Mesmerism, Animal Magnetism, and Witchcraft,.................101
"   VI.—Illustrated Books,...101
"   VII.—Encyclopedias, Dictionaries, Concordances, and other Works
of Reference,..102
"   VIII.—Periodicals, Newspapers, and Magazines,..........................104
"   IX.—Government and other Reports,...105
"   X.—Bibliographical Works, and Library and Booksellers' Cata-
logues,... 106

ADDENDA,........ 107
Section I.—Novels and Romances,..107
"   II.—Miscellaneous,..108

INDEX,...109

ANALYTICAL CATALOGUE

OF THE

Mercantile Library of San Francisco.

1861.

CLASS I.

NOVELS AND ROMANCES

PART I.

WORKS ARRANGED BY NAMES OF AUTHORS.

ABOUT, E. Germaine
— ACTRESS in High Life
ADAM Blair and Matthew Wald
ADVENTURES of Sir Frizzle Pumpkin
AGATHONIA ; a Romance. 18mo
AGNES. By Author of Ida May
AGUILAR, Grace. Home Scenes and
   Heart Studies
— Mother's Recompense
— Vale of Cedars ; or, the Martyr
— Woman's Friendship ; a Story of
   Domestic Life
— Home Influence ; a Tale for Moth-
   ers and Daughters
— Days of Bruce ; a Story from
   Scottish History. 2 vols
AINSWORTH, W. H. The Miser's Daugh-
   ter

AINSWORTH, W. H. Rookwood
— The Star Chamber. 2 vols
— Lancashire Witches. 2 vols
ALICE Sherwin ; a Tale. By C. J. M.
ALL's not Gold that Glitters
ALMOST a Heroine
ALONZO and Melissa
ALTON Locke : Tailor and Poet
AMY Lee ; or, Without and Within
ANDERSEN, Hans C. The Sand Hills of
   Jutland
— Story Book
— To be, or not to be
ANDERSON, Florence. Zenaida
ARABIAN Nights' Entertainments. 3 vols
ARABIAN Days' Entertainments
ARBOUVILLE, Countess. Christine Van
   Amburg, etc

1

ARMSTRONG, F. C.   The Young Middy
ARTHUR, T. S.   Twenty Years Ago, and
   Now
— The Hand but not the Heart
— Heart Histories and Life Pictures
— Tales from Real Life, etc
— The Good Time Coming
— What can Woman do ?
,— The Successful Merchant
— Temperance Tales
— The Angel and Demon
— Three Eras in a Woman's Life
— Lizzie Glenn
ARTHUR, King, and the Knights of the
   Round Table.   3 vols
ASPENWOLD
ATHERN, Anne.   Here and Hereafter
AUSTEN, Miss.   Sense and Sensibility
— Pride and Prejudice, and North-
— Emma ; a Novel   [anger Abbey
— Persuasion
— Mansfield Park
— Northanger Abbey
AZEGLIO, M.   The Challenge of Barletta
— Nicolo dei Lapi ; or, Last Days of
   The Florentine Republic

B ACHELOR of the Albany
   BALDWIN, J. G.   Flush Times of
   Alabama
BALLANTYNE, R. M.   The Coral Island
— Ungava
— Snowflakes and Sunbeams
BALLYSHAN Castle
BALZAC, H.   Veronique
— Cesar Birotteau
BANIN, J.   The Smuggler
BARCLAY, John.   Argenis ; or, the Loves
   of Poliarchus and Argenis
BARHAM, Rev. H.   Ingoldsby Legends
BARNES, J.   The Old Inn ; or Travelers'
   Entertainment
BARON Trenck
BASTILE, Chronicles of
BEDE, C.   Adventures of Mr. Verdant
   Green
BEHIND the Scenes in Paris
BELISARIUS ; a Fable
BELL J.   A Man,
BERGER, E.   Charles Auchester
BEN Sylvester's Word
BENNETT.   Clara Moreland
— Wild Scenes on the Frontiers
BERNARD, C.   Gerfaut
— Le Gentilhomme Campagnard. 2
   vols
BIERNATYKI.   The Hallig ; or Sheepfold
   in the Waters
BINDER, W. E.   Viola
— Madelon Hawley
BIRD, Dr. R. M.   Calavar
— Nick of the Woods
BLACK Mantle ; a Romance

BLONDE and Brunette
BOCCACIO, G. Decameron ; or Ten Days'
   Entertainment.   2 vols
BOOK of 1,000 Comical Stories
BORROW, G.   Lavengro
— The Romany Rye
BOURNE, W. O.   Gems from Fable Land
BOWMAN, A.   The Castaway
— The Kangaroo Hunters
BRACKINRIDGE, H.   Modern Chivalry
BRADFORD, A. C.   Nellie Bracken
BRADLEY, Mary E.   Douglas Farm
BRAY, Mrs.   Warleigh
— Trials of the Heart
— Trelawncy of Trelawne
— White Hoods
— Fitz, of Fitz-Ford
— The Protestant
,— The Talba
— Henry de Pomeroy
— Courtenay of Walreddin
— De Foix
BREMER, Frederika.   The Home
— Strife and Peace
— A Diary ; H— Family ; and other
   Tales
— The Neighbors, etc
— The President's Daughters ; and
— Hertha   [Nina
— The Home.   2 vols
— The Neighbors.   2 vols
— The H— Family.   2 vols
— The President's Daughters.   3
   vols
— New Sketches of Every Day Life.
   2 vols
— Strife and Peace.   2 vols
— Brothers and Sisters.   2 vols
— Father and Daughter
BREWSTER, Anne.   Compensation
BRISTED, C. A.   Sword and Gown
— Guy Livingstone
BROCK, Mrs. C.   Home Memories
BRONTE, Miss.   Villette
— Shirley
— The Professor
— Wuthering Heights
-- Jane Eyre
— Tenant of Wildfell Hall
BROOKS, Shirley.   Aspen Court
BROOKE, W.   Eastford
BROOKE, H.   The Fool of Quality. 2 vols
BROTHERS Clerks.   By Xariffa
BROUGH, J. C.   Fairy Tales of Science
BROWN, T. W.   Minnie Hermon
BROWN, C. B.   Arthur Mervin
— Wieland
— Edgar Huntley
— Jane Talbot
BROWN.   The Fudges in England
— The Younger
BRUNTON, Mrs.   Self-Control
— Discipline

BRYANT, J. D.   Pauline Seward
BULFINCH, T.   The Age of Chivalry
BULWER, Sir E.   Devereux
— Pelham
— Night and Morning
— The Caxtons
— My Novel.   2 vols
— Eugene Aram
— Godolphin
— Leila ; and Calderon the Courtier
— Rienzi
— The Disowned
— Zanoni
— Last Days of Pompeii
— Lucretia ;
— Ernest Maltravers
— Alice
— Paul Clifford
— Pilgrims of the Rhine
— Harold
— The Pelham Novels, etc
— What will he do with it ?
BULWER, Lady.   Behind the Scenes
BUNCE, A.   A Bachelor's Story
BURDETT, C.   Margaret Moncrieffe
BURKHARDT, C. B.   Fairy Tales, and
     Legends of many Nations
BURNEY, Miss.   Evelina
— The Secret

CAMPBELL, Major.   The Old Forest
     Ranger
CAMILLE
CARLEN, Emilie.   The Home in the Val-
     ley
— Woman's Life
CARLETON, W.   Traits and Stories of
     the Irish Peasantry.   2 vols
— The Black Baronet
CARLETON, R.   The New Purchase in
     the Far West
— German Romance.   2 vols
CARY, Alice.   Married, not Mated
CASTLE Builders
CATHARA Clyde ; a Novel.   By Inconnu
CERVANTES, S. M.   Don Quixote
— Trabajos de Persiles y Sigismunda
     2 vols
— The Wanderings of Persiles and
     Sigismunda
CHAMIER, Capt.   The Life of a Sailor
— Tom Bowling
CHANDLER, Ellen,   This, That, and the
     Other
CHILD, L. Maria.   Philothea
CHRONICLES of the Bastile
CLARKE, Mrs. M. C.   The Iron Cousin
CLASSIC Tales
CLEMENS, Hon. Jere.   The Rivals ; a
     Tale of Burr and Hamilton
— Mustang Gray
CLERMONT ; or the Undivided House-
     hold

COBDEN, J. C.   The White Slaves of
     England
COCKTON, H.   Valentine Vox
— The Love Match
— The Steward
COGGESHALL, W. T.   Easy Warren
— Home Hits and Hints
COLLINS, W.   The Dead Secret
— After Dark
— Hide and Seek
— The Queen of Hearts
CONSIENCE, H.   Vera ; or the War of
     the Peasants
— The Conscript
— The Curse of the Village ; Being
     Rich ; and Blind Rosa
— The Demon of Gold
— The Miser of Ricketicketack
— The Lion of Flanders
COOKE, J. E.   Henry St. John, Gentle-
     man
COOPER, J. F.   Novels.   33 vols
— Afloat and Ashore
— Bravo ; a Tale
— Chain-bearer ; or the Littlepage
     Manuscripts
— The Crater ; or Vulcan's Peak
— Deer Slayer ; or the First War
     Path.   A Tale
— The Headsman ; or the Abbey des
     Viguerons
— Heidenmauer ; or the Benedictines
— Homeward Bound ; or the Chase
— Home as Found
— Jack Tier ; or the Florida Reef
— The Last of the Mohicans.   A
     Narrative of 1757
— Lionel Lincoln ; or the Leaguer
     of Boston
— Mercedes of Castile ; or the Voyage
     to Cathay
— The Monikins
— Ned Myers ; or Life before the
     Mast
— Notions of the Americans
— Oak Openings ; or the Bee Hunt-
     er
— The Pathfinder
— The Pilot ; a Tale of the Sea
— The Pioneers
— The Prairie ; a Tale
— The Red-Skins ; or, Indians or
     Injins
— Satanstoe
— The Sea Lions ; or the Lost Seal-
     ers
— The Spy ; a Tale of the Neutral
     Ground
— Two Admirals ; a Tale
— The Water Witch ; or the Skim-
     mer of the Seas
— Wept of the Wish-ton-Wish ; a
     Tale

COOPER, J. F. Wing and Wing; or Le
　Feu Follet. A tale
— Wyandotte; or The Hutted Knoll
　A Tale
COQUETTE, The, or Florence de Lacy
CORA and the Doctor
COSTELLO, Miss. Catharine de Medicis
COTTIN, Mad. Elizabeth; or The Exiles
　to Siberia
COUNTERPARTS; or the Cross of Love
COURCILLON, E. Le Curé Manqué
COUSIN Cicily; or Ups and Downs
CRISNA, the Queen of the Danube
CROKER, T. C. Killarny Legends
CROSLAND, Mrs. Lydia. A Woman's
　Book　　　　　[Dessert
CRUIKSHANK, G. Three Courses and a
CRUISE of the Midge
CUMMINGS, Maria. The Lamplighter
— El Furéidés
CUPPLES, G. The Green Hand
CURTIS, Laura J. Christine
— Now-a-Days
CURTIS, G. W. Potiphar Papers
CYRIL Thornton

DACRE, Lady. Tales of the Peerage
　and Peasantry
— Adventures of a Chaperon
DAISY Chain. 2 vols
DASSENS, G. W. Popular Tales from
　the Norse
DAY, T. Sandford and Merton
DAYS of my Life
D'AZEGLIO. Challenge of Barletta
DEFOE, D. Robinson Crusoe
— Captain Singleton and Col. Jack
— Memoirs of a Cavalier, and Me-
　moirs of Captain Cronke
— Moll Flanders, and History of the
　Devil
— Roxana, the Fortunate Mistress,
　and Mother Ross
— The Great Plague and Fire of
　London, Storm of 1703, and
　True Born Englishman
— Life of Duncan Campbell; New
　Voyage; Political Tracts, etc
DEFOREST, J. W. Seacliff
DENISON, Mrs. C. W. Gracie Amber
— Old Hepsey
DEQUINCEY, T. The Avenger, etc
DERBY, G. H. Phœnixiana
DE STAEL, Mme. Corinne, ou L'Italie.
　Translated
DICKENS, Charles [Boz.] Dombey and
　Son　　　　　[Tales
— Old Curiosity Shop, and other
— Oliver Twist
— The same　　　　[Chuzzlewit
— Life and Adventures of Martin
— Life and Adventures of Nicholas
　Nickleby

DICKENS. Personal History of David
　Copperfield
— Posthumous Papers of the Pick-
　wick Club
• — Sketches by Boz, Illustrative of
　Everyday Life
— Barnaby Rudge
— Christmas Stories
— Home Narratives
— Home and Social Philosophy
— The World Here and There
— Bleak House
— Hard Times
— Little Dorrit. 2 vols
— A Tale of Two Cities. 2 vols
— New Stories
— Short Stories
DISRAELI, B. Vivian Gray
— The Young Duke
— Contarini Fleming
— Miriam Alroy
— Henrietta Temple
— Venetia
DOCTOR Oldham at Greystone, and His
　Talk There
DOCTOR Thorne. A novel by Anthony
　Trollope
DOESTICKS. What He Says
— Pluribustah
— History and Record of the Ele-
　phant Club
DOOMED Chief; or Two Hundred Years
　Ago
DORR, Julia C. Lanmere
DRURY, Anna. Misrepresentation
DHU, Helen. Stanhope Burleigh
DUMAS, A. The Count of Monte Cristo
— Edmond Dantes
— The Three Guardsmen
— The Forty-five Guardsmen
— Twenty Years After
— Bragelonne
— The Iron Mask
— The Queen's Necklace
— Isabel of Bavaria
— Adventures of a Marquis
— Emanuel Philibert
— Ingénue
— The Conscript
— The Mohicans of Paris
DUN Browne's Experience in Foreign
　Parts
DUPUY, E. A. The Planter's Daughter
DYNEVOR Terrace. 2 vols

EBONY Idol　　　[from the Past
　ECHOES of a Belle; or A Voice
EDGWORTH, Miss. Novels. 16 vols
EDITH Hall
EDITH; or The Quaker's Daughter
EFFINGHAM, C. The Virginia Come-
　dians. 2 vols

EGAN, P. The Flower of the Flock
ELIZABETH, Charlotte. Siege of Derry
ELLIOTT, S. H. A Look at Home; or Life in the Poor Houses of N. England
ELLIOTT, G. T. The Mill on the Floss
— Adam Bede
— Scenes from Clerical Life
ELLIOTT, W. Carolina Sports
ELLIS, Mrs. Chapters on Wives
— Look to the End; or The Bennets Abroad. 2 vols
— The Mother's Mistake
EMBURY, Mrs. Waldorf Family
EMILIA Wyndham
ERNESTIN; or The Heart's Longing
EROS and Anteros; or The Bachelor's Ward
ESTELLE Grant; or The Lost Wife
EVENINGS at Haddon Hall
EVANS, Augusta J. Beulah
EXPERIENCES of a Gaol Chaplain

FARNHAM, Eliza W. My Early Days
FARRAR, F. W. Eric; or Little by Little
— Julian Home; a Tale of College Life [2 vols
FENELON, F. Telamacus. Translated.
— Telamacus
FERN, Fanny. Rose Clark
— Ruth Hall
— Leaves from Fanny's Portfolio
— Fresn Leaves
— Little Ferns
FEUILLET, C. The Romance of a Poor Young Man
FIELD, Margaret. Bertha Percy; or L'Espérance
FIELD, J. M. Major Thorpe's Scenes in Arkansaw
FIELDING, H. Joseph Andrews
— Tom Jones
— Works
FISHER's River Scenes and Characters
FLETCHER, Mrs. J. C. Rosa, the Parisian Girl
FLORAIN, M. Numa Pompilius
— Gonzalve de Cordove
FORD, Mrs. Gracie Truman
FORESTERS, The
FOUR Books. Chinese Classical Works
FORD, Sallie R. Mary Bunyan
FRANK Fairlegh
FREYTAG, G. Debit and Credit
FRIARSWOOD Post Office
FROST, J. Wild Scenes in a Hunter's Life
FULLERTON, Lady. Ellen Middleton
— Grantley Manor
— The Lady Bird

GASKELL, Mrs. E. Right at Last
— Mary Barton
— Lizzie Leigh
— Ruth
— The Moorland Cottage
— North and South
— Agnes Gray
— My Lady Ludlow
GALT, J. Sir Andrew Wylie of that Ilk
— The Provost, and other Tales
— The Annals of the Parish, and Ayrshire Legatee
— The Entail
— Laurie Todd
GEORGE Melville. An American Novel
GEORGE Mason. The Young Backwoodsman
GERMAN Popular Tales, etc
GERMAN Fairy Tales and Popular Stories
GERSTAECKER, F. Each for Himself
— Wild Sports in the Far West
GILMAN, C. Recollections of a Southern Matron
GIRARDIN, E. Stories of an Old Maid
GLEIG, G. R. The Chelsea Pensioners
— The Country Curate
GLEIZE, J. A. Thalysie. 3 vols
— Selena
GLENWOOD; or the Parish Boy
GIDDINGS, J. R. The Exiles of Florida
GODWIN, W. Fleetwood
— Caleb Williams
GOETHE, J. W. Novels and Tales
— Wilhelm Meister
GOLDEN Legacy
GOLDSMITH, O. Vicar of Wakefield, and Deserted Village
GOODWIN, E. Lily White
GOODRICH, S. G. Peter Parley's Thousand and One Stories
GORE, Mrs. Progress and Prejudice
— Cecil
— The Hamiltons
— Mrs. Armytage
— Mothers and Daughters
— Abednego the Money Lender
GRANT, J. Jane Seton; or the King's Advocate
GRATTAN, T. C. Agnes de Mansfelt
— Jacqueline of Holland
— Legends of the Rhine
— The Heiress of Bruges
GRAYSON, E. Standish the Puritan
GREENHALGH, T. Lancashire Life
GREENWOOD, Grace. A Forest Tragedy and other Tales
GREY, Mrs. The Duke
— The Little Beauty
GRIFFIN, Gerald. Card Drawing
— The Half-Sir
— The Coiner
— The Rival
— Tracy's Ambition

GRIFFIN, Gerald. Duke of Monmouth
— Tales of the Jury Room
— Holland Tide, The Aylmers, The Hand and Word, and Barber of Bantry
GRIMM. Popular Tales, and Household Stories. 2 vols
GRINGO, Harry. Tales of the Marines
GUERRAZZI, F. D. Beatrice Cenci
— Isabella Orsini

HACKLANDER. The Countess of St. Albans
HAI Evn Yockdan. The Self-Taught Philosopher
HALIBURTON, Judge. Sam Slick, the Clock Maker
— Nature and Human Nature
HALL, Mrs. S. C. Midsummer Eve
— The Outlaw   [Trot
HALL, A. O. Old Whitey's Christmas
HALL, Rev. B. R. Frank Freeman's Barber Shop. A Tale
HALL, J. Legends of the West
HAMPDEN, A. Hartley Norman
HARP of a Thousand Strings, etc
HARRY Coverdale's Courtship
HARRY Harson; or The Benevolent Bachelor
HARRY Lee; or Hope for the Poor
HARRY Muir. A Story of Scottish Life
HARTMAN, T. Charity Green
HAU Kiou Choan. From the Chinese, etc. 4 vols
HAVEN, Alice B. The Coopers
— Loss and Gain
HARLAND, Marion. The Hidden Path
— Moss Side
— Alone
— Nemesis
HAWTHORN, N. The Marble Faun. 2 vols
— The Snow Image, and other twice told Tales
— Twice Told Tales. 2 vols
— The Blithedale Romance
— The Scarlet Letter
— House of the Seven Gables
— Mosses from an Old Manse
HAZLETT, Helen. The Heights of Eidelberg
— Heart's Ease. 2 vols
HEIR of Redcliffe. 2 vols
HELME, Mrs. The Farmer of Inglewood Forest
HELOISE; or The Unrevealed Secret
HENTZ, Caroline Lee. The Lost Daugh-
— Rena; or The Snow Bird   [ter
— Love and Marriage
— The Banished Son
— Eoline
— The Planter's Northern Bride. 2 vols

HENTZ, Caroline Lee. Helen and Arthur
— Marcus Warland
— Linda
— Robert Graham
— Courtship and Marriage
— Ernest Linwood   [Slick
HIGH Life in New York. By Jonathan
HOFFMAN, C. F. Greyslaer
HOGG, James. Brownie of Bodsbeck
HOLMES, Mrs. Meadow Brook
— Tempest and Sunshine
— Lena Rivers
— Homestead on the Hillside
— Cousin Maud a...osamond
— Dora Deane
— Maggie Miller, etc
HOLLAND, J. G. The Bay Path
HOME is Home. A Domestic Tale
HOME Comforts, etc
HOME and the World
HOOD, T. Tylney Hall
HOOD's Own
HOOK, T. Jack Brag
— Gilbert Gurney
— The Widow and the Marquis
— All in the Wrong
— The Parson's Daughter
— Maxwell
— Gervase Skinner
— Cousin William   [Greek
HOPE, T. Anastasius; or Memoirs of a
HOSMER, H. L. Adela, the Octoroon
HOUSEHOLD Words, Novels and Tales from. 11 vols
HOUSEHOLD of Bouverie. 2 vols
HOWITT, W. and Mary. Stories of English and Foreign Life
HOWITT, W. A Boy's Adventure in Australia
— Tallengetta, The Squatter's Home. 2 vols   [vols
HUBBACK, Mrs. May and December. 2
— The Three Marriages
HUGO, V. Bug-Jargal
— Hans of Iceland
— Hunchback of Notre Dame
HUNGERFORD, J. The Old Plantation
HUNT, L. Stories from the Italian Poets
— A Book for a Corner

IDA May
INCHBALD, Mrs. The Simple Story
— Nature and Art
INDIAN Fairy Book
INGOLDSBY, G. My Cousin Nicholas
IRVING, J. T. The Attorney
ISLAND Home
IVORS. 2 vols

JACKSON, D. Alonzo and Melissa
JAMES, G. P. R. The Cavalier

JAMES, G. P. R.   Leonora D'Orco
— Lord Montagu's Page
— Darnley
— Forest Days
— Rose D'Albert
— The Convict.   2 vols
— Arrah Neil
— Arabella Stuart
— Heidelberg
— Russell
— The Smuggler
— Morley Ernstein
— Agincourt
— The False Heir
— Castle Ehrenstein
— The Step-Mother.   2 vols
— Sir Theodore Broughton.   2 vols
— Man at Arms
— Beauchampe
— Philip Augustus
— D' l'Orme
JAMES, Marion.   The Elder Sister
— Ethel
JARVES, J. J.   Kiana
JAUFREY the Knight and Fair Brunis-
      sende
JEAFFRESON, J. C.   Isabel
JERROLD, D.   Cakes and Ale
— Mrs. Caudles' Curtain Lectures
— Punch's Letter Writer and
      Sketches of the English
— Punch's Letters to his Son
— Men of Character
— A man Made of Money and Chron-
      icles of Clovernook
JONES, H. Maria.   The Pride of the
      Village
— The Gipsey Mother
— Rosaline Woodbridge
— The Gipsey Chief
JONES, J. B.   Border War
— Freaks of Fortune
JUDD, S. Margaret.   A Tale.   2 vols
JUNO Clifford

KAVANAGH, Julia.   Daisy Burns
— Adele
— St. Gildas
— Grace Lee
— Nathalie
— Rachel Gray
— Seven Years
KENNEDY, Grace.   Dunallan
— Father Clement
KENNEDY, G. P.   Rob of the Bowl
— Swallow Barn
— Horse Shoe Robinson |2 vols
— The Hawks of Hawk's Hollow.
KINGSLEY, C.   Hypatia
— Alton Locke
— Two Years Ago
— Yeast

KINGSLEY, C.   Amyas Leigh
— Fool of Quality, by H. Brooke.   2
      vols
KINGSTON, W. H. G.   The Early Life of
      Old Jack
— Old Jack, a Man-of-Wars' Man
— Salt Water
— Fred Markham
KIRK, C. D.   Wooing and Warring in
      the Wilderness
KIRWAN.   The Happy Home
KIT Kelvin's Kernels
KNOW-NOTHING.   The

LAFOSSE, G. T.   Chroniques de
      l'œil de Bœuf.   Quarto
LAING, Caroline H.   The Old Farm
LAIRD of Norlaw   [House
LAMARTINE, A.   Genevieve
LAMB, C.   Rosamund Gray
LANCES of Lynwood
LAMPLIGHTER.   The
LANDON, Miss.   Romance and Reality
LANGDON, M.   Ida May
LASSELLE, Mrs. N. P.   The Belle of
      Washington
LEATHER Stocking and Silk
LE Courtisan Desabuse
LEE, Eliza.   Parthenia
— Canterbury Tales.   2 vols
LEE, Holme.   Sylvan Holt's Daughter
— Against Wind and Tide
— Hawksview
LELAND, Anna A.   Home
LEPEE, A. F. E.   De Tout in Peu
LE SAGE A. Rene Bachelor of Salamanca
— Asmodeus ; or the Devil on Two
— Le Diable Boiteaux   [Sticks
— Gil Blas.   2 vols
— Histoire de Gil Blas de Santillane
— Life of Guzman D'Alfarache.   2
      vols
LESLIE, Miss.   Pencil Sketches
LEVER, C.   Arthur O'Leary.   2 vols
— The O'Donohue
— Harry Lorrequer.   2 vols
— Tom Burke of Ours.   3 vols
— The Knight of Gwinne.   3 vols
— The Daltons.   4 vols
— The Fortunes of Glencore
— Roland Cashel.   2 vols
— The Martins of Cro' Martin
— Gerald Fitzgerald
— Maurice Tiernay, the Soldier of
      Fortune
— Jack Hinton.   2 vols
— Con Cregan
LEWIS, Lady T.   The Semi-Detached
      House
LLEWELLYN, E. L.   Title Hunting
LEYCESTER.   The
LIGHT and Darkness ; or The Shadow
      of Fate

LIGHTS and Shadows of Scottish Life
LINDEN, Liele. Chestnutwood. 2 vols
LINWOODS. The, 2 vols
LISTER, T. H. Granby
LOGAN. The Master's House
LONGFELLOW, H. W. Kavanagh
— Hyperion
LONZ Powers; or The Regulators. 2 vols
LORENZO Benoni
LOUD, J. Gabriel Vane
LOVER, S. Handy Andy
— Rory O'More
— Barney O'Rierdon
— Treasure Trove
LUCK of Ladysmede
LUCY Crofton

MABEL VAUGHAN
McCABE, W. B. Bertha
MACKENZIE, R. S. Tressilian and his
    Friends
MADEMOISELLE Mori. A Tale of Modern
    Rome
MAGDALEN Hepburn
MAGDALEN, the Enchantress
MAIDEN Aunt
MAILLARD, A. M. Miles Tremenhere
MAITLAND, J. A. Sartaroe
— The Lawyer's Story
— Diary of an Old Doctor
MANZONIA, A. The Betrothed. 2 vols
MARIAN Elwood; or How Girls Live
MARRYAT, Capt. Masterman Ready
— Poor Jack
— The Settlers in Canada
— The King's Own
— Pacha of Many Tales
— Peter Simple
— Percival Keene
— Rattlin, the Reefer
— Frank Mildmay
— Japhet in Search of a Father
— Newton Forster
— Midshipman Easy
— Snarleyow
— Jacob Faithful
— The Poacher
— The Phantom Ship
— The Privateersman
— The Pirate and Three Cutters
— The Mission; or Scenes in Africa
MARRYAT, Miss. Temper
MARTELL, Martha. Second Love
MARTIN Merrivale
MARY Staunton; or Pupils of Marvel
MARY Lindon   [Hall
MATCH Girl, The
MATRIMONIAL Brokerage in New York
MATTHEW Carnaby
MAURICE, J. K. N. Pepper Papers
MAXWELL, W. H. Captain O'Sullivan
— Matrimonial Misfortunes of Peter
    Clancey

MAXWELL, W. H. The Bivouac
— Stories of Waterloo
— Captain Blake
— Hector O'Halloran
MAYO, S. The Berber; or the Moun-
    taineer of the Atlas
— Kaloolah
McHENRY, J. O'Halloran
McINTOSH, Maria J. The Lofty and the
    Lowly. 2 vols
— Evenings at Donaldson Manor
— Violet
— Meta Grey
McLEOD, D. Pynnshurst
MELVILLE, H. The Piazza Tales
— Israel Potter
— Mardi. 2 vols
— Omoo, a Narrative of Adventures
    in the South Seas
— Typee, a Peep at Polynesian Life
    in the Marquesas
— White Jacket; or The World in a
    Man-of-War
— Moby Dick, the Whale
MELVILLE, G. J. W. Holmby House
MERKLAND; or Self-Sacrifice
MILLER, T. Godfrey Malvern
MILLER, Hugh. Scenes and Legends of ·
    the North of Scotland
MITFORD, M. Lay. Our Village. 2 vols
— Belford Regis
— Atherton, and other Tales
MISERIES of Human life
MODERN Pilgrims
MOUDY, Cheykh. Contes; Traduites de
    l'Arabe
MONTGOMERY, Cora. Eagle Pass
MOORE, T. The Epicurean and Alciphron
MORE, Margarita. Household of Sir
    Thomas More
MORE, Sir Thomas. Utopia; or the
    Happy Republic
MORGAN, Lady. O'Donnell
— Florence Macarthy
— The Wild Irish Girl
MORIER, D. R. Adventures of Hajji
— Zorab   [Baba
— Ayesha
MORRIS, R. Courtship and Matrimony
MOTHER'S Trials
MOULTON, Louise. My Third Book
MOWATT, A. Cora. The Fortune Hunter
MUGGE, T. ·Afraja
MULOCH, Miss. John Halifax
— Nothing New
— Agatha's Husband
— Avillion
— Olive
— The Ogilvies
— A Life for a Life
— A Hero
— Bread upon the Waters
— Alice Learmont

MUNCHAUSEN, Baron. Surprising Travels and Adventures
MURRAY, C. A. The Prairie Bird [der
MYERS, P. H. The Prisoner of the Border
MYRTLE, Minnie. The Myrtle Wreath

NAPIER, Sir C. William the Conqueror. A Historical Romance
NAVARRE. Reine de L'Heptameron de Nouvelles. 3 vols
NEALE, Flora. Thine and Mine
NEAL, J. C. Charcoal Sketches. 2 vols
NEAL, J. True Womanhood. A Tale
NEIGHBOR Jackwood
NELLIE of Truro
NEWMAN, J. H. Loss and Gain; or Story of a Convent
NEW England's Chattels; or Life in the Northern Poor House
NEW Priest in Conception Bay. 2 vols
NOBLE, L. The Lady Angeline
NORTH, W. The Slave of the Lamp
NOVELS, Chinese. Translated by J. F. Davis
NOVELS, Select. [Miscellaneous.] 2 vols
— Kenneth, Lafitte, and Tom Burke
.— The Dancing Feather, The Poor Cousin, Woman's Life, etc
— The Prairie Bird, Florence Sackville, Wife's Sister, etc [11 vols
— and Tales from Household Words.

OLD Brewery and the New Mission at the Five Points
OLD Doctor, The
OLD Forest Ranger
OLD Haun, the Pawnbroker
OLD House by the River
OLIPHANT, Mrs. The Athelings
— Adam Græme, of Mossgray
OLIVE Branch; or The White Oak Farm
OTIS, Mrs. H. Gray. The Barclays of Our First Families   [Boston
OUT of the Depths. The Story of a Woman's Life

PARAGREENS in Paris
PARDOE, Miss. A Life Struggle
— The Hungarian Castle. 3 vols
PARKMAN, F. Vassall Morton
PASCAL. Jacqueline; or Convent Life at Port Royal
PATTERSON, Sarah E. B. Masters and Workmen
PAULDING, J. K. The Puritan and his Daughter
PAUL Ferroll. A Tale
PAYSON, G. Totemwell
PEABODY, Mrs. Miss Slimmen's Window
PEACE; or The Stolen Will

PEACOCKE, Dr. J. S. The Creole Orphans
PEACOCKE, G. Headlong Hall
— Nightmare Abbey
— Maid Marian
— Crotchet Castle
PENINSULAR Scenes and Sketches
PEN Owen
PENTAMERONE, The; or Story of Stories
PERCE, E. The Last of His Name
PETER Schlemil in America
PETERSON, C. J. The Old Stone Mansion
— Kate Aylesford
PHELPS, Mrs. L. Ida Norman
PHELPS, S. D. Sunlight and Hearthlight
PICKERING, E. Agnes Serle
PINEY Wood's Tavern; or Sam Slick in Texas
POLLARD, E. Black Diamonds from Darkey Homes in the South
POOLE, J. Little Pedlington and the Pedlingtonians. 2 vols
POOR Fellow
PORTER, Jane. Scottish Chiefs. A Romance
— Thaddeus of Warsaw. A Novel
— The Pastor's Fireside
— The Lakes of Killarney
— Angela
PORTER, Miss A. M. The Hungarian Brothers
— The Recluse of Norway
PORTRAITS of My Married Friends
PRESBURG, R. F. The Mustee
PREVOST, Abbé. Manon Lescaut
PULZKY, Theresa. Tales and Traditions of Hungary

QUAKER Soldier
QUEVEDO, Francisco de. Visions. Translated from the Spanish
QUOD, John. The Attorney; or The Correspondence of J. Q.

RABELAIS, F. Works. Translated. 4 vols
— Œuvres de
RADCLIFFE, Ann. Mysteries of Udolpho
— Romance of the Forest
RANDOLPH, J. T. Cabin and Parlor; or Slaves and Masters
RAWSON, the Renegade; or The Squatter's Revenge
REACH, A. B. Clement Lorimer
READE, C. Love Me Little, Love Me Long
— Peg Woffington
— Christie Johnstone
— Never Too Late to Mend. 2 vols
— White Lies

READE, C. A Good Fight, etc
RECTORY of Moreland ; or My Duty
REGINALD Dalton
REID, Captain M. The White Chief
— The Boy Hunters
— Young Voyagers
— Young Yagers
— Desert Home
— Rifle Rangers
— Scalp Hunters
— Bush Boys
— War Trail
— Plant Hunters
— Ran Away to Sea
— Osceola, the Seminole
REVERIES of a Bachelor
REYNOLDS, G. W. M. The Opera
    Dancer
— Olivia ; or The Maid of Honor
RICE, Rosella. Mabel ; or Heart Histo-
    ries
RICHARD the Fearless
RILEY, H. H. Puddleford and its People
— The Puddleford Papers
RINALDO Rinaldini
RICHARDSON, S. Pamela. 4 vols
— Clarissa Harlowe. 8 vols
— Sir Charles Grandison. 7 vols
RITA. An Autobiography
RITCHIE. L. Schunderbannes, the Rob-
    ber of the Rhine
— Robert Oakland ; or The Outcast
    Orphan
RITCHIE, Miss. Twin Roses
ROBINSON, Solon. Hot Corn ; Life
    Scenes in New York
ROCHE, R. Maria. Children of the
    Abbey
ROE, A. S. Time and Tide ; or Strive
    and Win
— The Star and Cloud
— A Long Look Ahead
— True to the Last
— How Could He Help It·
ROMANCE and Its Hero
ROMAUNT. Island Home ; or the Young
    Castaways
ROPES, H. Cranston House
ROSA, the Parisian Girl
ROSE Douglas
RUFFINI. Doctor Antonio
— Lorenzo Benoni
— Dear Experience
RUSSELL, Martha. Leaves from the Tree
    of Idrasyl
RUTLEDGE

SAINT Pierre, I. B. de. Paul et
    Virginie
SAINTINE, X. B. Picciola
SALA, G. A. The Adventuress
SAND, Mad. Geo. Teverino

SANFORD and Merton
SAYMORE, Sarah E. Hearts Unveiled
SCARRON, Paul. Comical Romance
— His whole Comical Works
SCHOOLCRAFT, Mrs. H. R. The Black
    Gauntlet
SCHOOL Days at Rugby
SCOTT, Sir Walter. Waverly Novels.
    54 vols in 27
— Waverly Novels and Waverly
    Tales. 54 vols in 27
Vols 1, 2. Waverly ; or 'Tis Sixty
    Years Since
" 3, 4. Guy Mannering ; or The
    Astrologer
" 5, 6. The Antiquary
" 7, 8. Rob Roy
    Tales of My Landlord.
Vols 9, 10. Black Dwarf, and Old
    Mortality
" 11, 12. Heart of Mid-Lothian
" 13, 14. Bride of Lammer-
    moor, and Legend of
    Montrose
" 15, 16. Ivanhoe
" 17, 18. The Monastery
" 19, 20. The Abbot
" 21, 22. Kenilworth
" 23, 24. The Pirate
" 25, 26. The Fortunes of Nigel
" 27, 28. Peveril of the Peak
" 29, 30. Quentin Durward
" 31, 32. St. Ronan's Well
" 33, 34. Redgauntlet
    Tales of the Crusaders.
Vol 35. The Betrothed
" 36. The Talisman
Vols 37, 38. Woodstock ; or The
    Cavalier
    Chronicles of the Canongate.
Vol 39. The Highland Widow, and
    The Two Drovers
" 40. The Sergeant's Daughter,
    Aunt Margaret's Mirror,
    and The Tapestried Cham-
    ber, etc
Vols 41, 42. Saint Valentine's Day
" 43, 44. Anne of Geierstein ;
    or The Maiden of the
    Mist
    Tales of My Landlord.
Vols 45, 46. Count Robert of Paris
" 47. Castle Dangerous
    Waverly Tales.
Vol 48. Tales of a Grandfather,
    being Stories taken from
    Scottish History, in-
    scribed to Hugh Little-
    john. 1st Series
Vols 49, 50. The Same. 2d Series
" 51, 52. The same. 3d Series

Scott, Sir Walter. Waverly Tales
Vols 53, 54. The same, taken from
the History of France;
inscribed to Master
J. H. Lockhart. 4th
Series
Scott, Rosa. Marian Wallace
Scott, M. Tom Cringle's Log
Scouring of the White House
Sealsfield, C. The Cabin Book
Sears, E. H. Athanasia; or Fore-
gleams of Immortality
Sea Stories
Sedgwick, Miss C. M. New England
Male and other Miscellanies
— Redwood
— Clarence
— Hope Leslie. 2 vols
— Married or Single. 2 vols
Sewell, E. Katharine Ashton. 2 vols
— Cleve Hall
— Ursula. 2 vols
Shely, Mary W. Frankenstein
Shelton, F. W. Peeps from a Belfry
Sherwood, Mrs. Works. 16 vols
Sigourney, Mrs. L. H. Lucy Howard's
Journal
Simms, W. G. The Lily and the Totem
— The Forayers
— Catharine Walton
— Guy Rivers
— Richard Hurdis
— Border Beagles
— The Partisan
— Beauchampe
— The Yemasse
— Mellichampe
— Eutaw
— Confessions of a Blind Heart
— The Maroon
— Southward Ho
— Charlemont
— The Wigwam and the Cabin
— The Cassique of Kiawah
Sinclair, C. Lord and Lady Harcourt
— Modern Accomplishments'
— Modern Society; or The March of
— Modern Flirtations   [Intellect
— Beatrice
Siogvolk, P. Walter Ashwood
Sir Rohan's Ghost
Sister Agnes
Sisters of Soleure   [York. 2 vols
Slick, Jonathan. High Life in New
Slick, Sam. See Haliburton, T. C.
Smedley, F. E. Lewis Arundel
— Frank Fairleigh
— Harry Coverdale's Courtship
Smith, Irene B. The Elm Tree Tales
Smith, Horace. Zillah   [of Opinion
Smith, W. Thorndale; or The Conflict
Smith, Mrs. E. O. Newsboy   [villers
Smith, A. The Marchioness of Brin-

Smith, A. Adventures of Mr. Ledbury
— The Scattergood Family
Smith, J. F. Alice Arran; or One
Hundred Years Ago
— Dick Markham; or Smiles and
— Temptation   [Tears
— Rochester
— Gus Howard
— Stanfield Hall
— Amy Lawrence
— Fred Graham
— Henri de la Tour
— Charles Vavasseur
— Marion Barnard
— Dick Tarleton
— Harold Tracy
— Harry Ashton
— Woman and Her Master
— The Virgin Queen
— Minnie Gray
— Fred Arden
— Ellen de Vere
Smollett, Tobias. Select Works
— Roderick Random
Sorrows of Werter
Sortain, J. Count Arensberg. 2 vols
Souclie, F. Le Chateau des Pyrénées.
3 vols
— Marguerite
Southworth, Emma D. E. N. The
Discarded Daughter
— The Missing Bride
— The Deserted Wife
— The Curse of Clifton
— Retribution
— India
— The Wife's Victory, etc
— The Lost Heiress
— The Inebriate's Hut
— The Three Beauties
— The Lady of the Isles
— The Two Sisters
— Vivia
— Old Neighborhoods, etc
— The Haunted Homestead, and oth-
er Tales
Souvestrie, E. Man and Money
— Leaves from a Family Journal
— The Attic Philosopher
Stael. Corine; or Italy
Starbuck, O. Hampton Heights
Stephens, Mrs. H. Hagar, the Martyr
— Mary Derwent
Stephens, Anna S. The Heiress of
Greenhurst
Sterne, Laurence. Works
— Tristram Shandy
— Sentimental Journey
Stinson, A. L. Easy Nat
Stories for the Home Circle
Stories from Blackwood
Story of a Pocket Bible
Story, S. A. Caste

STOWE, H. B. Father Henson's Story
— The May Flower
— Dred. 2 vols
— Uncle Tom's Cabin. 2 vols
— The Minister's Wooing
STRICKLAND, Miss. Pilgrims of Walsing-
    ham
— Edward Evelyn
— Old Mackinaw
SUBALTERN, The
SUE, E. The Wandering Jew. 3 vols
— Atar Gull
— Mathilde; Memoirs d'une Jeune
    Femme
SWEAT, Mrs. Ethel's Love Life
SWELL Life at Sea
SWIFT, Jonathan. Tale of a Tub
SYLVIA'S World

TALES from the German
    TALES of the Genii
TALMON, Thrace. Edith Hale
— Captain Molly
TAUTPHŒUS, Baroness. The Initials
— Quits
— Cyrilla
TAYLOR, C. B. Legends and Records
TENANT House, etc
THACKERAY, W. M. Book of Snobs
— History of Pendennis. 2 vols
— Jeames' Diary, Legend of the
    Rhine, etc
— Duck of Barry Lyndon
— Mr. Brown's Letters to a Young
    Man About Town
— Paris Sketch Book. 2 vols
— Punch's Prize Novelists
— Shabby Genteel Story. with other
    Tales
— Yellow-Plush Papers
— Henry Esmond
— The Virginians
— The Newcomes. 2 vols
— Men's Wives and Fitz Boodles'
    Confessions
THEODOSIUS and Constantia
THINKS I to Myself, a Serio-Ludicro-
    Tragico-Comico Tale
THOMPSON, D. P. Gaut Gurley
THORPE, T. B. The Hive of the Bee
    Hunters
TIFFANY, O. Brandon; or One Hundred
    Years Ago
TIGHE. Lifford, A Novel
TOWNSEND, Virginia. While it was Morn-
— Living and Loving   [ing
TRELAWNEY, Capt. The Younger Son
TREVELYAN
TRIALS of Jessie Loring
TRIALS of Margaret Lindsay
TROLLOPE, A. Doctor Thorne
— The Three Clerks

TROLLOPE, A. The Kellys and O'Kellys
— The Bertrams
— Castle Richmond
TUPPER, M. F. Crock of Gold, The
    Twins, and Heart. 12 mo.
    Philadelphia
TURNER. Jack Hopeton
TUTHILL, Mrs. L. C. Reality

UMSTED, Mrs. Southwold
    UNCLE Ralph; A Tale

VALERIUS
    VALON, A. Le Chale Noir
VARRA, O. Eddies Round the Rectory
VARA; or The Child of Adoption
VERMOND, P. Chronique Populaires de
    Berry
VERNON Grove; or Hearts as They Are
VICAR of Wakefield   [Navarre
VILLOSLADA, F. N. Donna Bianca of
VINCARD, P. Le Banquet des Sept Gor-
    mands
VIOLET; or The Times We Live In
VOLTAIRE, F. M. A. de. Contes et Romans

WALDOR, A. Chas. Mandel. 2 vols
    WALPOLE, Horace. Castle of
    Otrano. A Gothic Story
WALKER, G. The Three Spaniards
WALTER Thornley; or a Peep at the Past
WARBURTON, E. Darien; or The Mer-
    chant Prince. 2 vols
WARD, Catharine G. The Cottage on
— The Fisher's Daughter [the Cliff
— Mysterious Marriage
WARD, R. P. Tremaine   [Palmyra
WARE, W. Zenboia; or The Falls of
— Julian. Scenes in Judea
— Aurelian; or Rome in the Third
    Century
WARNER, Misses. Say and Seal. 2 vols
— Dollars and Cents. 2 vols
— Wide, Wide World. 2 vols
— Queechy. 2 vols
— The Hills of Shatemuc
WARREN, S. Ten Thousand a Year
— Diary of a Physician
— Miscellanies
— Now and Then, and The Lily and
    the Bee, etc
WATSON, Rev. J. F. Tales and Takings
WEIL, G. Biblical Legends of the Mus-
    sulmans
WEIR, J. Lonz Powers; or The Reg-
    ulators. 2 vols
WENTZ, Sara A. Smiles and Frowns
WHICH; The Right or the Left
WHITE Acre v. Black Acre [the First
WHITEHALL; or The Days of Charles

WHITEHEAD, C. E. Wild Sports in the South
WHITE Slave; or Memoirs of a Fugitive
WHITTY, E. M. Knaves and Fools
WIEHER, F. M. The Widow Bedott
WIFE's Trials and Triumphs [Papers
WIGHT, O. F. Abelard and Heloise
WILD Flower, The
WILLIS, N. P. Paul Fane
WILLIS the Pilot
WINNIE and I
WINSCOM, Jane A. Onward
WINTER Lodge
WITCHES of New York. By Philander Doesticks
WOLFSDEN
WOMAN's Faith
WOOD, G. Future Life; or Scenes in Another World

WOODHILL; or The Ways of Providence
WORMLEY, E. Amabel
WUTHERING Heights

YEAST. A Problem
Yonge, Catharine. Daisy Chain. 2 vols
Yonge, Catharine. The Castle Builders
— Friarswood Post-Office
— Beechcroft
— The Heir of Redcliffe. 2 vols
— Richard the Fearless
— Heartsease. 2 vols
YULE-TIDE Stories

ZILLAH, the Child Medium

PART II.

ABBOT, by Scott
ABEDNEGO, the Money Lender, by Mrs. Gore
ABELARD and Heloise, by O, F. Wight
ACTRESS in High Life
ADAM Bede, by G. Elliott
ADAM Blair and Matthew Wald
ADAM Græme of Mossgray, by Mrs. Oliphant
ADELA the Octoroon, by H. L. Hosmer
ADELE, by Julia Kavanagh
ADVENTURESS, by G. A. Sala
ADVENTURES of a Chaperon, by Lady Dacre
ADVENTURES of Sir Frizzle Pumpkin
ADVENTURES of a Marquis, by A. Dumas
AFLOAT and Ashore, by J. F. Cooper
AFRAJA, by F. Mugge
AFTER Dark, by W. Collins
AGATHA's Husband, by Miss Muloch
AGATHONIA. A Romance
AGAINST Wind and Tide, by Holme Lee
AGE of Chivalry, by T. Bulfinch
AGINCOURT, by James
AGNES
AGNES Serle, by Ellen Pickering
AGNES Gray, by Mrs. Gaskell
AGNES de Mansfelt, by T. C. Grattan
A Good Fight, by C. Reade
A Hero, by Miss Muloch
ALCIPHRON, by T. Moore
ALICE Arran, by J. F. Smith
ALICE, by Bulwer
ALICE Learmont, by Miss Muloch
ALICE Sherwin
ALL in the Wrong, by T. Hook
ALL's not Gold that Glitters
ALMOST a Heroine
ALONE, by Marian Harland
ALONZO and Melissa, by D. Jackson
ALTON Locke, by C. Kingsley
AMABEL, by E. Wormsley
AMY Lawrence, by J. F. Smith
AMY Lee
ANASTASIUS, by T. Hope
ANGELA, by Jane Porter
ANNALS of the Parish, by John Galt
ANNE Geierstein, by Scott

ANTIQUARY, by Scott
AMYAS Leigh, by C. Kingsley
ARABELLA Stuart, by James
ARABIAN Days
ARABIAN Nights
ARRAH Neil, by James
ARTHUR O'Leary, by Lever
ASPEN Court, by Shirley Brooks
ATAR Gull, by Sue
ATHANASIA, by E. H. Seares
ATHELINGS, by Mrs. Oliphant
ATHERTON and other Tales, by M. R. Mitford
ATTORNEY; or Correspondence of John Quod
ATTIC Philosopher, by E. Souvestrie
ATTORNEY, by J. T. Irving
AUNT Margaret's Mirror, by Scott
AURELIAN, by Wm. Ware
AUSTRALIAN Crusoes, by Bowercroft
AVENGER, The, by T. DeQuincy
AVILLION, by Miss Muloch
AYESHA, by D. R. Movier
AYLMERS, by Gerald Griffin
AYRSHIRE Legends, by John Galt

BACHELOR of the Albany
BACHELOR of Salamanca, by A. R. Le Sage
BACHELOR's Story, by O. A. Bunce
BALLYSHAN Castle
BANISHED Son, by Caroline Lee Hentz
BANQUET des Sept Gourmands, par P. Vincard
BARBER of Bantry, by Gerald Griffin
BARCLAYS of Boston, by Mrs. Otis
BARNABY Rudge, by Dickens
BARNEY O'Rierdon, by S. Lover
BARON Trenck
BAY Path, by Dr. J. G. Holland
BEATRICE, by Catharine Sinclair
BEATRICE Cenci, by F. D. Guerazzi
BEAUCHAMPE, by Simms
BEAUCHAMPE, by James
BEECHCROFT, by Catharine Yonge
BEHIND the Scenes, by Lady Bulwer
BEHIND the Scenes in Paris. 2 vols

BEING Rich, by H. Conscience
BELFORD Keyes, by M. R. Mitford
BELINDA, by Miss Edgeworth
BELISARIUS. A Fable
BELL, J. A Man
BELLE of Washington, by Mrs. N. P. Lasselle
BEN Sylvester's Word
BERBER, by W. S. Mayo
BERENICE, by Mad. E. S. Lesdernier
BERTHA, by W. B. McCabe
BERTHA Percy, by Margaret Field
BERTRAMS, by A. Trollope
BETROTHED, by Scott
BETROTHED, by A. Manzoni
BEULAH, by Augusta J. Evans
BIBLICAL Legends, by G. Weil
BIRTHDAY Presents, by Mrs. Sherwood
BITTERSWEET, by Mrs. Sherwood
BIVOUAC, by W. H. Maxwell
BLACK Diamonds from Darkey Homes, by E. Pollard
BLACK Dwarf, by Scott
BLACK Gauntlet, by Mrs. Schoolcraft
BLACK Mantle
BLEAK House, by Dickens
BLESSED Family, by Mrs. Sherwood
BLIND Rosa, by H. Conscience
BLITHEDALE Romance, by N. Hawthorn
BLONDE and Brunette
BOOK for a Corner, by Leigh Hunt
BOOK of 1,000 Comical Stories
BOOK of Snobs, by Thackeray
BORDER Beagles, by Simms
BORDER War, by J. B. Jones
BOY's Adventures in Australia, by W. Howitt
BOY Hunters, by Mayne Reid
BRAGELONNE, by A. Dumas
BRANDON, by A. Tiffany
BRAVO, The, by Cooper
BRIDE of Lammermoor, by Scott
BROKEN Hyacinth, by Mrs. Sherwood
BROWNIE of Bodsbeck, by J. Hogg
BROWN's Letters to Man About Town. by Thackeray
BREAD Upon the Waters, by Miss Muloch
BROTHER Clerks, by Xariffa
BROTHERS and Sisters, by Miss Bremer
BUG Jargal, by Victor Hugo
BUSH Boys, by Mayne Reid
BUTTERFLY, by Mrs. Sherwood

CABIN Boy's Story
CABIN and Parlor, by J. T. Randolph
CABIN Book, by C. Sealsfield
CAKES and Ale, by D. Jerrold
CALAVAR, by R. M. Bird
CALEB Williams, by W. Goodwin
CALDERON the Courtier, by Bulwer
CAMILLE

CANTERBURY Tales, by Miss Lee
CAPT. Blake, by W. H. Maxwell
CAPTAIN Molly, by Thrace Talmon
CAPT. O'Sullivan, by W. H. Maxwell
CAPT. Singleton and Col. Jack, by D. Defoe
CARD Drawing, by Gerald Griffin
CAROLINE Mordaunt, by Mrs. Sherwood
CAROLINA Sports, by G. Elliott
CASSIQUE of Kiawah, by Simms
CASTAWAYS, by A. Bowman
CASTE, by S. A. Story
CASTLE Builders, by Catharine Yonge
CASTLE Dangerous, by Scott
CASTLE Ehrenstein, by James
CASTLE of Otranto, by H. Walpole
CASTLE Richmond, by A. Trollope
CASTLE Rackrent, by Miss Edgeworth
CATHERA Clyde, by Inconnu
CATHARINE Ashton, by E. M. Sewell
CATHARINE de Medicis, by Miss Costello
CATHARINE Walton, by Simms
CAUDLE Curtain Lectures, by D. Jerrold
CAVALIER, by James
CAXTONS, by Bulwer
CECIL, by Mrs. Gore
CESAR Birotteau, by Balzac
CHAIN Bearers, by Cooper
CHALE Noir, par A. Valon
CHALLENGE of Barletta, by M. D'Azzeglio
CHAPTER on Wives, by Mrs. Ellis
CHARCOAL Sketches, by J. C. Neale
CHARITY Green, by T. Hartman
CHARLEMONT, by Simms
CHARLES Auchester, by E. Berger
CHALES Mandel, de M. Waldor
CHARLES O'Malley, by Lever
CHARLES Vavasseur, by J. F. Smith
CHATEAU de Pyrénées, by F. Soulie
CHELSEA Pensioners, by G. R. Gleig
CHESTNUTWOOD, by Linden Lisle
CHILD Wife, by Dickens
CHILDREN of the Abbey, by R. Maria Roche
CHINA Manufactory, by Mrs. Sherwood
CHINESE Novels
CHRISTIE Johnstone, by C. Reade
CHRISTINE Van Amburg, by Countess Arbouville
CHRISTINE, by Laura J. Curtis
CHRISTMAS Stories, by Dickens
CHRONICLES of the Bastille
CHRONICLES of Clovernook, by D. Jerrold
CHRONIQUES de l'œil de Bœuf, par G. Lafosse
CHRONIQUES Populaires de Berry, P. Vermond
CLARA Moreland, by E. Bennett
CLARA Stephens, by Mrs. Sherwood
CLARISSA Harlowe, by S. Richardson
CLARENCE, by Mrs. Sedgwick
CLASSIC Tales

CLEMENT Lorimer, by A. B. Reach
CLERMONT
CLEVE Hall, by E. Sewell
COINER, The, by Gerald Griffin
COMICAL Romance, by Scarron
COMMON Errors, by Mrs. Sherwood
COMPENSATION, by Anne Brewster
CONFESSIONS of a Blind Heart, by Simms
CONSCRIPT, by A. Dumas
CONSCRIPT, The, by H. Consience
CONTARINI Fleming, by B. D'Israeli
CONTES ; Traduites de l'Arabe. Cheykh
    Mohdy
CONTES et Romans, par Voltaire
CONVENT of St. Clair, by Mrs. Sherwood
CONVICT, by James
COOPERS, The, by Alice B. Haven
COQUETTE, by Mrs. Foster
CORA and the Doctor
CORAL Island, by R. M. Ballantyne
CORINNE, by Mad. de Stael
COTTAGE on the Cliff, by Catharine G.
    Ward
COUNT of Arensberg, by J. Sortain
COUNT of Monte Cristo, by A. Dumas
COUNT Robert of Paris, by Scott
COUNTESS of St. Albans, by Hacklander
COUNTERPARTS
COUNTRY Curate, by G. R. Gleig
COURTENAY of Walreddin, by Mrs. Bray
COURTSHIP and Marriage, by Caroline
    Lee Hentz
COURTSHIP aud Matrimony, by R. Morris
COUSIN Cicily
COUSIN Maude and Rosamond, by Mrs.
    Holmes
COUSIN William, by T. Hook
CRANSTON House, by H. Ropes
CREOLE Orphans, by J. S. Peacocke
CRISNA; or the Queen of the Danube
CROCK of Gold, by M. F. Tupper
CROTCHET Castle, by G. Peacocke
CURE Manquè, by E. Courcillon
CURSE of Clifton, by Mrs. Southworth
CURSE of the Village, by H. Consience
ORATER ; or Vulcan's Peak, by Cooper
CRUISE of the Midge
CYRILLA, by Baroness Tautphœus
CYRIL Thornton

DAISY BURNS, by Julia Kavanagh
    Daisy Chain, by Catharine Yonge
DALTONS, by Lever
DANCING Feather
DARIEN, by E. Warburton
DARNLEY, by James
DAVID Copperfield, by Dickens
DAYS of Bruce, by Grace Aguilar
DAYS of my Life
DEAD Secret, by W. Collins
DEAR Experience, by Ruffini
DEBIT and Credit, by G. Freytag
DECAMERON, by Boccacio. 2 vols

DEER SLAYER, by Cooper
DE FOIX, by Mrs. Gray
DE L'ORME, by James
DEMON of Gold, by H. Consience
DEVEREAUX, by Bulwer
DESERTED Wife, by Mrs. Southworth
DESERT Home, by Mayne Reid
DIABLE Boiteaux
—   Translated
DIARY of an Old Doctor, by S. A. Mait-
    land
DIARY of a Physician, by S. Warren
DICK Markham, by J. F. Smith
DICK Tarleton, by J. F. Smith
DISCARDED Daughter, by Mrs. South-
    worth
DISCIPLINE, by Miss Brunton
DISOWNED, by Bulwer
DOCTOR Antonio, by Ruffini
DOCTOR Oldham
DOCTOR THORNE, by Anthony Trollope
DOESTICKS, What ho says
DOLLARS and Cents, by Miss Warner
DOMBEY and Son, by Dickens
DONNA Bianca of Navarre, by F. Villos-
    lada
DON Quixote, by Cervantes
DOOMED Chief
DORA Deane, by Mrs. Holmes
DOUGLAS Farm, by Mary E. Bradley
DRED, by Mrs. Stowe
DUDLEY Castle, by Mrs. Sherwood
DUKE of Monmouth, by Gerald Griffin
DUKE, The, by Mrs. Grey
DUNALLAN, by Grace Kennedy
DUN Browne's Experiences in Foreign
    Parts
DUNCAN Campbell, by D. De Foe
DYNEVOR Terrace.

EAGLE PASS, by Cora Montgomery
    EASTFORD, by W. Brooke
EASY Warren, by W. T. Coggeshall
EASY Nat, by A. L. Stimson
ECHOES of a Belle
EBONY Idol
ECONOMY, by Mrs. Sherwood
EDDIES round the Rectory, by O. Vara
EDGAR Huntley, by C. B. Brown
EDITH Hale, by Thrace Talmon
EDITH ; or the Quaker's Daughter
EDMOND Dantes, by A. Dumas
EDWARD Evelyn, by Miss Strickland
EDWARD Mansfield, by Mrs. Sherwood
ELDER Sister, by Marian James
ELEPHANT Club, by Doesticks
EL Furéidés
ELIZABETH ; or, Exiles to Siberia, by
    Mad. Cottin
ELLEN de Vere, by J. F. Smith
ELLEN Middleton, by Lady Fullerton
ELM Tree Tales, by Irene Smith

EMANCIPATION, by Mrs. Sherwood
EMANUEL-Philibert, by A. Dumas
EMELINE, by Mrs. Sherwood
EMMA, by Mrs. Austin
EMILIA Wyndham
EMILY and Her Brothers, by Mrs. Sherwood
ENGLISH Mary, by Mrs. Sherwood
ENTAIL, by John Galt
EOLINE, by Caroline Lee Hentz
EPICUREAN, by T. Moore
ERIC, by F. W. Farrar
ERNEST Linwood, by Caroline Lee Hentz
ERNEST Maltravers, by Bulwer
ERNESTINE ; or The Heart's Longing
ERMINA, by Mrs. Sherwood
EROS and Anteros
ERRAND Boy, by Mrs. Sherwood
ESTELLE, by Florian
ESTELLE Grant ; or The Lost Wife
ETHEL, by Marian James
ETHEL's Love Life, by Mrs. Sweat
EUGENE Aram, by Bulwer
EUTAW, by Simms
EVELINA, by Miss Burney
EVENINGS at Haddon Hall
EVENINGS at Donaldson Manor, by M. J. McIntosh
EXILES of Florida, by J. R. Giddings
EXPERIENCE of a Gaol Chaplain

FAIRCHILD Family, by Mrs. Sherwood
FAIRY Tales of Many Nations, by C. B. Burkhardt
FAIRY Tales of Science, by J. C. Brough
FALSE Heir, by James
FARMER of Inglewood Forest, by Mrs. Helme
FASHION and Famine, by Mrs. Stephens
FATHER and Daughter, by Miss Bremer
FATHER Clement, by Grace Kennedy
FATHER's Eye, by Mrs. Sherwood
FATHER Henson's Story, by Mrs. Stowe
FAULKLAND, by Bulwer
FISHER's Daughter, by Catharine D. Ward
FISHER's River Scenes and Characters
FITZ Boodle's Confessions, by Thackeray
FITZ, of Fitz Ford, by Mrs. Bray
FLEETWOOD, by W. Godwin
FLORENCE Dombey, by Dickens
FLORENCE De Lacey, the Coquette
FLORENCE Macarthy, by Lady Morgan
FLORENCE Sackville
FLOWER of the Flock, by Pierce Egan
FLOWER of the Forest, by Mrs. Sherwood
FLUSH Times in Alabama, by J. G. Baldwin
FOOL of Quality, by H. Brooke

FORAYERS, by Simms
FOREST Days, by James
FORESTERS
FOREST Tragedy, by Grace Greenwood
FORTUNE Hunter, by Anna C. Mowatt
FORTUNES of Glencore, by Lever
FORTUNES of Nigel, by Scott
FORTY-FIVE Guardsmen, by A. Dumas
FOUR Books, Chinese Novels
FRANK Fairlegh, by F. E. Smedley
FRANK Freeman's Barber Shop, by B. R. Hall
FRANK, Harry and Lucy, by Miss Edgeworth
FRANK Mildmay, by Capt. Marryat
FRANKENSTEIN, by Mrs. Shelley
FREAKS of Fortune, by J. B. Jones
FRED Arden, by J. F. Smith
FRED Graham, by J. F. Smith
FRED Markham, by W. H. G. Kingston
FRIARSWOOD Post Office, by Catherine Yonge
FUDGES in England, by Brown the Younger
FUTURE Life, by G. Wood

GABRIEL Vane, by J. Loud
GAUT Gurley, by D. P. Thompson
GEMS from Fable Land, by W. O. Bourne
GENEVIEVE, by A. Lamartine
GENTILHOMME Campagnard, by E. Bernard
GEORGE Mason, the Young Backwoodsman
GEORGE Melville
GERMAN Popular Tales
GERMAN Romance, by T. Carlyle
GERVASE Skinner, by T. Hook
GERALD Fitzgerald, by Lever
GERFAUT, by E. Bernard
GERMAINE, by E. About
GERMAN Fairy Tales
GHOST Seer, by Schiller
GILBERT Gurney, by T. Hook
GIL Blas, by A. R. Le Sage
— Translated
GYPSY Babes, by Mrs. Sherwood
GYPSEY Mother, by H. Maria Jones
GYPSEY Chief, by H. Maria Jones
GLENWOOD, or the Parish Boy
GODFREY Malvern, by T. Miller
GOLDEN CLEW, by Mrs. Sherwood
GOLDEN Legacy
GODOLPHIN, by Bulwer
GONZALVE de Cordove, par Florian
GRANBY, by T. H. Lyster
GRACE Lee, by Julia Kavanagh
GRACIE Amber, by Mrs. Denison
GRACIE Truman, by Mrs. Ford
GREYSLAER, by C. F. Hoffman
GRANTLEY Manor, by Lady Fullerton
GREEN Hand, by C. Cupples

2

Gus Howard, by J. F. Smith
Guy Carlton, by F. Forrester
Guy Livingstone, by C. A. Bristed
Guy Mannering, by Scott
Guy Rivers, by Simms
Guzman D'Alfarache, by A. R. Le Sage

HADJI Baba, by D. P. Morier
Hai Ebn Yockdan
Half-Sir, by Gerald Griffin
Hagar the Martyr, by Mrs. Stephens
Hallig, by Biernatzyki
Hamiltons, by Mrs. Gore
Hampton Heights, by C. Starbuck
Hand and Word, by Gerald Griffin
Handy Andy, by S. Lover
Hans of Iceland, by Victor Hugo
Happy Grandmother, by Mrs. Sherwood
Happy Home, by Kirwan
Hard Times, by Dickens
Harold, by Bulwer
Harry Coverdale's Courtship, by F. E. Smedley
Harp of a Thousand Strings, etc.
Harrington, by Miss Edgeworth
Harold Tracy, by J. F. Smith
Harry Ashton, by J. F. Smith
Harry Harson
Harry Lee, or Hope for the Poor
Harry Lorrequer, by Lever
Harry Muir, A Story of Scottish Life
Hartley Norman, by A. Hampden
Hau Kiou Choan
Haunted Homestead, and other Tales, by Mrs. Southworrh
Hawks of Hawk's-Hollow, by J. P. Kennedy
Headlong Hall, by G. Peacocke
Head of the Family, by Miss Muloch
Headsman, by Cooper
Heart, by Tupper
Heart Histories and Life Pictures, by T. S. Arthur
Heart of Midlothian, by Scott
Heartsease, by Catherine Yonge
Hearts Unveiled, by Sarah Saymore
Hector O'Halloran, by W. H. Maxwell
Hedoe of Thorns, by Mrs. Sherwood
Heidelberg, by James
Heidenmauer, by Cooper
Heights of Eidelberg, by Helen Hazlett
H. Family, by Miss Bremer
Heir of Redcliffe, by Catherine Yonge
Heiress of Greenhurst, by Mrs. Stephens
Heiress of Bruges, by T. C. Grattan
Helen, by Miss Edgeworth
Helen and Arthur, by Caroline Lee Hentz
Heloise, or the Unrevealed Secret
Henri de la Tour, by J. F. Smith
Henry Esmond, by Thackeray

Henry de Pomeroy, by Mrs. Gray
Henry Milner, by Mrs. Sherwood
Henry of Ofterdingen, by F. Von Hardenburg
Henry St. John, Gentleman, by J. E. Cooke
Henrietta Temple, by B. D'Israeli
Heptameron de la Reine de Navarre
Hermits' Dell
Her Age, by Mrs. Sherwood
Hertha, by Frederika Bremer
Hide and Seek, by W. Collins
Hidden Path, by Marian Harland
High Life in New York, by Jonathan Slick
Highland Widow, by Scott
Hills of Shatamuc, by Miss Warner
History of the Devil, by D. De Foe.
Hive of the Bee Hunters, by T. B. Thorpe
Holland Tide, by Gerald Griffin
Holmsby House, by G. I. W. Melville
Home, by Anna A. Leland
Home, by Miss Bremer
Home Comforts
Home Influence, by Grace Aguilar
Home and Social Philosophy, by Dickens
Home Memorie, by Mrs. C. Brock
Home and World
Home as Found, by Cooper
Home is Home
Home Hits and Hints, by W. T. Coggeshall
Home in the Valley, by Emilie Carlen
Home Narratives, by Dickens
Home Scenes, etc., by Grace Aguilar
Homeward Bound, by Cooper
Homestead on the Hillside, by Mrs. Holmes
Hoon's Own, by Thomas Hood
Hope Leslie, by Mrs. Sedgewick
Horse-Shoe Robinson, by J. P. Kennedy
Hot Corn ; or Life Scenes in New York, by Solon Robinson
Hours of Infancy, by Mrs. Sherwood
House of Seven Gables, by N. Hawthorne
Household of Sir Thomas More, by Margaret More
How Could he Help It, by A. S. Roe
Household of Bouverie
Hunchback of Notre Damé, by Victor Hugo
Hungarian Brothers, by Maria Porter
Hungarian Castle, by Miss Pardoe
Hypatia, by C. Kingsley
Hyperion, by Longfellow

IDA May, by M. Langdon
Ida Norman, by Mrs. L. Phelps
Idler, by Mrs. Sherwood
India, by Mrs. Southworth

INDIAN Fairy Book
INDIAN Pilgrims, by Mrs. Sherwood
INEBRIATE's Hut, by Mrs. Southworth
INFANT's Grave, by Mrs. Sherwood
INFIRMARY, by Mrs. Sherwood
INGENUE, by A. Dumas
INGOLDSBY Legends, by H. Barham.
INITIALS, by Baroness Tautphœus
INTIMATE Friends, by Mrs. Sherwood
IRON Cage, by Mrs. Sherwood
IRON Cousin, by Mrs. Cowden Clarke
IRON Mask, by A. Dumas
Isabel, by J. C. Jeaffreson
ISABEL of Bavaria, by A. Dumas
ISABELLA Orsini
ISLAND Home, by C. Romaunt
ISRAEL Potter, by H. Melville
IVANHOE, by Scott
IVORS

JACK Brag, by T. Hook
    JACK Hinton, by Lever
JACK Hopeton, by Turner
JACK Tier, by Cooper
JACOB Faithful, by Capt. Marryat
JACQUELINE, by B. Pascal
JACQUELINE of Holland, by T. C. Grattan
JANE Eyre, by C. Bronte
JANE Seton, or the King's Advocate, by
    J. Grant
JANE Talbot, by C. B. Brown
JAPHET in Search of a Father, by Capt.
    Marryat
JAUFREY the Knight and the Fair
    Brunissende
JEAME's Diary
JOHN Halifax, by Miss Muloch
JOSEPH Andrews, by Fielding
JULIAN Home, or College Life, by F. W.
    Farrar
JULIAN, by Wm. Ware
JULIAN Percival, by Mrs. Sherwood
JULIANA Oakley, by Mrs. Sherwood
JUNO Clifford

KALOOLAH, by W. S. Mayo
    KANGAROO Hunters, by A. Bow-
    man
KATE Aylesford
KATHERINE Ashton, by E. Sewell
KATHERINE Seward, by Mrs. Sherwood
KATIE Stewart
KAVANAGH, by Longfellow
KELLY and O'Kelleys, by A. Trollope
KENILWORTH, by Scott
KENNETH
KIANA, by J. J. Jarves
KILLARNEY Legends, by T. C. Croker
KING's Own, by Capt. Marryat
KNAVES and Fools, by E. M. Whitty
KNIGHT of Gwynne, by Lever
K. N. PEPPER Papers, by J. Maurice.

LADY Angeline, by L. Noble
    LADY Bird, by Lady Fullerton
LADY of the Isles, by Mrs. Southworth
LADY of the Manor, by Mrs. Sherwood
LAFITTE
LAIRD of Norlaw
LAKE of Killarney, by Jane Porter
LAMPLIGHTER, by Maria Cummings
LANCASHIRE Life, by T. Greenhalgh
LANCASHIRE Witches, by W. H. Ains-
    worth
LANCES of Lynwood
LANMERE, by Julia Dorr
LAST Days of Pompeii, by Bulwer
LAST of his Name, by E. Perce
LAST of the Mohicans, by Cooper
LATTER Days, by Mrs. Sherwood
LAURIE Todd, by John Galt
LAVENGRO, by Borrow
LAWYER's STORY, by J. A. Maitland
LEATHER Stocking and Silk
LEAVES from a Family Journal, by E.
    Souvestrie
LEAVES from the Tree of Igdrasyl, by
    Martha Russell
LEDBURY, Mr., Adventures, by A. Smith
LEGEND of Montrose, by Scott
LEGEND of the Rhine, by Thackeray
LEGENDS and Record, by C. B. Taylor
LEGENDS of the Rhine, by T. C. Grattan
LEGENDS of the West, by J. L. Hall
LEILA, by Bulwer
LENA Rivers, by Mrs. Holmes
LEONORA D'Orco, by James
LEWIS Arundel, by F. E. Smedley
LIFE of a Sailor, by Capt. Chamier
LIFE for a Life, by Miss Muloch
LIFE Struggle, by Miss Pardoe
LIGHTS and Shadows of Scottish Life
LIGHT and Darkness, or the Shadow of
    Fate
LILY and Totem, by Simms
LILY White, by E. Goodwin
LINDA, by Caroline Lee Hentz
LINWOODS,
LION of Flanders, by H. Consience
LIONEL Lincoln, by Cooper
LITTLE Beauty, by Mrs. Grey
LITTLE Beggars, by Mrs. Sherwood
LITTLE Dorrit, by Dickens
LITTLE Female Academy, by Mrs. Sher-
    wood
LITTLE Henry and his Bearer, by Mrs.
    Sherwood
LITTLE Mornere, by Mrs. Sherwood
LITTLE Pedlington, by J. Poole
LITTLE Woodman, by Mrs. Sherwood
LIVING and Loving, by Virginia Town-
    send
LIZZIE Leigh, by Mrs. Gaskell
LOFTY and the Lowly, by M. J. McIntosh
LONG Look Ahead, by A. S. Roe
LONZ Powers, by J. Weir

LOOK at Home, or Life in the Poor Houses of New England
LOOK to the End, or the Bennetts Abroad, by Mrs. Ellis
LORD and Lady Harcourt, by Catherine Sinclair
LORD Montague's Page, by James
LORENZO Benoni, by Ruffini
LOSS and Gain, by Alice B. Haven
LOSS and Gain, by J. H. Newman
LOST Daughter, by Caroline Lee Hentz
LOST Heiress, by Mrs. Southworth
LOVE and Marriage, by Caroline Lee Hentz
LOVE after Marriage
LOVE Match, by H. Cockton
LOVE me Little, Love me Long, by C. Reade
LOVER'S Stratagem
LUCK of Barry Lyndon, by Thackery
LUCK of Ladysmede
LUCRETIA, by Bulwer
LUCY Crofton
LUCY Howard's Journal, by Mrs. Sigourney
LUCY and her Dhaye, by Mrs. Sherwood
LYCESTERS, The
LYDIA, a Woman's Book, by Mrs. Crosland

MABEL; or, Heart Histories, by Rosella Rice
MABEL Vaughan
MADEMOISELLE Mori
MAGDALEN the Enchantress
MAGDALEN Hepburn
MAGGIE Miller, by Mrs. Holmes
MAID Marian, by G. Peacocke
MAIDEN Aunt
MAIL Coach, by Mrs. Sherwood
MAJOR Thorpe's Scenes in Arkansaw, by J. M. Field
MAN and Money, by E. Souvestrie
MAN at Arms, by James
MANON Lescaut, by Abbe Prevost
MAN made of Money, by D. Jerrold
MANSFIELD Park, by Miss Austin
MARBLE Faun, by N. Hawthorne
MARCHIONESS of Brinvilliers, by A. Smith
MARCUS Warland, by Caroline Lee Hentz
MARDI, by H. Melville
MARGARET, by S. Judd
MARGARET Moncrieffe, by C. Burdett
MARGUERITE, by F. Soulie
MARIAN Ellwood
MARIAN Wallace, by Scott
MARION Barnard, by J. F. Smith
MARRIED or Single, by Miss Sedgwick
MARRIED not Mated, by Alice Cary
MAROON, by Simms.
MARTIN Chuzzlewit, by Dickens

MARTIN Merivale, by Paul Creyton
MARTINS of Cro' Martin, by Lever
MARY Anne, by Mrs. Sherwood
MARY Barton, by Mrs. Gaskell
MARY Bunyan, by Sallie Ford
MARY Derwent, by Mrs. Stephens
MARY Lyndon
MARY Staunton
MASTERMAN Ready, by Capt. Marryat
MASTERS and Workmen, by Sarah E. B. Patterson
MASTER'S House, by Logan
MATCH Girl
MATHILDE, Memoirs d'un Jeune Femme, by Sue
MATRIMONIAL Brokerage in New York
MATRIMONIAL Misfortunes of Peter Clancy, by W. H. Maxwell
MATTHEW Carraby
MAURICE Tiernay, by Lever
MAXWELL, by T. Hook
MAY and December, by Mrs. Hubback
MAY Flower, by Mrs. Stowe
MEADOW Brook, by Mrs. Holmes
MELLICHAMPE, by Simms
MEMOIRS of a Cavalier, by D. De Foe
MEMOIRS of Capt. Cronke, by D. De Foe
MEMOIRS of Sergeant Dale
MEN of Character, by D. Jerrold
MEN's Wives, by Thackeray
MERCEDES of Castile, by Cooper
MERKLAND
META Gray, by M. J. McIntosh
MIDSHIPMAN Easy, by Capt. Marryat
MIDSUMMER Eve, by Mrs. S. C. Hall
MILES Tremenhere, by A. Maillard
MILL on the Floss, by G. Elliot
MINNIE Grey, by J. F. Smith
MINNIE Hermon, by T. W. Brown
MINISTER's Wooing, by Mrs. Stowe
MIRIAM Alroy, by B. D'Israeli
MISCELLANIES, by S. Warren
MISER's Daughter, by W. H. Ainsworth
MISER of Ricketictack, by H. Conscience
MISERIES of Human Life
MISREPRESENTATION, by Anna Drury
MISS Slimmen's Window, by Mrs. Peabody
MISSING Bride, by Mrs. Southworth
MISSION, or Scenes in Africa, by Capt. Marryat
MOBY Dick, by H. Melville
MODERN Accomplishments, by Catherine Sinclair
MODERN Chivalry, by H. Brackinridge
MODERN Flirtations, by Catherine Sinclair
MODERN Pilgrims, by G. Wood
MODERN Society, by Catherine Sinclair
MOHICANS of Paris, by A. Dumas
MOLL Flanders, by D. De Foe
MONASTERY, by Scott
MONEY Maker, by Jane Campbell

MONIKINS, The, by Cooper
MONK of Cimies, by Mrs. Sherwood
MORAL Tales, by Maria Edgeworth
MOORLAND Cottage, by Mrs. Gaskell
MORLEY Ernstein, by James
MOSSES from an Old Manse, by Hawthorne
MOSS Side, by Marian Harland
MOTHERS and Daughters, by Mrs. Gore
MOTHER's Mistake, by Mrs. Ellis
MOTHER's Recompense, by Grace Aguilar
MOTHER Ross, by D. De Foe
MOTHER-IN-LAW, by Mrs. Southworth
MOTHER's Trials
MOURNING Queen, by Mrs. Sherwood
MRS. Catherine Crawley, by Mrs. Sherwood
MUSTANG Gray, by Hon. Jer. Clemens
MCSTEE, by B. F. Presburg
MY Aunt Kate, by Mrs. Sherwood
MY Cousin Nicholas, by G. Ingoldsby
MY Early Days, by Eliza Farnham
MY Godmother, by Mrs. Sherwood
MY Lady Ludlow, by Mrs. Gaskell
MY Novel, by Bulwer
MYRTLE Wreath, by Minnie Myrtle
MY Three Uncles, by Mrs. Sherwood
MY Third Book, by Louise Moulton
MY Uncle Timothy, by Mrs Sherwood
MYSTERIES of Udolpho, by Ann Radcliffe
MYSTERIOUS Marriage, by Catharine G. Ward

NATHALIE, by Julia Kavanagh
NATURE and Art, by Mrs. Inchbald
NATURE and Human Nature, by Judge Haliburton
NED Myers, by Cooper
NEIGHBOR Jackwood
NEIGHBORS, by Miss Bremer
NELLY Bracken, by A. C. Bradford
NELLIE of Truro
NEMESIS, by Marian Harland
NEVER Too Late to Mend, by C. Reade
NEWCOMES, by Thackeray
NEW England Tale, by Miss Sedgwick
NEW England's Chattels, or Life in the Northern Poor House
NEW Priest in Conception Bay
NEW Purchase, by R. Carleton
NEWSBOY, by Mrs. E. O. Smith
NEW Stories, by C. Dickens
NEWTON Forster, by Capt. Marryat
NICHOLAS Nickleby, by Dickens
NICK of the Woods, by R. M. Bird
NIGHT and Morning, by Bulwer
NIGHTMARE Abbey, by G. Peacocke
NORMAN Leslie
NORTH and South, by Mrs. Gaskell
NOTHING New, by Miss Muloch
NOTIONS of the Americans, by Cooper

NOUR Mahal
NOVELS and Tales, by Goethe
NOW-A-DAYS, by Laura J. Curtis
NOW and Then, by S. Warren
NUMA Pompillius, by Florian
NUN, by Mrs. Sherwood

OAK Openings, by Cooper
OBEDIENCE, by Mrs. Sherwood
O'DONNELL, by Lady Morgan
O'DONOHUE, by Lever
OGILVIES, by Miss Muloch
O'HALLORAN, by J. McHenry
OLD Brewery and New Mission at the Five Points
OLD Curiosity Shop, by Dickens
OLD Doctor
OLD Farm House, by Caroline E. Laing
OLD Forest Ranger, by Major Campbell
OLD Haun, the Pawnbroker
OLD Hepsey, by Mrs. Denison
OLD House by the River
OLD Inn, by J. Barnes
OLD Jack, Early Life of, by W. H. G. Kingston
OLD Jack, a Man-of-Wars' Man, by W. H. G. Kingston
OLD Lady's Complaint, by Mrs. Sherwood
OLD Mortality, by Scott
OLD Mackinaw, by Miss Strickland
OLD Neighborhoods, by Mrs. Southworth
OLD Plantation, by J. Hungerford
OLD Stone Mansion, by C. J. Peterson
OLD Things and New Things, by Mrs. Sherwood
OLD Whitney's Christmas Trot, by A. O. Hall
OLIVE, by Miss Muloch
OLIVER Twist, by Dickens
OLIVER and the Jew Fagin, by Dickens
OLIVE Branch, or the White Oak Farm
OLIVIA, or the Maid of Honor, by G. W. M. Reynolds
OMOO, by H. Melville
ONWARD, by Jane A. Winscom
OPERA Dancer, by G. W. M. Reynolds
ORMOND, by Maria Edgeworth
ORPHAN Boy, by Mrs. Sherwood
ORPHANS of Normandy, by Mrs. Sherwood
OSCEOLA, the Seminole, by Mayne Reid
OUR First Families
OUR Village, by M. R. Mitford
OUTLAW, by Mrs. Hall
OUT of the Depths, The Story of a Woman's Life

PACHA of Many Tales, by Capt. Marryat
PAMELA, by S. Richardson
PARAGREENS in Paris

PARENTS' Assistant, by Mrs. Edgeworth
PARIS Sketch Book, by Thackeray
PARSON's Daughter, by T. Hook
PARTHENIA, by Eliza Lee
PARTISAN, by Simms
PASTOR's Fireside, by Jane Porter
PATHFINDER, by Cooper
PATRONAGE, by Miss Edgeworth
PAUL and Virginia, by B. St. Pierre
PAUL Clifford, by Bulwer
PAUL Fane, by N. P. Willis
PAUL FERROLL
PAULINE Seward, by J. D. Bryant
PEACE; or the Stolen Will
PEARL Fishing, etc., by Dickens
PEEPS from a Belfry, by F. W. Shelton
PEG Woffington, by C. Reade
PELHAM, by Bulwer
PELHAM Novels, by Bulwer
PENCIL Sketches, by Miss Leslie
PENDENNIS, by Thackeray
PENINSULAR Scenes and Sketches
PEN OWEN
PENTAMERONE; or, Story of Stories
PENNY Tract, by Mrs. Sherwood
PERCIVAL Keene, by Capt. Marryat
PERE la Chaise, by Mrs. Sherwood
PERSILE y Sigismunda, by Cervantes
—— —— Translated
PETER Schlemil in America
PETER Simple, by Capt. Marryat
PETER WILKINS
PEERVIL of the Peak, by·Scott
PHANTOM Ship, by Capt. arryat
PHILIBERT, by Dumas
PHILIP Augustus, by James
PHILOTHEA, by L. Maria Child
PHŒNIXIANA, by G. H. Derby
PIZZA Tales, by H. Melville
PICCIOLA, by X. B. Saintaine
PICKWICK Club, by Dickens
PILGRIMS of the Rhine, by Bulwer
PILGRIMS of Walsingham, by Miss
Strickland
PILOT, by Cooper
PINEY Wood Tavern, or Sam Slick in
Texas
PIONEERS, by Cooper
PIRATE, by Scott
PIRATE and Three Cutters, by Capt.
Marryat
PLANTER's Daughter, by Ellen A. Dupuy
PLANTER's Northern Bride. by Caroline
Lee Hentz
PLANT Hunters, by Mayne Reid
PLURIBUSTAH, by Doesticks
POACHER, by Capt. Marryat
POOR Boy and Merchant Prince, by W.
M. Thayer
POOR Cousin
POOR Fellow
POOR Jack, by Capt. Marryat
POPULAR Tales, by Miss Edgeworth

POPULAR Tales and Household Stories,
by Grimm
POPULAR Tales from the Norse, by G.
W. Dassens
PORTER's Common, by Mrs. Sherwood
PORTRAITS of my Married Friends
POTIPHAR Papers, by G. W. Curtis
PRAIRIE, by Cooper
PRAIRIE Bird, by C. A. Murray
PREACHER and King, by Bungener
PRECAUTION, by Cooper
PRESIDENT's Daughter, by Miss Bremer
PRIDE and Prejudice, by Miss Austin
PRIDE of Life
PRIDE of the Village, by H. Maria Jones
PRISONER of the Border, by P. H. Myers
PRIVATEERSMAN, by Capt. Marryat
PROCRASTINATION. by Mrs. Sherwood
PROFESSOR, by C. Bronte
PROGRESS and Prejudice, by Mrs. Gore
PROTESTANT, The, by Mrs. Bray
PROVOST and other Tales, by John Galt
Riley
PUDDLEFORD and its People, by H.
PUDDLEFORD Papers, by H. Riley
PUNCH's Letter Writer, by D. Jerrold
PUNCH's Letters to his Son, by D. Jerrold
PUNCH's Prize Novelists, by Thackeray
PURITAN and his Daughter, by J. K.
Paulding
PYNNSHURST, by D. McLeod

QUAKER SOLDIER
QUEECHY, by Miss Warner
QUEEN of Hearts, by W. Collins
QUEEN's Necklace, by A. Dumas
QUENTIN Durward, by Scott
QUITS, by Baroness Tautphœus

RACHAEL Gray, by Julia Kavanagh
RAN Away to Sea, by Mayne Reid
RATLIN the Reefer, by Capt. Marryat
RAWSON the Renegade, or the Squatter's
Revenge
REALITY, by Mrs. Tuthill
RECAPTURED Negro, by Mrs. Sherwood
RECLUSE of Norway, by Maria Porter
RECOLLECTIONS of a Southern Matron,
by C. Gilman
RECTORY of Moreland
RED Book, by Mrs. Sherwood
REDGAUNTLET, by Scott
REDSKINS, by Cooper
RED Rover, by Cooper
REDWOOD, by Miss Sedgwick
REGINALD Dalton
REINE Canziani
RENA; or the Snow Bird, by Caroline
Lee Hentz
RESIGNATION, by Countess Arbouville
REVERIES of a Bachelor
RETRIBUTION, by Mrs. Southworth
RICHARD Savage

RICHARD Hurdis, by Simms
RICHARD the Fearless, by Catharine
  Yonge
RIENZI, by Bulwer
RIFLE Rangers, by Mayne Reid
RIGHT at Last, Mrs. Gaskell
RINALDO Rinaldini
RITA; an Autobiography
RIVALS, by Hon. Jer. Clemens
RIVALS, by Gerald Griffin
ROB of the Bowl, by J. P. Kennedy
ROB Roy, by Scott
ROBERT Graham, by Caroline Lee
  Hentz
ROBERT Oaklands; or the Outcast Or-
  phans, by L. Ritchie
ROBINSON Crusoe, by D. De Foe
ROCHESTER, by J. F. Smith
RODERICK Random, by T. Smollett
ROLAND Cashel, by Lever
ROMAN Baths, by Mrs. Sherwood
ROMANCE and Reality, by Miss Landon
ROMANCE and its Hero
ROMANCE of Forest, by Ann Radcliffe
ROMANY Rye, by Borrow
ROMANCE of a Poor Young Man, by
  C. Feuillet
RORY O'More, by S. Lover
ROOKWOOD, by Ainsworth   [Jones
ROSALINE Woodbridge, by H. Maria
ROSA, the Parisian Girl
ROSAMUND Gray, by C. Lamb
ROSAMOND, by Miss Edgeworth
ROSARY, by Mrs. Sherwood
ROSA, the Parisian Girl
ROSE D'Albert, by James
ROSE Clark, by Fanny Fern
ROSE Douglas
ROXANA, by D. De Foe
RUSSELL, by James
RUTH, by Mrs. Gaskell
RUTH Hall, by Fanny Fern
RUTLEDGE

SAINT Gildas, by Julia Kavanagh
  SAINT Giles and St. James, by D.
  Jerrold
SAINT Hospice, by Mrs. Sherwood
SAINT Roman's Well, by Scott
SAINT Valentine's Day, by Scott
SALT WATER, by W. H. G. Kingston
SAM Slick, the Clockmaker, by Hali-
  burton
SANDFORD and Merton, by T. Day
SAND Hills of Jutland, by Hans C. An-
  dersen
SANTO Sebastiano
SARTAROE, by J. A. Maitland
SATANSTOE, by Cooper
SAY and Seal, by Misses Warner
SCALP Hunters, by Mayne Reid
SCARLET Letter, by N. Hawthorn
SCATTERGOOD Family, by A. Smith

SCENES and Legends of the North of
  Scotland, by H. Miller
. SCENES from Clerical Life, by G. Elliott
SCHOOL Days at Rugby
SCHOOL and Holiday
SCHUNDERHANNES, the Robber of the
  Rhine, by L. Ritchie
SCOTTISH Chiefs, by Jane Porter
SEA LIONS, by Cooper
SCOUT, by Simms
SEACLIFF, by J. W. De Forest
SEA Stories
SECOND Love, by Martha Martell
SECRET, by Miss Burney
SELENA, by J. A. Gleize
SELF-CONTROL, by Miss Brunton
SEMI-DETACHED House, by Lady Lewis
SENTIMENTAL Journey, by Sterne
SENSE and Sensibility, by Miss Austin
SETTLERS in Canada, by Capt. Marryat
SEVEN Years, by Julia Kavanagh
SHABBY Genteel Story, by Thackeray
SHEPHERD'S Fountain, by Mrs. Sherwood
SHIRLEY, by C. Bronte
SHORT Stories, by C. Dickens
SIEGE of Derry, by Charlotte Elizabeth
SIMPLE Story, by Mrs. Inchbald
SIR Andrew Wylie, by John Galt
SIR Charles Grandison, by S. Rich-
  ardson
SIR Frizzle Pumpkin
SIR Ralph Esher
SIR Rohan's Ghost
SIR Theodore Broughton, by James
SISTER Agnes
SISTERS of Soleure
SKETCHES, by Dickens
SIX Nights with the Washingtonians,
  by T. S. Arthur
SKETCHES of Every Day Life, by Miss
  Bremer
SKETCHES of the English, by D. Jerrold
SLAVE of the Lamp, by W. North
SLICK, Jonathan, High Life in N. York
SMIKE, by Dickens
SMILES and Frowns, by Sara A. Wentz
SMUGGLER, by J. Banin
SMUGGLER, by James
SNARLEYOW, by Capt. Marryat
SNOW-FLAKES and Sunbeams, by R. M.
  Ballantyne
SNOW Image, and other Tales, by N.
  Hawthorn
SOUTHWARD Ho! by Simms
SOUTHWOLD, by Mrs. Umsted
SORROWS of Werter
SPY, by Cooper
STANDISH, the Puritan, by F. Grayson
STANFIELD Hall, by J. F. Smith
STANHOPE Burleigh, by Helen Dhu
STAR and Cloud, by A. S. Roe
STAR Chamber, by W. H. Ainsworth
STARS and Angels

STEP-MOTHER, by James
STEWARD, by H. Cockton
STORIES of an Old Maid, by E. Girardin
STORY of a Pocket Bible
STORIES of Waterloo, by W. H. Maxwell
STORIES of English and Foreign Life, by Wm. and Mary Howitt
STORIES for the Home Circle
STORIES from the Italian Poets, by Leigh Hunt
STORIES from Blackwood's Magazine
STORY Book, by Hans Andersen
STRANGER at Home, by Mrs. Sherwood
STORY of a Feather, by Douglas Jerrold
STRIFE and Peace, by Miss Bremer
SUBALTERN
STUDENT, by Bulwer
SUNLIGHT and Hearthlight, by S. D. Phelps
SUCCESSFUL Merchant, by W. Arthur
SURGEON's Daughter, by Scott
SUSANNAH, by Mrs. Sherwood
SUSAN Gray, by Mrs. Sherwood
SWALLOW Barn, by J. P. Kennedy
SWELL Life at Sea
SWISS Cottage by Mrs. Sherwood
SWORD and Gown, by C. A. Bristed
SYLVAN Holt's Daughter, by Holme Lee
SYLVIA's World

TALBA, by Mrs. Bray
TALE of a Tub, by Swift
TALE of Two Cities, by Dickens
TALES, by Countess D'Arbouville
TALES of Fashionable Life, by Miss Edgeworth
TALES of the Genii
TALES of a Grandfather, by Scott
TALES of the Jury Room, by Gerald Griffin
TALES for the Marines, by Harry Gringo
TALES of the Peerage and Peasantry, by Lady Dacre
TALES from the German
TALES from Real Life, by T. S. Arthur
TALES and Novels, from Household Words, 11 vols
TALES and Takings, by Rev. J. F. Watson
TALES and Traditions of Hungary, by Theresa Pulzky
TALISMAN, by Scott
TALLANGETTA; The Squatter's Home, by W. Howitt
TAPESTRIED Chamber, by Scott
TELAMACUS, by Fenelon
TEMPER, by Miss Marryat
TEMPER and Temperament, by Mrs. Ellis
TEMPEST and Sunshine, by Mrs. Holmes
TEMPTATION, by J. F. Smith
TENANT House
TENANT of Wildfell Hall, by Miss Bronte

TEN Thousand a Year, by S. Warren
TEVERINO, by G. Sand
THADDEUS of Warsaw, by Jane Porter
THALYSIE, by J. A. Gleizes
THEODORE, by De Welte
THEODOSIUS and Constantia
THEOPHILUS and Sophia, by Mrs. Sherwood
THINE and Mine, by Flora Neale
THINKS I to Myself
THIS, That and the Other, by Ellen Chandler
THORNDALE, by W. Smith
THOUSAND and One Stories, by Peter Parley
THREE Beauties, by Mrs. Southworth
THREE Clerks, by A. Trollope
THREE Courses and a Dessert, by Cruikshank
THREE Guardsmen, by A. Dumas
THREE Marriages
THREE Spaniards, by Walker
TIGHE Lifford
TIME and Tide, by A. S. Roe
TITLE Hunting, by E. L. Lewellyn
To be, or not to be, by Hans Andersen
TOM Bowling, by Capt. Chamier
TOM Burke of Ours, by Lever
TOM Cringle's Log, by M. Scott
TOM Jones, by Fielding
TOTEMWELL, by G. Payson
TOUT en Peu, by T. A. E. Lépéé
TRACY's Ambition, by Gerald Griffin
TRAITS and Stories of the Irish Peasantry, by W. Carleton
TRAVELS and Adventures, by Baron Munchausen
TRELAWNEY of Trelawne, by Mrs. Bray
TREMAINE, by R. P. Ward
TRESSILIAN and his Friends, by R. S. Mackenzie
TREVELYAN
TRIALS of Jessie Loring
TRIALS of the Heart, by Mrs. Bray
TRIALS of Margaret Lindsay
TRISTRAM Shandy, by Sterne
TRUE to the Last, by A. S. Roe
TRUE Womanhood, by J. Neal
TWENTY Years After, by A. Dumas
TWIN Roses, by Anna Cora Mowatt
TWICE Told Tales, by N. Hawthorn
TWINS and Heart, by M. F. Tupper
TWIN Roses, by Mrs. Ritchie
Two Admirals, by Cooper
Two Drovers, by Scott
Two Sisters, by Mrs. Southworth
Two Sisters, by Mrs. Sherwood
Two Years Ago, by C. Kingsley
TYLNEY Hall, by T. Hood
TYPEE, by H. Melville

UNCLE RALPH
UNCLE Tom's Cabin, by Mrs. Stowe

UNDIVIDED Household, by Hon, Jer. Clemens
UNGAVA, by R. M. Ballantyne
UPS and Downs
URSULA, by E. Sewell
USEFUL Little Girl, by Mrs. Sherwood
UTOPIA, by Sir T. More

VALE of Cedars, by Grace Aguilar
VALENTINE Vox, by H. Cockton
VALERIUS
VANITY Fair, by Thackeray
VARA, or the Child of Adoption
VASSALL Morton, by F. Parkman
VENETIA, by B, D'Israeli
VERDANT Green, Adventures of, by C. Bede
VERNON Grove
VERONIQUE, by H. Balzac
VERA, by H. Consience
VICAR of Wakefield, by Goldsmith
VICAR of Wrexhill
VICTORIA, by Mrs. Sherwood
VILLAGE Doctor, by Countess Arbou- ville
VILLETTE, by C. Bronte
VIOLA, by W. E. Binder
VIOLET, by M. J. McIntosh
VIOLET; or The Times we Live In
VIRGIN Queen, by J. F. Smith
VIRGINIA Comedians
VIRGINIANS, by Thackeray
VISIONS of Francis Quevedo
VIVIA, by Mrs. Southworth
VIVIAN Grey, by B. D'Israeli

WALDORF Family, by Mrs. Em- bury
WALTER Ashwood, by P. Siogvolk
WALTER Thornley
WANDERING Jew, by Sue
WARLEIGH, by Mrs. Bray
WAR Trail, by Mayne Reid
WATER Witch, by Cooper
WAVERLY, by Scott
WAPT of Wish-ton-Wish, by Cooper
WHAT can Woman do? by Arthur
WHAT will he do with it? by Bulwer
WHEAT and Tares
WHICH; the Right or the Left
WHILE it was Morning, by Virginia Townsend
WHITE Acre versus Black Acre
WHITE Chief, by Mayne Reid
WHITEHALL
WHITE Hoods, by Mrs. Bray
WHITE Jacket, by H. Melville
WHITE Lies, by C. Reade
WHITE Slave
WHITE Slaves of England, by J. C. Cobden

WIDE, Wide World, by Miss Warner
WIFE's Trials and Triumphs
WIDOW and Marquis, by T. Hook
WIDOW Barnaby
WIDOW Bedott Papers, by F. M. Wicher
WIELAND, by C. B. Brown
WIFE's Sister
WIFE's Victory, by Mrs. Southworth
WIGWAM and Cabin, by Simms
WILD Flower
WILD Irish Girl, by Lady Morgan
WILD Nell
WILD Scenes in a Hunter's Life
WILD Scenes on the Frontier, by E, Bennett
WILD Sports in the Far West, by F. Gerstaecker
WILD Sports in the South, by O. E. Whitehead
WILKINS Wylder
WILHELM Meister, by Goethe
WILLIAM the Conquerer, by Sir C. Napier
WILLIS the Pilot
WING and Wing, by Cooper
WINNIE and I
WINTER Lodge
WITCHES of New York, by Philander Doesticks
WOLFSDEN
WOMAN's Faith
WOMAN's Friendship, by Grace Aguilar
WOMAN's Life, by Emilie Carlen
WOMAN and her Master. by J. F. Smith
WOMAN in White, by Wilkie Collins
WOODCRAFT, by Simms
WOODHILL
WOODSTOCK, by Scott
WOOING and Warring in the Wilderness, by C. D. Kirk
WORLD Here and There, by Dickens
WUTHERING Heights, by Miss Bronte
WYANDOTTE, by Cooper

YEAST, a Problem, by C. Kingsley
YELLOWPLUSH Papers, by Thack- eray
YMMASSEE, by Simms
YOUNG Duke, by B. D'Israeli
YOUNG Foresters, by Mrs. Sherwood
YOUNG Fur Traders
YOUNG Middy, by F. C. Armstrong.
YOUNG Voyagers, by Mayne Reid
YOUNG Yagers, by Mayne Reid
YOUNGER Son, by Capt. Trelawney
YULE-TIDE Stories

ZANONI, by Bulwer
ZENOBIA, by Wm. Ware
ZENAIDA, by Florence Anderson
ZILLA, by H. Smith
ZILLAH, the Child Medium
ZOHRAB, by D. R. Morier

CLASS II.

RELIGION.

ALEXANDER, A. Evidences of the Authenticity, etc., of the Scriptures

ANSPACH, Rev. F. R. The Two Pilgrims

APELEUTHERUS, or an Effort to obtain Intellectual Freedom

APOLOGY for Professing the Religion of Nature, etc.

ARTHUR, T. S. Advice to Young Men

BABBAGE, C. Ninth Bridgewater Treatise

BAGSTER, ——. Genuineness, etc , of the Word of God

BALLOU, Rev. M. The Divine Character indicated

BARCLAY, R. Apology for the Principles and Doctrines of the Quakers

— Catechism and Confession of Faith

BARRETT, B. F. Lectures on the New Dispensation

— The Golden Reed, or True Measure of a True Church

— Doctrines of the New Jerusalem Church

BARROW, J. Of Contentment, Patience and Resignation

BATES, E. Doctrines of the Friends

BEDE's Ecclesiastical History and Anglo-Saxon Chronicle

BEECHER, E. The Conflict of Ages

BEECHER, Miss. Appeal to the People as Interpreters of the Bible

— Common Sense applied to Religion

BEHMEN, J. Aurora, that is the Day Spring, etc.

— Election of Grace

— His Epistles

— Teutonic Philosophy

— Theosophic Philosophy

— His Third Book, of the Three-fold Life of Man

BENTON, J. A. The California Pilgrim

BIBLE

— with References

— with the Apocrypha

BIDEL, Die, nach Dr. Martin Luther's Uebersetzung

BLEDSOE, A. T. Theodicy; or, a Vindication of the Divine Glory

BOOK of Common Prayer

BOOK of Mormon

BOSSUET, J. B. Sermons Choisies

BRONSON, O. A. New Views of Christianity, etc.

BROUGHAM, Lord. Discourse on Natural Theology

BROWN, A. M. Wreath around the Cross

BROWNE, T. Pseudoxia Epidemica

— Religio Medici

BUNGENER, L. F. Trois Sermons sous Louis XV. 3 vols.

BUNSEN, C. C. Signs of the Times for Religious Liberty

BUNYAN, J. Grace Abounding

— Pilgrim's Progress

BURNAP, G. W. Expository Lectures on the Doctrine of the Trinity

BURNET, G. Four Discourses

— Life of God in the Soul of Man

BURROWES, Rev. G. Commentary on the Song of Solomon.

BUSH, G. Anastasis, or the Doctrine of the Resurrection of the Body

BUSHNELL, H. God in Christ

CAHAGNET, L. A. Celestial Telegraph

CASSIODORUS. Historia Ecclesiastica. Folio, 1472

CAVE, E. Lives and Acts of Apostles

CHALMERS, T. Miscellanies. 4 vols.

CHANNING, W. E. Discourses

— His Works

CHAPIN, E. H. Extemporaneous Discourses

CHEEVER, Rev. N. T. Voices of Nature to the Soul of Man

CHEEVER, G. A Reel in the Bottle

CHILD, Mrs. Progress of Religious Ideas. 3 vols

CHILLINGWORTH, W. The Religion of the Protestants

CHRISTIAN Advices; Yearly Meeting of the Friends in London
CHRISTIAN Library, Vol. 1
CHUBB, T. Tracts
CICERO, M. T. On the Immortality of the Soul
— On the Nature of the Gods
CLARENDON, Earl. View of the Dangerous Errors in Hobbes' Leviathan
CLARKE, Dr. S. Demonstration of the Being and Attributes of God
— See Leibnitz
CLOWES, J. Dialogues on the Theological Works of Swedenborg
COIT, Rev. T. Puritanism
COLEMAN, L. The Apostolic and Primitive Church
COLERIDGE, S. T. Constitution of Church and State; and Sermons
— Confessions of an Enquiring Spirit
— Hints towards the Formation of a more Comprehensive theory of Life
COLLIBER, S. On the Nature and Existence of God
CONCORDANCE of the Book of Common Prayer
CRUDEN, A. Concordance to the Old and New Testaments
CUMMINGS, J. Apocalyptic Sketches

DANA, M. S. B. Letters on the Trinity
D'AUBIGNE. History of the Reformation
DAVIS, A. J. Divine Revelations of Nature
DES VOEUX. Lettres sur les Miracles
DE WETTE. Human Life, or Practical Ethics
— Theodore, or the Skeptic's Conversion
— Introduction to the Old Testament
DEWEY, O. Discourses on Various Subjects
— Discourses on Unitarianism
— Discourses on Human Life
DIAL, The. A Magazine. 4 vols
DICK, T. His Complete Works.
DIDRON, M. Christian Iconography. 2 vols.
DODDRIDGE, P. Family Expositor
DORR, B. Churchman's Manual
DOW, Lorenzo, Writings of
DRELINCOURT, C. The Christian's Consolation against the Fear of Death
DWIGHT, T. The Father's Book

ECONOMY of Human Life
EDWARDS, J. On the Will.
ELIZABETH, C. English Martyrology, abridged from Fox

ENCYCLOPEDIA of Religious Knowledge. (Fessenden & Co's.)
ENTHUSIASM, Natural History of
ERSKINE, Lord. On the Evidence of Revealed Religion
EUSEBIUS. Ecclesiastical History
EVANS, F. W. History of the Shakers
EVANS, S. Examples of Youthful Piety
— Account of the Religious Society of Friends
EVELYN, J. History of Religion. 2 vols

FABER, Rev. F. W. All for Jesus
— FANATICISM
FATHERS, Apostolic
FICHTE, J. G. Destination of Man
FOSTER, J. On Natural Religion and Social Virtue
— His Life and Correspondence
FOX, J. Acts and Monuments. 8 vols
— See Elizabeth, C.
FOX, W. J. Religious Ideas
FREE-THINKERS. A Discourse
FULLER, Rev. Andrew. Works
— Principal of his Works and Remains
FURNESS, W. H. History of Jesus

GLANNIL, J. Discourses, Sermons, etc
— On Preaching
— A Blow at Modern Sadducism
GLEIGH, G. R. History of the Bible
GORRIE, P. D. Churches and Sects of the United States
GREENLEAF, S. On the Testimony of the Four Evangelists
GREEN, Rev. G. Concordance of Prayer Book
GREGG, W. Creed of Christendom
GREGORY, O. Evidences of the Christian Religion
— Letters on Christian Religion
GURNEY, J. J. On the Evidences of Christianity

HALL, Rev. R. Works. 3 vols
— Miscellaneous Works
HAMPDEN, R. D. Life of Thomas Aquinas
HANNA, Rev. W. Life and Writings of Chalmers. 4 vols
HARE, J. Guesses at Truth. 2 vols
HARRINGTON's Sermons
HARRIS, J. The Great Commission
— The Great Teacher
HATCH, Cora. Discourses on Religion, etc
HAYDEN, W. B. The Phenomena of Modern Spiritualism
HEADLEY, J. T. Sacred Mountains
— Sacred Scenes and Characters
HECKER, J. T. Questions on the Soul

HENNELL, C. C.   On the Origin of
  Christianity
HILL, T.   Geometry and Faith
HITTELL, J. S.   The Evidences against
  Christianity. 2 vols
HOBBES, T.   His Complete English
  Works
— Ecclesiastical History from Moses
  to Luther
HOLBACK, Baron.   Good Sense
HOLBEIN, H.   The Dance of Death
HOWARD, L.   Ecclesiastes and Wisdom,
  translated
HUMAN Nature.   On the Divine Institu-
  tion of Rewards and Punish-
  ment
HUMAN Progression, Theory of
HUMAN Soul.   Enquiry into its Nature,
  etc
HUME, ?.   Philosophical Works
HUTCHINSON, F.   On Witchcraft
— System of Moral Philosophy

IAMBLICUS.   On the Mysteries of the
  Egyptians, etc
INGRAHAM, Rev. J. H.   The Prince of
  the House of David
— The Throne of David

JENYNS, S.   Works
— Job Abbot, or Reasons for embrac-
  ing the Doctrines of the New
  Christian Church
JONES, J.   Ecclesiastical Researches
JOSEPHUS, F.   Works
JULIAN, The Emperor.   Two Orations
JUSTIN Martyr.   Dialogue with Trypho
  the Jew

KANT, E.   Religion within the
  Boundary of Pure Reason
KEMPIS, T. A.   Imitation of Christ
KIP, Rev. W. J.   Catacombs of Rome
KITTO, J.   Cyclopedia of Biblical Lit-
  erature. 2 vols
— Scripture Lands Described
— Cyclopedia of Biblical Literature
KORAN, The, & Mohammed.   Trans-
  lated by G. Sale
KRUMACHER, F. A.   Parables
KURTZ, J. H.   The Bible and Astron-
  omy

LEIBNITZ and Clarke.   On Principles of Natural Philosophy
  and Religion
LEWIS J.   Merits of Protestantism demonstrated. 4 vols
LATNER in Oxford

MACKAY, R. W.   On the Progress
  of the Intellect as exemplified

in the Religious Development of
  the Greeks, etc.
MAGOON, E. L.   Proverbs for the People
— Republican Christianity
MALEBRANCHE, N.   On the Search after
  Truth, also on Nature and
  Grace
MAN, Ideal
MANT, R.   Horæ Liturgicæ
MARRIEL, F. D.   Theological Essays
McILVAINE, C. P.   Evidences of Chris-
  tianity
MENU, The Ordinances of
METAPHYSICAL Essays on the Formation,
  etc., of Spiritual and Material
  Beings
MIDDLETON, C.   On the Miraculous
  Powers of the Christian Church
— On the Conformity between Po-
  pery and Paganism
MILMAN, H. H.   History of the Jews.
  3 vols
MILTON, J.   His Prose Works
MINUCIUS, Felix.   Octavius
MISCELLANEA Sacra.   On the History of
  the Apostles
MISHNA, The.   Eighteen Treatises
MOORE, G.   Power of the Soul over the
  Body
MORE, H.   Apocalypsis Apocalypseos
— Conjectura Cabalistica
— On the Grand Mystery of Godli-
  ness
— Inquiry into the Mystery of In-
  iquity
MORE, Hannah.   Sacred Dramas
— Practical Piety
— The Spirit of Prayer
— Essay on St. Paul
MURRAY, L.   The Power of Religion
MORELL, J. D.   Philosophy of Religion
MORGAN, ——   The Moral Philosopher
MORMONS ; or Latter-Day Saints, and
  Joseph Smith
MOUNTFORD, W.   Euthanasy
MUDIE, R.   Man, as a Moral and Ac-
  countable Being
MYLES, W.   Chronological History of
  the Methodists

NEALE, E.   The Closing Scene
NEANDER, Dr. A.   History of the Chris-
  tian Religion. 2 vols
— History of Christian Dogmas. 2
  vols
— Christian Life in the Early and
  Middle Ages
— History of the Christian Church
  during the first three Centuries
— The Emperor Julian and his Gen-
  eration

NEWCOMB, H. Christianity Demonstrated
NEWMAN, F. W. The Soul, her Sorrows and Aspirations
NOBLE, Rev. S. Appeal in behalf of the New Church
NOIR, M. L'A. Lamps of the Temple
NORTON, A. Statement of Reasons for not believing the Doctrines of the Trinitarians
— Translation of the Gospels. 2 vols
NOYES, R. G. Translation of Job
— Translation of the Proverbs, Ecclesiastes and the Canticles
— Translation of the Hebrew Prophets
— Translation of the Book of Psalms

PAINE, M. Discourse on the Soul and Instinct
PAINE, T. Theological Works
PALEY, W. Natural Theology
PALFREY, J. G. On the Jewish Scriptures and Antiquities
— On the Evidences of Christianity
PARKER, T. Discourse on Religion
PASCAL, B. Pensées
PECK, Rev. J. T. Central Idea of Christianity
PENN, W. No Cross, no Crown
PHILLIPS, S. Three Plain Discourses
PLATO against the Atheists
— Apology of Socrates, etc
PLOTINUS. Five Books
— His Select Works
PLUTARCH's Morals
PRAYER, Common, and Administration of the Sacraments
PRESTON, J. A Liveles Life
PRIAULX, O. de B. Quæstiones Mosaicæ
PRIESTLY, J. On Christian Truth, Piety, etc
PROCLUS. Elements of Theology

RAMSAY, Chevalier. On the Principles of Natural and Revealed Religion
RANKE, L. History of the Popes of Rome during the 16th and 17th Centuries
RAUCH, F. A. On the Human Soul
REED, A. Martha; a Memorial
REEL in a Bottle
RIPLEY, H. J. The Four Gospels, with Notes
— Acts of the Apostles, with Notes
ROBERTSON, Rev. F. Sermons
ROBBINS, C. History of the Second Church in Boston
ROBINSON, Rev. S. The Church of God, an Essential Element of the Gospel

ROGERS, H. Eclipse of Faith
— Reason and Faith
ROSS, A. View of the Religions in the World
ROWLAND, H. A. Common Maxims of Infidelity
RUPP, J. D. History of the Religious Denominations in the U. S.

SACRED Edict of the Emperor Kang-He.
SAINT Augustine, Confessions of
SALE, George. See Koran
SALLUST on the Gods and the World
SALVATION, Philosophy of the Plan of
SCOTT, Rev. W. A. The Bible and Politics
— Daniel, a Model for Young Men
— The Giant Judge
— Queen Esther
SCRIVER, C. Cotswold's Emblems
SERMONS, Unitarian
SHERLOCK, Bishop T. His Works
SMITH, C. B. Christian Metgphysics
SMITH, J. P. Scripture and Geology
SMITH, Sidney. His Works
— Miscellaneous Sermons
SMITH, J. The Book of Mormon
SPANISH and English New Testament
SPIRITUAL Despotism
SPOFFORD, J. Pagano-Papismus
SPRING, G. Power of the Pulpit
SPURGEON, Rev. C. H. Sermons. 6 vols
— Gems
STEBBINGS, Rev. H. History of the Christian Church. 2 vols
STRAUSS, D. F. Life of Christ
STURM, C. C. Morning Communings with God
SWEDENBORG, E. Angelic Wisdom concerning Divine Love and Wisdom
— Angelic Wisdom concerning Divine Providence
— Delights of Wisdom concerning Conjugial Love
— Four Leading Doctrines
— Heaven and Hell
— Heavenly Arcana
— Four Treatises
— Spiritual Diary
— True Christian Religion
— Dictionary of Correspondences.
SYMBOLS, Book of
SYNESIUS on Providence. See Plotius

TAYLOR, Jeremy. Holy Living and Dying
TAYLOR, Rev. W. Seven Years' Street Preaching in San Francisco
TAYLOR, R. On the Origin, Evid etc., of Christianity

TEMPLE, E.   The Christian's Daily
    Treasure
— Of Truth
TERTULLIAN'S Apology for the Primitive
    Christians
TESTAMENTUM Novum Græcum
THEISM, Christian
THOMAS, F. S.   The Psychologist
THEOS Mathos.   Early Magnetism, etc.,
    as veiled in the Poets and
    Prophets
TILLOTSON, J.   His Works   12 vols
TOLAND, J.   Christianity not Mysterious
— Collection of Pieces from his MSS
— Letters to Serena
— Tedradymus
TORRUBIA, P. P. T.   Ejercicios Espirit-
    uales
TRACTS of the American Unitarian As-
    sociation
TRAVIS, G.   Letters to E Gibbon
TRENCH, R. C.   Sermons
TURNER, S.   The Sacred History of the
    World.   3 vols
TUCKER, A.   The Light of Nature Pur-
    sued.   2 vols

ULLMAN, C.   Worship of Genius
    and Essence of Christianity

VENN, H.   The Complete Duty of
    Man

VOICES of Nature to the Soul of Man

WEIL, G.   Biblical Legends
    WHEELER, D.   His Gospel Labors
    in the Pacific Islands
WHISTON, W.   Astronomical Principles
    of Religion
WHITE, Rev. J.   The Eighteen Chris-
    tian Centuries
WHITING, W.   Sermons and Memoirs
    of Rev. Jos. Harrington
WILBERFORCE, S.   History of the Prot-
    estant Episcopal   Church in
    America
WILLIAMS, W. R.   Lecture on the
    Lord's Prayer
— Religious Progress
WOLLASTON, W.   Religion of Nature
    Delineated
WORCESTER, N.   Last Thoughts on Im-
    portant Subjects
WRIGHT, R.   Sixteen Unitarian Mis-
    sionary Discourses

YOUNG, E.   Night Thoughts of Life,
    Death and Immortality
YOUTHFUL Pilgrims of the Society of
    Friends

ZANCHIUS, J.   Of Absolute Predes-
    tination

CLASS III.

JURISPRUDENCE, AND GOVERNMENT.

SECTION I.

Law of Nations, Treaties, and Diplomacy.

BURLAMAQUI, J. Principles of Natural and Politic Law

GROTIUS, H. De Jure Belli ac Pacis. 5 vols

LAURENCE, W. R. Visitation and Search
LYMAN, T. Diplomacy of the United States

PUFFENDORF'S Laws of Nature and Nations. Folio

TRESCOTT, W. H. Diplomatic History of the Administrations of Washington and Adams

UNITED States Diplomatic Correspondence, from 1783 to '89. 7 vols

VATTEL, E. Law of Nations

WEBSTER, D. Works. 6 vols
WHEATON, H. Elements of International Law

SECTION II.

Statute Law.

ARMY Regulations of the United States for 1857

BIGELOW, J. R. State Constitutions

CONSTITUTION of the United States
CONSTITUTION and Laws of California. Original Editions
CODE of Procedure in the Courts of the State of New York
CORPUS Juris Civilis. Quarto, 1868

DUER, W. A. Constitutional Jurisprudence of the U. S.

HENNINGS' Statutes at Large of the State of Virginia. 16 vols

INDIANA, Laws of

LABATT, H. J. The Practice Act of California
LEYES de California, from 1852 to '59. 7 vols
LEYES del Teritoria de Nuevo Mexico

MOULTON, R. K. Constitutional Guide

SAN Francisco Ordinances, etc., 1854
SHEARER, L. Digest of Decisions of the Supreme Court of California
STATUTES of California from 1850 to 1861. 8 vols
UNITED States Statutes at Large, from 1789 to 1851. 10 vols
UNITED States. Acts and Resolutions passed at the 1st Session 31st Congress
— Public and General Statutes, 1749—1847

WOOD, W. H. R. Digest of the Laws of California, 1850 to '60

SECTION III.

Common, Chancery, and Miscellaneous Law, State Trials, etc.

ANTHON, J. American Precedents
ARNOLD, J. Law of Marine Insurance

BECK, T. R. and J. R. Elements of Medical Jurisprudence. 2 vols
BENEDICT, E. C. American Admiralty Jurisdiction, etc
BLACKSTONE, W. Commentaries on the Law of England
BOUVIER, J. Law Dictionary
BURR, Aaron. Report of his Trial. 2 vols

BURTON, J. H.   Criminal Trials in Scotland.   2 vols

BRYNSHOCK, C.   Treatise on the Law of War

CASE of the Black Warrior

CHITTY, J.   On Commerce and Manufactures, and the Contracts relating thereto

CHITTY and Hulme, J. W.   On Bills of Exchange

CHITTY, Jun.   On Contracts not under Seal

CICERO.   On the Laws; translated.

CODE de Napoleon ; translated

CROSBY, F.   Everybody's Lawyer and Counsellor in Business

CUSHING, L. S.   The Law and Practice of Legislative Assemblies.   2 vs

— Manual for Deliberative Assemblies

DE LOLME, J. L.   History of the English Constitution.   2 vols

— The English Constitution compared with a Republican Form, etc

DUER, W. A.   Lectures on the Constitutional Jurisprudence of the United States

DUER, J.   Marine Insurance

EDEN, R. H.   Law of Injunctions

EDWARDS, C.   The Juryman's Guide in the State of New York

ELIÇABIDE, M. C.   Le Procé de Fastes Criminels.   1840

EVERY Woman her own Lawyer

FEUERBACH, A. R.   Remarkable Criminal Trials

FREEDLEY, E. T.   The Legal Adviser

GAMBOÁ, F. X.   The Mining Ordinances of Spain.   2 vols

GERBALD, J.   Trial for Sedition in Edinburgh, 1794

GETZ, G.   Precedents in Conveyancing

HALL, B. F.   Opinions of the Attorney Generals of U. S.   5 vols

HARE and Wallace.   Select American Decisions   • |

HART, J. B.   Treatise on Practice of Courts of California

HOFFMAN, D.   Course of Legal Study

HOLCOMBE, J. P.   Leading American Cases

— The Law of Debtor and Creditor

HOLTHOUSE, H. J.   Law Dictionary

HOWARD, B. C.   Report of the Dred Scott Case

JUSTINIAN.   Corpus Juris Civilis.   4to, 1688

KENT, J.   Commentaries on American Law.   4 vols

KINNE, A.   Questions for Kent's Commentaries

LEVIN, W.   Legal and Commercial Common-place Book

LIEBER, F.   Legal and Political Hermeneutics

LIVINGSTON, J.   Law Register

LOUISIANA, Civil Code of

MACKENZIE, A. S.   Proceedings in the Court Martial of

MANSFIELD, E. D.   The Legal Rights of Women

MARSHALL, J.   The Federal Constitution

MENU.   Ordinances of

NAPOLEON, Louis.   Le Procé de Fastes Criminels.   1840

ODD Fellows.   Digest of the Laws of the Order

OLIVER, B. L.   Forms of Practice

— Practical Conveyancing

PETERS, R.   United States Digest

PHILLIPS, W.   On Marine Insurance

POWELL, J. J.   Essay on the Laws of Contracts

PROCEEDINGS of the Court Martial of A. S. Mackenzie

RAY, J.   Medical Jurisprudence

RECOPILACION de Renas Militares

REEVES, J.   Law of Shipping

ROBERTS, W.   Voluntary and Fraudulent Conveyances

ROSCOE, H.   Digest of the Law of Evidence

SEDGWICK, T.   On the Measure of Damages

SELWYN, W.   Law of Nisi Prius

SHARSWOOD, G.   Lectures on Commercial Law

SMITH, J. W.   Mercantile Law

STORY, J.   Equity Jurisprudence

— Equity Pleadings

— Conflict of Laws

— Law of Agency

— Law of Bailments

— Bills of Exchange

— Law of Partnership

— Promisory Notes

STORY, W. W.   On Contracts not under Seal

— On Sales

TA-TSING-TEU-LEE, being the Fundamental Code, etc., of China
TAYLOR, A. J. Medical Jurisprudence
TOWNSEND, W. C. Modern State Trials. 2 vols.
TURNER, W. R. Documents and Charges against, in 1851

UNITED States versus Limantour. 4 vols
UNITED States. Digest of the Decisions in Common Law and Admiralty
— Annual Digest of Decisions for 1847-8-9

SECTION IV.

Government and Politics.

ABOUT, E. The Roman Question
ADAMS, N. A South-side View of Slavery
ADDRESSES and Messages of the Presidents of the United States
AMERICAN State Papers. 21 vols. folio
AMERICANS' Guide. The Constitution, etc.
ARISTOTLE. Politics and Economics
— Organon, etc. 2 vols.

BECCARIA, C. B. Essay on Crimes and Punishments
BENTHAM, J. Tratados de Legislation. 8 vols
BENTON, T. H. Abridgement of Debates in Congress. 13 vols.
— Thirty Years' View, from 1820 to 1850. 2 vols
— The Dred Scott Decision examined
BLACK WARRIOR, Case of the
BLAKEY, R. History of Political Literature. 2 vols
BREESON, J. A Plea for the Indians
BLUNT, J. Sketch of the Formation of the Confederacy of the U. S.
BONAPARTE, Prince Napoleon. Napoleonic Ideas
BROUGHAM, Lord. Political Philosophy. 3 vols
BROWNLOW and Pryne. Ought Slavery to be Perpetuated
BURKE, E. Reflections on the French Revolution
BURGH, J. Political Disquisition
BYRDSALL, F. History of the Loco-Foco Party

CAMP, G. S. Democracy
CARBONARI, Memoirs of the Society of
CARLYLE, T. Latter Day Pamphlets
CARY, H. C. The Slave Trade
CICERO. Political Works. Translated
CLUSKEY, M. W. The Political Text Book

3

COCKE, W. A. Constitutional History of the United States to the close of Jackson's Administration.
COE, J. The True American [2 vols
COMTE, A. Republique Occidentale
CONGRESS, Debates and Proceedings from 1834 to 1854. 30 vols
— Register of Debates in, from 1825 to 1837. 29 vols
— Cases of Contested Elections, from 1789 to 1834
CONGRESSIONAL Globe to 1860. 38 vols. Quarto
CORRESPONDENCE Relative to Com. Perry's Expedition to Japan
CUSHING, L. Manual for Deliberative Assemblies
— Law and Practice of Deliberative Assemblies. 2 vols
CYCLOPEDIA of Political and Constitutional Knowledge. 4 vols

DE TOCQUEVILLE, A. Democracy in America
DOCUMENTS relative to Central American Affairs
DWIGHT, T. The History of the Hartford Convention

ELLIOT, J. Debates in the States Conventions. 4 vols
EXECUTIVE Papers of the 1st Session of the 19th Congress of the U. S.
FEDERALIST, The
FILANGIERI, C. Ciencia de la Legislacion. 6 vols
FLANDERS, H. Exposition of the Constitution of the United States

GOURDON, E. Histoire du Congrés de Paris
GUIZOT, F. History of Representative Government in Europe

HAMMOND, J. D. History of Political Parties in the State of New York
HAMILTON, A. The Federalist
— Works. 7 vols
HELPER, H. R. The Impending Crisis at the South
HILDRETH, R. Theory of Politics
HUMBOLDT, A. Essay on New Spain

ILLUMINES, Essai sur la Secte des

JENKINS, J. S. Political Parties in the State of New York
JOHNSON, A. B. Guide to the Understanding of our American Union

KNIGHT, C. Cyclopedia of Political, Constitutional and State Knowledge

LAMARTINE, A.   Trois mois ou Pouvoir
LIEBER, F.   Manual of Political Ethics.
   2 vols
— Civil Liberty and Self-government

MADISON, James.   Debates on the Federal Constitution
MAPS and Views to accompany Presidents' Messages from 1853 to '59
MICHELET.   The People.   Translated
MONROE, Jas.   View of the Conduct of the Executive in 1794, '5 and '6
MUNICIPALIST, The

NEW York State Register, 1858, by J. Disturnell

OHIO.   Annual Report of Statistics for 1857 and 1858.   2 vols
ORMSBY, R McK.   History of the Whig Party

PARSONS, C. G.   Inside View of Slavery, etc
PHILLIPPO, J.   The United States and Cuba
POSCHE, T. and C. Goepp.   The New Rome; or the U. States of the World
PRESIDENTS' Messages and Documents from 1853 to 1860

REPORT of the Committee on the Harper's Ferry Invasion
RIPLET'S Strength of Nations

SECRET Proceedings and Debates in the Convention of 1787
SIDNEY, A.   Discourses concerning Government

TREMENHEERE, H. S.   The Constitution of the United States

VIRGINIA.   Journal of the House, from 1757 to 1691.   3 vols
— Journal of the House, from 1850 to 1856.   5 vols
— Documents of the House of Delegates, from 1850 to '56.   12 vols
— Proceedings in the Convention, 1775-6.   2 vols
— Journal of Convention in 1778
— Journal of the Senate in 1778-9

WARDEN, R. B.   Familiar and Forensic View of Man and Law
WHEELER, H. G.   History of Congress, Biographical, etc.   2 vols
WIRT, W.   Letters of the British Spy
WOOD, J.   The Suppressed History of the Administration of John Adams

SECTION V.

Political Economy, Finance, Money and Commerce.

ANDERSON, D.   History of Commerce.   6 vols
ANDERSON, J. D.   Report on the Commerce of Canada and the U. S.

BANKS, History of
BASCOM, J.   Political Economy
BISCHOFF, G.   History of the Woolen Trade, etc.   2 vols

CAMELS.   Reports of the Secretary of War upon
CAREY, H. C.   Letters to the President on the Foreign and Domestic Policy of the Union, etc
CENSUS of the State of New York for 1845
CENSUS Seventh of the United States, 1850
CENSUS of the United States for 1855
CHEVALIER, M.   On the Probable Fall in the Value of Gold
CLEAVELAND, J.   The Banking System of the State of New York
COBBETT, W.   Porcupines' Works.   12 vols
COLWELL, S.   The Ways and Means of Payment; or Analysis of the Credit System
COMMERCIAL Relations of the U. S. with Foreign Countries
COMMERCE and Navigation of the U. S. of America.   Reports to 1860. 6 vols
— Of British America with the U. S. since 1829
COOLIDGE, R. H.   Report on Sickness in the Army of the U. S., from 1835 to 1855
CORDOVA, J. de.   Texas, her Resources and Public Men
CORMERE.   M.   Recherches sur les Finances.   2 vols
CHAIK, G. L.   History of British Commerce.   2 vols

DE BOW, G. D. B.   Statistical View of the United States
DE Quincey, T.   Logic of Political Economy
DREW, T. R.   Lectures on the Restrictive System
DYMOND, J.   Inquiry into War

EMIGRANT Ships, Report on the Sickness, etc., of
ENLISTMENTS, Messages of the Presidents in regard to

ENTZ, J. F. Exchange and Cotton Trade between England and the U. S.

FINANCES. Reports of the Secretary of the Treasury on the state of the Finances, from 1790 to June, 1860. 12 vols

FLAGG, E. Report of the Commercial Relations of the United States. 4 vols, 4to

FLORIDA. War Documents relating to

FOLGER, R. M. Tables of British Sterling and U. S. Currency

FONBLANQUE, A., Jr. How we are Governed

FREEDLEY, E. T. Practical Treatise in Business, Money, etc

FRENCH, B. F. The Iron Trade in the U. S. from 1621 to 1857

GIBBON, J. S. The Banks of New York, and Clearing House

GOUGE, W. M. Fiscal History of Texas

HILDRETH, P. Banks and Paper Currency

HOLCOMBE, J. P. The Merchants' Book of Reference

HUMBOLDT, A. Ensayo Politico sobre la Nueva España. 4 vols

JAPAN. Report of the Secretary of State of the Expedition to

KELLY, P. Universal Cambist

KETTELL, T. P. Southern Wealth and Northern Profits

LIEBER, F. Property and Labor
— The Penitentiary System of the United States

MACGREGOR, J. Commercial Statistics. 5 vols

MAN of Business in his various relations

MANSFIELD, E. D. Statistics of Ohio for 1858

MASON, J. The Laws of the Circulation, etc., of Wealth

MERCHANTS' and Bankers' Register for 1860

MILL, J. S. Principles of Political Economy. 2 vols

MILL, J. S. On Liberty

NICOLLET, J. N. Report of the Upper Mississippi River

PACIFIC Railroad Reports. 10 vols. Quarto

PACKARD, F. A. Inquiry into the Separation of Convicts in Prisons

PHILIPS, W. Propositions concerning Protection and Free Trade

PICKIN, T. Statistical View of the Commerce of the United States

POST Offices in the United States in 1851

POTTER, A. Political Economy

PRISON Discipline Society Reports, from 1846 to 1854. 3 vols

QUARANTINE and Sanitary Convention in New York, 1859

RAINEY, T. Ocean Steam Navigation and Post

REPORTS of Commerce and Navigation of the U. S., to June, 1860

REPORT of Secretary of Treasury, to June 30, 1860

REPORT of Mutual Life Insurance Co., New York, 1859

REPORTS of the Prison Discipline Society from 1826 to 1854. 3 vols

REUSS, W. F. The Trade between England and the U. S., 1833

ROCKWELL's Report of Railroad and Canal Routes from Atlantic to Pacific Ocean

ROGERS, H. J. American Code of Marine Signals
— Marine Telegraphic List of Merchant Vessels

SAMPSON, M. B. Rationale of Crime and its Treatment

SAY, J. B. Political Economy

SMITH, A. Wealth of Nations

SMITH, E. P. Political Economy

ST. LEONARD, Lord. A Handy Book of Property

WATERSTON, W. Cyclopedia of Commerce

WAYLAND, F. Political Economy

WEIGHTS and Measures. Report of the Secretary of the Treasury

CLASS IV.

PHILOSOPHY, SCIENCE, AND THE ARTS.

SECTION I.—PHILOSOPHY.

1. *Metaphysics.*

ABERCROMBIE, J. On the Intellectual Powers
— Philosophy of the Moral Feeling
ARISTOTLE. Metaphysics

BAILEY, S. Essays on the Formation, etc., of Opinions
BRAY, C. The Philosophy of Necessity. 2 vols
BROWN, T. Philosophy of the Human Mind
BURTON, R. Anatomy of . Melancholy.

CAPACITY and Genius
CUDWORTH, R. Intellectual System of the Universe

DAVIS, A. J. Principles of Nature and a Voice to Mankind
DESCARTES, R. Meditations Metaphysiques
— Meditationes de Primâ Philosophiâ

EDWARDS, J. On the Will

FERRIER, J. F. Metaphysics
FOWLER, O. S. Memory, etc., applied to Self-Education

HAMILTON, Sir W. Philosophy
— Lectures on Metaphysics. 2 vols
HAVEN, J. Mental Philosophy
HELVETIUS. On Man

KANT, E. Critic of Pure Reason
— Metaphysics of Ethics

LEIBNITZ. Œuvres
LOCKE, J. On the Human Understanding

MACKAY, R. Progress of the Intellect, etc. 2 vols
METAPHYSICAL Essays
MOORE, G. Man and his Motives

MUDIE, R. Man in his Intellectual Faculties

PARR, S. Metaphysical Tracts of the 18th Century

SCHELLING. Systeme de l'Idealisme Transcendentale
SPINOSA, Essai Metaphysique sur les Principes de

TAYLOR, Isaac. The World of Mind
THOMSON, W. Outline of the Laws of Thought
TILBERGHIER, G. Essai sur la Generation et des Connaissances Humaines
TYLER, S. Discourse on the Baconian Philosophy

UPHAM, T. C. On the Will

WIGAN, A. L. The Duality of the Mind

2. *Moral, Social and Ethical.*

ABERCROMBIE, J. Philosophy of the Moral Feelings
ALISON, A. Essays on Taste
ALPHA
ARISTOTLE. Nicomachean Ethics. Translated
ATKINSON, H. G. Laws of Man's Nature

CAREY, H. C. Principles of Social Science. 3 vols
CHANDLER, Mary. The Elements of Character
CHAPONES, Mrs. Letters on the Improvement of the Mind
CICERO. De Finibus
— Tusculan Disputations. Translated
— Offices. Translated
COLLINS, T. W. Humanics

DE Wette. Human Life. Translated

FULLOM, S. W. The History of Woman. 2 vols

HANGER, C. H. Proverbial and Moral Thoughts
HICKOK, L. P. System of Moral Science
HILDRETH, R. Theory of Morals
HUTCHINSON, F. On the Passions and Affections
— System of Moral Philosophy

JOUFFROY, T. S. Introduction to Ethics

MUDIE, R. Man in his Relations to Society

PASSIONS, The. Historical Illustrations of their Origin, Progress, etc

SMITH, Adam. Theory of Moral Sentiments
SPENCER, H. Social Statics

VAN DOREN, H. Mercantile Morals

WAYLAND, W. Elements of Moral Science
WHEWELL, W. Elements of Morality

3. Logic and Oratory.

ARISTOTLE. Treatise on Rhetoric

BAILEY, S. Theory of Reasoning
BAUTIN, M. Art of Extempore Speaking
BLAIR, H. Rhetoric and Belles Lettres

CICERO's Orators and Oratory

DAVIES, C. Logic of Mathematics

GERHART, E. V. Introduction to Philosophy and Logic

HAMILTON, Sir W. Logic

MILLS, J. S. System of Logic

WHATELY, R. Elements of Logic

4. General and Miscellaneous Works.

ANTONINUS, A. V. Meditations. Translated
APULEIUS. Works. Translated

BELL, J. D. A Man
BOETIUS, A. M. Consolations of Philosophy
BUCKE, C. Beauties, Harmonies and Sublimities of Nature
BURGH, J. Dignity of Human Nature
BURNETT, F. Doctrina Antiqua de Rerum Originibus
— Archæologiæ Philosophicæ

BURNETT, C. M. Philosophy of Spirits
BUTLER, W. A. History of Ancient Philosophy. 2 vols

COMTE, A. Philosophie Positive. 6 vols
— Ensemble du Positivisme
COUSIN, V. History of Philosophy

DENDY, W. L. Philosophy of Mystery
DICK, T. On the Improvement of Society

EPICTETUS. Works. Translated

GURNEY, J. J. Thoughts on Habit and Discipline
GUAYS, L. B. The True System of Religious Philosophy

HARTLEY, D. Observations on Man. 3 vols
HENRY, C. S. History of Philosophy
HERDER, J. G. Philosophy of History
HICKOK, Dr. L. P. Rational Cosmology
HUME, D. Philosophical Works. 4 vols

JOHNSON, E. Nuces Philosophicæ

LOCKE, John. Philosophical Works

MAURICE, F. D. Ancient Philosophy

PLUTARCH's Morals

RITTER, H. History of Ancient Philosophy

SALVERTE, E. Philosophy of Magic, etc. 2 vols
SCHILLER. Æsthetic and Philosophic Letters
SCHLEGEL, F. Philosophy of Life and Philosophy of Language
SCHMUCKER, S. S. System of Mental Philosophy
STALLO, J. B. Principles of the Philosophy of Nature
SWEDENBORG, E. Principia. Translated

TENNEMAN. Manual of the History of Philosophy

UPHAM, T. C. Disordered Mental Action

VIGNY, A. Servitude et Grandeur Militaires

WHEWELL, W. Philosophy of the Inductive Sciences. 3 vols

SECTION II.—Science and the Arts.

1. Mathematics.

COURTENAY, E. The Differential and Integral Calculus

Davies, C. Logic of Mathematics
— Treatise on Shades and Shadows
— Elements of Algebra
— Elements of Surveying and Navigation
— Elements of Descriptive Geometry
— Elements of Geometry and Trigonometry
— Elements of Differential and Integral Calculus
— Elements of Analytical Geometry
— University Arithmetic
Davies, C. and W. G. Peck. Mathematical Dictionary
De Morgan, A. Essay on Probabilities

Lardner, D. Treatise on Arithmetic

Powell, B. History of Natural Philophy

Scholfield, N. Elements of Plane Geometry and Mensuration
— Higher Geometry and Trigonometry

Vallejo, J. Compendio de Matematicas. 2 vols
Ward, J. The Young Mathematician's Guide

2. physics.—(A.) Astronomy.

ARAGO, M. The Comet
Blunt, C. F. The Beauty of the Heavens; illustrated
Brewster, Sir D. More Worlds than One

Dick, T. Practical Astronomer
— Celestial Scenery
— Sidereal Heavens

Fontenelle. Plurality of Worlds

Grant, R. History of Physical Astronomy
Herschel, Sir J. W. F. Outlines of Astronomy
— Treatise on Astronomy
Hind, J. R. The Solar System

Jones, Rev. G. Observations on the Zodiacal Light

La Place, P. S. System of the World. 2 vols

Manilius, M. Five Books. Translated.
Mitchell, O. M. Planetary and Stellar Worlds
— Popular Astronomy

Nichols, J. P. Architecture of the Heavens

Smyth, C. P. Teneriffe; an Astronomer's Experiment

United States Astronomical Expedition to Southern Hemisphere, 1849 to 1852-3. 3 vols

Walker, S. C. Planet Neptune
Whewell, W. Plurality of Worlds
Whiston, W. Astronomical Principles of Religion

(B.) Mechanics.

APPLETON'S Dictionary. 2 vols
Artizan Club Illustrations to Bourne on the Steam Engine

Babbage, C. Economy of Machinery
Barlow, P. Treatise on the Strength of Timber
Brees, S. C. Railway Practice, with folio vol. of Plates
Bourne, J. Catechism of the Steam Engine
— Treatise on the Steam Engine; illustrated by the Art. Club
— Treatise on the Screw Propeller

Colburn Z. and A. L. Holley. The Locomotive Boilers of European Railways

Douglas, Gen. Sir H. The Construction of Military Bridges
Downing, S. Elements of Practical Hydraulics
Duggan's Theoretical and Practical Treatise on Bridge Building. Folio

Easton, A. Practical Treatise on Street and Horse-power Railways
Ewbank, T. Machines for Raising Water, etc

Francis, J. B. Lowell Hydraulic Experiments. 4to

Gillespie, W. M. Manual of the Principles and Practice of Road-making

Jamieson, A. Dictionary of Mechanical Science

KELT, T.　Mechanic's Text Book
KING, C.·　Memoir of the Construction, etc., of Croton Aqueduct
KING, W. II.　Lessons and Notes on the Steam Engine

LARDNER, Dr. D.　Treatise on Mechanics
— The Steam Engine
LATHAM, J. II.　The Construction of Wrought Iron Bridges

MAHON, D. H.　Elementary Course of Civil Engineering
MORINS' Mechanics

NEVILLE, J.　Hydraulic Tables
NICHOLS, P.　The Mechanic's Companion

PATENT Office Reports. 1847—1860
PEIRCE, B.　Physical and Celestial Mechanics
PRACTICE of Surveying and Leveling, by an Engineer
PRESCOTT, G. B.　Theory and Practice of the Electro-Telegraph

SHAFFNER, T. P.　The Telegraph Manual
SMITH. B.　Report of Italian Irrigation
STEVENSON, D.　Canal and River Engineering
STORROW, C. S.　Treatise on Water Works

TAIT, T.　The Strength of Materials
TREDGOLD, T.　Treatise on the Steam Engine, Locomotive, Marine and Stationary. 4 vols. 4to
— Principles of Warming and Ventilating

VOSE, G. L.　Hand-Book of Railroad Construction

WEALE, J.　Examples of Railway Making
WEISBACH, J.　Mechanics of Machinery and Engineering. 2 vols
WISE, J.　A System of Æronautics

(C.) Chemistry, Electricity, Galvanism, and Mechanism.

B AIN, A.　Elements of Chemistry
BAKEWELL, F. C.　Manual of Electricity
BELL, W. E.　Carpentry made Easy
BOOTH and Morfits.　Encyclopedia of Chemistry
BRANDE, W. T.　Manual of Chemistry. 2 vols
BUCKMASTER, J. C.　Inorganic Chemistry

CHAUDET, M.　L'Art de l'Essayeur
COOKE, J. P., Jr.　Elements of Chemical Physics

DE LALANDE, L. J. L.　Traite de Physiology Végétale
DELEUZE, J. P. F.　Instructions in Animal Magnetism
DONOVAN, M.　Treatise on Chemistry

ESDAILE, J.　Natural and Mesmeric Clairvoyance

FARRADAY, M.　Chemistry and Physics
— Chemical Manipulations
FEUCHTWANGER, Dr. L.　Treatise on Fermented Liquors
FRESENIUS, C. R.　Instructions in Chemical Analysis

GRAHAM, T.　Elements of Chemistry. 2 vols
GRIFFIN, J.　Chemistry of the Non-Metallic Elements
— Chemical Recreations
GRIFFIN, F. W.　Compendium of Qualitative Analysis

KANE, R.　Elements of Chemistry
KNAPP, Dr.　Chemistry applied to the Arts. 4 vols
,
LARDNER, D.　Treatise on Heat
LARDNER and Walker's Manual of Electricity, etc. 2 vols
LIEBIG, J.　Animal Chemistry
— Agricultural Chemistry
— Complete Works on Chemistry
— Familiar Letters on Chemistry
LOCKE, J.　Terrestrial Magnetism
LOWIG, Dr. C.　Principles of Organic Chemistry. 8vo

METCALFE, S. J　Caloric, its Agencies, etc. 2 vols
MILLER, W. A.　Elements of Chemistry
MURPHY, Rev.·R.　Principles of Electricity, Heat, etc
MUSPRATT, Dr. S.　Chemistry as applied to Arts, etc. 2 vols

PARNELL, E. A.　Elements of Chemical Analysis

REICHENBACH, C.　Magnetic Letters
— Dynamics of Magnetism

SECCHI, A.　Electrical Rheometry
STOCKHARDT, · J. A.　Principles of Chemistry
SWEDENBORG, E.　Principles of Chemistry

TURNER, E. Elements of Chemistry. 2 vols

VICAT, L. J. Treatise on Cements

YOUMAN, E. L. Class Book of Chemistry

(*D.*) *General and Miscellaneous Works.*

ALMEIDA, T. Recreacion Filosophica. 11 vols
ANNUAL of Scientific Discovery, and Year Book of Facts, from 1850 to 1860. 11 vols
ARNOTT, N. Elements of Physics

BELVILLE, J. H. Manual of the Barometer
BISCHOFF, G. Chemistry, Physiology and Geology. 3 vols
BLODGET, L. Climatology of the U. S.
BREWSTER, W. Letters on Natural Magic

COMSTOCK, J. C. Natural Philosophy

ÉCLER. Letters on Natural Philosophy

FARRADAY, M. Lectures on the Forces of Matter

GAUSS. Theoria Motus. Translated by C. H. Davis
GROVE, W. R. Correlation of Physical Forces

HARE, R. Explosiveness of Nitre
HIGGINS, W. M. The Earth
HUNT, R. The Poetry of Science

LARDNER, D. Treatise on Geometry

MULLER, J. Principles of Physics and Meteorology

NICHOLS, J. P. Cyclopedia of Physical Sciences

PESCHEL, C. F. Elements of Physics. 3 vols
PHILOSOPHICAL Transactions, from 1800 to 1830, abridged. 2 vols
PIERCE, B. Elementary Treatise on Sound
PIKE, B., Jr. Catalogue of Instruments, etc. 2 vols

QUACKENBOS, G. P. Natural Philosophy

ROHAULTUS, J. Tractatus Physicus

SILLIMAN, B., Jr. First Principles of Physics
SOMERVILLE, Mrs. Connection of the Physical Sciences
SWEDENBORG, E. The Physical Sciences

TIMB, J. Year Book of Facts for 1859
TURNBULL, W. Treatise on the Strength of Timber

WELLS, D. A. Annual of Scientific Discovery. 10 vols
WIDDUPP, J. The Physical Constitution of Celestial Bodies
WOODBURY, Capt. D. P. Treatise on the Arch

YEAR Book of Facts in Science and Art, for 1869 and '60. 2 vols

3. NATURAL HISTORY.—(*A.*) *Geology, Mineralogy, Metallurgy, and Mining.*

BAKEWELL, R. Introduction to Geology
BUCKLAND, W. Geology and Mineralogy
BUDGE, J. The Miner's Guide

CALICOTT on the Deluge
CALVERT, J. The Gold Rocks of Great Britain

DANA, J. D. System of Mineralogy
DAVIES, T. A. Answer to Hugh Miller and Theoretic Geologists
DE LA BECHE, Sir H. The Geological Observer

FEUCHTWANGER, L. A Popular Treatise on Gems
FOSTER and Whitney. Geology of Lake Superior

GEIKIE, A. Story of a Boulder
GOLD Fields of Australia and California

HAIR, T. H. Views of the Collieries of Northumberland, etc. Folio
HITCHCOCK, Prof. E. Outline of the Geology of the Globe
— Elementary Geology
HOPKINS, E. Connection of Geology and Terrestrial Magnetism

JACOBS, W. The Precious Metals. 2 vols
JOURNAL des Mines. 19 vols

LEE, C. A. Elements of Geology
LESLEY, J. P. The Iron Manufacturers' Guide
— Manual of Coal and its Topography

LYELL, Sir C. Manual of Elementary Geology
— Principles of Geology. 5 vols
— Wonders of Geology. 2 vols
— Geological Excursions in the Isle of Wight
— Petrifactions and their Teachings
— The Medals of Creation. 2 vols

MILLER, Hugh. Popular Geology
— Testimony of the Rocks
— Footprints of the Creator
— Old Red Sand-stone
MARCOU, J. Geology of North America, Prairies of Texas, and the Rocky Mountains
MOORE, N. F. Ancient Mineralogy

OVERMAN, F. Treatise on Metallurgy
OWEN, D. D. Geology of Wisconsin, Iowa, etc

PAGE, D. Elements of Geology
PHILLIPS, J. A. Manual of Metallurgy
— Mining and Metallurgy
PHILLIPS, J. Treatise on Geology. 2 vols
PHILLIPS, G. J. System of Mining for Coals and Metals
PIGGOTT, A. S. The Chemistry and Metallurgy of Copper

SHEPARD, C. U. Mineralogy
SMEE, A. Elements of Electro-Metallurgy
SMITH, J. P. Scripture and Geology
SWALLOW, G. C. Reports of the Geology of Missouri

THOMSON, T. Outlines of Mineralogy and Geology. 2 vols
TRIMMER, J. Practical Geology and Mineralogy
TUOMEY, M. Report of the Geology of South Carolina. Quarto
TYSON, P. T. Geology and Industrial Resources of California

WHITNEY, J. D. The Metallic Wealth of the United States

(B.) *Botony, Agriculture and Horticulture.*

ALLEN, R. L. The American Farm
ALLEN, J. F. Treatise on the Grape Vine
ANDREWS, G. H. Treatise on Agricultural Engineering. 2 vols

BARRY, P. The Fruit Garden
BEECHER, H. W. Fruit, Flowers and Farming

BOUSSINGAULT, J. B. Rural Economy
BRECK, J. The Flower Garden
BRIDGMAN, T. Young Gardeners' Assistant
BROWNE, D. J. The Trees of America
— Manual of Modern Farming
BUCHANAN, R. The Culture of the Grape and Wine-Making

CAMPBELL, J. L. Agriculture
CAIRD, J. Prairie Farming in America
COLE, S. W. The American Fruit Book
— The American Vetinarian
COLMAN, H. European Agriculture
CULPEPPER, N. British Herbal

DADD, G. H. The American Reformed Cattle Doctor
— Nature and Treatment of Diseases of Cattle
DOWNING, A. J. Rural Essays
— Fruit and Fruit Trees of America

ELLIOTT, F. R. The American Fruit Growers' Guide
EMERSON, G. The American Farmers' Encyclopedia
EVANS, G. The Dairyman's Manual
EVELYN, J. Philosophic Discourse of Earth

FAIRHOLT, F. W. Tobacco; its History, etc
FESSENDEN, T. American Gardener
FIELD, T. W. Manual of the Cultivation of the Pear Tree
FISKE, J. Grape Culture
FLINT, C. L. Milch Cows and Dairy Farming
FLORA Columbiana

GARDEN, Manual of the
GILPIN, W. S. Practical Hints upon Landscape Gardening
GORDON and Glendenning. The Pinetum
GRAY, A. Botanical Text Book
— Genera of Plants of the U. S. 2 vols
— Plantæ Wrightianæ
GUENON, M. F. Treatise on Milch Cows

HARVEY, W. H. Nereis Boreali-Americana
HENFREY, A. Elementary Course of Botany
HENSLOW, Rev. J. S. Physiological Botany
HIND, J. Farriery
HYDE, J. F. The Chinese Sugar Cane

ILLUSTRATED Register of Rural Affairs for 1855–6–7

JOHNSTON, J. W. F.   Practical Agriculture

KEMP, E.   How to lay out a Garden, etc
KERR, J.   Poultry
KLIPPART, J. H.   The Wheat Plant; its
Culture, etc
LAMBERT, A. B.   Description of the
Genus Pinus, with folio vol. of
Plates
LIEBIG, Baron.   Letters on Modern
Agriculture
LINCOLN, Mrs.   Familiar Lectures on
Botany
LOUDON, J. C.   Arboretum et Fruticetum
Britanicum.   8 vols
— The Villa Gardener
LOUDON, Mrs.   Gardening for Ladies
LOW, D.   Domestic Animals of the Brit-
ish Isles

MAGNE, J. H.   How to Choose a Good
Milch Cow
McCULLOCH, Prof.   Reports on Sugar
Cane and Hydrometers
MECHI, J.   How to Farm Profitably
MOORE, T.   Illustrations of Orchidaceous
Plants.   Colored
MUNN, B.   The Practical Land Drainer

NASH, J. A.   The Progressive Farmer

OLCOTT, H. S.   The Chinese and African
Sugar Canes
OUR Farm of four Acres, and what we
made of it

PARDEE, R. G.   Manual for the Cultiva-
tion of the Strawberry
PATENT Office Reports.   1847—1860
PRESCOTT, H. P.   Tobacco and its
Adulterations
PURSH, F.   The Plants of North Amer-
ica.   2 vols

RANDALL, H. S.   Sheep Husbandry in
the South
REPORT of the Third Annual Fair of
the California Horticultural So-
ciety in 1859
REPTON, H.   Landscape Gardening and
Architecture
REEMELIN, C.   The Vine Dresser's Manual

SKEARINGTON, G.   Modern System of
Farriery
SMITH, Sir J. E.   English Flora.   4 vols
SOWERBY, J. E.   The Ferns of Great
Britain
STEPHENS, H.   The Farmer's Guide.   2
vols

THOMAS, J. J.   Farm Implements and
their Use

THORNTON, R. J.   Elements of Botany.
2 vols
THURBER, Prof.   American Weeds
TRANSACTIONS of the California State
Agricultural Society for 1856,
'57, '58 and '59
— Horticultural Society for 1859

UPTON, R. A.   The Housekeeper and
Gardener

VOLNEY, C. F. C.   View of the Soil and
Climate of the United States
WATSON, A.   The American Home Gar-
den
WARDEN, J. A.   Manual for the Cultiva-
tion of Hedges
WELLS, D. A.   The Year Book of Agri-
culture for 1856–7

(C.) Zoology.

AGASSIZ, L.   Classification of In-
sects
— and A. A. Gould.   Principles of
Zoology
— Contributions to the Natural His-
tory of the United States.   2 vols
ALLEN, R. L.   History, etc., of the
Domestic Animals
AUDUBON, J. J.   The Birds of America.
5 vols.   Elephant folio
— Ornithological Biography.   5 vols.
Royal 8vo
— and J. Bachman.   The Quadru-
peds of America.   3 vols

BAIRD, S. F., Cassin and Lawrencé.
Birds of North America.   2
vols.   4to
BECHSTEIN, J. M.   On Cage and Cham-
ber Birds
BELL, T.   History of British Quadrupeds
— Natural History of British Reptiles
— British Stalk Eyed Crustacea
BEMENT, C. N.   American Poulterer's
Companion
BEWICK, T.   History of Quadrupeds
BINNEY, A.   Terrestrial Moluks of the
United States.   3 vols
BIRDS of America, by J. J. Audubon.
4 vols elephant folio, and 5 vols
imperial 8vo
BIRDS.   Natural History of
BOULTON, J.   Illustrations of British
Song Birds
BROWN, Capt. T.   Taxidermist's Manual
BRODERIP's Zoological Recreations
BROWNE, D. J.   American Poultry Yard
BUFFON, G. L. L.   Natural History

CASSIN, J.   The Birds of California,
Texas, Oregon, etc

Cuvier, G. L. Animal Kingdom
Cuvier, Baron. The Animal Kingdom.
8 vols

Dana, J. D. Custrace of the United State Exploring Expedition
— Zoophytes. Quarto, with the plates, folio
Dixon, Rev. E. S. The Dovecote and Aviary
— Poultry; their Breeds and Management

Donovan, E. The Insects of China, by Westwood. 4to

Elephant, Natural History of

Forbes, Prof. E. Natural History of the European Seas

Gibbes, R. W. Mosasaurus, and the three new allied Genera
Girard, C. Fresh Water Fishes of North America
Giraud, J. P., Jr. The Birds of Long Island
Godman, J. D. American Natural History. 3 vols
Goldsmith, O. Animated Nature
Good, J. M. The Book of Nature
Gosse, P. H. The Aquarium
Gould, A. A. Molusca and Shells of the Exploring Expedition

Hamilton, G. Elements of Vegetable and Animal Physiology
Harlan, R. Fauna Americana
Holbrook, J. E. North American Herpetology. 4 vols. 4to
Huish, R. Natural History and Management of Bees
Humphrey's and Westwood's British Moths. 2 vols
Hunt, V. D. The Horse and his Master

Insects, Natural History of

Jaeger, B. Life of North American Insects
Jardine, Sir W. Naturalists' Library. 40 vols
Jesse, E. Gleanings in Natural History. 3 vols
— Anecdotes of Dogs
Johnston, G. History of British Zoophytes
— Introduction to Conchology
Jones, T. K. The Animal Kingdom

Leidy, J. Flora and Fauna within Living Animals
— Extinct Species of Fossil Ox

Lewes, G. H. Studies in Animal Life

Melsheimer, Dr. F. E. Catalogue of the Coleoptera of the U. S.
McDie, R. The Feathered Tribes of the British Islands. 2 vols

Natural History, Knight's English Cyclopedia. 4 vols

Owen, R. The Classification and Distribution of Mammalia

Plinius, C., Secundus. Natural History; translated. Folio, 1634

Quadrupeds, Natural History of

Richardson and Gray's Zoology of the Voyage of the Erebus and Terror
Ruschenberger, W. S. W. Natural History. 2 vols

Say, T. Conchology, etc. 8 vols
Smith, J. V. C. Natural History of Fishes of Massachusetts
Sowerby, G. B. Conchological Manual
— Conchological Illustrations
Swainson, W. Habits and Instincts of Animals
— Animals in Menagéries
— Geology and Classification of Animals
— Natural History of Quadrupeds
— Natural History of Birds. 2 vols
— Natural History of Fishes. 2 vols
— Shells and Shellfish
— and Shuckbard's History of Insects
Swedenborg, E. Animal Kingdom
— Economy of the Animal Kingdom

Treasury of Natural History

Waterhouse, G. R. Natural History of Mammalia. 2 vols
Westwood and Humphrey's British Moths. 2 vols. 4to

Youatt, W. Sheep; their management, etc
— Cattle
— The Dog
— The Horse
— The Pig; management, etc

(D.) *Anthropology and Ethnology.*

Cabell, S. L. Testimony of Science to the Unity of Mankind
Combe, G. Constitution of Man
— Principles of Physiology

DARWIN, C.   The Origin of Species

ETHNOLOGICAL Transactions.   2 vols

HALE, H.   Ethnography of the U, S. Exploring Expedition

KNOX, R.   Races of Men

LATHAM, R. G.   Natural History of the Varieties of Man
— Man and his Migration
— Native Races of the Russian Empire.   2 vols
LAWRENCE, W.   Lectures on Man

NOTT, J. C. and G. R. Gliddon.   Types of Mankind
— Indigenous Races of the Earth

PICKERING, C.   The Races of Man

SMITH, C. H.   Natural History of the Human Species

(E.) *Miscellaneous Works.*

BAILEY, J. W.   Microscopic Observations of Soundings
— Microscopic Observations in South Carolina
BUCKLAND, F. T.   Curiosities of Natural History.   2 vols
BUTLER, H. D.   The Family Aquarium

CATLOW, A.   Drops of Water in the Microscope

DARWIN, C.   Voyage of a Naturalist
DAVIS, A. J.   Principles of Nature
DAVIS, C. H.   Law of Deposit of Flood Tide
DRAYSON, Capt. A. W.   The Earth we Inhabit
EDWARDS, A. M.   Life Beneath the Waters
EPISODES of Insect Life.   3 vols

GARDINER, Wm.   The Music of Nature
GARLICK, T.   Treatise on Artificial Propagation of Fish
GOBINEAU, Count.   The Moral and Intellectual Diversity of the Races of Mankind
GOSSE, P. H.   Evenings at the Microscope
GUYOT, A.   Earth and Man

HERBERT, H. W.   Hints to Horse-keepers
— The Horse of America.   2 vols
HERSCHEL, Sir W.   The Study of Natural History
HERSCHEL, Sir J.   Manual of Scientific Inquiry

HIGGINS, W. M.   The Earth
HUMBOLDT, A.   Views of Nature
— Cosmos.   5 vols

JACKSON, J. R.   What to Observe
JARDINES, Sir W.   Naturalist's Library.   40 vols

KIDDER, K. P.   Guide to Aparian Science
KINGSLEY, C.   Glaucus ; or Life beneath the Waters

LAWSON, T.   Meteorological Register, for 1826, '27, '28, '29 and '30
LEWES, G. H.   Sea Side Studies
LORD, E.   The Epoch of Creation

MACLISE, J.   Comparative Osteology. Folio
MAUNDER, S.   Treasury of Natural History
MAURY, M. F.   Directions to accompany Wind and Current Charts
— The Physical Geography of the Sea
MILLER, H.   Footprints of the Creator
MUDIE, R.   Guide to the Observation of Nature

NATURAL History.   Reports of the Regents of the University of New York on the Condition of the State Cabinet of N. H.
NATURE Delineated

OGILVIE, G.   The Master Builder's Plan
OWEN, R.   Paleontology

PETERMAN and Milner's Physical Atlas
PRITCHARD, J. C.   Natural History of Man.   2 vols

RENNIE, J.   Bird Architecture

SCHOUW, J. F.   The Earth, Plants and Man
SCHUBERT, G. H.   Mirror of Nature
SMELLIE, W.   The Philosophy of Natural History
SWAINSON, W.   Discourse on Natural History
— Taxidermy and Biography of Zoologists

TATTERSALL, G.   Pictorial Gallery of English Race Horses

VESTIGES of Creation

WHITE, Gilbert.   Natural History of Selborne
WINSLOW, C. F.   The Preparation of the Earth for Intellectual Races

4. MEDICINE, PHYSIOLOGY, PHRENOLOGY, AND PHYSIOGNOMY.

BEAUMONT, W. Physiology of Digestion
BEECHER, Miss C. E. Letters to the People on Health, etc
BINNS, E. Anatomy of Sleep
BLACKWELL, E. Laws of Life

CAREY, M. The Malignant Fever in Philadelphia in 1803
CARPENTER, W. B. Principles of Human Physiology
— Principles of Comparative Physiology
CHINESE Works on Surgery, Medicine, etc. 5 vols
CLARK, Dr. J. H. Sight and Hearing
COMBE, G. Constitution of Man
COMBE, A. Principles of Physiology
COPLAND, J. Dictionary of Practical Medicine. 4 vols
CORNANO, L. On Health and Long Life

DRAPER, J. W. Human Physiology
DUNGLISON, R. Dictionary of Medical Science
DUNSFORD, H. Advantages of Homœopathy

FRANCKE, H. New Theory of Disease, applied to Water

GALT, J. M. The Treatment of Insanity

HITTELL, J. S. New System of Phrenology
HOBSON, B. Works in Chinese on Surgery, Medicine, etc. 5 vols
HOOKER, W. Medical Delusions
— Physician and Patient

JOHNSON, E. Domestic Practice of Hydropathy
— Results of Hydropathy
JOHNSTON, J. F. The Chemistry of Common Life. 2 vols
JONES, T. W. Defects in Sight and Hearing

KIRKES, W. and J. Page's Manual of Physiology

LARDNER, Dr. Animal Physics
LAVATER, C. ·Essays on Physiognomy
— L'Art de connaitre les Hommes par la Physiognomie. 10 vols
LAWRENCE, W. Comparative Anatomy, Physiology, etc
LAZARUS, M. E. Passional Hygiene
LEAD Pipe, Reports in regard to Poisoning by the use of

LYZARS, J. The Use and Abuse of Tobacco
MOORE, G. Health, Disease and Remedy
— Power of the Soul over the Body
— Use of the Body in Relation to the Mind

MUDIE, R. Man in his Physical Structure and Adaptation

NEWNHAM, W. Human Magnetism
NIGHTINGALE, Florence. Notes on Nursing
OTTO, Dr. F. J. Manual of the Detection of Poisons

PAINE, M. Institutes of Medicine
— Materia Medica
— Medical and Physiological Commentaries
PARIS, J. A. Treatise on Diet
PHILIP, A. P. W. The Means of Preserving Health

QUAIN and Wilson's Anatomical Plates. Quarto

REDFIELD, J. W. Comparative Physiognomy
RICE, N. P. Trials in Illustrating the Discovery of Etherization
RIDGE, B. Health and Disease, their Laws, etc
RUSH, J. The Philosophy of the Human Voice

SANITARY Economy ; its Principles, etc
SEWALL, T. Phrenology
SMITH, M. G. Treatise on Teeth
SPURZHEIM, J. G. Phrenology
— Phrenology in connection with Physiology   [gy
STILLING, J. H. Theory of Pneumatolo-

TAYLOR, A. S. Poisons
TICKNOR, C. Philosophy of Living
TRALL, R. T. Hydropathic Encyclopedia. 2 vols

UPHAM, T. C. Imperfect and Disordered Mental Action

VEGETABLE Substances for the Food of Man

5. Fine Arts, Sports, and Amusements.

AGNEL, H. R. Book of Chess
ALEXANDRE, A. The Beauties of Chess
ALLSTON, W. Lectures on Art
AMERICAN Anglers' Guide, by J. J. Brown

ANGELL, Dr. D. M, Ladies' and Gentlemen's Mirror of Fortune
APPLETON's Encyclopedia of Drawing

BELL, Sir C. Anatomy of Expression
BERTRAND, C. F. Le Parfumeur Impérial
BLAINE, D P. Encyclopedia of Rural Sports
BOOK of Costume
BROWN. J. J. The American Anglers' Guide
BURGESS, N. G. The Photograph and Ambrotype Manual
BYRN, M. L. Artist and Tradesman's Companion

CHESS Hand Book
COALE, G. B. Manual of Photography
CRAVEN's Walkers' Manly Exercises
— Recreations in Shooting

DALRIO, E. The Game of Chess, after a new Method
DE LA MOTTE, F. Book of Ornamental Alphabets

FIELD, G. Treatise on Colors and Pigments
FIELDING, T. H. Synopsis of Practical Perspective
— Theory of Painting and Lithography
FISKE, D. W. Book of the First American Chess Congress

GOETHE. Theory of Colors
GREENER, W. Science of Gunnery

HAND Book of Games
HAWKER, Col. P. Instructions upon Guns and Shooting
HERBERT, H. W. Frank Forester's Field Sports. 2 vols
— Fish and Fishing in the U. S.
— American Game in its Seasons
— Frank Forester's Sporting Scenes. 2 vols
— Frank Forester's Horse and Horsemanship. 2 vols. Quarto
HOYLE's Games
HUMPHREYS, H. N. Origin and Progress of Writing

JAENISCH, C. F. The Chess Preceptor
JARVES, J. J. Art Hints
JEWITT, E. Manual of Illuminated Missal Painting
JOPLING, J. Isometrical Perspective

KLING, J. The Chess Euclid

LANZI, L. History of Painting in Italy. 3 vols

LEAF and Flower Pictures, and how to make them
LEWIS, W. The Chess-Board Companion
— Treatise on the Games of Chess
LEWIS, E. J. The American Sportsman
LOSSING, B. J. History of the Arts, etc

MAHON, D. H. Industrial Drawing, etc
MONROE, J. Science and Art of Chess
MONTEZ, Lola. The Arts of Beauty
MORPHY, P. Triumphs of, in Europe
— Games of Chess, with notes, by Lowenthal
MULLER, C. O. Ancient Art, and its Remains

PHILIDOR, A. D. Studies of Chess. 2 vols
PUGIN, A. W. Floriated Ornaments. Folio
PUTNAM, J. D. R. The Rowers' Manual

REYNOLDS, Sir J. Notes and Observations on Pictures
— Works. 2 vols
RICAUTI, J. A. Sketches for Rustic Work. Quarto
RUSKIN, J. Modern Painters. 5 vols
— Lectures on Architecture and Painting
— The Seven Lamps of Architecture
— The Stones of Venice. 3 vols
— Pre-Raphaelitism
— The Political Economy of Art
— The Elements of Drawing
— The True and Beautiful in Nature, Art, etc
— Beauties of

SARRATT, J. H. Treatise on the Game of Chess. 2 vols
— New Treatise on the Game of Chess. 2 vols
SCROPE, W. Days of Deer Stalking
SMITH, H. Festivals, Games and Amusements
SOCIABLE, or 1001 Amusements
STAUNTON, H. The Chess Tournament
— The Chess-Players' Hand Book
— The Chess-Players' Companion
STEWART, W. C. The Practical Angler

TOMLINSON, C. Amusements in Chess

WALKER, G. Chess and Chess-Players
WALKER's Manly Exercises
WALTON, J. and C. Colton. Complete Angler
WALPOLE, H. Anecdotes of Painting in England. 3 vols
WHIST, Laws and Practice of
WHYLE, J. C. History of the British Turf. 2 vols

WILKINSON on Color
WORTHEN, W. E. Appleton's Encyclopedia of Drawing

6. USEFUL ARTS, ARCHITECTURE, MANUFACTURING, AND CIVIL ENGINEERING.

ADAMS, R. and J. Works on Architecture. Imp. Folio
ALLEN and Lewis. Rural Architecture
ALLEN, C. B. Cottage Building
ANDERSON, W. Mercantile Letter Writer
ANNUAL of Scientific Discovery for 1858-9
ANTISELL, Dr. T. The Manufacture of Hydro-Carbon Oils
— Hand Book of the Useful Arts
APPLETON's Dictionary. 2 vols
ARNOTT, N. Chimney Valves and Ventilations
ARTIZAN, The, from 1842 to 1860. 17 vols. Quarto. London
ARTS and Sciences. Knight's English Cyclopedia. 2 vols

BACHE, A. D. and McCulloch's Reports in Relation to Sugar, etc
BAKEWELL, F. C. Great Facts of Inventions during the present Century
BARLOW, P. Materials and Construction
BARTLET, W. H. C. Elements of Analytical Mechanics
— Elements of Mechanics
BASHFORTH, F. Treatise on the Construction of Oblique Bridges
BEALE, L. S. How to work with a Microscope
BECKMANN, J. History of Inventions and Discoveries. 2 vols
BELL, W. E. Carpentry made Easy
BIGELOW, J. The Useful Arts. 2 vols
BISCHOFF, J. History of Woolen and Worsted Manufactories. 2 vols
BLACK, W. Practical Treatise on Brewing
BOHN, H. G. Guide to the Knowledge of Pottery, Porcelain, etc
BOTH, M. L. New Clock and Watch Makers' Manual
BRANDE, W. T. Dictionary of Science and Art
BREWSTER, Sir D. Treatise on Optics
BROWN, R. Domestic Architecture. Quarto
BUILDER, The, from Dec., 1842, to Jan., 1859. 16 vols. Folio. London
BURROWES, T. H. Pennsylvania School Architecture
CARPENTER, W. B. The Microscope and its Revelations
CLEAVELAND, H. W., and Backus. Village and Farm Cottages

CRITTENDEN, S. W. and S. H. Book Keeping, by Single and Double Entry
DESIGNS for Furniture Shop Fronts, etc. Folio
DODD's Curiosities of Industry
DOWNING, A. J. The Architecture of Country Houses
— Treatise on the Theory and Practice of Landscape Gardening

EASTLAKE, C. L. Materials for a History of Oil Painting

FAIRBURN, W. Useful Information for Engineers

GALTON, F. The Art of Travel
GARDE. Meuble Ancien et Moderne. Folio
GRIFFITH, W. Marine and Naval Architecture
GULLICH, T. J., and J. Timbs. Painting Popularly Explained
GWILT, J. Encyclopedia of Architecture

HAMILTON, R. An Introduction to Merchandise
HAMMOND, J. H. The Farmers' and Mechanics' Architect
HATFIELD, R. G. The American House Carpenter
HERRING, R. Samples with prices of paper. Quarto
HISTORY of Silk, Cotton, Linen, Wool, etc
HUNT, T. F. Designs for Parsonages, Alms Houses, etc
— Architettura Campestre. Quarto
— Examples of Tudor Architecture. 4to
HUNT, R. History of Manufactures in Metals. 3 vols

INK, History of

JOHNSON, J. Typographia; or The Printer's Instructor. 2 vols

LAFEVER, M. The Architectural Instructor. Quarto
LAMBREQUER, L. Tapisserie Anciene et Moderne. Folio
LANGSTROTH, L. Practical Treatise on the Hive and Honey Bee
LARDNER, D. Lectures on Science and Art
— Treatise on the Manufacture of Porcelain and Glass
— Railway Economy in England and America
LAW, H. Rudiments of the Art of Constructing and Repairing Roads

LEUCHARS, R. B. Treatise on the Construction of Hot Houses

MAPES, J. J. American Repository of Arts, etc. 4 vols. 1840–43
MASON, G. C. The Application of Art to Manufactures
MECHANICKS' Register. 4 vols. London, 1825
MUIRHEAD, J. P. The Inventions, etc., of James Watt. 3 vols
MULLALY, J. The Laying of the Ocean Telegraph in 1857–8

MUNSELL, J. Chronology of Paper Making

NICHOLSON, J. B. Manual of the Art of Book-binding

PATENT Office Reports from 1847 to 1860
PORCELAIN and Glass Manufactures

ROBINSON, P. F. Rural Architecture. Quarto
— Designs for Farm Buildings. Quarto
RONALD and Richardson's Chemical Technology. 4 vols

SAVAGE, W. Dictionary of the Art of Printing
SCIENTIFIC and Literary Treasury, by J. Maunder
SILK Manufactures
SILLOWAY, W. Text-book of Carpentry
SLOAN, S. The Model Architecture. 2 vols. Quarto
— Constructive Architecture. Quarto
SMITH, J. Panorama of Science and Art. 2 vols
STOKES, J. Cabinet Maker and Upholsterers' Manual
STUART, R. Dictionary of Architecture

TIMPERLEY, C. H. Dictionary of Printers and Printing
TOMLINSON, C. Cyclopedia of the Useful Arts. 2 vols
TREDGOLD, T. Warming and Ventilating Public Buildings

URE, A. Dictionary of Arts, Manufactures and Mines

WEBSTER, E. The Phonographic Teacher
WELLS, D. A. The Science of Common Things
— Familiar Science
— Things not Generally Known
WETHERILL, C. M. The Manufacture of Vinegar

WHEELER, G. Rural Homes
— Homes for the People
WILCOX, C. M. Rifles and Rifle Practice
WILKIE, G. The Manufacture of Iron in Great Britain
WILSON, J. Treatise on Punctuation

7. COOKERY AND DOMESTIC ECONOMY.

BEECHER, Miss. Treatise on Domestic Economy
— Domestic Receipt Book
BLACK, W. Treatise on Brewing
BREAKFAST, Dinner and Tea, Viewed Classically, Theoretically and Practically

COOK's Complete Guide, by a Lady
COOLEY, A. J. Cyclopedia of 6,000 Receipts
CORNER Cupboard; or Facts for Everybody

DONOVAN, M. Domestic Economy. 2 vols

HALL, Mrs. The Ladies' New Book of Cookery
HALL, Miss. Practical American Cookery
HAND Books for Home Improvement
HENDERSON, A. History of Ancient and Modern Wines
HENDERSON, W. A. and D. Hughson. Modern Domestic Cookery

INQUIRE Within. 3,700 Facts worth Knowing
IRVING, L. Modern and Domestic Cookery
IRVING, Miss. 1,000 Receipts in Domestic Cookery

JOHNSTON, J. F. The Chemistry of Common Life. 2 vols

LESLIE, Miss. More Receipts

MANN, Mrs. H. Christianity in the Kitchen
MANUAL of Domestic Economy

REDDING, C. History and Description of Modern Wines
RUNDELL, Mrs., and Mrs. Birch. New System of Domestic Cookery

SAVERIN, B. Physiologie du Gout
SIMMONDS, P. L. Curiosities of Food
SIMPSON, L. F. Hand Book of Dining
SOYER, A. The Pantropheon
— Culinary Campaign in the Crimean War

WALSH, J. H. Manual of Domestic Economy

YOUMANS. E. L. Hand Book of House-hold Science

8. MILITARY AND NAVAL WORKS.

ATLAS of the Battles of the American Revolution
BERYMAN, Capt. W. M. The Militia-man's Manual and Sword Exercise
BLAND, W. Hints on the Form of Ships and Boats
BRACK, F. Tactique de Trois Armes, Infanterie, Cavalrie, etc
BRACK, F. De. Advance Posts of Light Cavalry
BLUNT, J. Shipmaster's Assistant *
BOWDITCH, N. American Practical Navigator

CAVALRY Tactics. 2 vols
COFFIN, E. S. Marine Traverse Tables
COLON, F. Juzgados Militaires. 5 vols
COOKE, E. W. Sixty-five Plates of Shipping and Craft
COOPER, Capt. S. System of Instruction for Militia and Volunteers
CROWEN, T. J. System of Cookery

DECKER. Tactique de Trois Armes
DANA, R. H. The Seaman's Friend
DOUGLAS, Gen. Sir H. Naval Warfare with Steam

EPHEMERIS; or Nautical Almanac

FORBEST, R. Illustrated Hand-book of Military Engineering .

GRAFTON, H. D. Treatise on Camp and March
GREENER, W. Gunnery in 1858

HALLECK, H. W. Elements of Military Art and Science
HARDEE. Col. W. J. Rifle and Light Infantry Tactics. 2 vols
HOYT, E. Treatise on Military Art

JOMINI. Precis de l'Art de la Guerre
— Tableau des Principales Combinacions de la Guerre
— Atlas pour les Dernieres Guerres
— Des Guerres de Frederic II, Comparées au Systeme Modérne
— Tableau des Principales Combinacions de la Guerre

KINGSBURY, C. P. Treatise on Artillery and Infantry

MACAULAY, J. I. Field Fortification
MAURY, M. F. Sailing Directions
MILITARY Maxims of Napoleon

ORDENANZA Militar. 2 vols

PLANS of the principal Battles in Europe from 550 to 1800

REGLAMENTO para el exercicio de la Infanteria
— mandato observar en la Republica Mexicana
REPORT on Small Arms for the United States Service
ROYAL Military Chronicle, 1811

SCOFFERN, J. New Resources of Warfare
SCOTT, Gen. Infantry Tactics. 4 vols. 24mo
STRAITH, Major H. Fortification and Artillery
STUART, C. The Naval Dry Docks of the United States. Quarto

TURNER, J. Pallas Armata

WARD, J. H. Manual of Naval Tactics

9. ALCHEMY, MAGIC, AND GENERAL AND MISCELLANEOUS WORKS.

ABANO, P. de. Magical Elements
AGRIPPA, H. C. Of Occult Philosophy and Geomancy
ALCHEMY and the Alchemists
APPLETON's Dictionary
ARBATEL. Of Magic

BREWSTER, D. Letters on Natural Magic
BUTLER, T. P. The Philosophy of the Weather
COAST Survey. Annual Reports, from 1851 to 1859, with Charts

ENNEOMOSER, J. History of Magic. 2 vols
HOPE, T. Origin and Prospects of Man. 3 vols
HUMBOLDT, A. Cosmos. 5 vols
HITCHCOCK, E. A. Remarks of Alchemists
LIEBER, F. Vocal Sounds of Laura Bridgeman

NICOLSON, W. British Encyclopedia

PATENT Office Reports. 1847—1859
PETERSON, R. E. Familiar Science*

SMITHSONIAN Contributions to Knowledge. 11 vols

4

CLASS V.

VOYAGES, TRAVELS, AND PERSONAL ADVENTURES.

SECTION I.

IN AMERICA.

ABBOTT, J. C. C. South and North; or, Impressions during a Trip to Cuba
ABERT, Lieut. J. W, Report of his examination of New Mexico in 1846
ADALBERT, Prince. Travels in the South of Europe and Brazil, and a Voyage up the Amazon. 2 vols
ADAMS, J. C., Hunter, of California. Adventures of
— The Lost Hunter
ALEXANDER, Capt. J. E. Transatlantic Sketches
ALLEN, P. History of the Expedition of Lewis and Clarke 2 vols
AMERICAN Adventures by Land and Sea 2 vols
ASHE, T. Travels in America in 1806

BALLENTINE's Hudson's Bay; or, Every Day Life in the Wilds of North America
BARD, S. Waikna; or, Adventures on the Mosquito Shore
BARROW, J. Arctic Voyages
BARTRAM, W. Travels through North and South Carolina, etc

BARTLETT, J. R. Personal Narrative in Texas and New Mexico
BARTLET, Washington. Manuscript Journal of Cruises, from 1833 to 1837. Folio
BATES, Mrs. D. B. Four Years on the Pacific Coast
BEECHEY, Capt. F. W. Voyage to the Pacific Coast in 1826. 2 vols
BELCHER, Capt. Sir E. Arctic Voyage in Search of Sir John Franklin. 2 vols
BELLE Brittan on a tour to Newport, etc
BERMUDA, a Colony, a Fortress, and a Prison
BINGHAM, H. 21 Years in the Sandwich Islands

BISHOP, H. E. Floral Home; or First Years in Minnesota
BOND, J. W. Minnesota and its Resources
BONNEVILLE, Capt. Adventures of, by Washington Irving
BORTHWICK, J. D. Three Years in California
BOURNE, B. F. Captive in Patagonia
BRYANT, E. What I saw in California
BUFFUM, E. G. Six Months in Gold Mines of California
BURNEY, J. Buccaneers in America. Quarto

CABOT, J. E. Tour to Lake Superior
CADDELL, C. M. Jesuits' Missions in Japan and Paraguay
CALDERON de La Barca, Mme. Life in Mexico. 2 vols
CANADA, The Backwoods of
CARLTON, R. The New Purchase in the West
CHAMBERS, W. Things as they are in America
CHASTELLUX, M. Travels in North America in 1780. 2 vols
CHEEVER, Rev. H. T. Life in the Sandwich Islands
COKE, Hon. H. J. Ride over the Rocky Mountains, to Oregon and California
COLTON, W. Three Years in California
COLUMBIA, British, Report on the House of Commons, 1859. Folio
COMBE, G. Notes on the United States of America. 2 vols
COOKE, Lieut. Col. Report of his March from Santa Fé to San Diego
Cox, Ross. Adventures on the Columbia River
COULTER, John. Adventures on the Coast of South America and California. 2 vols
— Adventures in the Pacific
COZZENS, F. S. Acadia

DANA, R. H. Two Years before the Mast
— To Cuba and Back

DAVIS, W. H. El Gringo; or Mexico and her People
DAVENPORT, R. A. Perilous Adventures, etc
DELANO, A. A Life on the Plains and in the Diggings
DE VEAUX. Falls of Niagara
DE VRIES, D. P. Voyages to America in 1632
DONIPHAN, Capt. Expedition and Conquest of New Mexico
DRAGOON Campaigns to the Rocky Mountains, 1836
DRAKE, Cavendish and Dampier. Their Lives and Voyages
DRAKE, S. G. Indian Captivities
— Tragedies of the Wilderness
DUFFERIN, Lord. Letters from High Latitudes
DUNDONALD, Admiral Earl. Services in South America. 2 vols
DUNIWAY, Mrs. Crossing the Plains and Living in Oregon
DWIGHT, T. Travels in New England and New York. 4 vols

EDWARDS, F. S. Campaign in New Mexico with Col. Doniphan
ELLIS, W. Polynesian Researches. 4 vols
EMORY, Major. Report of the Mexican Boundary Commission, vol. 1
EWBANKS, T. Life in Brazil

FALCONER, T. The Discovery of the Mississippi and S. W. Oregon
FAMIN, C. Chile, Paraguay, Uraguay et Buenos-Ayres
FARNHAM, J. T. Life, Adventures and Travels in California, etc
FARNHAM, Mrs. Life in Prairie Land
— California, In-Doors and Out
FEATHERSTONHAUGH, G. W. Excursions through the Slave States. 2 vols
FEMALE Life Among the Mormons
FERRIS, B. G. Utah and the Mormons
FERRY, G. Vagabond Life in Mexico
FOSTER, L. Wayside Glimpses North and South
FRANKLIN, Sir J. His Thirty Years in the Arctic Regions
FREMONT, J. C. Expedition to the Rocky Mountains, and to Oregon and North California
— Life and Explorations, by C. W. Upham
— Life, by J. C. Smucker
FROEBEL, J. Seven Years Travel in Central America

GASS, P. Lewis and Clarke's Journal
GIBBES, R. W. Cuba for Invalids

GIBBON, Lieut. L. Exploration Amazon
GILLIS, Lieut. The United States Astronomical Expedition to Chile. 3 vols. Quarto
GISBORNE, L. The Isthmus of Darien in 1852
GLADSTONE, T. H. The Englishman in Kansas
GOSSE, P. H. A Naturalist's Sojourn in Jamaica
GRAVES, Mrs. Woman in America
GRAHAM, J. D. Report on the Mexican Boundary
GREEN, T. J. Texian Expedition against Mier
GREEN, N. W. Fifteen Years among the Mormons
GREELEY, H. Overland Journey from New York to San Francisco
GREGG, J. Commerce of the Prairies. 2 vols
GRUND, F. J. Aristocracy in America. 2 vols

HALE, C. E. Kansas and Nebraska
HAMMOND, S. H. Wild Northern Scenes
HARDY, Lieut. Travels in Mexico in 1825-8
HAYES, Dr. J. J. Arctic Boat Journey in 1854
HEAD, G. Forest Scenes in North America
HEADLEY, J. T. The Adirondack
HENRY, J. Sketches in Moravian Life
HERNDON, W. D. Exploration of the Amazon. 2 vols
HINES, G. Oregon
HOFFMAN, C. F. A Winter in the West. 2 vols
HOLTON, P. F. Twenty Months in New Granada and the Andes
HOUSTON, Mrs. Texas and the Gulf of Mexico
HOWE, Mrs. Julia W. A Trip to Cuba
HUGHES, J. T. Doniphan's Expedition and Conquest of New Mexico
HUMBOLDT, A. Von. Travels in the Equinoctial Regions of America. 6 vols
— The same, abridged
— The Island of Cuba
HUNDLEY, D. R. Social Relations in the Southern States
HUNTER, J. Memoirs of his Captivity among the Indians

ICELAND, Greenland and the Faroe Islands
INGRAHAM, J. H. The Sunny South
IRVING, J. T. Indian Sketches. 2 vols
IRVING, W. Adventures of Captain Bonneville

Je▮▮▮t, J. R.   Captivity among the Savages of Nootka Sound
Johnston, Capt. A. R.   Journal in New Mexico
Jones, J. M.   The Naturalist in Bermuda

Kane, Dr. E. K.   U. S. Grinnell Expedition in Search of Sir John Franklin
— Arctic Explorations, the Second Expedition. 2 vols
Keating, H. H.   Expedition to St. Peter's River, in 1823. 2 vols.
Kelly, J. W.   Excursions to California, etc. 2 vols
Kendall, G. W.   Expedition across the Great Southwestern Prairies. 2 vols
Kidder, D. P., and J. C. Fletcher.   Brazil and the Brazilians
King, Rev. T. Starr.   The White Hills of New Hampshire
Kip, L.   Army Life on the Pacific

Labat, R. P.   Voyage aux Iles Francaise dé l'Amerique dans 1694
Lacroix, F.   Patagonie, Terre-de-Feu, etc
Lafayette in America in 1824-5, by A. Lavasseur. 2 vols
Lanman, C.   The Wilds of America. 2 vols
Latrobe, C. J.   The Rambler in Mexico
Lette, J. M.   California Illustrated
Levasseur, A.   Lafayette in America. 2 vols
Lewis and Clarke's Expedition to the Pacific. Quarto
Lewis and Clarke.   Abridgment of
Liancourt, R.   Travels in the United States from 1795 to 1797. 2 vols. Quarto
Long, Major.   Expedition to the Rocky Mountains. 2 vols
Long, J.   Voyages and Travels of an Indian Interpreter and Trader
Lyell, C.   Travels in North America, in 1841-2. 2 vols
— Second Visit to America. 2 vols
Lyon, Capt. G. F.   Journal of a Residence and Tour in Mexico 1826

Mackay, C.   Life and Liberty in America '
Mackenzie, A.   Voyages from Montreal to the Pacific in 1789-93
Marcy, Capt. E. B.   Exploration of the Red River in 1852
Marryat, Capt.   Diary in America
Marryat, Frank.   Mountains and Molehills

Martineau, H.   Society in America. 2 vols.
McClintock, Capt.   Discovery of the Fate of Sir John Franklin
McDougal, G. F.   Voyage of the Resolute in search of Sir John Franklin, in 1852
McGowan, E.   Narrative of his adventures and Persecutions by the Vigilance Committee
McKenney, T. L.   Tour to the Lakes of the Chippeway Indians
McLean, J.   Notes of 28 Years' Service in the Hudson Bay Territories. 2 vols
Mears, J.   Voyages to the Northwest Coast in 1788-9. Quarto.
Michaux, F. A.   Travels in the United States
Mollhausen, B.   Journey from the Mississippi to the Coast of the Pacific. 2 vols
Montgomery, Cora.   Eagle Pass
Moodie, Mrs.   Roughing it in the Bush
— Life in the Clearings
Morrell, Capt B.   Four Voyages to the South Sea and Pacific, 1722-3
Morse, J.   Report on Indian Affairs
Mulany, J.   Trip to New Foundland
Murray, Hon. C. A.   Travels in America in 1834-5-6. 2 vols
Murray, Miss A.   Letters from the United States and Canadas

Norman, B. M.   Travels in Yucatan

Olmsted, F. L.   Journey through Texas
— Journey to the Seaboard Slave States
— Journey through the Back Country
Osborn, Lieut. S.   Stray Leaves from an Arctic Journal
Ossoli, Countess.   At Home and Abroad

Page, T. G.   La Plata and the Argentine Confederation and Paraguay
Palmer, J. W.   The New and Old; or California and India
Parker, S.   Tour to the Rocky Mountains
Parkman, F.   Prairie and Rocky Mountain Life
Parsons, C. G.   Tour Among the Planters
Parry, W. E.   Three Voyages to Discover a Northwest Passage. 2 vols
Perkins, E. T.   Na Motu; or Reef Roving in the South Seas

PAYNE. R. M. The Geral-Milco

PIKE, L. M. Explorations in the Western Territory. 4to

PITCAIRN's Island and its Inhabitants

POLAR Seas and Regions

PORTE Crayon's Virginia Illustrated

PRAIRIE Traveller

REID, Mayne. Wild Life; or Adventures on the Frontier

— The Wood Rangers

REVERE, Lieut. J. W. Tour of Duty in California

RICHARDSON, J. Arctic Searching Expedition.

— Journal of a Boat Voyage in the Arctic Sea

RIGSBY, J. The Shoe and Canoe. 2 vols

ROBINSON, C. Voyages and Discoveries in America to 1573

ROBINSON, A. Life in California

ROBINSON, Mrs. Kansas

ROSS, A. Adventures of the First Settlers in Oregon

— Adventures in Oregon and the Rocky Mountains. 2 vols

— Fur Traders in the Far West. 2 vols

RUXTON; G. F. Adventures in Mexico, etc

— Life in the Far West

RYAN, W. R. Adventures in California. 2 vols

SALA, G. A. A Journey due North in 1856

SARTORUS, C. Mexico, Landscapes, Sketches, etc. Quarto

SCARLET, Hon. P. C. South America and the Pacific. 2 vols

SCENES in the Rocky Mountains. Oregon, California, etc

SCHOOLCRAFT, H. R. Journal through the Northwest of the United States

— Expedition to Itasca Lake in 1832

— Travels in the Mississippi Valley

SEWELL's Journal during a Summer tour with Children

SEYD, E. California and its Resources

SHEA, J. G. Discovery, etc., of the Mississippi Valley

SIMPSON, Sir G. Journey Round the World in 1841–2. 2 vols

SIMPSON, J. H. Military Reconnaisance to the Navajo Country

SITGREAVE, Capt. L. Expedition to the Zuni and Colorado River

SMITH, Capt. J. Travels and History of Virginia.

SMITH, E. R. Tour Among the Araucanian Indians of Chile

SMITH, S. C. Chile con Carné

SMUCKER, S. M. Arctic Explorations in the 19th Century

SQUIER, E. G. The States of Central America.

— Notes on Central America

— Nicaragua. 2 vols

STANSBURY, H. Expedition to the Great Salt Lake

STEPHENS, J. L. Incidents of Travel in Central America, Chiapas and Yucatan

— Incidents of Travel in Yucatan

STEVENSON, W. B. Twenty Years' Residence in South America. 2 vols

STEWART, C. S. Brazil and La Plata

STOUT, F. B. Nicaragua : Past, Present and Future

STRAIN, J. G. Journey to Chili, etc

STREET, A. B. Woods and Waters

SUBALTERN in America

SWAN, J. G. The Northwest Coast

TAYLOR, B. El Dorado

TAYLOR, W. California Life Illustrated

TERNAUX Compans, H. Voyages de l'Amerique. 20 vols

— Essai sur l'Ancien Gundisramanca

— Histoire de Mexique, par Alvaro Tezo. 2 vols

TEN Months in Mexico

THORNTON, J. Q. Oregon and California in 1848. 2 vols

TOMES, R. Panama in 1855

TOMLINSON, W. P. Kansas in 1858

TRAIN, G. F. Young America in Wall Street

TRAVELS to the Western Slope of the Cordilleras

TROLLOPE, Mrs. Domestic Manners of the Americans

TROLLOPE, A. West Indies and the Spanish Main

TURNBULL, B. Cuba and the Slave Trade

TYTLER, P. F. Discoveries on the North Coast of America

VANCOUVER, Capt. G. Voyage to the North Pacific in 1790. 3 vols. Quarto and Atlas of Plates

VEILE, Mrs. Following the Drum

VENEGAS, Padre. Noticia de la California. 3 vols. 1757

WAFER, L. Voyage to the Isthmus of America, 1699

WARD, H. G. Mexico in 1829. 2 vols

WARREN, T. R. Dust and Foam

WATERTON, C. Wandering in South America

WHITEFIELD, G. Voyage from London to Savannah

WIERZBICKI, F. P. California as it is,
and as it May Be. 1849
WILLIAMS, T. and J. Calvert. Fiji and
the Fijians
WILLIAMS, J. J. Isthmus of Tehuante-
pec
WILLIS, N. P. Health Trip to the Trop-
ics
WILSON, R. A. Mexico
WINTERBOTHAM, W. View of America.
5 vols
WISE, Lieut. Los Gringos
— Scampavias
WORTLEY, Lady B. Stuart. Travels in
the United States and Canada

SECTION II.

IN EUROPE, THE LEVANT, AND EGYPT.

ABOUT, E. Greece and the Greeks
ADALBERT, Prince. Travels in
the South of Europe, etc. 2
vols
ADDISON, J. Remarks on several parts
of Italy
ANDERSON, J. Bible Lights from Bible
Lands
ARCULF, Bishop. Travels in the Holy
Land, A. D. 700
ARTHUR, W. Italy in Transition in 1860
ATTACHE in Madrid
AULDJO, J. Visit to Constantinople

BAIRD, H. M. Modern Greece
BALLOON Travels of Robert Merry
BARVELL, G. The Pedestrian in France
BARTLETT, D. W. Paris with Pen and
Pencil
BARTLETT, W. H. The Nile Boat
— Forty Days in the Desert, on the
Track of the Israelites
BARTOL, C. A. Pictures of Europe
BEATTIE, W. The Waldenses, illustra-
ted, by Bartlett
BEATY's Illustrations of Hanoverian and
Saxon Scenery
BELLE Smith Abroad
BENEDICT, E. C. A Run through Eu-
rope
BERNARD the Wise. Voyage to Pales-
tine, in 867
BINNS, J. 29 Years in Europe and the
United States
BORROW, G. The Bible in Spain
BRACE, C. L. Hungary
— Home Life in Germany
— The Norse-Folk
BROCKEDON, W. Illustrations of the
Passes of the Alps. 2 vols
BROQUIERES, B. Travels in Palestine,
in 1432-3
BROWNE, J. R. Yusef

BROUGHTON, Lord. Visits to Italy, from
1816 to 1854. 2 vols
BRYANT, W. C. Letters from Spain
BUCHANAN, R. Clerical Furlough in the
Holy Land
BULLARD, Mrs. Sights and Scenes in
Europe   [vols
BULWER. England and the English. 2
BUNBURY, Selina. A Summer in North-
ern Europe
BURCKHARDT, J. L, Egypt and Nubia
BURRITT, Elihu. Thoughts on Things
at Home and Abroad

CASS. France, Its King and Court
CASTELLAN, A. L. Description of
Turkey. 3 vols
CHANNING, W. A Physician's Vacation
CHARLES, P. Notabilities in France and
England
CHESTERTON, G. L. Peace, War and Ad-
venture. 2 vols
CHATEAUBRIAND, M. Itineraire de Paris
a Jerusalem
CHOPIN, M. Ruissie. 2 vols
CHOULES, J. O. Cruise of the North
Star
COCKS, C. Bordeaux, its Wines, etc
COLMAN, H. European Life and Manners.
2 vols
COLTON, Rev. W. Land and Sea in the
Bosphorus and Egean
— Ship and Shore in Madeira, Lis-
bon, etc
COSAS de España; or Going to Madrid
COXE, A. C. Impressions of England
CRAWFORD, Mabel. Life in Tuscany
CUNNINGHAM, P. Hand-Book of London
CURTIS, G. W. Notes of a Howadji
CURZON, R. Monasteries of the Levant
— Armenia

DE CUSTINE, M. Russia
DE FOREST, J. W. European Acquaint-
ance
DE LAGNY, G. The Knout and the
Russians
DENDY's Wild Hebrides
DE STAEL, Mad. Alemagne
— Germany. 2 vols
DICKENS, C. Pictures from Italy
DIDDIN, Dr. T. F. Tour in France and
Germany. 3 vols
DITSON, G. L. The Crescent and the
French Crusaders
— France, Egypt and Ethiopia
DIX, J. A. A Winter in Madeira
DORE, by a Stroller in Europe
DUFFERIN, Lord. Letters from High
Latitudes
DUNN Browne's Experiences in Foreign
Parts
DUVALLON, B. Vue de la Españole

DWIGHT, H. E.   Travels in Germany

EDWARDS, Rev. J. E.   Random Sketches of European Travel

EOTHEN, A.   Traces of Travel

EUROPE.   Reminiscences of an Old Traveler

EUROPEAN Life, Legend and Landscape, by an Artist

FIELD, H. M.   Summer Pictures; from Copenhagen to Venice

FORBES, J.   Norway and its Glaciers

FORD, R.   The Spaniards and their Country

— Gatherings from Spain

FORESTER, T.   Norway and its Scenery

— Mesopotamia and Assyria

FRONTIER Lands of the Christian and Turk.   2 vols

FURNISS, W.   Views across the Sea

GARDNER, A. K.   The French Metropolis

— Old Wine in New Bottles

GELL and Gandy's Pompeiana

GILLEY's Narrative

GLIMPSES of Europe, by a Merchant

GREELEY, H.   Glances at Europe

GREENWOOD, Grace.   Haps and Mishaps of a Tour in Europe

GREGOROVIUS, F.   Corsica, Picturesque, Historical, etc

GUILLEMARD, R.   Adventures of a French Sergeant

GUROWSKI.   Russia as it is

HALL, Mrs.   Ireland, its Scenery, Character, etc.   3 vols

HAMILTON, J.   Sinai, the Hedjaz, etc

HAUSSEY, Baron D.   Great Britain in 1833.   2 vols

HAWKES, F. L.   Monuments of Egypt, and a Voyage up the Nile

HEAD, F. R.   Life and Adventures of Bruce the Traveler

HEADLEY, J. T.   Letter from Italy; and the Alps and the Rhine

— Rambles and Sketches

HERSCHEL, R. H.   Notes of a Journey to Syria and Palestine

HILLARD, G. S.   Six Months in Italy

HOLLAND, Lord.   Foreign Reminiscences

HONAN, M. B.   Personal Adventures in Italy

FOOD, T.   Up the Rhine.   2 vols

HOPPIN, J. M.   Notes of a Theological Student

HORNBY, Mrs. E.   In and Around Stamboul

HORWITZ, O.   Brushwood picked up on the Continent

HOWITT, W.   Students' Life in Germany

— German Experiences

HOWITT, W.   Rural Life in England.   2 vols

HOWITT, Anna M.   Art Student in Munich

HUGHES, T. M.   Overland Journey to Lisbon.   2 vols

HUNT, F. K.   The Rhine and its Scenery

HUSSAR, The

INGRAHAM, Rev. J. H.   The Pillar of Fire

IRISH, The, at Home and Abroad

JARVES, J. J.   Italian Sights and Papal Principles

— Parisian Sights and French Principles

JOHNSON, Anna.   Peasant Life in Germany

— Cottages of the Alps

JOHNSON, Mrs. S. B.   Hadji in Syria

KAVANAGH, Miss.   A Summer and Winter in the Two Sicilies

KHARTOUM and the Nile

KIRKLAND, Mrs.   Holidays Abroad

KIRWAN.   Men and Things as I saw them in Europe

KITTO, J.   Scripture Lands

KOHL, J. G.   Travels in England and Wales

— Austria

— Russia

LAMARTINE, A.   Visit to the Holy Land

LEPSIUS, Dr.   Letters from Egypt, Ethiopia and Syria

LINDSAY, Lord.   Letters on Egypt, Edom and the Holy Land

LOFTUS, W. K.   Travels and researches in Chaldea, etc

LYNCH, W. F.   Expedition to the Dead Sea

M.   Letters from Three Continents

MacGAVOCK, R. W.   A Tennesseean Abroad

MACKENZIE, Sir G. S.   Travels in Iceland in 1810

MACKENZIE, A. S.   A Year in Spain

MacLEOD, D.   Pynnshurst, his Wanderings, etc.

MADRID in 1835, by a resident officer

MARIGNY, T.   Voyages in the Black Sea

MARTINEAU, Harriet.   Feats on the Fiord

MAUNDERELL, H.   Journey from Aleppo to Jerusalem in 1697

MAUNDEVILLE, Sir J.   Travels in Palestine from 1322 to 1356

MAXWELL, J. S.   The Czar, his Court and People

McCORMICK, R. C.   St. Pauls to St. Sophia

McCLELLAN, Capt. G. B. Report to Secretary of War from Seat of War in Europe. 8 vols. Washington, 1857
MILES, P. Rambles in Iceland
MILLER, Hugh, First Impressions of England
— Cruise of the Betsy
MILNER, J. Russia
MITCHELL, D. G. Battle Summer
— Fresh Gleanings
MONRO, V. Summer Rambles in Syria, etc
MORAN, B. Footpath and Highway
MORRIS, E. Joy. Life and Love in Norway
— Corsica
MOSLEM and Christian. 3 vols

NELIGAN, Rev. W. H. Rome, its Churches etc
NORTON, C. E. Notes of Travel and Study in Italy
NOYES, J. O. Roumania

OSBORN, H. S. Palestine, Past and Present
OSCANYAN, C. The Sultan and his People
OSSOLI, Margaret Fuller. At Home and Abroad

PAGET, J. Hungary and Transylvania. 2 vols
PAINE, Caroline. The Tent and Harem
PALESTINE. Early Travels in
PARROTT, F. Journey to Ararat
PFEIFFER, Ida. Journey to Iceland
PINKERTON, J. Collection of Voyages and Travels. 6 vols
Poco Mas. Adventures in Spain
POOLE, S. Englishwoman in Egypt
PORTER, Rev. J. L. Five Years in Damascus. 2 vols
POST, H. N. V. Visit to Greece and Constantinople in 1827
PRIME, S. Travels in Europe and the East
PRIME, W. C. Boat Life in Egypt and Nubia
— Tent Life in the Holy Land
PRIME, S. I. Letters from Switzerland

REACH, A. B. Claret and Olives from the Garonne and Rhone
ROBINSON, Dr. E. Biblical Researches in Palestine, etc. 3 vols
ROMAIC Beauties and Trojan Humbugs
RUSSELL, R. M. Palestine
RUSH, R. Memoranda of a Residence in the Court of St. James

SALA, G. A. Journey due North

SCENES of the Holy Land. 2 vols
SEWELL, Miss. Journal of a Summer Tour
SHELLEY, Mrs. Rambles in Germany and Italy
SILLIMAN, Prof. B. Visit to Europe in 1851. 2 vols
SIX Years' Travel in Russia by an English Lady
SKETCHES of Switzerland. 2 vols
SLADE, A. Turkey and the Turks
SLAVEHOLDER Abroad; or Billy Buck's Visit with his Master to England
SMITH, A. Story of Mont Blanc
SMITH, J. V. C. Pilgrimage to Egypt
SÆWULFS' Travels in Palestine in 1102 and 1103
SOUTHGATE, H, Travels in Armenia, Persia, etc. 2 vols
SPAIN. A Year in
SPALDING, W. Italy and the Italian Islands. 3 vols
SPOTISWOODE, W. Tarrantasse's Journey through Russia in 1856
STANHOPE, Lady H. Travels. 3 vols
STEPHENS, J. L. Travels in Greece, Turkey, Russia and Poland. 2 vols
— Travels in Egypt and Arabia Petrea. 2 vols
ST. JOHN, C. Wild Sports of the Highlands
ST. JOHN, B. Purple Tints of Paris
— Village Life in Egypt. 2 vols
ST. JOHN, J. A. Egypt and Nubia
STOWE, Mrs. H. B. Sunny Memories of Foreign Lands. 2 vols
SWEAT, Margaret J. Highways of Travel

TAYLOR, Bayard. Travels in Greece and Russia
— Northern Travel
— Landscapes from Egypt
— The Lands of the Saracen
— At Home and Abroad
— Views Afoot
THOMSON, W. M. The Land and the Book. 2 vols
THORNBURY, W. Life in Spain, Past and Present
TYNDALL, the Glaciers of the Alps
TRAIN, G. F. The American Merchant in Europe, Asia, etc
TRI-COLORED Sketches of Paris
TROLLOPE, Mrs. Belgium and Western Germany in 1833
TUCKERMAN, H. T. Italian Sketch Book
— Sicily, a Pilgrimage
— A Month in England
TUDELA, Benjamin of. Travels in Palestine from 1160 to 1173

TWEEDIE Rev. Dr. Ruined Cities of the East

UHLEMANN, M. Three Days in Memphis

VERT, Mod. le. Souvenirs of Travel. 2 vols

VON RAUMER, F. England in 1841. 2 vols

VUES-DE la Hollande, et de la Belgique

WAKEFIELD, E. G. England and America

WALLIS, S. T. Spain, Her Institutions, etc

WANDERINGS of a Pen and Pencil

WARBURTON, E. The Crescent and the Cross

WARD, M. F. English Items

WARREN, J. E. Vagamundo; or The Attaché in Spain

WELD, C. R. The Pyrenees

WHITE, C. Three Years in Constantinople. 3 vols

WILKES, G. Europe in a Hurry

WILLIBALDS' Travels in Palestine in 721–27

WILLIS, N. P. The World Here and There

— Fun Jottings

— Summer Cruise in the Mediterranean

— Famous Persons and Places

— Pencilings by the Way

WISE, Lieut. Scampavias from Gibel-Tarek to Stamboul

YOUNG Americans Abroad

SECTION III.

IN ASIA, AFRICA, AUSTRALIA AND OCEANICA.

AFRICA. Discovery and Adventure in

ALEXANDER, Sir J. E. Travels in Africa

— Passages in the Life of a Soldier. 2 vols

ALLEN, Capt. W. The Expedition to the Niger in 1841. 2 vols

ANDERSON, A. British Embassy to China in 1792–4

ANDERSON, J. Lake Ngami

ATKINSON, T. W. Oriental and Western Siberia

BALL, B. L. Rambles in Eastern Asia, etc

BARROW, J. Travels in China. Quarto

BARTH, H. Travels in North and Central Africa in 1849 to 1855. 3 vols

BINGHAM, H. 21 Years in the Sandwich Islands

BLAKESLEY, Rev. J. W. Four Months in Algeria

BOWRING, Sir J. The Kingdom and People of Siam. 2 vols

BRUCE, J. Travels to discover the Source of the Nile in 1768–73. 8 vols and Atlas of Plates

BURCKHARDT, J. L. Travels in Arabia. 2 vols

BURTON, Capt. R. F. Travels in Central Africa

— Pilgrimage from Medina to Mecca

CADDELL, C. M. The Mission of Japan and Paraguay

CANÓT, Captain; or Twenty Years of an African Slaver

CAPPER. South Australia

CAVES. French in Algeria

CHINA, Pictorial, Descriptive and Historical

CLACY, Mrs. C. Lady's Visit to the Gold Diggings of Australia in 1853

— Lights and Shadows of Australian Life. 2 vols

COBBOLD, R. H. Pictures of the Chinese, by themselves

COOKE, G. W. China; being the Times' Special Correspondence

COLLINS, P. McD. Voyage down the Amoor River

COURET, L. du. Life in the Desert

CRAWFORD, J. Journal of an Embassy to Siam. 2 vols

— The Indian Archipelago. 3 vols

CULBERTSON, M. S. Darkness in the Flowery Land

CUMMING, R. C. Five Years in South Africa

CURTIS, G. W. Nile Notes of a Howadji

DAVIS, J. F. Description of China and its Inhabitants

— The Chinese

D'EWES, J. China, Australia and the Pacific Islands. 2 vols

DISCOVERIES and Adventures in Africa

DITSON, G. L. Circassia

DOWNING, C. T. Stranger in China

DRURY, R. Adventures during Fifteen Years' Captivity in Madagascar

DUBOIS, Abbé. Manners and Customs of the People of India. 2 vols

EARL, G. W. Native Races of the Indian Archipelago. 2 vols

— The Eastern Seas

ELGIN, Earl of. Mission to China and Japan, by L. Oliphant

ELLIS, H. T. Hongkong to Manilla

ELLIS, Rev. W. Three Visits to Madagascar in 1853–4–6

ERMAN, A. Travels in Siberia. 2 vols

FOOTE, A. H. Africa and the American Flag

FORBES, F. E. Five Years in China

FORBES, J. Residence in India

— Eleven Years in Ceylon. 2 vols

— Oriental Memoirs. 2 vols and Atlas of Plates

GIBSON, W. M. The Prisoner of Weltevreden

GIRONIERE, P. Twenty Years in the Phillipine Islands

GOLDEN Dagon ; or Up and Down the Irawaddi

GRANT, Dr., and the Nestorians, by Rev. F. Laird

GUTZLAFF, C. Three Voyages on the Coast of China in 1831

HARCOURT'S Algeria

HARRIS, Capt. W. C. Wild Sports in Southern Africa

HAWKES, Rev. F. S. Narrative of Com. Perry's Expedition to Japan. 4to

HEBER, Reginald. Journey through India in 1824. 3 vols

HELL, X. Travels in the Steppes of the Caspian Sea

HILDRETH, R. Japan as it Was and Is

HODSON, Major. Twelve Years in India

HOUGH, W. British Exploits in India, Afghanistan and China

HOWITT, W. Land, Labor and Gold in Australia. 2 vols

HOWITT, ·R. Australia, Historical and Descriptive

HUC, M. Journey through Tartary, Thibet, etc. 2 vols

— Journey through the Chinese Empire. 2 vols

— Christianity in China, Tartary, etc. 3 vols

INDIA, Pictorial, Descriptive, etc

IRELAND, J. B. Wall Street to Cashmere

JAPANESE Manners and Customs

JOHNSON, Capt. Travels in Southern Abyssinia. 2 vols

JOURNAL of the French Embassy to China in 1698

KELLY, W. Victoria in 1853 and in 1858. 2 vols

KEPPEL, H. Expedition to Borneo. 2 vols

KIDD, S. China

KRAPF, J. L. Travels in Eastern Africa

LANDER, R. and J. Exploration of the Niger. 2 vols

LAURIE, Rev. T. Dr. Grant and the Nestorians

LAY, G. T. Chinese as they are

LAYARD, A. H. Nineveh and Babylon

— Nineveh and its Remains

LIVINGSTON, Rev. D. Travels in South Africa

LOVIOT, Fanny. Lady's Captivity among Chinese Pirates

LOW, H. Sarawak and Inhabitants, etc

MACFARLANE, C. Japan

MACKAY, A. Western India

MACKENZIE, Mrs. C. Life in the Mission, etc.; or Six Years in India. 2 vols

MALCOLM, Sir J. Memoir of Central India. 2 vols

MALCOLM, H. Travels in Southeastern Asia. 2 vols

MARRYAT, F. S. Borneo and the Indian Archipelago

MEREDITH, Mrs. C. My Home in Tasmania

MILNE, W. C. Life in China.

MINTURN, R. B. Jr. From New York to Delhi

NOTES of Travel in Zanzibar, etc

OLIPHANT, L. Earl of Elgin's Mission to China and Japan

PAINE, Caroline. The Tent and Harem

PALMER, J. W. New and the Old ; or California and India

PARK, Mungo. Life and Travels

PARKYNS, M. Life in Abyssinia. 2 vols

PARROT, F. Journey to Ararat

PECK, G. W. Melbourne and the Chincha Islands

PERRY, Commodore M. Expedition to Japan. 3 vols. Quarto

PHILIPS, Gov. Voyage to Botany Bay, etc

POLO, Marco. Travels

PRINSEP, H. T. Thibet, Tartary and Mongolia

PULSZKY, Francis. The Tri-color on the Atlas ; or Algeria

RENAUDOT, E. Ancient Accounts of India and China

RENNELLS, J. The Geographical System of Herodotus. 4 vols

RICHARDSON, J. Mission to Central Africa in 1850–1. 2 vols

RILEY, J. Narrative of his Shipwreck in 1815

RILEY, W. W. Sequel to Riley's Narrative

ROVING in the Pacific, from 1837 to 1849.
2 vols

RUSSELL, M. Polynesia

RUSSELL, W. H. India. 2 vols

SHAKSPEARE, Capt. H. The Wild Sports
of India

SIDNEY, S. Three Colonies of Australia

SMITH, G. Visit to the Consular Cities
of China

SOUTHGATE, Rev. H. Tour through
Armenia, Persia, etc. 2 vols

SPIER, Mrs. Life in Ancient India

SPRY, H. H. Modern India. 2 vols

STEINMITZ, A. Japan and her People

SWAINSON, W. New Zealand and its
Colonization

TAYLOR, B. Journey through India,
China and Japan

— Journey through Central Africa

TAYLOR, C. Five Years in China

THOMAS, Rev. C. W. Adventures and
Observations on the West Coast
of Africa

THOMPSON, A. S. The Story of New
Zealand. 2 vols

THUNBERG, C. P. Voyages au Japon.
4 vols

TIFFANY, O. The Canton Chinese

TOMES, R. The Americans in Japan

TWELVE Years in China

VECILLOT, L. Les Français en Algerie

WARD, W. India and the Hindoos

WARD, H. The Cape and the Kaffirs

WESTGARTH, W. Australia, Port Philip
and New South Wales

WILLIAMS, S. W. Middle Kingdom. 2
vols

WILSON, Rev. J. L. Western Africa

WINTERBOTHAM, W. China

WOOD, W. M. Fankwei; or the San
Jacinto in the Seas of China and
Japan

SECTION IV.

VOYAGES AROUND THE WORLD, MISCELLA-
NEOUS COLLECTIONS, AND PERSONAL
NARRATIVES.

ANSON, Admiral. Voyage around
the World in 1740. 4to

BATES, Mrs. D. B. Four Years on the
Pacific

BEECHEY, Capt. F. W. Voyage to the
Pacific and Behring's Strait, in
1825–28. 2 vols

BELCHER, Capt. Sir E. Voyage round
the World, in 1836–42. 2 vols

— Voyage of the Samarang to the
Eastern Seas, in 1843–6. 2 vols

BERNARD, W. D. Voyage of the Nemesis

BOUGAINVILLE, L. Voyage round the
World, in 1766–9. 4to

BROWNE, J. Ross. Etchings of a Whaling Cruise

BRUCE, J. His Life and Voyages, by F.
B. Head

BUCKINGHAM, J. S. America, Historical
and Descriptive. 3 vols

— Canada, Nova Scotia, etc

BURNEY, J. The Buccaneers of America.
4to

CHURCHILL's Collection of Voyages and
Travels. 6 vols. Folio. 1754

CIRCUMNAVIGATION of the Globe

CLEVELAND, R. J. Voyages and Commercial Enterprises

COGGESHALL, G. Voyages, from 1802
to 1841

COLNETT, Capt. J. Voyage to the South
Atlantic and Pacific Oceans.
4to

COLTON, W. The Sea and the Sailor

COOK, J. Voyages round the World. 2
vols

Cox, W. Russian Discoveries between
Asia and America. 4to

DAVENPORT, R. A. Perilous Adventures

DIARY, in MSS., of a Whaling Voyage
to the South Seas

DICKENS, C. World Here and There

DIXON, Capt. G. Voyage round the
World, 1790. 4to

DUFFERIN, Lord. A Yacht Voyage, etc.,
in 1856

ELLIS, W. Polynesian Researches. 4
vols

ERSKINE, J. E. Cruise among the Islands of the Pacific

FRANKLIN, Sir John. Thirty Years in
the Arctic Regions

FROST, J. Incidents and Narratives of
Travel

GERSTAECKER, F. Narrative of a Journey round the World

GILLIS, Lieut. J. M. U. S. Naval Astronomical Expedition to Southern Hemisphere. 3 vols. 4to.
1849 to 1852

GOODRICH, F. B. Man upon the Sea;
or Adventures, Explorations, etc

HABERSHAM, Lieut. A. W, My Last
Cruise

HAKLUYT, R. Navigations and Discoveries, 1589. Folio
HALL, W. H. Voyage of the Nemesis
HAWKSWORTH, J. Account of Voyages in the Southern Hemisphere. 3 vols. 4to. London, 1783
HAYES, J. E. Arctic Boat Journey
HUMBOLDT, A. Cosmos. 5 vols

JARVES, J. Sandwich Islands

KANE, Dr. Arctic Voyage. 2 vols
— Grinnell Expedition
KRUSENSTERN, L'Admiral. Voyage au tour du Monde. 2 vols

LA PEROUSE. Relation a la Recherche de par La Billardiére. 6 vols. 4to, and Atlas of Plates, etc
LA PLACE, D. M. Voyage au tour du Monde, par les Mers de l'Inde et de Chine. 4 vols., and Atlas of Plates
LEE, Lieut. S. P. Report of the Cruise of the Dolphin
LETTERS from Three Continents, by M.
LISIANSKI, W. Voyage round the World in 1803 to 1806. Quarto
LITTLE, G. Life on the Ocean
LOCKMAN, J. Travels of the Jesuits. 2 vols. 1743

McCLINTOCK, Capt. The Fate of Sir John Franklin Discovered
MACGILLVRAY, W. Travels of A. von Humboldt
MARATIME and Inland Discoveries. 3 vols
MARTIN, J. M. British Colonial Library. 12 vols
MEARES, J. Voyages in 1788-9, from China to Northwest Coast. 4to
MOFRAS, Duflot. Exploration de Oregon, Californie, et la Mer ver mielle, dans 1840 to 1842. 2 vols., and Plates
MOLLHAUSEN, B. Journey to Coasts of Pacific, in 1858. 2 vols
MORRISON and Himmalch, Notes of the Voyage of, from Canton, in 1857
MORRELL, Capt. B. Four Voyages in the South Sea and Pacific Ocean, 1823-31
MURRAY, H. Travels of Marco Polo

NORDHOFF, C. Whaling and Fishing
NORTHERN Regions

OLMSTEAD, F. A. Incidents of a Whaling Voyage

PFEIFFER, Ida. A Lady's Second Journey round the World. 2 vols
PERKINS, E. T. Na Motu; or Reef Rovings in South Seas
PINKERTON, J. Collection of Voyages and Travels. 6 vols. 4to
PITCAIRN's Island
POLAR Seas and Regions

REID, M. Odd People
RICHARDIERE, B. de la. Bibliotheque des Voyages. 6 vols
RICHARDSON, J. Arctic Expedition in Search of Sir John Franklin
ROBBINS, A. Loss of the Brig Commerce
ROGERS, Woodes C. Voyage round the World. London, 1712
ROVINGS in Pacific in 1837-39
RUSCHENBERGER, W. S. W. Voyage round the World in 1835-6
— Three Years in the Pacific, from 1835-6-7
RUSSELL, Rev. M. Polynesia

SANTAREN, V. Americus Vespucius and his Voyages
SCARLETT, Sir J. C. South America and Pacific. 8vo
SEEMAN, B. Voyage of H. M. S. Herald during the years 1845-51. 2 vols
SIMPSON, Sir Geo. Journey round the World. 2 vols
SWAN, J. G. Northwest Coast of America.

TAYLOR, J. BAYARD. Cyclopedia of Modern Travels
TRAIN, G. F. The American Merchant
— Spread Eagleism
VANCOUVER, G. Voyage to North Pacific and North Atlantic Oceans in 1790-95. 3 vols. 4to, and Folio Atlas
VOYAGES round the World, from the Death of Capt. Cook
VOYAGES of the Adventure and Beagle. 4 vols

WHITECAR, W. B. Four Years in a Whale Ship, 1856-7-8-9
WILKES, C. U. S. Exploring Expedition. 5 vols., and Atlas
WILLIAMS, T., and Calvert J. Fiji and the Fijians
WILLIS, N. P. Famous Persons and Places
WRANGEL, Admiral. Expedition to the Polar Sea in 1820

SECTION V.

GEOGRAPHICAL AND TOPOGRAPHICAL
WORKS, ATLASES, GUIDE BOOKS AND
STATISTICS.

ALMANAC National de la Repub-
lique Française
AMERICA and the West Indies, Geo-
graphically Described, by Long,
Porter and Tucker
AMERICAN Ethnological Society's Trans-
actions. 2 vols
AMERICAN Almanac, from 1830-to 1860.
31 vols
APPLETON. Travelers' Guide and Hand
Book for 1860 .
— Illustrated Hand Book of Ameri-
can Travel
ATLAS to Australia and Gold Regions

BALDWIN, T., and J. Thomas' Gazetteer
of the United States
BAIRD, R. The West Indies and North
America
BARINGTON, A. Treatise on Physical
Geography
BEATTIE, W. The Waldenses of Pied-
mont, etc. Illustrated
BELDEN, E. D. The City of New York
BOSTON Municipal Register for 1857
— Directory for 1855-6
BOYD, W. C. Guide through Italy
BRINGTON, D. G. Notes on the Florida
Peninsula
BUTLER, S. Atlas of Ancient Geography
BYERS and Kellom's Hand-Book to the
Nebraska and Kansas Gold
Fields

CALIFORNIA Register, 1857-9
CALLICOT, T. C. Hand-Book of Uni-
versal Geography
CANADA Directory
CENSUS of the United States for 1850.
Quarto
— of the State of New York for 1845
and 1855. 2 vols. Folio
CHELTENHAM, Guide to
CHURTON, E. The Railroad Book of
England
CINCINNATI, 1856
CLARK, B. The British Gazetteer of
Great Britain. 3 vols
COAST Survey of the United States.
Report from 1851 to 1859. 4to
— Sketches accompanying the same
COLTON. Atlas of the World. 2 vols.
Imperial quarto
COLUMBIA, Descriptive of the District of
CORNWALLIS, K. The New El Dorado
in British Columbia

DELESERT, E. Voyage dans les deux
Océans, en 1844-7
DIRECTORIES. San Francisco. 5 vols
1852-60
— New York, '56-60. 2 vols
— Sacramento, 1856
— Marysville 1855
— Boston, 1855-1856
DISTURNELL's New York State Register

ELLET, C. Physical Geography of the
United States
ENGEL, M. Memoires, etc., Geograph-
iques des Pays de l'Asie et de
l'Amerique. 4to
FINDLAY, A. G. Directory of the Pa-
cific Ocean. 2 vols .
FINDEN's Views of the Ports and Har-
bors of Great Britain. 2 vols.
Quarto
FORD, R. Hand-Book for Travelers in
Spain. 2 vols
FORESTER, T. Paris and its Environs
FRANCIS, C. S. Strangers' Hand-Book
to the city of New York
FROST, J. Great Cities of the World

GALIGNANI's New Paris Guide for 1860
GALTON, J. The Art of Travel
GELL, Sir W. Topography of Rome,
with an Atlas
GEOGRAPHY, New English Encyclopedia
of. 4 vols. Quarto
GOLD Fields of St. Domingo
GOLDSMITH, Rev. J. A Geographical
View of the World. 2 vols
GORDON, P. Geography Anatomized
GUIDE of Rome and its Environs
GUYOT, A. Physical Geography

HALL, Mr. and Mrs. Hand-Book of
Dublin and Wicklow
— Ireland, its Scenery, Character,
etc. 3 vols
HARGRAVE, E. H. Australia, and its
Gold Fields
HARPER's Gazetteer of the World
HAYLING Island. Topographical, etc
HAYWARD's Gazetteer of Massachusetts
HOLLANDE et la Belgium. Illustrated
HUNT, F. M. The Rhine Book

ITALIE, Nouveau Guide du Voyageur en

JOHNSON, Prof. A. K. Atlas of the
World. Folio
— Atlas of Physical Geography.
Abridged. Folio
KNIGHT, C. Gazetteer of London
— Cyclopedia of all Nations
LIPPINCOTT's Pronouncing Gazetteer of
the World

LIEBER, O. M. Survey of South Carolina

MACKAY; R. W. S. The Canada Directory for 1854

MALTE Brun, C. Universal Geography
— and Balbi's System of Geography

MANDEVILLE, J. W. Report of the Surveyor General of California for 1859

— Marlette, Report for 1855

MAP of Central America

MAP of the Seat of War in Florida

MAPS of the United States' Coast Survey, complete

MAPS and Plans to Alison's History of Europe

MARTIN, M. Australia

MATTHEW, F. Emigration Fields in North America

McCULLOCH, J. R. Geographical Dictionary. 2 vols

MURRAY, J. Hand-Book for Modern London
— Hand-Book for Southern Germany
— Hand-Book for Northern Italy
— Hand-Book for the Ionian Islands, Greece, Turkey, etc
— Hand-Book for the Continent
— Hand-Book for France
— Hand-Book for London
— Hand-Book for Spain. 2 vols
— Hand-Book for Syria and Palestine
— Hand-Book for India. 4 vols

MURRAY, H. Encyclopedia of Geography. 3 vols

NEW South Wales Almanac and Remembrancer

O'FLANAGAN, J. R. The Blackwater in Munster

OUR Globe. Picturesque Illustrations. Oblong folio

PARIS, Versailles et les Provinces ou 18eme Siecle. 2 vols

PARIS tel qu'il est, etc

PARRY, W. E. Arctic Voyages

PEAKS and Passes, by the Alpine Club

PLATT, J. Manners and Customs of all Nations

PHILADELPHIA in 1852

PITKIN, T. Statistical View of the United States

RENNELL, J. The Comparative Geography of Western Asia. 2 vols

RICHARDS, T. A. Appleton's Hand-Book of Travel in the United States

RITCHIE, J. S. Wisconsin and its Resources

RINGGOLD, C. Charts of the Bay of San Francisco, etc., with Sailing Directions

ROME, Topographical Map of. 4 sheets

SMITH, J. C. Gazetteer of the World

SOMERVILLE, Mary. Physical Geography

STRABOS' Geography, literally translated. 3 vols

STRAHLENBERG'S Description of Europe and Asia

STRICKLAND, W. P. Old Mackinaw and its surroundings

TAYLOR, R. C. Statistics of Coal

THOMAS and Baldwin, Gazetteer

THOMPSON, J. Gazetteer and Geographical Dictionary

TOPOGRAPHICAL Map of the Road from Missouri to Oregon

VADE-Mecum of the East Indies

WADDINGTON, A. The Frazer River Mines

WETMORE, A. Gazetteer of Missouri

WINGATE'S Maryland Register for 1857

WINTERBOTHAM, W. United States. 5 vols

YEDDO, Japanese Map of

CLASS VI.

HISTORY.

SECTION I.

1. EUROPEAN HISTORY.

ABBOTT, J. S. C. The Empire of
    Austria
— The Empire of Russia
— The French Revolution of 1789
ALISON, A. History of Europe. 6 vols
ALLEN, J. Battles of the British Navy.
    2 vols
ALLEN, T. History and Antiquities of
    London and Westminster. 4 vols
ANCELOT, Mme. Les Salons de Paris
ANQUETIL, M. Histoire de France. 5
    vols
ANNALS of British Legislation. 5 vols
ARNOLD, T. History of Rome
— History of the Later Roman Com-
    monwealth
ARTHUR, W. Italy in Transition; or
    Scenes and Events in 1860
ATHENS, its Grandeur and Decay
AYOLA, J. Historia de Gibraltar
AZEGLIO. Italy and France in 16th
    Century

BAIRD, H. M. Modern Greece
BARKER, W. B. Lares and Penates ; or
    Citicia and its Government
BELL, R. History of Russia. 3 vols
BLANC, Louis. History of Ten Years.
    2 vols
BONAPARTE, N. Memoirs of the History
    of France during his Reign 3
    vols
BONNECHOSE, E. D. Le Quatre Con-
    quêtte d' l'Angléterre. 2 vols
BRITISH Expedition to the Crimea, Rus-
    sell's Lectures
BRODIE, G. The British Empire from
    Charles I. to the Restoration. 4
    vols
BROWNE, J. History of the Highland
    Clans of Scotland. 4 vols
BUCHANAN, G. History of Scotland. 2
    vols
BUCKLE, H. T. History of Civilization
    in England. Vol. 1
BULWER. Athens. 2 vols
BUSK, M. History of Spain and Por-
    tugal

BURNETT, Bishop. History of the Re-
    formation of the Church of
    England. 2 vols
— History of his own time, from the
    Restoration of Charles I. to the
    Treaty of Utrecht. 2 vols

CÆSAR's Commentaries
CARLYLE, T. French Revolution. 3 vols
CARRELL, A. History of the Counter
    Revolution in England
CASS, Louis. France, its King and
    Court
CASTLENAU, M. de. Reigns of Francis
    II. and Charles IX. of France
CHAMBERS, W. and R. Pictorial His-
    tory of the Russian War
CHAMBERS, R. Traditions of Edinburgh
— Domestic Annals of Scotland. 2
    vols
CHARLES X. and Louis Philippe in the
    Revolution of 1830
CHESNEY, Col. The Russo-Turkish
    Campaigns of 1828-9
CHRONICLES, Six Old English
COBBETT, W. The Protestant Reform-
    ation
COIT, T. W. Puritanism
COLLETTA, P. History of Naples from
    1734 to '56. 2 vols
CONDE, J. A. History of the Arabs in
    Spain. 3 vols
COX, W. History of the House of
    Austria. 4 vols
CRIGHTON, A., and Wheaton, H. Scan-
    dinavia
CROMWELL and the English Crown, by
    F. Guizot
CROWE, E. C. History of France. 3
    vols

D'AUBIGNE, J. H. M. History of the
    Reformation
DAVIES, C. M. History of Holland. 3
    vols
DIONYSIUS Halicarnassus. Roman An-
    tiquities. 4 vols. Quam
DITSON, G. L. Crescent and French
    Crusaders
DIX, W. G. The Unholy Alliance
DORAN, Dr. New Pictures and old Panels

DUNHAM, S. A. History of Spain and Portugal. 5 vols
— History of Denmark, Sweden and Norway. 3 vols
— History of Poland
— History of the Germanic Empire. 3 vols
— History of the Middle Ages. 4 vols
DWIGHT, Theo. The Roman Republic of 1848

EATON, C. Rome in the 19th Century. 2 vols
ECCLESTON, J. Introduction to English Antiquities
ETHELWERD's Old English Chronicle
EUROPE, History of, from 1815. 2 vols
EUROPE, and the Allies of the past and To-day
EUSEBIUS. Ecclesiastical History

FAIRFAX Correspondence. 4 vols
FERGUSON, A. History of the Roman Republic
FLAGG, E. Venice. 2 vols
FLETCHER, J. History of Poland
FLORIAN, M. Moors of Spain
FLORENCE of Worcester's English History to Edward I
FRANCE and England, by de Loisnion
FROISSART, Sir J. Chronicles of England, France and Spain. 2 vols
FORSTER, J. Historical and Biographical Essays. 2 vols
FOX, C. J. History of the Reign of James II

GALLOIS, M. L. Histoire de la Revolution de 1848. 5 vols
GAY, Madame. Celebrated Saloons
GEIGER, E. G. History of the Swedes
GELDART, Mrs. T. Popular History of England
GEOFFREY of Monmouth's British History
GEORGE, A. Queens of Spain. 2 vols
GEIGER, E. G. History of the Swedes
GIBBON, E. Decline and Fall of the Roman Empire. 6 vols
— History of the Roman Empire abridged, by W. Smith
GILDAS' Old English Chronicle
GODWIN, Parke. History of France. Vol. 1 •
GODWIN, W. History of the Commonwealth of England. 4 vols
GOLDSMITH, O. History of England
GORDON, T. History of the Greek Revolution. 2 vols
GOURDONF. Congress de Paris
GRATTAN, T. C. History of the Netherlands

GRAMMONT's Court of Charles II
GREEK and Roman Antiquities. 2 vols
GRENVILLE Papers, The Correspondence of Richard Grenville, Earl Temple and Right Hon. Geo. Grenville. 4 vols
GRETTON's Viciscitudes of Italy
GROTH, E. History of Greece. 12 vols
GUIZOT, F. History of Civilization. 4 vols
— English Revolution of 1640

HALL, E. The Puritans and their Principles
HALLAM, H. Constitutional History of England
— Middle Ages
HANCOCK, T. The Friends in Ireland in the Rebellion of 1798
HASTINGS, Warren. State of the East Indies
HEADLEY, J. T. Imperial Guard of Napoleon
HEEREN, A. H. L. Ancient Greece
HERBERT, W. History of the Livery Companies of London. 2 vols
HINMAN, R. Letters of Charles and James II. to Governors of Connecticut
HISTORY of the Protestant Church in Hungary
HOOKE, N. History of Rome
HOPKINS, S. The Puritans of the time of Edward VI, and Elizabeth
HOVEDEN, Roger de. Annals of England and Europe, from 732 to 1201
HUBER, V. A. The English Universities. 3 vols
HUME, D. History of England. 6 vols
HUNTINGDON, Henry of. Chronicle of England to Henry II

INGULPH. Chronicle of the Abbey of Croyland
IRELAND, W. H. History of the County of Kent. 2 vols. 4to
INVING, W. The Conquest of Granada

JAMES, G. P. R. History of Chivalry
JESSE, J. H. Memorials of London. 2 vols
— England under the Stuarts. 3 vols
— The Pretenders
JOHNSTON, J. K. Atlas to Alison's Europe
JOLY, J. C. Historia de la Compania de Jesus. 7 vols

KEIGHTLEY, T. History of England. 5 vols
KELLY, W. K. History of Russia
KEYSER, R. The Religion of the Northmen

Koch, C. W. The Revolutions of Europe

Kohlrauchs, F. History of Germany

Labaume, E. Account of the French Campaign in Russia

Laing, S. Sea Kings of Norway. 3 vols

Lamartine, A. History of the Revolution of 1848
— The Restoration of Monarchy in France. 4 vols
— History of Turkey. 3 vols
— History of the Girondists. 3 vols

Lawson. History of the Episcopal Church of Scotland. 2 vols

Liddell, H. G. History of Rome

Lingard, Dr. J. History of England. 13 vols

Livius' History of Rome, literally translated. 4 vols

Lodge, E. Illustrations of British History. 3 vols

Louis Philippe. Mon Journal. Evénements de 1815

Louis XIV. Memoirs of the Reign of, by the Duke de St. Simon. 4 vols

Macaulay, T. B. History of England. 4 vols

Machiavelli, N. History of Florence, and other works

MacGeoeghegan, Abbe. History of Ireland

Mackintosh, Sir J. History of England, with continuation to 1860. 10 vols

Mahon, Lord. History of England. 2 vols

Mallet, P. H. Northern Antiquities

Malmesbury, Wm. of. Chronicle of the Kings of England

Malte Brun. Tableau de la Pologne. 2 vols

Martin, R. M. History of the British Possessions in the Mediterranean
— The British Colonial Library. 10 vols •

Matthew of Westminster. Great Britain to 1307

Matthew Paris' English History from 1235 to 1273

Maxwell, W. H. History of the Irish Rebellion of 1798

M'Elheran, J. The Condition of Women of the Gothic and Celtic Races

Menzel, W. History of Ge⬛⬛ 3 vols

Michaud, J. F. History of the Crusades. 3 vols

Michelet, M. History of France. 2 vols

Mignet, F. A. History of the French Revolution

Miller, T. History of the Anglo-Saxons

Milner, Rev. T. Russia; its Rise, Progress, &c

Monumens des Grands-Maitres de l'order de St. Jean. 2 vols

Monstrelet, E. Chronicles of War of France from 1400 to 1516. 2 vols

Moore, T. History of Ireland. 4 vols

Moses, M. The Revolution in France in 1830

Motley, J. L. The Rise and Progress of the Dutch Republic. 3 vols

Napier, W. F. P. History of the Peninsular War. 5 vols

Napoleon's Historical Miscellanies. 3 vols

Neander, A. History of the Early Christian Church

Nennius' Old English Chronicle

Newman, T. W. Regal Rome

Nicholas, N. H. History of the Royal Navy. 2 vols

Nicolini, G. B. History of the Jesuits. 2 vols

Niebuhr, B. G. Lectures on Roman History. 3 vols
— History of Rome. 2 vols
— The same, from first Punic War to Death of Constantine

Normanby, Marquis. A Year of Revolution, 1848, in Paris. 2 vols

Odericus Vitalis' Ecclesiastical History of England and Normandy

Orosius' History, in English, by B. Thorpe

Palgrave, Sir F. History of Normandy and England. 2 vols
— History of the Anglo-Saxons

Pardoe, Miss. Episodes of French History
— Court and Reign of Francis I. of France. 2 vols
— Court and Reign of Louis XIV. of France. 2 vols

Persecutions of the Protestants in France

Prescott, W. H. Reign of Ferdinand and Isabella. 3 vols
— Philip II. 3 vols

Ranke, L. History of the Popes. 2 vols
— History of Servia
— Civil Wars and Monarchy in France

5

RAUMER, K.   Contributions to the History, etc., of German Universities

REUMONT, A. de.   The Carafas of Maddaloni, Naples under Spain

RICHARD of Cirencester's Old English Chronicle

ROBERTSON, W.   Reign of the Emperor Charles V

— History of Scotland

ROGER of Wendover's History of England to 1235

ROJOUX et Mainguet.   Histoire de Angleterre.   2 vols

ROLLIN, L.   La Décadence de l'Angleterre.   2 vols

ROME, History of

ROME.   2 vols

RONDELET, A.   Essai Historique sur le Pont de Rialto

RUSSELL, W. H.   The British Expedition to the Crimea

— The War, by the Times' Correspondent

SALLUST, C. C.   Histories

SAXTON, L. C.   Fall of Poland.   2 vols

SCHILLER, J. C. F.   Thirty Years' War

— Revolt of the Netherlands

SECRET Societies of the Middle Ages

SEGUR, Count P.   The Expedition of Napoleon to Russia.   2 vols

SCHMITZ, L.   History of the Middle Ages

SCOTT, Sir W.   History of Scotland.   2 vols

S. E. O.   Hungary and its Revolutions

SFORZOSI.   History of Italy

SIBORNE, Capt. W.   Details of the Battle of Waterloo

SINDING, Rev. P. C.   History of Scandinavia

SISMONDI, J. C. L.   History of the Italian Republic

— History of the Fall of the Roman Empire.   2 vols

SMEDLEY.   Sketches of Venetian History

SMIBERT, T.   The Clans of the Highlands of Scotland

SMYTHE, W.   French Revolution.   3 vols

SOUTHEY, R.   Chronicles of the Cid

SPALDING, W.   Italy and the Italian Islands

SPEED, J.   The Historie of Great Britaine.   Folio.   1614

STEBBING, Rev. H.   History of the Reformation.   3 vols

STEPHENS, A. J.   History of English Constitution.   2 vols

STUART and Revett.   Antiquities of Athens

SWITZERLAND, History of

TABLEAU de l'Histoire de Europe. 3 vols

TACITUS.   Works.   Translated.   2 vols

TAYLOR, W. B. S.   History of the University of Dublin

TAYLOR, W. C.   History of Ireland.   2 vols

TEFFT, B. F.   Hungary and Kossuth

THIER's Consulate and Empire.   3 vols

— French Revolution.   2 vols

THIERRY, A.   The Conquest of England by the Normans.   2 vols

— History of the Tiers Etat

THIRLWALL, C.   History of Greece.   8 vols

THORP, W.   Destinies of the British Empire

THUCYDIDES.   History of the Peloponnesian War

TOUCHARD, Lafosse.   Histoire de Paris.   4 vols

TUEL, J. E.   Illustrated History of the War in Italy

TURNER, S.   Sacred History of the World

TYTLER, P. F.   History of Scotland.   7 vols

UNGEWITTER, F. H.   Europe, Past and Present

VOLTAIRE.   Siécle de Louis XIV

WADE, J.   British History Chronologically Arranged

WAKEFIELD, E. G.   England and America compared

WALDENSES, The, by W. Beattie.   Quarto

WALPOLE, H.   Journal of the Reign of George III

WHEATON, H.   History of the Northmen

WHITE, J.   History of France to 1848

WOODWARD, R. B.   History of Wales

WORCESTER, Florence of.   Chronicles of England to Edward I

WRAXALL, L.   The Armies of the Great Powers

WRAXALL, N. W.   Historical Memoirs

— Posthumous Memoirs

WRIGHT, T.   History of Scotland.   3 vols

— History and Topography of the County of Essex

ZSCHOCKKE, H.   History of Switzerland

SECTION II.

ASIATIC HISTORY.

ALEXANDER, D. A.   History of the Israelitish Nation

AUBER, P.   Rise and Progress of British Power in India.   2 vols

BARCLAY, J. T. The City of the Great King

BASNAGE. History of the Jews

BJORNSTJERNA. British Empire in the East

BONOMI, J. Nineveh, and its Palaces

BRITISH India, Historic Account of

BROOKES, Rajah. Journal of Events in Borneo, etc

CALLERY and Ivan. History of the Insurrection in China

CHAMICH, M. History of America. 2 vols

CHARLEVOIX, F. X. Histoire du Japan China, Ava, Siam, etc. 9 vols

CHRONICLE of the Crusades

COKE, W. Russian Discoveries between Asia and America

CRIGHTON, A. History of Arabia

FRAZER, J. B. Historic Account of Persia

— Mesopotamia and Assyria

GUTZLAFF, C. Sketch ot Chinese History. 2 vols

HOUGH, Major. British Military Exploits in India, etc

HUNT, G. H. Outram and Havelock's Persian Campaign

JOSEPHUS. Works. Translated by Whiston

KAEMPFER, E. Histoire de l'Empire du Japon. 2 vols. Folio

LAYARD, A. H. Nineveh and Babylon

— Nineveh and its Remains

LUCKNOW, Defense of, by a Staff Officer

MACFARLANE, C. History of British India

MALCOLM, H. F. India and the Mutineers

MARLES, M. Histoire de l'Inde. 6 vols

MARTIN, R. M. The Indian Empire, its History, etc. 4 vols

— History of the Possessions of the East India Company. 2 vols

MARTINEAU, Harriet. British Rule in India

MEMORABLE Year of the War in China, Mutiny in India, etc

MENDELSSOHN, M. Jerusalem. 2 vols

MILMAN, H. H. History of the Jews 3 vols

MUNDAY, Capt. R. Events in Borneo, from Journals of Sir J. Brooke. 2 vols

MURRAY, H. Historical and Descriptive Account of British India. 3 vols

MUTINY in India; an illustrated History. 4 vols

OCKLEY, S. History of the Saracens

OSBORN, H. S. Palestine, Past and Present

POCOCKE, E. India in Greece

POLYBIUS. General History. 2 vols

RAFFLES, Sir S. History of Java. 2 vols., and quarto plates

ROBERTSON, W. Ancient India

RUSSELL, M. Palestine

THORPE, W. Destinies of the British Empire

WARD, W. India and Hindoos. 2 vols.

— History of the Hindoos [4to

WEBB, J. Antiquity of China

WILLIAMS, S. W. The Middle Kingdom. 2 vols

WILSON, H. H., and J. Mill. History of British India. 9 vols

WINTERBOTHAM, W. Chinese Empire

SECTION III.

AFRICAN HISTORY.

CHAMPOLION, Figeac. Egypte Ancienne

DE PAUW. Egyptians and Chinese

HAWKES, F. L. Monuments of Egypt

HERODOTUS, edited by Rawlings. 4 vols

KENRICK, J. Ancient Egypt

— Primitive History

LEPSIUS, Dr. R. Egypt and Ethiopia.

MARTIN, R. M. History of Southern Africa

RUSSELL, Rev. M. Ancient and Modern

— Nubia and Abyssinia [Egypt

— History and Condition of the Barbary States

SHARPE, S. History of Egypt

WILKINSON, G. Ancient Egyptians. 6 vols

SECTION IV.

AMERICAN HISTORY.

ADAIR, J. History of the American Indians

AMERICAN Archives. 10 vols. Folio

ARMSTRONG, Gen. J. Notices of the War of 1812. 2 vols

BANCROFT, G. History of the United States. 8 vols

BARBER, J. W. Historical Collections for Massachusetts

BARCLAY, S. Recollections of the American Revolution

BEAMISH, N. L. Northmen in America

BELISLE, D. W. History of Independence Hall, Philadelphia

BENNETT, J. C. History of the Saints

BEVERLEY's History of Virginia. 1705

BLUNT, J. The Formation of the Confederacy of the United States

BOND, H. Genealogies and History of Watertown, etc

BOTTA, C. The War of Independence of the United States. 2 vols

BOWEN, A. The Naval Monument

BRADDOCK, Gen. The Expedition of, in 1775

BROADHEAD, J. R. History of the State of New York to 1664

BUNNER, E. History of Louisiana

BURGOYNE's Campaign and the Battles of Bemis Heights

BURGESS, T. Battle of Lake Erie

BURNETT, J. Notes on the early Settlement of the Northwest Territory

BURNEY, J. History of the Buccaneers of America. 4to

BYRDSALL, F. The Loco-Foco, or Equal Rights Party

CAMPBELL, J. W. History of Virginia to 1781

CAMPBELL, W. W. Border Warfare of New York

CAPRON, E. S. History of California

CARLETON, J. H. Battle of Buena Vista

CATLIN, G. The North American Indians. 2 vols

CHALMERS, G. The Revolt of the American Colonies. 2 vols

CHASLES, P. Études sur la Literature et les Moeurs des Anglo-Americaines

CLINTON, Sir H. Narrative of his Campaign in America

COGGESHALL, G. American Privateers and Letters of Marque

COLLINS, L. Historical Sketch of Kentucky

CONTRIBUTIONS to American History, 1858; being Memoirs of the Historical Society of Pennsylvania. Vol. 6

COOPER, J. F. History of the Navy of the United States to 1853

CORTES, H. Dispatches of his Conquest of Mexico

COWELL, B. Spirit of '76 in Rhode Island

CURTIS, G. T. History of the Constitution of the United States. 2 vols

CUTTS, J. M. Conquest of California and New Mexico in 1846–7

DE FOREST, J. W. History of the Indians of Connecticut

DENNY, Major E. Records of Upland Co., Pa., and Military Journal

DOCUMENTS Relating to the Colonial History of the State of New York. 10 vols. Quarto

DONIPHAN's Expedition and Conquest of New Mexico

DOUGLASS, W. Planting of the British Settlements in America. 2 vols. 1749

DRAKE, S. G. History of Boston, from 1630 to 1670

DUNN, J. History of Oregon Territory

DU PRATZ, M. History of Louisiana

DWIGHT, T. History of Connecticut

—— The Hartford Convention

ELLETT, Mrs. Domestic History of the American Revolution

ELLIOT, C. W. New England. 2 vols

FAIRBANKS, G. R. History of St. Augustine, Florida

FELT, J. B. Annals of Salem. 2 vols

FITZGERALD, J. E. The Charter, etc., of the Hudson's Bay Company

FLINT, T. Indian Wars in the West

FLORIDA, The War in

FOOTE, Rev. H. W. Sketches of Virginia

FORBES, A. History of California

FORREST, W. S. Historical Sketch of Norfolk, Va., etc

FRANCIS, Dr. J. W. Old New York

FRENCH, B. F. Historical Collection of Louisiana. 5 vols

FROTHINGHAM, R. History of the Siege of Boston and Battle of Lexington

GIBBS, G. Memoirs of the Administrations of Washington and Adams. 2 vols

GIBBES, R. W. Documentary History of the Revolution in South Carolina. 2 vols

GIDDINGS, J. The Exiles of Florida

GLEIG, R. The Campaigns of the British Army at Washington and New Orleans

GORDON, W. History of the Rise, Progress and Establishment of the

Independence of the United States. 4 vols

GRAHAM, J. History of the United States till 1688. 2 vols

GREEN, C., and S. Y. Wells. View of the Shakers

GREENHOW, R. History of Oregon and California

GUROWSKI, Count. America and Europe

HALE, S. History of the United States. 2 vols

HALIBURTON, T. C. Rule and Misrule of the English in America

HALL, R. B. History of Eastern Vermont

HAMILTON, J. C. History of the United States. 6 vols

HAWKES, Rev. F. L. The Protestant Episcopal Church in Virginia
— The Protestant Episcopal Church in Maryland
— History of North Carolina, from 1584 to 1729. 2 vols

HAZARD, S. Pennsylvania Archives. 12 vols

HEADLEY, J. T. The Last War with England. 2 vols

HELPS, A. The Spanish Conquest in America. 3 vols

HENRY, W. S. Campaign Sketches of the War with Mexico

HILDRETH, R. History of the United States. 6 vols

HILDRETH, S. P. Pioneer History of the Northwest Territory

HINES, G. Oregon, its History, Condition, etc

HISTORICAL Magazine. 3 vols [vols
HISTORICAL Collections of Louisiana. 5
— of South Carolina. 2 vols
— of Pennsylvania. Vols. 6 and 7
— of New York. 4 vols
— of Florida

HISTORY of the United States. 2 vols

HOLMES, A. Annals of America to 1826. 2 vols

HOTCHKIN, J. H. History of the Settlement of Western New York

HOWE, Gen. Sir W. Narrative of his conduct in America

HOWE, H. Virginia Historical Collections

HOWITT, Mary. Popular History of the United States. 2 vols

HUNTER, J. The Founders· of New Plymouth

HUTCHINSON, T. History of Massachusetts. 3 vols

HYDE, J. Jr. Mormonism

ICELAND, Greenland and the Faroe Islands

INGERSOLL, J. History of the late War with England. 2 vols

IRVING, T. Conquest of Florida, by De Soto

IZARD, Ralph. Correspondence during the Revolution

JAMES, W. Account of Military Occurrences in the War between Great Britain and the United States. 2 vols
— Naval Occurrences in the late War between Great Britain and the United States

JAMES, J. J. History of the Sandwich Islands

JOHNSON, Capt. C. General History of the Pyrates, 1724

KENDALL, G. W. War with Mexico; illustrated. Imperial folio

KNOX, J. P. Historic Account of St. Thomas, St. Croix and St. Johns

LANMAN, J. H. History of Michigan

LEE, H. The Campaign of 1781, in the Carolinas
— Memoirs of the War in Southern Department of the United States

LEWES, G. H. Biographical History of Philosophy. 2 vols

LIVERMORE, A. A. The War with Mexico, reviewed

LOSSING, B. J. Field-Book of the Revolution. 2 vols
— Mount Vernon, and its Associations
— National History of the United States. 2 vols

LOUISIANA Historical Collections, by B. B. French. 5 vols [etc

LUNT, G. Three Eras of New England,

MACARTNEY, W. Origin and Progress of the United States

MARSHALL, C. Passages from his Remembrancer

MARTIN, R. M. History and Geography of Canada
— History of Nova Scotia, Cape Breton, etc
— History of the West India Islands

MATHER, I. Remarkable Providences in New England

McGEE, T. D'A. Irish Settlers in North America

McINTOSH, J. Origin of the North American Indians

McSHERRY, J. History of Maryland

MEADE, Bishop. Old Churches, etc., of Virginia. 2 vols

MEEK, A. B. Romantic Passage in Southwestern History

MEXICAN War, and its Heroes, etc
MIALL, J. G. Footsteps of our Forefathers
MINOT, G. R. Continuation of the History of Massachusetts, from 1748. 2 vols
MIRANDA, F. His attempt to effect a Revolution in South America
MOLINA, J. History of Chili. 2 vols
MOORE, Frank. Diary of the American Revolution. 2 vols
MOORE, G. H. The Treason of Major-General Charles Lee
MORGAN, L. H. League of the Iroquois
MORTON, N. New England's Memorial
MOULTRIE, W. Memoirs of the American Revolution. 2 vols
MURRAY, H. British America. 2 vols

NEILL, E. D. History of Minnesota
NEW Ipswich, History of
NEW York, State Documents relating to, from 1603-78. 10 vols. 4to
— Historical Society Collections. 4 vols
NILES, H. Principles and Acts of the American Revolution

O'CALLAGHAN, E. B. Documentary History of New York. 4 vols
ONDERDONK, H., Jr. Revolutionary Incidents of Queens Co.

PALFREY's New England. 2 vols
PARKMAN, F. J. History of the Conspiracy of Pontiac
PATTON, J. H. History of the United States
PEARCE, S. Annals of Luzerne County
PECK, Rev. G. Wyoming; its History,
PENNSYLVANIA Records. 16 vols [etc
PENNSYLVANIA Archives, from 1664 to 1790. 12 vols
PETERSON, G. History of Rhode Island
PITKIN, T. Political and Civil History of the United States. 2 vols
PLANS of the Battles of the American Revolution. Folio
PRESCOTT, W. H. Conquest of Mexico
— Conquest of Peru

RAMSEY, A. C. History of the Mexican War
RECORDS of the Colony of Rhode Island, by J. R. Bartlett. 2 vols
REED, J. History of Rutland, Mass
RHODE Island Colonial Records, by J. R. Bartlett. 2 vols
RICHMOND in By-Gone Days
RIDGELEY, D. Annals of Annapolis
RIPLEY, R. S. War with Mexico
RIVERO and Von Tschudes' Peruvian Antiquities

RIVERS, W. J. Sketch of the History of South Carolina to 1719
ROBERTSON, W. History of America
ROBINSON, F. Account of the Organization of the Army of the United States. 2 vols
RUPP, J. D. History of Lancaster County, Pa

SAFFELL, W. T. R. Records of the Revolutionary War
SARGENT, W. The Expedition of Gen. Braddock in 1755
SCHOOLCRAFT, H. R. American Indians
— The Indian Tribes of the United States. 5 vols. 4to
SEARS, E. H. Pictures of the Olden Time, etc
SHERMAN, H. The Governmental History of the United States
SIMCOE, Col. J. G. Operations of the Queen's Rangers in the American Revolution
SIMMS, W. G. History of South Carolina
SMITH, W. History of the State of New York to 1732. Hist. Col. Vol. 4
SMITH, J. Jay. American Historical and Literary Curiosities. 2 vols
SMITH, E. R. The Araucanian Indians of Chile
SOLIS, A. de. Conquesta de Mejico
SOULE, F., J. H. Guion, and J. Nisbet. Annals of San Francisco
SOUTH Carolina, History to 1719, by W. J. Rivers
SPARKS, J. Correspondence of the American Revolution. 4 vols
SPRAGUE, J. T. History of the Florida War
SQUIER, E. G. The Serpent Symbol, etc
— The States of Central America
— Aboriginal Monuments of New York
— Nicaragua
— and Davis, E. H. Ancient Monuments of the Mississippi Valley
STONE, W. L. Border Warfare of the American Revolution, and Life of Brant. 2 vols

TARLETON, Col. History of the Campaign in 1781. Quarto
TAYLOR, W. C. Manual of Ancient History
THACHER, J. Military Journal during the American Revolution
THOMAS, G. Account of Pennsylvania and New Jersey, 1698
THOMPSON, B. F. History of Long Island. 2 vols
THORNTON, J. The Landing of the Pilgrims at Cape Ann, Mass

TOMLINSON, W. P. History of Kansas in 1858
TRANSACTIONS of the American Antiquarian Society. 3 vols
TRESCOTT, W. H. Administrations of Washington and Adams
TUCKER, G. History of the United States. 4 vols
TRUMBULL, H. Discovery of America, Landing at Plymouth, etc

VALENTINE, T. D. History of the City of New York
VENEGAS, M. Natural and Civil History of California. 2 vols. London, 1749

WADDINGTON, A. The Frazer River Mines Vindicated
WARBURTON, E. The Conquest of Canada. 2 vols
WASHINGTON, G. His Revolutionary Orders
WATSON, J. F. Annals of Philadelphia and Pennsylvania. 2 vols
WHEELER, H. G. The Congress of the United States. 2 vols
WHITTLESEY, C. Ancient Works in Ohio
WIERZBICKI. California as it is, 1849
WILKINSON, Eliza. Letters during the American Revolution
WILLIARD, Emma. Historia de los Estados Unidos
WILLETT, W. M. Narrative of the Military Actions of Col. Marinus Willett
WILLIAMS. J. S. The Invasion and Capture of Washington
WILLIAMSON, H. History of North Carolina. 2 vols
WILLSON, M. American History
WILSON, R. A. New History of the Conquest of Mexico
WILSON, D. Mexico and its Religion
WINTERBOTHAM, W. View of America. 5 vols
WINTHROP, J. History of New England. 2 vols
WOOD, J. The Administration of John Adams

YOAKUM, H. History of Texas. 2 vols
YOUNG, A. Chronicles of the Pilgrim Fathers
— Chronicles of Massachusetts

ZARATE, A. de. Histoire de Peru. 2 vols

SECTION V.

SPECIAL HISTORY.

ANDREWS, A. History of British Journalism. 2 vols

BANKS, History of
BEAMISH, N. L. Northmen in America
BELCHER, J. The Clergy of America
BELISLE, D. W. History of Independence Hall, Philadelphia
BLAKEY, R. History of Political Literature. 2 vols
BOSSUET. Sur l'Histoire Universelle
BROOKE, R. Fields of Battle in England of the 15th Century
BURNHAM, G. P. History of the Hen Fever
BYRDSALL, F. History of the Locofoco Party

CHATEAUBRIAND. Analyse de l'Histoire de France
CHILD, L. Maria. Progress of Religious Ideas. 3 vols
CLARKSON, T. The African Slave Trade
CRAIK, G. L. History of British Commerce. 3 vols
COUSIN, V. History of Philosophy. 2 vols

EDWARDS, E. Memoirs of Libraries. 2 vols
EUROPE, and the Allies of the Past and To-day
EVANS, F. W. The Shakers, their Origin, etc
EVELYN, J. History of Religion. 2 vols

FRENCH, B. F. The Iron Trade of the United States, from 1621 to 1857
FULLOM, S. W. The History of Woman. 2 vols

GIBBONS, J. S. The Banks of New York and the Panic of 1857
GLEIG, G. R. History of the Bible

HALL, E. The Puritans and their Principles
HALLAM, H. Literature of Europe. 2 vols
HAMMOND, J. D. Political History of New York. 3 vols
HENNELL, C. C. The Origin of Christianity
HENRY, C. S. History of Philosophy. 2 vols
HERBERT, W. The Livery Companies of London. 2 vols
HIGGINS, G. Celtic Druids

HISTOIRE, ou Anecdotes sur la Revolu-
tion de Russie, en 1762
HISTORIC Doubts relative to Napoleon
Bonaparte
HISTORY of the Protestant Church in
Hungary
HOME, H. History of Man. 3 vols
HONE, W. Ancient Mysteries
HOOD, G. History of Music in New
England
HYDE, J. History of Mormonism

IAMBLICUS. On the Mysteries of the
Egyptians, etc
ILLUMINES, Essai sur la Secte de

JEAFRESON. Novels and Novelists. 2
vols
JOSEPHUS, F. History of the Jews

LAURIE's History of Free Masonry
LAWSON, W. J. History of Banking
LEVI, L. Annals of British Legislation.
5 vols
LOSSING, B. J. History of the Fine Arts

MAHAWANSO, The
MILLINGEN, J. G. The History of Duelling. 2 vols
MOSHEIM, J. L. Ecclesiastical History.
4 vols
MYLES, W. Chronological History of
the Methodists

NEANDER, A. The Planting of Chris-
tianity
NEWMAN, F. W. History of English
Universities. 3 vols

ORMSBY, R. McK. History of the Whig
Party
PICTURES from Battle Fields
PRESCOTT, G. B. Account of the Elec-
tric Telegraph

RAUNER, K. Von. The German Univer-
sities
RELIGIOUS Society of Friends, and the
Indians
RHEES. The Public Libraries of the
United States
RITTER, H. History of Philosophy. 3
vols
ROBBINS, C. History of the Old North
Church in Boston
ROSS, A. View of all Religions in the
World
RUPP, J. D. Religious Denominations
in the United States
RUSSELL, M. Palestine

SABINE, L. Notes on Duels and Duelling

SAVIGNY, C. Von. History of the Ro-
man Law
SCHLEGEL, F. History of Literature
SISMONDI. Historic View of the Liter-
ature of the South of Europe
— Italian Republics
STANTON, H. B. Reforms and Reformers
STEPHENS, H. L. Comic Natural His-
tory of the Human Race

TAYLOR, W. B. S. The University of
Dublin
TENNEMANN. History of Philosophy
THOMAS, I. History of Printing in
America. 2 vols
TICKNOR, H. Spanish Literature. 3 vols

VOLTAIRE. Louis XIV
— Louis XV

WESTON, G. The Progress of Slavery
in the United States
WHEWELL, W. History of the Inductive Sciences. 3 vols
WILBERFORCE, S. History of the Church
in America

SECTION VI.

GENERAL HISTORY AND CHRONOLOGY.

ARNOLD, T. Lectures on Modern
History

BAYLE, P. Historical Dictionary. 5
vols. Folio
BLAIR, H. Chronological Tables
BLANC, L. Ten Years. 2 vols
BUCKE, C. Ruins of Ancient Cities

DICTIONNAIRE Historique; ou Histoire
abregée. 6 vols
DIODORUS Siculus. Historical Library.
2 vols
DRUMMOND, W. Origines. 4 vols

GOODRICH, S. G. History of all Nations.
2 vols
GREENE, G. W. Historic Studies

HAYDN, J. Dictionary of Dates; new
Edition, to 1859
HEEREN, A. H. L. Manual of Ancient
History
HERDER, J. G. Philosophy of History
HISTORICAL Magazine. Vols. 1, 2 and 3

KEIGHTLEY, T. Outlines of History
KOEPPEN, A. L. The World in the
Middle Ages. Folio

LAVOISNE, M. Complete Genealogical,

Historical and Geographical Atlas

MICHELET, M. Modern History
MILLER, S. Retrospect of the 18th Century. 4 vols
MORERI, L. Le Grand Dictionnaire Historique. 10 vols. Folio
MUNSELL, J. Every Day Book of History and Chronology

OXFORD Chronological Tables. Folio

PERCE, E. The Battle Roll, an Encyclopedia of Battles, etc

RAWLINSON, R. Historic Evidences
ROLLIN, C. Ancient History. 4 vols

SCHLEGEL, F. The Philosophy of History
— Lectures on Modern History
SEAMAN, E. C. The Progress of Nations in Civilization, etc
SCHLOSSER, F. C. History of the 18th Century. 6 vols
SMITH, J. T. Comparative History of Chronological Eras
SMYTH, W. Lectures on Modern History. 2 vols
STRETCH, L. M. The Beauties of History, etc

TOULOTTE, M. A. C. T. Riva Histoire de la Barbarie. 3 vols
TREASURY of History
TYTLER, A. F. Universal History. 6 vols

SECTION VII.

BIOGRAPHY.

ABELARD and Heloise, Romance of, by O. W. Wight
ABBOTT, J. Romulus
— King Charles I
— Hannibal
— King Alfred
— Nero
— Darius the Great
— Xerxes
— Cyrus
— Mary Queen of Scots
— Pyrrhus
— William the Conqueror
— Cleopatra
— Julius Cæsar
— Alexander the Great
— Madame Roland
— Josephine
— Maria Antoinette
— Peter the Great

ABBOTT, J. Henry 4th, King of France
ABBOTT, J. S. C. History of Napoleon Bonaparte. 2 vols
— Napoleon at St. Helena
— Kings and Queens
ADAMS, J. Q. Memoir of, by Josiah Quincy
ADAMS, Miss Hannah. Memoir by herself
ADDISON, Joseph. Life of, by L. Aikin
AGUILAR, Grace. Women of Israel. 2 vols
AIKIN, Lucy. Court of Charles I. 2 vols
ALBERMARLE, Earl of. Memoirs of the Marquis of Rockingham. 2 vols
ALCOTT, Dr. W. A. Forty Years in the Wilderness of Pills and Powders
ALEXANDER the Great. Life of, by J. Williams
ALEXANDER, Col. Sir J. E. Passages in the Life of a Soldier. 2 vols
ALFRED the Great. Life of, by J. Abbott
— Life of, by Asser
— Life of, by Dr R. Pauli
ALISON, Sir A. Life of Marlborough. 2 vols
ALLEN, W. The American Biographical Dictionary
ALLEN, E. Life of, by J. Sparks
AMERICAN Biography, by J. Belknap. 3 vols
APPLETON's New Cyclopedia of Biography
AQUINAS, T. Life of, by R. D. Hampden
ARAGO, F. Biographies of Distinguished Men. 2 vols
ARDECHE, M. History of Napoleon. 2 vols
ARMSTRONG, J. Life of Gen. Richard Montgomery
ARNOLD, Dr. T. Life and Correspondence of, by A. P. Stanley
— Life of Hannibal
ARNOLD, Benedict. Life of, by J. Sparks
ARTIST's Married Life of Albert Dürer
AUSTIN, J. T. Life of Elbridge Gerry. 2 vols
AUSTIN, Miss. Memoirs of the Duchess of Orleans
AUTOBIOGRAPHY, a Collection of Lives written by the parties themselves. 33 vols

BAKER, G. E. Life of Wm. H. Seward
BALDWIN, J. G. Party Leaders
BALLANTYNE, J. Chronicle of the Hundredth Birth-Day of Robert Burns
BANCROFT, A. Life of Washington. 2 vols
BARKER, Jacob. Incidents in the Life of
BARNUM, P. T. Life, by Himself

BARRETT, B. F. Life of Swedenborg
BARRINGTON, Sir J. Sketches of his
    own time
BARROW, Sir J. Memoirs of Naval
    Worthies of Queen Elizabeth's
    Reign
— Life of Peter the Great. 2 vols
— Life of Lord George Anson
— Life of Admiral Howe
BARTLETT, D. W. The Heroes of the
    Indian Rebellion
— Presidential Candidates for 1860
— Life of Joan of Arc
— Life of Lady Jane Grey
— Modern Agitators
BARTRAM, J., and H. Marshall's Memoirs,
    by W. Darlington
BAUER, J. Lives of Alex. and William
    · Humboldt
BAYLE, P. Great Biographical Diction-
    ary. 5 vols. Folio
BAYNE, B. Essays in Biography and
    Criticism
BEATTIE, W. Life and Letters of Thos.
    Campbell
BECKET, T. A'. Life of, by Robertson
— Life of, by H. H. Milman
BECKFORD, W. Memoirs of. 2 vols
BECKWOURTH, J., Life and Adventures of,
    by T. D. Bonner
BEDFORD, H. Life of St. Vincent de
    Paul
BEHMEN, J. Memoirs of
— Life of, by F. Okely
BELKNAP, J. American Biography. 3
    vols
BELL, H. C. Life of Mary Queen of
    Scots. 2 vols
BELL, R. Lives of the English Poets.
    2 vols
— Life of George Canning
BENNETT, J. Gordon. Memoirs of his
    Life and Times
BERKELEY, H. Memoirs of Madame
    d'Arblay
BERNAL Diaz. Memoirs, by himself. 2
    vols
BINNEY, H. Eulogy on John Marshall
BIOGRAPHIE Nouvelle des contemporairs.
    20 vols
— Universelle des contemporairs,
    depuis 1788 jusqu' a nos jours.
    5 vols
BLACKSHEAR's Memoirs of S. F. Miller
BLESSINGTON, Lady. Life and Corres-
    pondence. 2 vols
BOGART, W. H. Daniel Boone, and the
    Hunters of Kentucky
BONAPARTE, Napoleon. Life of, by L'Ar-
    deche. 2 vols
— Life of, by W. Scott
— Life of, by W. Grimshaw
— Life of, by J. G. Lockhart

— Maitland's Narrative of his Sur-
    render
— Court and Camp of
— and his Marshals, by J. T. Headley.
    2 vols
— Dictated to his Generals. 7 vols
— by J. S. C. Abbott. 2 vols
— at St. Helena, by J. S. C. Abbott
— by Count Lebedoyére. 2 vols
— by Ardéche. 2 vols
— in Exile, by O'Meara. 2 vols
— Captivity at St. Helena. 2 vols
— Life, by Hazlitt. 4 vols
— Napoleon Dynasty
— Napoleon Code
— Correspondence with his brother
    Joseph. 2 vols
— Gallery, outline Illustrations of
    his Life, etc.
— Court and Camp
BONNER, T. D. Life and Adventures of
    J. Beckwourth
BOONE, D. Life of, by J. M. Peck
— and the Hunters of Kentucky
BOSWELL, J. Life of Samuel Johnson.
    10 vols
— Life of Samuel Johnson. 2 vols
BOWEN, F. Life of B. Lincoln
— Life of J. Otis
— Life of Baron Steuben
BRAINERD, D. Life of, by W. B. O.
    Peabody
BRANT, Thayendanega. Life of, by W.
    L. Stone. 2 vols
BREWSTER, D. Life, Writings and Dis-
    coveries of Sir J. Newton. 2
    vols
— Martyrs of Science
BREWSTER, W. Life and Time, by A.
    Steele
BRIALMONT, M., and G. R. Gleig. Life
    of the Duke of Wellington. 4
    vols
BRINLEY, T. The Life of Wm. T. Porter
BRISTED, C. A. Five Years in an Eng-
    lish University
BROCK, Rev. W. Biographical Sketch
    of Sir H. Havelock
BRONSON, O. A. The Convert
BROUGH, R. B. Life of Sir John Fal-
    staff, illustrated
BROUGHAM, Lord. Statesmen of the
    Time of George III
— Philosophers of the Time of
    George III
— Men of Letters of the Time of
    George III
BROWN, T. N. Life and Times of Hugh
    Miller
BROWN, J. Sixty Years' Gleanings in
    Life's Harvest
BROWNE, C. B. Life of, by W. H. Pres-
    cott

Browning, H. C. Life of Goethe, from his Autobiographical Papers
Browning, M. 24 Years of the Life of a Hunter
Bruce, J. Life of, by F. B. Head
Bryan, M. Biographical Dictionary of Painters and Engravers
Bryant, W. C. Discourse on Life and Genius of Irving
Buckingham, Duke of. Memoirs of the Court of George IV. 2 vols
Buckingham, J. S. Autobiography. 2 vols
Burgess, Tristam. Memoir and Speeches
Burke, E. Life of, by M. Prior. 2 vols
Burnap, G. W. Life of L. Calvert
Burns, Robert, Life of, by J. G. Lockhart
— Life of, by T. Carlyle
Burns, J. Mothers of the Wise and Good
Burr, Aaron. Memoirs of, by M. L. Davis. 2 vols
— Private Journal during his Residence in Europe. 2 vols
Bush, G. Mahomet
Busoni, M. P. Memoirs, etc., de la Duchesse d'Orleans
Buxton, Sir F., Memoirs of, by his Son
Byron, Lord. Life of, by J. Galt

Cabot, S. Life of, by C. Hayward
Cæsar, Julius. Life of, by J. Abbott
Caldwell, C. M. D. Autobiography
Calvert, L. Life of, by G. W. Burnap
Campan, Mad. The Court of Marie Antoinette. 2 vols
Campbell, F. Frederick the Great and his Times. 2 vols
Campbell, T. Life and Letters of, by W. Beattie. 3 vols
Campbell, W. Life of DeWitt Clinton
Campbell, J. Lives of the Lords Chancellors of England. 7 vols
— Lives of the Chief Justices of England. 2 vols
Canning, G. Life of, by R. Bell
Captains of the Old World, by H. W. Herbert
Carlyle, T. History of Frederick II. 2 vols
— Life of John Sterling
— Life of Robert Burns
— Life of Schiller
Carruthers, R. Life of Alexander Pope
Carson, Kit. Life and Adventures, as related by himself
Catherine II. Memoirs of, by herself
— Court and Reign of, by S. M. Smucker
Cavendish, G. Life of Cardinal Wolsey

Celebrated Men, Lives and Criminal Trials of
Cellini, B. Memoirs, by himself
Chadwick, W. Life and Times of Dan. De Foe
Chalmers, T. Memoirs of, by Rev. W. Hanna
Chambers, R. Life and Works of Robert Burns. 4 vols
Channing, E. T. Life of W. Ellery
Channing, W. E. Memoir of
Charlemagne. History of, by G. P. R. James
Charles I. Memoirs of the Court of, by Lucy Aiken. 2 vols
Charles I. Life of, by Abbott
Charles II. Beauties of the Court of, by Mrs. Jameson
Charles V. Life of, by W. Robertson, edited, with an account of his life after his abdication, by W. H. Prescott. 3 vols
— Cloister Life of, by W. Stirling
Charles IX., and his times
Chasles, P. Notabilities in France and England
Chateaubriand, F. A. Autobiography. 2 vols
Chatterton. Life of, by J. Dix
Child, L. M. Isaac T. Hopper
Choate, Rufus. Reminiscences of, by E. G. Parker
Chorley, H. F. Life of Mrs. Hemans
Cibber, C. Life, by himself
Cicero. Life of, by C. Middleton
Claiborne, J. F. H. Life and Times of Gen. Sam. Dale
Clarke, Mrs. Charlotte. Life
Clarkson Thos. Biographical Sketch of, by T. Taylor
Claxton, T. Autobiography
Clay, H. Life of, by E. Sargent
Clayton, J. W. Personal Memoirs of Charles II. 2 vols
Cleaveland, H. R. Life of Hendrick Hudson
Cleopatra. Life of, by Abbott
Clinton, De Witt. Life of, by J. Renwick
— Life of, by W. Campbell
Clive, Lord. Life. 3 vols
Cloquet, J. Recollections of Lafayette. 2 vols
Corbett, W. Life of Andrew Jackson
Cockburn, H. Memorials of his Time
Cœur, Jacques, Life of, by Mrs. Costello
Colden, C. D. Life of Robert Fulton
Coleridge, H. Lives of the Northern Worthies. 3 vols
Coleridge, S. T. Biographia Literaria
— Reminiscences of, by J. Cottl
Columbus, C. Life and Voyages W. Irving. 3 vols

COLTON, C. Life and Speeches of Henry Clay. 2 vols

COMMINES, P. Memoirs. 2 vols

COMPTON, B. Life of R. C. Trench

CONKLIN, M. C. Memoirs of the Mother and Wife of Washington

COOPER, J. T. Lives of Distinguished Americal Naval Officers

COPWAY, G. Recollections of a Forest Life

CORMENIN, Viscount De. (Timon.) Orators of France

CORNE, H. Le Cardinal de Richelieu

CORNEILLE and his Times, by F. Guizot

COSTELLO, Miss. Life of Jacques Cœur, the French Argonaut

COTTLE, J. Reminiscences of S. T. Coleridge

COUGHLAN, Mrs. Memoirs, by herself

COURTENAY, T. P. Memoirs of Sir Wm. Temple. 2 vols

COUSIN, V. La Société Française au XVII Siécle. 2 vols

COWPER, Wm. Life and Works, by Southey. 8 vols

COX, W. Memoirs of the Duke of Marlborough. 2 vols

CRANMER, T. Life and Times of

CREASY, E. S. Memoirs of Eminent Etonians

CREICHTON, Capt. J. Memoirs of

CROCKETT, Col. David. Life, by himself

CROLY, G. Life and Times of George IV

CROMWELL, O. Letters and Speeches, etc. 2 vols

— Life of, by J. T. Headley

— Life of, by M. Russell

— A Vindication, by D'Aubigné

CROSBY, Hon. N. Obituaries of Eminent Americans, who died in 1858-9. 2 vols

CUNNINGHAM, Allan. Painters and Sculptors of Great Britain. 5 vols

— Life and Works of Burns

CURTIS, Joseph. Memoirs of

CURWEN, S. Journal and Letters from 1775 to 1784

CUSTIS, Geo. Washington Parke. Recollections and Memoirs of Washington

CYRUS the Great, by Abbott

D'ARBLAY, Mme. Memoir of, by H. Berkeley

DARIUS the Great. Life of, by Abbott

DARLINGTON, W. Memoirs of John Bartram and H. Marshall

D'AUBIGNE, T. Agrippa, Life of

— Cromwell

DAVIDSON, L. M. Memoir of, by C. M. Sedgwick

DAVIDSON, M. M. Biography of, by W. Irving

DAVIE, W. R. Life of, by F. M. Hubbard

DAVIS, M. L. Memoirs of Aaron Burr. 2 vols

DAVIS, Elizabeth. A Balaklava Nurse. Autobiography. 2 vols

DAVY, J. Life of Sir Humphrey Davy. 2 vols

DECATUR, S. Life of, by A. S. Mackenzie

DE QUINCEY, T. Autobiographical Sketches

DES CARTES. Life of

DE WITT, C. D. Histoire de Washington

DEXTER, Timothy. Life of, by S. L. Knapp

DEXTER, S. Reminiscences

DIARY of a Member of the Howard Association of New Orleans

DICKENS, C. Memoirs of Joseph Grimaldi. 2 vols

DISTINGUISHED Men of Modern Times

DIXON, W. H. William Penn

DIXON, E. H. Scenes in the Practice of a New York Surgeon

DODDINGTON, G. B. Diary of, Autobiography. Vol. 22

DORAN, Dr. Queens of England of the House of Hanover. 2 vols

— Monarchs Retired from Business

DOUBLEDAY, T. The Political Life of Sir R. Peel. 2 vols

DOUGLAS, Stephen A. Life and Speeches of

DOVER, Lord. Life of Frederick II. 2 vols

DRAKE, Cavendish, and Dampier. Lives and Voyages of

DUER, A. The Artist's Married Life

DUPPA, R., and T. De Quincey. Lives of Michael Angelo and Raphael

DWIGHT, Theo. The Character of Jefferson

— Life of Gen. Garibaldi

— Life of, by W. B. Sprague

EATON, Gen. W. Life of, by C. C. Felton. Sparks' Biography

— Life of, from his Manuscripts, etc

EDWARDS, J. Life of, by S. Miller

EDWARD the Black Prince. Life of, by G. P. R. James

ELDER, W. Life of Dr. Kane

ELDON, Lord. Life of, by H. Twiss

ELIZABETH, Queen. Life of, by J. Abbott

ELIOT, J. Life of, by C. Francis

ELLERY, W. Life of, by E. T. Channing

ELLET, Mrs. Women Artists of all Ages

— Women of the Revolution. 3 vols

ELLIOT, J. Life of, by C. Francis

ELLIS, G. E. Life of A Hutchinson

— Life of William Penn

ELLIS, G. E.   Life of John Mason
ELTON, R.   Memoir and Remains of Jonathan Macy
ELWOOD, T.   Life, by himself
ENGLISH Cyclopedia of Biography. 6 vols. 4to
EUGENE, Prince.   Memoirs, by himself
EVERETT, E.   Life of Washington
— Life of John Stark
EVERETT, A. H.   Life of Patrick Henry
— Life of Gen. Warren
EXMOUTH, Admiral. Life of, by E. Ostler

FABER, G. S.   Napoleon the Man of Prophecy
FARMER, J.   Genealogical Register of the First Settlers in New England
FARRAR, Mrs.   Life of John Howard
FELTON, C. C.   Life of W. Eaton
FEMALE Biography, by M. Hays
FENELON, F.   Lives of Ancient Philosophers
FERDINAND and Isabella, The Reign of, by W. H. Prescott. 3 vols
FERGUSON, W.   Notes and Recollections of a Professional Life
FERGUSON, J.   Life of, by himself
FERN, Fanny. Life and Beauties of
FEUERBACH. Remarkable Criminal Trials
FICHTE, J. G.   Memoir of, by W. Smith
FIELD, Rev. W.   Life, Writings and Opinions of Dr. S Parr. 2 vols
FITCH, J.   Life of, by C. Whittlesey
FLANDERS, H.   Lives of Chief Justices of the United States. 2 vols
FLINT, T.   Recollections of the Last Ten Years
FORSTER, J.   Life and Adventures of Oliver Goldsmith
— Statesmen of the Commonwealth of England. 5 vols
FORSYTH, W.   The Captivity of Napoleon at St. Helena. 2 vols
FOSTER, J.   Life and Correspondence, edited by Ryland. 2 vols
Fox, Maria, Memoirs of
Fox, C. J., Memoirs of, by Lord John Russell. 2 vols
— Memoirs of, by J. Trotter
Fox, John.   Acts and Monuments of the Christian Martyrs. 8 vols
FRANCIS II. and Charles IX. of France, by M. Castelnau.   Folio
FRANCIS, G. H.   Orators of the Age
FRANCIS, C.   Life of S. Bale
— Life of John Eliot
FRANKLIN, B.   Autobiography
— Life of, by J. Sparks
FREDERICK II.   History of, by T. Carlyle. 2 vols
— His Court and Times. 2 vols
— by Lord Dover. 2 vols

FREDERICK II.   Life of, by T.B. Macaulay.   Vols. 1 and 2
FREER's Life of Henry IV.   2 vols
FREMONT, J. C.   Life of, by S. M. Smucker
— Life and Travels, by C. Upham
FROST, J.   Pictorial Life of Andrew Jackson
— Life of Gen. Taylor
FRY, Elizabeth. Brief Memoir of
FULLER, Dr. T.   History of the Worthies of England. 3 vols
FULLER, Robt.   Life, by C. D. Colden
— by J. F. Reigart
— by J. Renwick

GALT, J.   Life of Cardinal Wolsey
— Life of Lord Byron
GANNELL, W.   Life of Roger Williams
— Life of S. Ward
GARDNER, C. K.   Dictionary of the Officers of the United States Army
GARIBALDI, Life of.   by T. Dwight
GARLAND, H.   Life of John Randolph. 2 vols
GASKELL, E. O.   Life of Charlotte Bronte. 2 vols
GAVARD, M.   Les Rois de France. Portraits
GEORGES, The, Four Kings of England, by S. W. Smucker
GEORGE II.   Memoirs of the Reign of, by Lord Hervey. 2 vols
GEORGE IV.   Life and Times of, by G. Croly
GEORGI, A.   My Life and Acts in Hungary
GEORGIAN Era.   Memoirs of Eminent Persons in the Reign of the Georges. 4 vols
GERRY, E.   Life of, by J. T. Austin. 2 vols
GIBBON, E.   Life of Mahomet
— Memoir of his Life and Writings, by himself
GILFILLAN, G.   The Bards of the Bible
GLEIG, G. R.   Memoirs of Warren Hastings. 3 vols
— Lives of British Military Commanders. 3 vols
GODWIN, P.   Hand-Book of Universal Biography
GOETHE.   Autobiography
— Life of, by H. C. Browning
— Life of, by G. H. Lewes. 2 vols
GOLDONI, F. D.   Memoirs, by himself
GOLDSMITH, O.   A Biography, by W. Irving
— Life and Adventures of, by J. Forster
GOODRICH, S. G.   Recollections of a Lifetime.   2 vols

GORTON, S., Life of, by J. M. Mackie
GORTON, J. Biographical Dictionary. 4 vols
GRAHAM, J. Life of Gen. Morgan
GRANT, Mrs. Memoirs of an American Lady
GRANT, J. Random Recollections of the House of Lords
— The British Senate. 2 vols
— Life of Mary of Lorraine
GRAYDON, A. Memoirs of his own time
GREELEY, Horace, Life of, by J. Parton
GREENE, G. W. Biographical Studies
GREENE, N. Life of, by G. W. Greene
— by W. G. Simms
GREENHOW, Horatio. Memorial of, by H. T. Tuckerman
GRESHAM, T. Life of
GREY, Lady J. Life of, by W. Bartlett
GRIMALDI, J. Life of, by C. Dickens. 2 vols
GRIMSHAW, W. Life of Napoleon
GRISWOLD, R. W. Poets of America
— Prose Writers of America
— Female Poets of America
— Poets of England
— The Republican Court, with Portraits
GILFORD, W. Memoir, by himself
GUIZOT, F. Oliver Cromwell and the English Commonwealth. 2 vols
— Corneille and his Times

HALDANE, R. and J. Memoirs of, by A. Haldane
HALE, D. Memoir of, by J. P. Thompson
HALE, Mrs. S. J. Woman's Record
HALL, J. Life of T. Posey
HALL, Mrs. M. Lives of the Queens of England before the Conquest
HALLOCK, W. A. Life of Justin Edwards
HAMILTON, A. Life of, by J. Renwick
— by his son, J. C. Hamilton. 7 vols
HAMMOND, Capt. M., Memoir of
HAMMOND, J. Life and Times of Silas Wright
HAMPDEN, John. Memorials of, by Lord Nugent. 2 vols
HAMPDEN, R. D. Life of Thomas Aquinas
HANNIBAL. Life of, by T. Arnold
— by Abbott
HANDEL. Life of, by Schoelcher
HARTE, W. History of Gustavus Adolphus. 2 vols
HASTINGS, Warren. By G. R, Gleig. 3 vols
HAVELOCK, Gen. Life of, by J. T. Headley
HAWKS, F. L. New Cyclopedia of Biography
HAWKINS, J. W. Life of, compiled by his son
HAWTHORNE, N. Life of Franklin Pierce

HAYDON, B. R. Autobiography. 2 vols
HAYS, M. Female Biography
HAYWARD, C. Life of John Cabot
HAZLITT, W. Life of Napoleon. 4 vols
HEADLEY, J. T. Life of Washington
— Washington and his Generals. 2 vols
— Napoleon and his Marshals. 2 vols
— General Havelock
— General Scott
— Life of Cromwell
— Life of Andrew Jackson
HEADLEY, P. C. Life of Lafayette
— Josephine the Empress
— Mary Queen of Scots
HEBER, Reginald. Life of, by his Widow 2 vols. Quarto
— The same. 12mo
HEMANS, Mrs., Memorials of, by H. F. Chorley
HENRY, Patrick. Life of, by A. H. Everett
— by Wm. Wirt
HENRY IV. of France, by Abbott
HERBERT, W. H. Captains of the Old World, by Freer. 2 vols
— Persons and Pictures
— Captains of the Roman Republic
— Memoirs of Henry VIII. and his Six Wives
HERBERT, Edward Lord. Life, by himself
HERVEY, Lord. Memoirs of George II. 2 vols
HILDRETH, R. Lives of Infamous Judges
HILL, G. C. Biography of Capt. John Smith
— Life of Gen. Putnam
HILL, Rev. Rowland. Life, by Jones and Sherman
HILLARD, G. S. Life of Captain John Smith
HITTELL, T. S. Adventures of J. C. Adams, Hunter of California
HOBART, N. Life of Swedenborg
HOFFMAN, C. F. Jacob Leisler
HOLBERG, Lewis. Memoir, by himself
HOLBROOK, S. F. Three-score Years
HOLBROOK, J. Ten Years among the Mail Bags
HOLLAND, Lady. Memoir of Rev. Sidney Smith. 2 vols
HOLLIDAY, J. Life of William, Earl of Mansfield. Quarto
HOLMES, E. Life of Mozart
HOOD, T. Memoirs of, by his Daughter and Son. 2 vols
HOOD, E. P. John Milton
HOPPER, I. Life of, by L. M. Child
HOUDIN, R. Memoirs of
HOUSSAYE, A. Men and Women of the 18th Century. 2 vols
— Philosophers and Actresses. 2 vols

HOUSSAYE, A. Le Roi Voltaire
HOUSTON, S. Life of
HOWARD, J. Life of, by Mrs. Farrar
HOWE, Adm'l. Life of, by Sir J. Barrow
HOWLAND, Jno. Life of, by E. M. Stone
HUBBARD, F. M. Life of W. R. Davie
HUBBARD, J. N. Life and Times of Maj. Van Campan. 2 vols
HUDSON, H. Life of, by H. R. Cleaveland
HUISH, R. Memoirs of Daniel O'Connell
HUMBOLDT, Alexander and William. Lives of, by Klencke
— Lives of, by J. Bauer
HUMBOLDT, A. Von. Life, Travels and Books
HUME, D. Life of, by himself
HUNDRED Boston Orators, by J. S. Loring
HUNT, Leigh. Autobiography. 2 vols
HUNT, F. Lives of American Merchants. 2 vols
HUNTER, J. The Separatists of the time of James I
HUTCHINSON, A., Life of, by G. E. Ellis
HUTCHINSON, Col. Memoirs of, by his Widow
HUTTON, W. Life, by himself

IMPEY, Sir J. E. Memoir of, by E. B. Impey
INDIAN Biography, by B. B. Thacher
ITURBIDE, A. Memoires de
IRVING, W. Washington. 5 vols
— Oliver Goldsmith
— Lives of Columbus, and his Companions. 3 vols
— Mahomet and his Successors. 2 vols
— Biography of Margaret M. Davidson
IRVINGIANA; a Memorial of Washington Irving
JACKSON, Andrew. Life of, by J. Parton 2 vols
— Pictorial Life of, by J. Frost
— Life of, by W. Cobbett
— Life of, by J. Jenkins
— Life of, by J. T. Headley
JAMES, G. P. R. Lives of Eminent Foreign Statesmen. 5 vols
— Life of Charlemagne
— Life and Times of Louis XIV. 2 vols
—· Life of Richard Cœur-de-Lion. 2 vols
— Life of Edward the Black Prince. 2 vols
JAMES II. Memoirs of the Reign of, by Lord Lonsdale
JAMESON, Mrs. Memoirs of Celebrated Female Sovereigns. 2 vols
— Stories and Memoirs
— Characteristics of Women

JAMESON, Mrs. Beauties of the Court of Charles II
— Memoirs of the Early Italian Painters
JAY, John. Life of, by Wm. Jay. 2 vols
— Life of, by J. Renwick
JEFFERSON, T. The Youth of
— Life of, by H. S. Randall. 3 vols
JENKINS, J. Life of Jackson
JENNY Lind. Memoranda of her Life, by N. P. Willis
JERROLD, Douglas. Life and Remains, by his Son
JESSE, J. H. The Pretenders and their Adherents
— The Court of England under the Stuarts. 3 vols
JOHNSON, G. W. Memoirs of John Selden
JOHNSON, C. Lives of English Highwaymen and Pirates
JOHNSON, S. English Poets
— Life of, by James Boswell. 10 vols
JOHNSONIANA. Supplement to Boswell
JONES and Sherman. Life of Rev. Rowland Hill
JONES, J. Paul, Life of, by A. S. Mackenzie. 2 vols
JONES, Sir W. Life of, by Lord Tinemouth
JOSEPH. Story of
JOSEPHINE, The Empress. Life of, by J. S. Memes
— by Abbott
— by P. C. Headley
JUDSON, Rev. A. Life and Letters of, by F. Wayland
JUDSON, Emily C. Life and Letters
JUNOT, Mad. Memoirs of Napoleon, his Court, etc

KANE, E. K. Life of, by W. Elder
KAVANAGH, Julia. The Women of France
KEATS, J. Life, Letters, etc
KENNEDY, J. P. Life of Wm. Wirt
KINGS and Queens, by J. S. C. Abbott
KINGSLEY, C. Sir Walter Raleigh, and other Papers
KINGSLEY, J. L. Life of Ezra Stiles
KING, Lord. Life and Letters of John Locke. 2 vols
KING, Vice Presid't. Obituary Addresses on his Death
KIRKLAND, S. Life of, by S. C. Lothrop
KIRKLAND, Mrs. Memoir of Washington
KLENCKE. Lives of Alex. and W. Humboldt
KNAPP, F. Life of Gen. Steuben
KNAPP, S. L. Life of Timothy Dexter
KNIGHT, Helen C. Life of James Montgomery
KNOX, John. Life of, by T. McCrie

KOTZEBUE, A. Von. Life and Literary Career, by himself
LACKINGTON, J. Memoirs of, by himself
LAERTUIS, Diogene. Lives of Ancient Philosophers
LAFAYETTE. Recollections of his Private Life, by J. Cloquet
— Life of, by P. C. Headley.
LAMARTINE, A. Life of Mary, Queen of Scots
— Memoirs of Celebrated Characters. 2 vols
LAMB, Gen. J. Memoirs of, by J. Q. Leake
LANCELOTT, F. The Queens of England. 2 vols
LASCASAS, Count. Memoirs of Napoleon. 4 vols
LASALLE, R. C. de. Life of, by J. Sparks
LATHROP, J. C. Life of S. Kirkland
LAUQUIER et Carpentier. Vie Anecdotique de Louis Philippe
LAURENCE, A. Extracts from his Diary and Correspondence
LAURENS, H. Narrative of his Confinement in the Tower of London in 1780
LAW, J. Life of, by A. Thiers
LAWRENCE, E. Lives of British Historians. 2 vols

LEAKE, J. Q. Life of Gen. J. Lamb
LEBEDOYERE, Count. Memoirs of Napoleon. 2 vols
LEDERHOSE, C. F. Life of Philip Melancthon
LEDYARD, J. Life of, by J. Sparks
LEE, Arthur. Life of, by R. H. Lee. 2 vols
LEE, C. Life of, by J. Sparks
LEE, R. H. Memoir and Correspondence of
L'ENCLOS, Ninon de. Her Memoirs and Letters. 2 vols
LEO X. Life of, by W. Roscoe
LEIBNITZ, G. W. von. Life of, by J. M. Mackie
LEISLER, J. Administration of, by C. F. Hoffman
LESLIE, C. R. Autobiographical Recollections
LEWES, G. H. Life of Goethe. 2 vols
LIEBER, F. Life of G. B. Niebuhr. 2 vols
LILLY, Sir W. Life of, by himself. Autobiography
LINCOLN, B. Life of, by F. Bowen
LINCOLN, R. W. Lives of the Presidents of the United States
LIND, Jenny, Memoranda of the Life of, by N. P. Willis
LINN, Dr. L. F. Life and Public Services of

LIVES of the Most Eminent Literary and Scientific Men of France. 2 vols
— Eminent British Statesmen. 7 vols
— Eminent Men of Italy, Spain and Portugal. 3 vols
— Eminent Literary and Scientific men of Great Britain
— British Physicians
LIVINGSTON, J. Portraits and Biographies of Eminent Americans. 4 vols
LOCKE, John. Life and Letters of, by Lord King
LOCKHART, J. G. Life of Sir Water Scott. 10 vols
— Life of Napoleon
— Life of Robert Burns
LODGE, E. Portraits of Illustrious Personages of Great Britain. 8 vols
LONDSDALE, Lord. Memoir of the Reign of James II
LORENZO de Medici, by W. Roscoe
LORING, J. S. Hundred Boston Orators
LOSSING, B. J. Biographies of the Signers of the Declaration of Independence
LOTHROP, S. K. Life of S. Kirkland
LOUIS XIV. Life of, by G. P. R. James. 2 vols
LOUIS XVI. Life of, by A. Renée
LOVE of Country; or Sioieski and Hedrig
LOWE, Sir H. The Captivity of Napoleon at St. Helena. 2 vols
LUCKNOW, The Defense of; a Diary of the Events of
LUTHER, M. Life of, by Michelet
LYMAN, S. P. Life of Daniel Webster

MACAULAY, T. B. Life of Frederick the Great
— Life of Wm. Pitt
— Biographical and Historical Sketches
— New Biography of Illustrious Men
MACILWAIN, G. Memoirs of Dr. J. Abernethy
MACKENZIE, A. S. Life of Stephen Decatur
— Life of Com. O. H. Perry. 2 vols
— Life of Paul Jones. 2 vols
MACKIE, J. M. Life of S. Gorton
— Life of Wang, Chief of the Chinese Insurrection
— Life of Leibnitz
MACKINTOSH, Sir Jas. Memoirs of, by A. J. Mackintosh. 2 vols
MADDEN, R. R. Life of the Countess of Blessington
— The Infirmities of Genius. 2 vols
MADISON, James. Life and Times, by W. C. Rives. Vol. 1

MAGOON, E. L. Living Orators of Amer-
ica
— Orators of the Revolution
— Orators of France
— Orators of the Age
MAHOMET. Life of, by Edward Gibbon
— Life of, by G. Bush
— and his Successors, by Washing-
ton Irving. 2 vols
MAITLAND. The Surrender of Napoleon
MALIBRAN, Madame. Memoirs of, by the
Countess Merlin. 2 vols
MANSFIELD, Earl. Life of, by J. Holliday
MANSFIELD, E. D. Life of Gen. Scott
MARCH, C. W. Daniel Webster
MARIE Antoinette. Life of, by Abbott
— Memoirs of the Court of, by Mad.
Campan. 2 vols
MARLBOROUGH, Duke of. Memoirs of, by
W. Coxe. 3 vols
— The same, by Sir A. Alison
MARLBOROUGH, Duchess of. Memoirs of,
by Mrs. Thomson. 2 vols
— Private Correspondence. 2 vols
MARMONTEL. Memoirs, by himself
MARQUETTE, Father. Life of, by J.
Sparks
MARSHALL, J. Life of George Wash-
ington. 2 vols
— Eulogy on
MARTHA; a Memorial, by A. Reed
MARQUETTE. Life of, by J. Sparks
MARTYRS of Science, by D. Brewster
MARY, Queen of Scots. Life of, by H. G.
Bell
— by P. C. Headley
— by A. Lamartine
— by D. McLeod
— by Abbott
MARY of Loraine, by J. Grant
MASON, J. Life of, by G. E. Ellis
MASSON, M. Celebrated Children of all
Ages
— Life of Milton
MATHER, C. Life of, by W. B. O. Peabody
MATHER, J. Remarkable Providences
MATTHIAS and his Impostures, by W. L.
Stone
MAUNDER, S. Biographical Treasury
MAXWELL, W. H. Life of Wellington
— Victories of Wellington [3 vols
McHARG, C. K. Life of Talleyrand
McLeod, D. Life of Sir W. Scott
— Life of Mary Queen of Scots
McCRIE, T. Life of John Knox
MELANCTHON, P. Life of, by C. F. Led-
derhose
MKMES, J. S. Life of Empress Josephine
MEMOIRS of Celebrated Characters, by
A. Lamartine. 2 vols
MEMORIAL; or Life and Writings of an
only Daughter
MEN of the Time

MEN and Women of the 18th Century,
by A. Houssaye. 2 vols
MERLIN, Countess. Memoirs of Madam
Malilban. 2 vols
METHODIST, The; or Incidents and
Characters. 2 vols
MEZZOFANTI, Cardinal. Life of, by C.
W. Russell
MICHELET, M. Life of Luther
MIDDLETON, C. Life of Cicero
MILLER, S. F. The Bench and Bar of
Georgia. 2 vols
— Memoirs of Gen. D. Blackshear
MILLER, Hugh. Life and Times of, by T.
N. Brown
— My Schools and Schoolmasters
MILLER, S. Life of Jonathan Edwards
MILMAN, H. H. Life of Thomas A'
Beckett
MILTON, J., Patriot and Poet, by E. P.
Hood
— Life of, by D. Masson. Vol. 1
MITCHELL, Col. J. Life of Wallenstein,
Duke of Friedland
MITFORD, Miss. Recollections
MODERN British Plutarch, by W. C.
Taylor
MONTGOMERY, Gen. R. Life of, by J.
Armstrong
MONTGOMERY, James. Memoirs of, by J.
Holland and J. Everett. 5 vols
— Life of, by Helen C. Knight
MONTGOMERY, H. Life of Gen. Z. Taylor
MONTEZ, Lola. Lectures and Auto-
biography of
MOODY, C. P. Biographical Sketches
of the Moody Family
MOORE, T. Memoirs and Journal, edited
by Lord J. Russell. 2 vols
— Life and Letters of Lord Byron
— Letters of Lord Byron
— Life of Richard Brinsley Sheridan.
2 vols
MORE, Hannah. Life of, by H. Thomp-
— Life of, by R. Ward   [son
MORE, T. Household of, by M. More
MORGAN, Gen. D. Life of, by J. Graham
MORGAN, Lady. Life of Salvator Rosa.
2 vols
— Passages from my Autobiography
MORPHY, P. Exploits and Triumphs of,
in Europe
MORERI, L. Dictionnaire Historique, etc.
10 vols. Folio
MORRIS, Gouverneur. Life and Corres-
pondence of, by J. Sparks. 3
vols
MOTHERS of the Wise and Good, by J.
Burns
MOWATT, Anna Cora. Autobiography
of an Actress
— Mimic Life
MOZART. Life of, by E. Holmes

6

MUHLENBERG, Major-Gen. Life of, by
H. A. Muhlenberg
MUIRHEAD, J. P. Life of James Watt
MUNDY, Major-Gen. Life and Correspondence of Admiral Rodney.
2 vols

NAPOLEON. Memoirs dictated to his Generals. 7 vols
— Court and Camp
— Life of, by J. S. C. Abbott. 2 vols
— at St. Helena, by J. S. C. Abbott
— Life of, by Ardèche. 2 vols
— in Exile, by B. E. O'Meara. 2 vols
— Correspondence with his Brother Joseph. 2 vols
— Life of, by J. G. Lockhart. 2 vols
— Captivity at St. Helena. 2 vols
— Narrative of his Surrender, etc., by Capt. Maitland
— Life of, by W. Hazlitt. 4 vols
— Life of, by W. Grimshaw
— Memoirs of, by Count Lascasas. 4 vols
— by Count Lebedoyere. 2 vols
— and his Marshals, by J. T. Headley. 2 vols
— Napoleon Dynasty, by the Berkley Men
— his Court, etc., by Madam Junot
— Napoleon Code
NAPOLEON Gallery, Outline Illustrations of his Life, etc
NAPOLEON III. Life of, by S. Smucker
NELSON. Life of, by R. Southey
NELSONIAN Reminiscences, by G. S. Parsons
NERO. Life of, by Abbott
NEWTON, Sir J. Life, Writings, etc., of, by D. Brewster. 2 vols
NIEBUHR. Reminiscences of, by F. Lieber
NOLTE, V. Fifty Years in both Hemispheres
NORTHCOTE, J. Life of Sir Joshua Reynolds. 2 vols
NUGENT, Lord. Memorials of John Hampden. 2 vols

OATMAN Girls. Captivity of
O'CONNELL. Memoirs of, by R. Huish
OGLETHORPE, Jas. Life of, by W. B. O. Peabody. S. A. Biog. Vol. 2
OKELY, F. Life of Jacob Behmen
OLD England's Worthies, Illustrated. Folio
O'MEARA, B. E. Napoleon in Exile. 2
O'NEAL'S Bench and Bar   [vols
ORATORS, Living, of America, by E. L. Magoon
— of the Revolution, by E. L. Magoon
— of France, by Timon
— of the Age, by G. H. Francis

OSTLER, E. Life of Admiral Exmouth
OTIS, Jas. Life, by W. Tudor
OXBERRY'S Dramatic Biography. 6 vols

PAINE, R. T. Memoir of, by his Parents
PAINTERS and Sculptors. Lives of, by A. Cunningham
PALFREY, W. Life of, by J. E. Palfrey
PARENTY, Abbe. Life of St. Angela Merici of Bresica
PARK, Mungo. Life and Travels of
PARKER, E. G. Reminiscences of Rufus Choate
— The Golden Age of American Orators
PARR, Dr. S. Life, Writings and Opinions of, by Rev. W. Field. 2 vols
PARSONS, Chief Justice. Memoirs of, by his Son
PARSONS, G. S. Nelsonian Reminiscences
PARTON, J. Life and Times of Aaron Burr
— Life of Horace Greeley
— Life of Jackson. 2 vols
PATRIOT Preachers of the American Revolution
PAULDING, J. K. Life of Washington. 2 vols
PAULI, Dr. R. Life of Alfred the Great, and a Translation of Orosius
PEABODY, W. B. O. Life of Cotton Mather
— Life of Alexander Wilson
— Life of J. Putnam
— Life of D. Brainerd
— Life of J. Sullivan
— Life of Gen. Oglethorpe
PEARCE, R. Memoirs and Correspondence of Marquis Wellesley. 3 vols
PECK, J. M. Life of Daniel Boone
PECK, Rev. J. T. The True Woman
PELLICO, Silvio. Mie Prigioni, in French and Italié
PENN, W. Life of, by G. E. Ellis
— Life of, by W. H. Dixon
PEPYS, S. Diary and Correspondence. 5 vols
PERRY, O. Life of, by A. S. Mackenzie
PERTHES, F. Memoirs of. 2 vols
PESTALOZZI, J. H. Life, Education, Principles, etc
PETER the Great. Life of, by J. Barrow
PHILIP II. Reign of, by W. H. Prescott. 3 vols
PHILOSOPHERS, Ancient. Their Lives, etc., by Diogenes Laertius
— Lives of, by Fenelon
PIERCE, Franklin. Life of, by Nathaniel Hawthorne
PIKE, Z. M. Life of, by H. M. Whiting
PINKNEY, W. Life of, by H. Wheaton

PIONEER Women of the West, by Mrs. Ellet
PITT, Wm. Life of, by Macaulay
PLETTERHAUS, Louisa. Journal of a Poor Young Lady
PLUTARCH's Lives. Translated
POETS, English. Lives of, by S. Johnson
— Female, of America, by R. W. Griswold
— and Poetry of America, by R. W. Griswold
— of England, by R. W. Griswold
— of Europe, by H. W. Longfellow
POPE, Alexander. Life of, by R. Carruthers
PORTRAITS of Eminent Conservatives and Statesmen, with Memoirs. 2 vols., folio
PORTRAIT Gallery of Distinguished Poets, Philosophers, Statesmen, etc. 3 vols
POSEY, T. Life of, by J. Hall
POTTER, Major Roger Sherman. Life and Adventures
PREBLE, E. Life of, by L. Sabine
PRENTISS, S. S. Memoir of, edited by his Brother. 2 vols
PRESCOTT, W. H. Life of C. B. Brown
— Ferdinand and Isabella. 3 vols
— Reign of Philip II. 3 vols
PRESIDENTS of the United States, by R. W. Lincoln
PRETENDERS, The. By J. H. Jessee. 3 vols
PRIME, S. I. The Bible in the Levant; or, Life of C. N. Righter
PRIOR, J. Life of Edmund Burke. 2
— Life of Oliver Goldsmith [vols
PRISON Life; or, Biographies of Picciola, Silvio Pellico, etc
PROSE Writers of America, by R. W. Griswold
PULASKI, Count. Life of, by J. Sparks
PUTNAM, I. Life of, by F. Bowen
— Life of, by W. B. O. Peabody
— A Biography, by G. C. Hill
PYRRHUS. Life of, by Abbott

QUEENS of England before the Conquest. By Mrs. M. Hall
QUEENS of England. Lives of, by A. Strickland. 12 vols
— By F. Lancelot. 2 vols
— of France. Memoirs of, by Mrs. F. Bush. 2 vols
— of Spain. Annals of, by A. George. 2 vols
QUINCY, Josiah, Jr. Memoir of, by his Son
QUINCY, Josiah. Memoir of John Quincy Adams

RACHEL. Memoirs, by Madame de B.

RALE, S. Life of, by C. Francis
RALEIGH, Sir Walter. By C. Kingsley
— Life of, by Mrs. Thompson
RANDOLPH, J. Life of, by H. Garland. 2 vols
RANDALL, H. S. Jefferson. 3 vols
RED JACKET. Life and Times of, by W. L. Stone
REED, J. Life of, by J. Renwick
— Life of, by H. Reed
REED, A. Martha, a Memorial
REGISTER of Agents, Army and Navy Officers, etc., for 1849
— of Officers and Agents in the Services of the United States, on the 13th of September, 1855
— The same, 1857
REIGART, J. F. Life of Robert Fulton
REMINISCENCES of an Officer of the Zouaves
RENEE, A. Louis XVI. et sa Cour
RENWICK, J. Life of D. Rittenhouse
— Life of Count Rumford
— Life of J. Reed
— Life of John Jay
— Life of Hamilton
— Life of De Witt Clinton
REYNOLDS, Sir J. Life of, by J. Northcote. 2 vols
RIBAULT, J. Life of, by J. Sparks
RICHARD Cœur de Lion. Life of, by G. P. R. James. 2 vols
RITCHIE, Mrs. Mimic Life
— Autobiography of an Actress
RITTENHOUSE, D. Life of, by J. Renwick
RIVES, W. C. Life and Times of James Madison. Vol. I
ROBERTSON, T. Charles V; with an account of the Emperor's After Life, by Prescott. 3 vols
— Life of T. A'Becket
ROBINSON, Mrs. Mary. Memoirs of, by herself
ROBINSON, Henrietta. Life of, by D. Wilson
ROCKINGHAM, Marqus. Memoirs of the Earl of Albemarle. 3 vols
RODNEY, Admiral. Life of, by Major General Mundy
ROGERS, Samuel. Recollections of
ROLAND, Madame. Life of, by Abbott
ROMILLY, Sir S. Life of, by his Sons. 2 vols
ROMULUS. Life of, by Abbott
ROPER, W. Life of Sir Thomas More
ROSA, Salvator. Life of, by Lady Morgan. 2 vols [12 vols
ROSE, H. J. Biographical Dictionary
ROSCOE, W. Life and Pontificate of Leo X. 2 vols
— Life of Lorenzo de Medici
ROSCOE, H. Lives of Eminent Lawyers

ROTH, E. Life of Napoleon III
ROUSSEAU, J. J. Confessions de
RUMFORD, Count. Life of, by J. Renwick
RUPERT, Prince, and the Cavaliers; by E. Warburton
RUSSELL, Lady Rachael. Letters, 2 vols
RUSSELL, Lord J. Memoirs of Charles James Fox. 2 vols
— Memoirs, Journal, etc., of Thomas More. 2 vols
RUSSELL, W. Extraordinary Men
— Extraordinary Women
RUSSELL, C. W. Life of Cardinal Mezzofanti
RUSSELL, Rev. M. Life of Oliver Cromwell
RYLAND, J. E. Life of John Foster

SABINE, L. Life of Preble
— The Loyalists of the American Revolution
SALLE, R. de la. Life of, by J. Sparks
SAMPSON, W. Life, by himself.
SANDERSON, J. Biography of the Signers of the Declaration of Independence. 9 vols
SANTAREM, Viscount. Researches respecting Americus Vespucius
SAVAGE, J. Our Living Representative Men
SCHILLER, F. Life of, by T. Carlyle
— Life of, by Pellarbie
SCHIMMELPINNCK, Mary A. Autobiography of. 2 vols
SCHOELCHER, V. Life of Handel
SCORESBY, W. Records of his Life, by his Son
SCOTT, Winfield. His Life and Services, by E. D. Mansfield
— Life of, by J. T. Headley
SCOTT, Sir Walter. Life of, by D. McLeod
— Memoirs of, by J. G. Lockhart. 10 vols
— Life of Napoleon
SCOTT, Rev. W. A. Esther, the Hebrew Persian Queen
— Daniel, a Model for Young Men
SEDGWICK, C. Life of Lucretia M. Davidson
SEDGWICK, M. Memoir of Joseph Curtis
SELDEN, J. Memoirs of, by G. W. Johnson
SEWARD, W. H. Life, by G. E. Barker
— Life and Public Services of
— Life of John Quincy Adams
SEYMOUR, C. B. Self-made Men
SHAKSPEARE. His Times and Contemporaries, by G. Tweddell
— by F. Guizot

SHAW, S. His Journal
SHEAHAN, J. W. Life of Stephen A. Douglas
SHELLEY and Byron. Last Days of, by E. J. Trelawney
SHELLEY, Lady. Shelley Memorials
SHERIDAN, R. B. Memoirs of, by T. Moore. 2 vols
— Life of, by J. Watkins. Quarto
SHERMAN, Mrs. Memoir of, by her husband
SHIEL, R. L. Sketches of the Irish Bar. 2 vols
SIDNEY, R. P. Life and Times
SIDNEY, A. Life of, by G. Van Sautvoord
SIGURD, the Crusader. Saga from 1107–18
SIMON, Duke de Saint. Memoirs of the reign of Louis XIV. 4 vols
SIMMS, W. G. Life of Captain John Smith
— Life of Gen. Nathaniel Greene
SMEDLEY, E. Venetian History
SMILES, S. Life of George Stephenson
— Self-Help
— Biographies   [C. Hill
SMITH, Capt. John. A Biography, by G.
— Life of, by G. S. Hillard
— by W. G. Simms
SMITH, T. Asheton. Reminiscences of
SMITH, W. Life of Fichte
SMITH, Sidney. Life and Letters, by Lady Holland. 2 vols
SMITH, J. P. Romantic incidents in Lives of Queens of England
SMUCKER, S. M. History of the Four Georges
— History of Napoleon III
— Court and Reign of Catharine II
— Life and Explorations of J. C. Fremont
SOCRATES. Life, Teachings and Death of
SOTO, De. Life of, by L. A. Wilmer
SOUTHEY, R. Life of Nelson   [vols
— Life and Works of W. Cowper. 8
— Lives of the British Admirals. 5 vols
SOVEREIGNS, Female. Lives of, by Mrs. Jamieson
SPARKS, J. Life of Franklin
— Life of Washington
— Life and writings of Washington. 12 vols
— Life and writings of Franklin. 7
— Life of J. Ribault   [vols
— Life of Ledyard
— Life of Pulaski
— Life of La Salle
— Life of Father Marquette
— Life of C. Lee
— Life of Gouverneur Morris. 3 vols

SPRAGUE, W. B. Life of Timothy Dwight

ST. ANGELA Merici. Life of, by Abbe Parentz

STANHOPE, Lady II. Memoirs of. 3 vols

STANLEY, Rev. A. P. Life and Correspondence of Dr. T. Arnold

STAPLETON's Canning and his Times

STARK, J. Life of, by E. Everett

STARLING, E. Noble Deeds of Woman

STATESMEN of the Commonwealth of England, by J. Forster

STEPHENS, A. Memoirs of J. Horne Tooke. 2 vols

STEPHENSON, G. Life of, by S. Smiles

STEELE, A. Life and Times of William Brewster

STERLING, J. Life of, by T. Carlyle

STEUBEN, Baron. Life of, by F. Bowen

STEUBEN, Gen. Life of, by F. Knapp

STILES, E. Life of, by J. L. Kingsley

STILLING, J. H. Autobiography of

STILLING, W. The Cloister Life of Charles V

STIRLING, W. A., Earl of. Life of, by W. A. Duer

ST. JOHN, J. A. Lives of Celebrated Travelers. 3 vols

STOCKTON, Com. R. F. Life, and Conquest of California

STOCQUELER. Life of Wellington 2 vols

STONE, W. L. Life of Joseph Brandt, (Thayendanegea.) 2 vols

— Life and Times of Red Jacket

— Matthias and his Impostures

STONE, E. M. Life of John Howland

STORY, J. Life and Letters. 2 vols

STRATTON, R. B. Captivity of the Oatman Girls

STRICKLAND, Agnes. Queens of England. 12 vols

— Queens of Scotland. 8 vols

STUART, J. W. Life of Jonathan Trumbull

SUETONIUS. Lives of the Twelve Cæsars, etc

SULLIVAN, W. The Public Men of the Revolution

SULLIVAN J. Life of, by W. B. O. Peabody

SULLY, Duke of. Memoirs. 4 vols

SWEDENBORG, E. Life of, by B. F. Barrett

— Life of, by N. Hobart

TALLEYRAND, Prince. Life of, by C. K. McHarg

TAYLOR, W. C. The Modern British Plutarch

TAYLOR, Gen. Z. Life of, by H. Montgomery

— Life of, by J. Frost

TAYLOR, T. Biographical Sketch of Thomas Clarkson

TEFFT, B. F. Webster and his Masterpieces. 2 vols

TEIGNMOUTH, Lord. Life of Sir William Jones

TEMPLE, Sir W. Memoirs of, by T. B. Courtenay. 2 vols

THACHER, J. American Medical Biography

THATCHER, B. B. Indian Biography. 2 vols

THAYER, W. M. The Poor Boy and Merchant Prince, Amos Lawrence

THIERS, A. The Mississippi Bubble; a Memoir of John Law

THOMPSON's Life of G. Villars. 3 vols

THOMPSON, H. Life of Hannah More

THOMPSON, J. P. Memoirs of David Hale

THOMSON, Mrs. A. T. Life of Sir Walter Raleigh

— Memoirs of the Duchess of Marlborough. 2 vols

THOREAU, H. Walden; or, Life in the Woods

THORSEBY, R. Diary and Letters from 1677 to 1724. 4 vols

TIMBS, J. School-Days of Eminent Men

— Stories of Inventors and Discoveries

TODD, Rev. J. Memoirs of H. Kinke White

TONE, Theobald W. Life by himself. Autobiography. Vol 19

TOOKE, J. Horne. Memoirs of, by A. Stephens. 3 vols

TRELAWNEY, E. J. The Last Days of Shelley and Byron

TRENCH, R. C. Life of Compton

TROLLOPE, A. Decade of Italian Women. 2 vols

TROTTER, J. Memoirs of Charles Jas. Fox

TROUIN, M. Memoirs de

TRUMBULL, Jonathan. Life of, by J. W. Stuart

— Autobiography, Letters, etc

TUCKER, J. S. Memoir of Admiral Earl St. Vincent. 2 vols

TUCKERMAN, H. T. Sketches of Eminent American Painters

— Memorial of Horatio Greenough

— Essays, Biographical and Critical

— Thoughts on the Poets

TUDOR, W. The Life of James Otis

TWEDDELL, G. Shakspeare

TWISS, H. Life of Lord Eldon. 2 vols

UNIVERSAL Biography. Handbook of, by P. Godwin

Upham, C. W. Life of Sir Henry Vane
— Life and Explorations of J. C.
    Fremont

Van Campen, Major. Life and Times
    of, by G. N. Hubbard. 2 vols
Vane, H. Life of, by C. W. Upham
Vandenhoff, G. Leaves from an Ac-
    tor's Note Book
Van Stanwood, G. Lives of Chief
    Justices of the Supreme Court
    of the United States
— Life of Algernon Sidney
Van Schaack, P. Life and Selections
    from his Works
Vasari, G. Lives of Eminent Painters
    and Sculptors. 5 vols
Vaux, J. H. Swindler and Thief;
    Memoirs by himself.
Veron, Dr. L. Memoirs d'un Bourgeois
    de Paris. 6 vols
Vespucius, Americus. Researches con-
    cerning, by Viscount Santarem
Vidocq. Memoirs of, by himself. Aut.
    Vols 25 to 28. 4 vols
Villars, Geo. Life of, by Thompson.
    3 vols
Vincent, Earl St. Life of, by J. S.
    Tucker. 2 vols
Voltaire, le Roy. Par A. Houston
— Memoirs by himself
— Louis XIV
— Louis XV

Wallenstein. Life of, by Col. J.
    Mitchell
Walpole, H. Royal and Noble Authors
    of Great Britain. 5 vols
Warburton, E. Prince Rupert and the
    Cavaliers. 3 vols
Ward, R. Life of Hannah More
Ward, S. Life of, by W. Gammell
Warren, J. C. Life of, from his Auto-
    biography and Journals. 2 vols
Warren, Joseph. Life of, by A. H.
    Everett
Washington. Life of, by Washington
    Irving. 5 vols
— by John Marshall. 2 vols
— by M. L. Weems
— by J. K. Paulding. 2 vols
— by A. Bancroft. 2 vols
— by J. T. Headley
— by Harriet Kirkland
— by E. Everett
— by J. Sparks
— and his Generals, by J. T. Head-
    ley. 2 vols
— in Domestic Life
— Recollections and Memoirs of, by
    G. Washington Parke Curtis
Watkins, J. Memoirs of Richard Brins-
    ley Sheridan. 4to

Watt, J. Life of, by J. Muirhead. 3 vols
Wayland, F. Memoirs of A. Judson
Wayne, Gen. Anthony. Life of, by J.
    Armstrong
Webster, D. Life of, by S. P. Lyman
— and his Masterpieces, by R. F.
    Tefft. 2 vols
— and his Contemporaries, by C. W.
— Life and Memorials of   [March
Weems, M. L. Life of Washington
Wellesley, Marquis. Memoirs and
    Correspondence. 3 vols
Wellington. Life of, by an Old Soldier
— by J. H. Stocqueler. 2 vols
— Life of, by Yonge. 2 vols [3 vols
— Memoirs of, by W. H. Maxwell.
— Victories of, by W. H. Maxwell
Wharton, Grace and Philip. The
    Queens of Society
Wheaton, H. Life of W. Pinkney
White, H. K. Life of, by Rev. J. Todd
Whiting, H. M. Life of Z. M. Pike
Whitman, Sarah H. Edgar Poe and his
    Critics
Whittlesey, C. Life of John Fitch
Wight, W. O. Abelard and Heloise
William the Conqueror. Life of, by
    Abbott
Williams, Roger. Life of, by W. Gam-
    mell
Williams, Rev. J. Life and Actions of
    Alexander the Great
Willis, N. P. Jenny Lind
— The Convalescent
Wilmer, L. A. Life of Ferdinand de
    Soto
Wilson, D. Life of Henrietta Robinson
Wilson, A. Life of, by W. B. O. Pea-
    body
Wirt, W. Memoirs of, by J. P. Ken-
    nedy. 2 vols
— Life of Patrick Henry
Wolsey, Cardinal. Life of, by J. Galt
— Life of, by G. Cavendish. 2 vols
Women of Israel, by G. Aguilar
— of the Revolution, by Mrs. Ellet.
    2 vols
— of France, by Julia Kavanagh
Wood, W. Personal Recollections of
    the Stage
Wright, T. Biographia Britannica Lit-
    eraria. 2 vols
Wright, Silas. Life and Times of, by
    J. Hammond
Wyatt, T. Memoirs of the Generals,
    Commodores, etc., of the Revo-
    lution

Xerxes. Life of, by Abbott

Yonge, C. D. Parallel Lives of Ancient
    and Modern
— Life of Wellington. 2 vols

CLASS VII.

MISCELLANEOUS.

SECTION I.

ANCIENT LITERATURE, ANTIQUITIES AND
MYTHOLOGY.

ADAIR, J. History of the American
Indians. 4to
ANTHON's Classical Dictionary
— Dictionary of Greek and Roman
Antiquities
ANTONINUS, A. V. Meditations. Trans-
lated
APULEIUS. Metamorphoses. Translated
ARCHÆOLOGY, Northern. Guide to
ARISTINETUS. Love Epistles
ATHENÆUS. Deipnosophists; or the
Banquet of the Learned
ARISTOPHANES. Comedies
ARISTOTLE. Metaphysics. Translated
— Nicomachean Ethics. Translated
— Politics
— Organon and Socical Treatises. 2
vols
— Rhetoric and Poetic

BEAMISH, N. L. Northmen in America
BOETIUS, A. M. S. Consolations of
Philosophy. Translated
BOHN, H. G. Classical Library. 80 vols
BRAND, J. Popular Antiquities of Great
Britain. 3 vols
BUTLER's Atlas of Ancient Geography

CÆSAR. Commentaries. Translated
CALLIMACHUS. Works
CATULLUS and Tibullus. Poems
CICERO, M. T. Five Books. De Fini-
bus. Translated
— Oratory and Orators
— Academics
— Laelius
— Immortality of the Soul. Trans-
lated
— Tusculan Disputations. Trans-
lated
— Tusculan Questions. Translated
— Nature of the Gods. Translated
— Orations, Offices, and Laelius.
Translated. 4 vols
— Letters to his Friends

CICERO, M. T. Cato Major, etc
— Political Works. Translated
CORY, I. Fragments of Ancient Phœ-
nician Authors, etc. Translated

DEMOPHILUS. Pythagorean Sentences.
Translated
DEMOSTHENES. Orations
— on the Crown, and on the Embassy
— The Olinthiac, and other Orations
DE PAUW. Egyptians and Chinese
DWIGHT, M. A. Grecian and Roman
Mythology

EPICTETUS. Works
ESCHYLUS. Translated. 2 vols
Esop's Fables. A new version, by T.
James
EURIPIDES. Tragedies. Translated. 2
vols

FLORUS, Sallust and Valerius Paterculus.
Translated
FRAGMENTS, Political, of Archytas,
Charondas, etc. Translated
GREEK Anthology, for use in Westmin-
ster, Eton, etc
GREEK Romances of Heliodorus, Longus
and Tatius

HELIODORUS, Longus and Tatius' Greek
Romances
HERODOTUS
HESIOD. Calimachus and Theogenes.
Translated
HIGGINS, G. Celtic Druids
HOMER's Illiad and Odyssey. Trans-
lated by A. Pope. 2 vols
— Iliad, literally translated
— Odyssey. Translated
— Translated
HORACE. Translated
— Works of, translated by Smart
HORATIUS. Opera. Edited by T. Kidd

IAMBLICUS. On the Mysteries of the
Egyptians, etc

JUSTIN Cornelius. Nepos and Eutropus.
Translated

JUVENAL. Persius Sulpicia and Lucil-
ius. Translated

KEIGHTLEY, T. The Mythology of Ancient Greece and Italy

LAERTIUS, D. Lives of the Philosophers
LAYARD, A. H. Nineveh and Babylon
— Nineveh and its Remains
LEMPRIERE'S Classical Dictionary. Ed-
ited by Anthon
LIVY'S History of Rome. Translated.
4 vols
LUCAN's Pharsalia. Translated
LUCIAN of Samosata. Translated
LUCRETIUS. De Rerum Natura
LUCRETIUS on the Nature of Things.
Translated

MALLET, P. H. Northern Antiquities
MANILIUS, M. Five Books. Translated
MATERNUS, J. T. Translated
MAXIMUS Tyrius. Dissertations. Trans-
lated
McINTOSH, J. Origin of the North
American Indians
McPHERSON, D. Antiquities of Kertch.
Folio
MULLER, C. O. Introduction to a Sci-
entific System of Mythology

OCELLUS. Translated
ORPHEUS. Mystical Hymns of
OVID. Metamorphoses, Amours, Art of
Love, etc. Translated
— The Fasti, Tristia, Epistles, etc.
Translated

PERSEUS' Satires. Translated
PETERS, W. Poets and Poetry of Greece
and Rome
PETRONIUS Arbiter. The Satyricon.
Translated
PHÆDRUS. Translated
— and Terence. Translated
PHILOSTRATUS. Translated
PIGOTT, G. Manual of Scandinavian
Mythology
PINDAR's Odes. Literally translated
PLATO's Works. Literally translated.
6 vols
— against the Atheists. Translated
— Apology of Socrates, Crito and
Phædo
PLAUTUS. Comediæ Tres
— Comedies. Literally translated.
2 vols
PLINIUS, C., Secundus. Natural History.
Translated
PLOTINUS. Five Books. Translated
— Select Works. Translated
PLUTARCH's Lives. Translated
— Morals. Translated

POLYBIUS. General History. Translated
PORPHYRY. Select Works. Translated
PROCLUS. Commentaries on the Timæus
of Plato. Translated
— Fragments of his Lost Writings.
Translated
— On the Theology of Plato. Trans-
lated
PROPERTIUS' Elegies. Translated

QUINCTILIAN. Institutes of Oratory.
Translated

RHODIUS Apollonius. Argonautics
RIVERO, M. Peruvian Antiquities

SALLUST. Florus and Valerius Pater-
culus. Translated
— on the Gods and the World.
Translated
SALLUST, C. C. His Histories. Trans-
lated
SENECA, L. A. His Works. Translated
SOPHOCLES. Tragedies. Translated
SQUIER, E. G. Aboriginal Monuments
of New York
— Nicaragua
— and Davis, E. H. Ancient Monu-
ments of the Mississippi Valley
SMITH's Dictionary of Greek and Ro-
man Geography. 2 vols
SMITH, W. Dictionary of Greek and
Roman Antiquities
SOPHOCLES. Tragedies in English Prose
SUETONIUS. Lives of the Twelve Cæsars
STRABO. Geography. Translated. 2
vols
SYNESIUS on Providence. Translated

TACITUS. Translated. 2 vols
TERENCE. Comedies and the Fables
of Phædrus. Translated
TERENTIUS Afer, P. Comediæ
TERTULLIAN. Apology for the Primitive
Christians
THEOGNIS. Works. Translated
THEOCRITUS. Bion, Moschus and Tyr-
teus. Translated
THUCYDIDES. Peloponnesian War.
Translated
TIBULLUS. Poems. Translated

VALERIUS. Paterculus, Florus and
Sallust. Translated
VIRGIL. Translated by Davidson

WHITTLESEY, C. Ancient Works in
Ohio   [vols
WILKINSON, G. Ancient Egyptians. 6

XENOPHON's Anabasis. Translated
— Cyropedia and Hellenies. Translated

SECTION II.

POETRY.

AIKIN, J. Select British Poets
AINSLIE, H. Scottish Songs and
AKENSIDE, M. Poems
  Ballads
ALDRICH, T. B. Ballad of Babie Bell,
  and other Poems
— The Course of True Love never
  did run Smooth
ALGER, W. R. The Poetry of the East
ALLSTON, W. Poems
ARIOSTO, L. Orlando Furioso, transla-
  ted by Rose. 2 vols
ARNOLD, T. Poems. 2 vols
ARTHUR Carryl
AYTOUN, W. E. Lays of the Scottish
  Cavaliers, etc

BAILY, J. Festus ; a Poem
— The Mystic, and other Poems
— The Age
BALLADS, Old. 4 vols
— and Songs
— Ancient Spanish
BARTON, R. Poems
BARLOW, Joel. The Vision of Columbus
BEATTIE, J. Poetical Works
BEAUMONT and Fletcher's Beauties, by
  Leigh Hunt
BERANGER, P. J. De. Œuvres Com-
  pletes. 2 vols
— 200 of his Lyrical Poems. Trans-
  lated
— Dernier Chanson
BERNI, F. Orlando Inamorato. Trans-
  lated
BIDDLE, H. P. Poems
BOCALINI, T. Advertisements of Par-
  nassus
BON Gaultiers' Ballads. Translated
BOURNE, V. Poetical Works
BOWRING, J. Specimens of the Polish
  Poets
BRITISH Poets
BROOKS, C. T. Songs and Ballads from
  the German
BROWN, T. Fudges in England
BROWNING, R. Poems. 2 vols
BROWNING, Elizabeth B. Napoleon III.
  in Italy, and other Poems
— Poems. 2 vols
— Aurora Leigh
— Men and Women
— Prometheus Bound, and other
  Poems
BRYANT, W. C. Poems
— Selections from American Poets
BULWER, E. L. The Siamese Twins,
  and other Poems

BURNS, R. Poetical Works
— Life and Works, by Chambers. 4
  vols
— Works, edited by A. Cunningham
BUTLER, S. Poetical Works
— Hudibras. 2 vols
BUTTURA, A. I. Poeti Italiani
BYRON, Lord. Works

CAMOENS. Les Lusiades. 2 vols
CAMPBELL, T. Poetical Works
CARY, H. F. Early French Poets
CARY, Alice. Poems
CARY, Phœbe. Poems
CHANDLER, Maria F. The Spirit Hart
CHATTERTON, T. Poems. 2 vols
CHAUCER, G. His Works
— Poetical Works
— Riches of
CHURCHILL, C. Poems. 3 vols
COFFIN, N. W. America, and other
  Poems
COLERIDGE, S. T. Poetical Works. 2
  vols
COLLINS, W. Poetical Works
COMENS, Le. Les Lusiades ou les Por-
  tugais
CONRAD, R. T. Aylmere, and other
  Poems
COOK, Eliza. Poems
COOPER, Miss. The Rhyme and Reason
  of Country Life
COSTELLO, L. S. Early Poetry of France
COWPER, W. Poems
CROLY, G. Beauties of the British
  Poets

DANA, C. A. The Household Book of
  Poetry
DANTE. Translated by J. C. Wright
DAVENANT, W. Works. Folio
DAVIDSON, L. M. Poetical Remains
DAVIDSON, M. M. Poetical Remains
DIBDIN, C. Sea Songs
DIVINE Songs
DE PORTE'S Poets and Poetry of Ger-
  many. 2 vols
DONALDSON, S. J. Lyrics and Poems
DONNE, J. Poetical Works
DRAKE, J. R. Culprit Fay
DRYDEN, J. Poems. 5 vols
— Poems

EDWARDS, C. The History and Poetry
  of Finger-Rings
ELLIS, G. Early English Metrical Ro-
  mances
ELPHINSTONII, J. Poetæ Sententiosi
  Latini
EMERSON, R. W. Poems
ENGLISH and Scottish Ballads
EVANS T. Old Ballads

FAIRCHILD, S. L. Last Night of Pompeii
FALCONER, W. Poetical Works
FR*** Hearts, that Failed 300 years
    ago, by the Author of New
    Priest
FLORIAN. Estelle, Pastorale. 18mo
FRITHIOF'S Saga
FULLER, Frances and Meta. Poems

GAY, J. Poetical Works. 2 vols
GEMS of Spanish Poetry. Spanish and
    English
GESNER, M. Œuvres Choises
GOETHE's Poems and Ballads
GOLDSMITH'S Poems
— Beattie and Campbell's Poems
GOULD, Hannah. Poems. 3 vols
GRAY, T. Poetical Works
GRIFFIN, Gerald. Poems and Plays
GRISWOLD, R. W. Poets and Poetry of
    England
— Poets and Poetry of America
— Female Poets of America
GUARINI, B. Il Pastor Fido

HALL, Mrs. S. C. Book of British
    Ballads. 2 vols
HALL, S. C. Book of Gems
HALLECK, F. Poetical Works
— Selections from the British Poets
    2 vols
HANGER, C. H. Proverbial and Moral
    Thoughts
HASTINGS, Sybil. Harvestings, etc
HEBER, Reginald. Poetical Works
HEINE, H. Fammtlichte Werke
HEMANS, Felicia. Poetical Works
HERBERT, G. Poetical Works
HERRICK, R. Hesperides. 2 vols
HERVEY, T. K. The Book of Christmas
HEWITT, M. E. Poems
HOLMES, O. W. Poems
HOLLAND, J. Poems
— Bitter Sweet
HOMER. Iliad and Odyssey, by Pope. 3
    vols
HOOD, T. Whims and Waifs
— Poems. 4 vols
HORACE, Translated
HOSMER, W. H. C. Poems. 2 vols
HOUSMAN, R. F. English Sonnets
HOWARD, H. Poetical Works
HOWE, Mrs. The World's Own, etc
HOWELL, J. Dodona's Grove
HOWITT, Mary. Pictorial Calendar of
    the Seasons
HUNT, Leigh. Poetical Works. 2 vols
HUSBAND and Wife

JENKS, J. W. Rural Poetry of the Eng-
    lish Language
JONES, E. The Emperor's Vigil, etc
KEATS, J. Poetical Works

KEMBLE, Frances A. Poems
KEWEN, E. J. C. Idealina, and other
    Poems
KINGSLEY, C. Poems
— Andromeda, and other Poems

LANDON, Miss. Complete Works
LELAND, C. G. Poetry and Mystery of
    Dreams
LEIGHTON, A. Poems
LINEN, James. Songs of the Season,
    and other Poems
LOCKHART, J. G. Ancient Spanish
    Ballads
LONGFELLOW, H. W. Poems. 2 vols
— The Courtship of Miles Standish
— Ballads and other Poems
— Poets and Poetry of Europe
— Voices of the Night
— Hiawatha
LOWELL, J. R. Poems
— The Bigelow Papers
LUNT, G. Age of Gold, and other
    Poems
LYDE, A. F. Buds of Spring

MACAULAY, T. B. Lays of Ancient
    Rome
MACFARLANE, J. The Night Lamp, etc
MACKAY, C. English Songs
— Voices from the Mountains and
    Crowd
MACPHERSON's Poems of Ossian. 2 vols
MARSH, Mrs. G. P. Wolf of the Knoll,
    and other Poems
MARVELL, A. Poetical Works
MASSEY, G. Poems and Ballads
MEEK, A. B. Songs and Poems of the
    South
MEREDITH, O. Lucile
— Poems
MIDNIGHT, and other Poems
MILMAN, H. H. Nala, and other Poems
MILTON, J. Paradise Lost
— Poetical Works
— Poetical Works and Life, by G.
    Gilfillan. 2 vols
MONTGOMERY, James. Poetical Works.
    2 vols
— Poetical Works; with a Memoir
— 9 vols
MOORE, Frank. Songs and Ballads of
    the Revolution
MOORE, T. Poetical Works
— 6 vols
— Lalla Rookh
MORFORD, H. Rhymes of Twenty Years
MORMONIAD
MOTHERWELL, W. Poems
— Minstrelsy, Ancient and Modern
MULOCH, Miss. Poems

NACK, J. Romance of the Ring

NOBLE, L. L.   The Lady Angeline, etc
NORTON, Mrs.   The Dreams, and other Poems
NOTHING New
NOTHING to Wear
NOTHING to Say
NOTHING to Do
NOTHING to Eat
NOTHING to You

OLIVE and the Pine
ORPHEUS.   Mystical Hymns of
OSGOOD, Frances S.   Poems
OSSIAN's Poems, by McPherson.   2 vols

PARNELL, T.   Poetical Works
PARTON, J.   The Humorous Poetry of the English Language
PERCIVAL, J. G.   Poetical Works.   2 vols
—   Clio.   No. 3
—   The Dream of a Day, and other Poems
PERCY, T.   Reliques of Ancient English Poetry
PETER, W.   Poets and Poetry of Greece and Rome
PETRARCH.   One Hundred Sonnets. Translated
—   A Selection of his Sonnets and Odes.   Translated
—   Triumphs of.   Translated
—   Sonnets, Triumphs and other Poems
PHELPS, S. W.   Sunlight and Hearthlight
PINDAR, Peter.   Works
POE, E. A.   Poems, (in Works.)
—   Eureka, a Prose Poem
POEMS, by the Author of John Halifax, etc
POETI Italiani, Dante, Petrarca, Ariosto, Tasso
POETRY of the Passions
POPE, A.   Poetical Works, edited by R. Carruthers.   2 vols
—   by Cary
PRAED, W. M.   Poetical Works
PRIOR, M.   Poetical Works.   2 vols
PROCTER, Anne.   Legends and Lyrics

RACINE, J.   Œuvres de.   8 vols
READ, T. B.   Sylvia, and other Poems
REYNARD the Fox, from the German of Goethe
RICHARDS, W. E.   Electron, a Telegraphic Epic
RITSON, J.   Ancient Songs and Ballads.   2 vols
ROBIN Hood.   Ballads and Songs, by J. Ritson.   2 vols
ROGERS, S.   Poetical Works
ROGERS, C.   Modern Scottish Minstrel.   5 vols

RUSTIC Rhymes, by the Author of Winter in the Country

SAGA of Frithiof
SAXE, J. G.   Poems
—   The Money-King, and other Poems
SCHILLER.   Minor Poems
—   Poems and Ballads
SCOTT, Sir W.   Poetical Works
—   10 vols
—   Lady of the Lake; illustrated. 8vo
SCOTTISH Songs and Ballads, by Ainslie
SECUNDUS, J.   The Kisses
SHAKSPEARE, W.   Poems
SHELLEY, P. B.   Poetical Works
—   Works.   2 vols
—   Works.   3 vols
SHENSTONE, W.   Poetical Works
SIGOURNEY, Mrs. L. H.   Poems, illustrated
SIMMS, W. G.   Egeria; or Voices of Thought
SKELTON, J.   Poems.   3 vols
SMITH, Horace and James.   Poetical Works
SMITH, Alex.   Poems
—   City Poems
SONGS and Ballads, from the German
SONGS and Ballads of the Revolution
SONGS of England and Scotland.   2 vols
SOUTHEY, Caroline.   Solitary Hours
SOUTHEY, R.   Complete Poetical Works
SPENSER, E.   Poetical Works
SPIRIT Harp.   A Gift, the Poetical Beauties of Harmonial Philosophy.
STEADMAN, E. C.   Poems
STREET, A. B.   Poems
SWIFT, J.   Poems.   3 vols

TAIT, J. R.   Dolce far Niente
TAPPAN, W. B.   Poems
TASSO, T.   Godfrey of Boulogne; or the Recovery of Jerusalem. Translated
—   Jerusalem Delivered
TAYLOR, J. Bayard.   Poems of the Orient
TEGNERS' Saga of Frithiof
TENNYSON, A.   Poems
—   In Memoriam
—   Maud, and other Poems
—   Idyls of the King
THACKERAY, W. M.   Ballads
TUPPER, M. F.   Poetical Works
—   Proverbial Philosophy
TURNER, G. A.   The Discovery of Sir J. Franklin, and other Poems
TWO Millions, by the Author of Nothing to Wear
TYPHON; or the Giants' War with the Gods

VAUGHAN, H. Sacred Poetry
VERITAS ; a Poem
VISIN of Rubeta

WALKER, J. Rhyming Dictionary
WATSON, J. T. Poetical Quotations
WATTS, J. Floræ Lyricæ, and Divine
    Songs
WELBY, Miss A. Poems, by Amelia
WHITE, K. Poetical Works
WHITE, H. K. Poetical Remains
WHITMAN, W. Leaves of Grass
WHITNEY, Anne. Poems
WIELAND. Oberon
WITHER, G. Fair Virtue. The Shep-
    herd's Hunting
WORDSWORTH, W. Complete Poetical
— 9 vols   [Works
— Yarrow Revisited
WRIGHT, T. Early Political Songs of
    England
WYATT, Sir T. Poetical Works

YOUNG, E. Poetical Works
— Night Thoughts

SECTION III.

DRAMA.

BAILEY, Joanna. Dramatic Works
BEAUMARCHAIS, P. Theatre de
BEAUMONT and Fletcher. Works. 2
    vols

CALIDAS. Sacontala. Translated. 4to
CAMILLE. Translated
COLERIDGE, S. T. Dramas
CORNEILLE, Pierre et Thomas. Thea-
    tre de

DAVENANT, W. Works
DODSLEY, R. Collection of Old Plays.
    12 vols
DRYDEN, J. His Works, including his
    Plays. Scott's edition. 18 vols
DUMAS, A. Royalists and Republicans
DUMAS, A. Jr. The Demi Monde ; a
    satire on Society

EURIPIDES. Translated

FOUR Old Plays

GOETHE. Faust. Translated, and in
    the Original
— Herman and Dorothea. Transla-
    ted
— Iphigenia in Tauris. Translated
GOETHE, W. J. Dramatic Works

HOWE, Julia W. The World's Own

HUNT, Leigh. Selections from Beau-
    mont and Fletcher

JERROLD, D. Comedies
— Comedies and Dramas
JONSON, Ben. His Works

LAMB, C. Specimens of the English
    Dramatic Poets
LAOU-SENG-URH. A Chinese Drama
LONGFELLOW, H. W. Spanish Student

MASSINGER and Ford. Dramatic Works
MODERN Standard Drama. 27 vols
MOLIERE, J. B. P. Œuvres. 2 vols
MORGAN, Lady. Dramatic Scenes from
    Real Life

RACINE, J. Theatre Complete
— Œuvres de. 2 vols

SCHILLER, F. Don Carlos, Infant der
    Espanien
— Don Carlos. Mary Stuart and
    Bride of Messina
— The Ghost Seer
— Wallenstein Dramatische Gedicht
— Early Dramas
SHAKSPEARE, W. Plays, edited by
    Johnson, Stevens, etc. 17 vols
— Dramatic Works
— Complete Works. 7 vols
— Dramatic and Poetical Works
— Supplement to his Plays
— By W. Hazlitt. 4 vols
SHERIDAN, R. B. Dramatic Works
SOPHOCLES. Tragedies. Translated
SOUVENIR, Dramatic

TERENTIUS, Afer. Comediæ

VOLTAIRE, F. M. M. Theatre de

WEBSTER, J. His Works. 4 vols
WYCHERLEY, Congreve, Vanbrugh, and
    Farquhar's Dramatic Works

SECTION IV.

EDUCATION, ELEMENTARY WORKS.

BERNARD, H. National Education
    in Europe
BROWN, G. The Grammar of English
    Grammars

CHESTERFIELD, Lord. Letters to his Son
CHESTERFIELD, Lady. Letters to her
    Daughters
COBBETT, W. Le Maitre d'Anglais

DEGERANDO, M. Self Education

DWIGHT, T. The Father's Book

ESSAYS on Education. 2 vols

FOWLER, W. C. English Grammar

GARNET, J. M. Lectures on Female Education
GRAMMAIRE Anglais

HABITS of Good Society; or Hand-book for Ladies and Gentlemen
HALL, B. R. Teaching a Science
HAND-BOOK for Home Improvement
HERVY, G. W. The Rhetoric of Conversation
HISTORY of Education

KRAISTER, C. Glossology

LOCKE, J. Thoughts on Education
LORD, D. N. Characteristics and Laws of Figurative Language

PAGE, D. P. Theory and Practice of Teaching
POTTER, A. Handbook for Readers and Students

MILTON, J. Treatise on Education
MANN, E. J. Deaf and Dumb
MANSFIELD, E. D. American Education

PHELPS, Mrs. Hours with my Pupils
PRIAULX, O. de B. National Education

SCHMIDT, H. I. Education
SPURZHEIM, J. G. View of the Elementary Principles of Education

UPTON, R. A. Home Studies

YOUNG Student's Library. Folio, 1692

SECTION V.

PHILOLOGY, TECHNOLOGY AND NAMES.

ANDREWS, S. P. Discoveries in Chinese

BARTLETT, J. R. Glossary of Words and Phrases used in the United States
BOWDITCH, N. P. Suffolk Surnames
BOWRING, J. The Language and Literature of Holland

CRABBE, G. Synonyms of the English Language

DICTIONNAIRE Technologique, 3 vols

DICTIONARY of Love
DICTIONARY of Modern Slang, Cant and Vulgar Words
DWIGHT, B. W. Modern Philology ; its Discoveries, etc

ELWYN, A. L. Glossary of Supposed Americanisms

FERGUSON, H. English Surnames
FOWLER, W. C. The English Language

HALLIWELL, J. O. Archaic Words. 2 vols
HAZEN, E. Popular Technology. 2 vols

JOHNSON, E. Nuces Philosophicæ
JOURDAN, J. L. Dictionnaire de des Termes des les Sciences Naturelles. 2 vols

KRAISTER, C. Glossology
[2 vols
LATHAM, R. G. The English Language.
LOWER, M. English Surnames. 2 vols

MARSH, G. P. Lectures on the English Language

NOTES and Queries

OSWALD, J. Ethnological Dictionary of the English Language

PEGGE, S. Anecdotes of the English Language

ROGET, P. M. Thesaurus of English Words and Phrases

SPIERS, A. Manual of Commercial Terms in English and French
SWINTON, W. Rambles among Words

TOOKE, J. H. Diversions of Purley
TRENCH, R. C. The Study of Words
— Glossary of English Words

WELSFORD, H. The English Language

SECTION VI.

HERALDRY AND GENEALOGY.

BARRINGTON, A. Introduction to Heraldry
BOND, Dr. H. Genealogies of Watertown, Waltham and Weston, Mass
BURKE, J. B. The Landed Gentry of England. 4 vols

BURKE, J. B.   British Peerage and Baronetage
— General Armory
BURKE, J. and J. B.   The Royal Families of England and Scotland. 2 vols

DODD, C. R.   Manual of Dignities, etc

FARMER, J.   Genealogical Register of the First Settlers of New England

HOLGATE, J. B.   American Genealogy. Vol 1.   4to

MOODY, C. P.   Sketches of the Moody Family

SMIBERT, T.   Clans of Scotland

SECTION VII.

NUMISMATICS.

ACKERMAN, J. Y.   Numismatic Manual
BUSHNELL, C. J.   Tradesmens' Cards. Political Tokens, Election Medals, etc

DICKESON, M. W.   The American Numismatic Manual.   Quarto

ECKFELDT and Dubois.   New Varieties of Gold and Silver Coin
— Manual of the Coins of all Nations.   Quarto

HUMPHREYS, H. N.   The Coin Collector's Manual.   2 vols
— The Coinage of the British Empire

SECTION VIII.

DRESSES AND COSTUMES.

BOOK of Costume; or, The Annals of Fashion
BOOK of Costume, Colored.   Quarto

COBBOLD's Pictures of the Chinese, by themselves

HOPE, T.   Costume of the Ancients. 2 vols

MARTIN, C.   Illustrations of the Civil Costumes of England
                                        [vols
SHAW, H.   Dresses and Decorations. 2

WAHLEN, A.   Moeurs et Costumes de tout les Peuples du Monde. Colored.   4 vols.   Quarto

SECTION IX.

FREE MASONRY.

ADAMS, J. Q.   Letters on the Masonic Institution

CATALOGUE of Books on Masonry

PARVIN, T.   Proceedings of the Grand Lodge of Iowa

WEBB, T. S.   The Free Mason's Monitor

SECTION X.

CRITICISM, ESSAYS, AND LETTERS.

ADAMS, Mrs. John.   Letters
ADVENTURER, The.   British Essayist.   3 vols
AFTERNOON of Unmarried Life
AGUECHEEK
AGUILAR, Grace.   Essays and Miscellanies
ALISON, A.   Miscellaneous Essays
ALLSTON, W.   Lectures on Art, and Poems
ALPHA and Omega.   2 vols
AUTOCRAT of the Breakfast Table

BACON, Francis Lord.   Essays
— On the Human Understanding
BACON, Delia.   Philosophy of Shakspeare's Plays
BADEAU, A.   The Vagabond
BAILEY, Rev. J.   Life Studies
BANCROFT, G.   Literary and Historical Miscellanies
BARKER, E. H.   Literary Anecdotes and Reminiscences.   2 vols
BARTLETT, J.   Collection of Familiar Quotations
BAYNE, P.   Essays.   2 vols
BEECHER, Henry Ward.   Star Papers
— New Star Papers
— Life Thoughts
BELSHAM, W.   Essays
BENTHAM, J.   The Book of Fallacies
BIBLIOTHEQUE Portative Ecrivans Francois.   5 vols
BLESSINGTON, Lady.   Conversations with Byron
BONAPARTE's Confidential Correspondence with Josephine
— With his Brother Joseph.   2 vols

BOVEE, C. N. Thoughts, Feelings and Fancies
BOWEN, F. Critical Essays
BRITISH Essayists, including the Spector, Tattler, Guardian, Lounger, Adventurer, Connoisseur, Rambler, World, Mirror, Idler, and Looker-on. 38 vols
BROUGHAM, J. A Basket of Chips
BUCKINGHAM, J. T. Specimens of Newspaper Literature, etc. 2 vols
BUNGAY, G. W. Offhand Takings
BURNS and Clarinda. Correspondence
BUSHNELL, Rev. H. Nature and the Supernatural

CABINET Album of Original and Selected Literature
CAMPBELL, Lord John. Shakspeare's Legal Acquirements
CAP Sheaf, by Lewis Myrtle
CARLYLE, T. Essays
— Heroes and Hero Worship
— Past and Present
— Sartor Resartus
— Letters and Speeches of Oliver Cromwell. 2 vols
CARROLL, Anna E. The Star of the West
CARY, H. F. Early French Poets
CHAPIN, E. H. Humanity in the City
CHASLES, P. Anglo-American Literature and Manners
CHATEAUBRIAND, F. A. Mélange Politiques et Litteraires
CHATFIELD, P. The Tin Trumpet
CHILD, L. Maria. Letters from New York. 2 vols
CLARK, W. G. Literary Remains
CLARKE, L. G. Knick-knacks [vols
CLAY, H. Private Correspondence. 2
COLLINGWOOD, Admiral. Selection from his Correspondence
COLLINS, S. Miscellanies
COLTON, Rev. C. C. Lacon on Many Things in Few Words
CONNOISSEUR, The. British Essayists. 2 vols
CONVERSATIONS of Goethe with Eckerman and Soret. 2 vols
COPELAND, R. M. Country Life
COZZENS, F. S. The Sparrowgrass Papers
CRAIK, G. L. Sketches of the Literature of England to the Reign of Elizabeth. 2 vols

D'ARGENS, M. Chinese Letters
— Jewish Spy
DE QUINCEY, T. Historical and Critical Essays. 2 vols
— Miscellaneous Essays
— Biographical Essays

DE QUINCEY, T. The Cæsars
— Note Book of an Opium Eater
— Essays on Philosophical Writers and Men of Letters. 2 vols
— Theological Essays and other Papers. 2 vols
— Narrative and Miscellaneous Papers. 2 vols
— Klosterheim; or the Masque
— Miscellanies, Chiefly Narrative
— Miscellanies
— Letters to a Young Man
D'ISRAELI, Isaac. Amenities of Literature. 2 vols
— Miscellanies of Literature. 3 vols
— Curiosities of Literature. 4 vols
DITSON, G. L. The Para Papers
DREAM Life, by Ik. Marvel
DUCHENE, P. Letters

ELDER, W. Periscopics
ELLET, Mrs. Characters of Schiller
EMERSON, R. W. Essays; 1st and 2d Series
— Nature
— Representative Men
— English Traits
ESSAYS and Reviews. 2 vols
EVERETT, A. H. Essays
FENN, J. The Paston Letters
FICHTE, J. G. Nature of the Scholar
FOSTER, Mrs. Hand-Book of Modern European Literature
FOSTER, J. Essays in a Series of Letters
— on the Evils of Popular Ignorance
— Critical Essays on the Eclectic Review. 2 vols
— Lectures at the Broadmead Chapel, Bristol. 2 vols
FOSTERIANA; or Thoughts, Reflections, etc., of John Foster
FOX, W. J. Lectures to the Working Classes. 4 vols
FRANKLIN, Benj. Letters to, from his Family and Friends
FREE-THINKER; or Essays of Wit and Humor. 3 vols
FRIENDS in Council. 4 vols
FULLER, Margaret. Life Without and Life Within

GERVINUS, G. G. Shakspeare
GIBBON, E. Miscellaneous Works, edited by Lord Sheffield
GILES, H. Lectures and Essays. 2 vols
GILFILLAN, G. Modern Literature and Literary Men. 2 vols
GOETHE, J. W. Conversations with Eckerman and Soret. 2 vols
— Correspondence with a Child. 2 vols
— Essays on Art
GRAY, T. His Letters

GREEK Literature. History of
GRUMBLER, A. Miscellaneous Thoughts
GUARDIAN, The. British Essayists. 3 vols
GUNN, T. B. The Physiology of New York Boarding Houses

HAMMOND, S. H., and L. Mansfield. Country Margins
HANNAY, J. Satire and Satirists
HARBAUGH, Rev. H. The True Glory of Woman
HASHEESH Eater. Passages from the Life of
HAZLITT, W. The Plain Speaker. 2 vols
— Table Talk. 2 vols
— The Round Table
— Criticisms on Art
— Characters of Shakspeare's Plays
— Lectures on the English Poets
— Lectures on English Comic Writers
— The Dramatic Literature of the Age of Elizabeth
HOME, H. Elements of Criticism
HOMES of American Authors, illustrated
HONE, W. The Every-Day Book. 2 vols
— The Year Book
— Ancient Mysteries and Plays
HOOD, T. Prose and Verse
HORTENSIUS. Union of Reason and Elegance
HOWITT, A. M. The Art Student in Munich
HUDSON, H. N. Lectures on Shakspeare. 2 vols
HUNT, L. Indicator
— Stories from the Italian Poets
— The Town
— Selections from English Authors
— Imagination and Fancy
— Essays and Miscellanies
— Men, Women and Books. 2 vols
— The Palfrey
— Worth and Wealth

IDLER, The. British Essayists. 2 vols

JAMES, J. A. The Young Man's Friend
JAMESON, Mrs. Sacred and Legendary Art. 2 vols
— Sketches of Art, Literature and Character
JEAFFRESONS, J. C. Novels and Novelists
JEFFERSON, T. Observations on the Writings of, by H Lee
JEFFREY, F. Contributions to the Edinburgh Review
JERROLD, B. Specimens of Douglas Jerrold's Wit
JONES, Rev. T. G. Recreations of a Southern Barrister

LAHARPE, M. De. Abrégé du Lycée, ou cours de Literature. 2 vols
LAMB, C. Life and Works
— Essays of Elia
LAMENNAIS, F. De la Société Premier
LANDOR, W. S. Pericles and Aspasia. 2 vols
— Selections from his Writings
LANMAN, C. Essays for Summer Hours
LIVING in the Country
LOOKER-ON, The. British Essayists. 3 vols
LOUNGER, The. British Essayists. 2 vols
LUDEWIG, H. E. Literature of the American Aboriginal Languages
LUTHER, Martin. Table Talk

MACAULAY, T. B. Essays. 5 vols
— Essays and Poems. Vol. 7
MACKINTOSH, J. Miscellaneous Works
MAHONY, Rev. F. Reliques of Father Prout
MALONE, E. Inquiry into the Authenticity of the Shakspeare Papers
MARIANA, J. P. Letters of a Turkish Spy
MARTINEAU, Rev. J. Miscellanies
MASSON, D. British Novelists and their Styles
MAURY, A. Principles of Eloquence
MAYO, A. D. Symbols of the Capital; or Civilization in New York
MICHELET, M. J. Love
— Woman
MILLEDULCIA. A Thousand Pleasant Things, etc
MOIR, D. M. Sketches of Poetical Literature of the Last Half Century
MONTAGUE, Lady Mary W. Letters
MONTAIGNE, M. Essays. Translated. 3 vols
MONTGOMERY, James. Lectures on Literature, etc
— Lectures. 2 vols
— Letters. 4 vols
MORE, Hannah. Moral Sketches
MORRIS, Gov. L. Papers of
MOSAICS, by the Author of Salad for the Solitary, etc
MULLER, F. Characteristics of Goethe. Translated. 3 vols

NEELES, H. Literary Remains
NOTT, E. Lectures on Temperance

OBSERVER, The. British Essayists. 3 vols
OSGOOD, S. Mile-Stones in our Life-Journey
— The Hearth-Stone

OUGHT American Slavery to be Perpetuated? A Debate
OWEN, R. Dale. Footfalls on the Bounds of another World

PARSONS, T. Essays
PASCAL, B. Thoughts, Letters and Opuscules
— Provincial Letters
PASHA Papers
PASTON Letters, edited by J. Fenn
PERSIAN Letters
PHIPPS, J. The State of Man, as held by the People called Quakers
PRESCOTT, W. H. Miscellanies
PROUT, Father. Reliques of
PURSUIT of Knowledge under Difficulties. 2 vols
PUTNAM's Hand-Book of Literature and Fine Arts

RAMBLER, The. British Essayists. 3 vols
READE, C. The Eighth Commandment
READINGS for the Young, from Walter Scott. 2 vols
REASON Why? of Things which are Imperfectly Understood
REED, H. Lecture on English History and Tragic Poetry
— Lectures on English Literature
RICHTER, J. Paul. Extracts from
ROBERTSON, Rev. F. W. Lectures and Addresses
ROCHEFOUCAULD. Maximes et Pensees
— Moral Reflections and Maxims
ROGERS, S. Recollections of the Table Talk of
ROGERS, H. The Greyson Letters
RURAL Hours, by a Lady
RUSH, R. Occasional Productions, etc

SAVARIN, B. Physiologie du Gout
SCHILLER. His Letters. Translated
— Correspondence with Goethe. Translated
SCHLEIERMACHER. Introduction to the Dialogues of Plato
SCHLEGEL, A. W. Dramatic Art and Literature
— Esthetic and Miscellaneous Works
SCOTT, Rev. W. A. Trade and Letters
— The Wedge of Gold
SEARS, E. H. Regeneration
SEARS, Edwards and Felton. Classical Studies
SELDEN, J. Table Talk
SEWELL, W. Introduction to the Dialogues of Plato
SHAHMAH in Pursuit of Freedom
SHELLEY, P. B. Essays, Letters, Translations, etc
SIGOURNEY, Mrs. L. H. Past Meridian

SISMONDI, J. C. L. The Literature of the South of Europe. 2 vols
SMITH, Sidney. Miscellanies. 2 vols
SMUCKER, S. The Four Georges
SMYTH, W. Lectures on the French Revolution. 2 vols
SOANE, G. New Curiosities of Literature. 2 vols
SOUTHEY, R. Selections from his Letters, by J. Waters. 4 vols
— Common-Place Book. 2 vols
SPALDING, W. History of English Literature
SPECTATOR, The
— British Essayists. 8 vols
— Selections from
SPENCE, Rev. J. Anecdotes and Characters of Men and Books
STARS and Angels
STEPHEN, J. Essays

TAIT, W. Magdalenism in Edinburg
TALFOURD, T. N. Critical and Miscellaneous Writings
TATLER, The. British Essayists. Vols. 1 to 4. 4 vols
— and Guardian
TAYLOR, H. Notes from Life; in seven Essays
TELEGRAPH. Story of, and History of the Atlantic Cable
TENSAS, M. D. Odd Leaves of a Louisiana Swamp Doctor
THACKERAY, W. M. English Humorists of the 18th Century
— The Four Georges
THOMASON, Rev. D. R. Review of Dr. Bellows' Lecture on the Theatre
THOMSON, W. Outline of the Laws of Thought
TICKNOR, G. History of Spanish Literature. 3 vols
TITCOMB, Timothy. Letters to Young People
— Gold Foil, etc., from Proverbs, etc
TODD, J. Hints to Young Men of the United States
TOM Brown at Oxford. Vol. 1
— School Days at Rugby
TRANSCENDENTALISM
TUCKERMAN, H. T. The Optimist
— Characteristics of Literature
— Rambles and Reveries
TUPPER, M. F. Rides and Reveries of the late Mr. Esop Smith
TWELFTH Night at the Century Club

VERPLANCK, G. C. Discourses and Addresses

W. The Owl Creek Letters
WALPOLE, H. Private Correspondence. 4 vols

WALSH, R. Didactics
WARREN, S. Miscellanies
WARREN, Gen. Inauguration of the Statue of, 1857
WASHINGTON, George. Maxims of
— Political Legacies
WHEAT and Tares
WHEWELL, W. Philosophy of Discovery
WHIPPLE, E. P. Essays and Reviews
— Lectures
WHITE, R. G. Shakspeare's Scholar
WHITTIER, J. G. Old Portraits and Modern Sketches
— Literary Recreations and Miscellanies
WILLIS, N. P. The Rag Bag
— Out-Doors at Idlewild
— Rural Letters

— Pencilings by the Way
— People I have met
WILLS, W. H. Odd Leaves from Household Words
WILMER, C. A. Our Press-Gang, an Exposition of American Newspapers
WILLMOTT, R. A. Pleasures of Literature
WILSON, Prof. J. Noctes Ambrosianæ. 4 vols
— Recreations of Christopher North
WOMAN'S Thoughts about Women
WORLD, The. British Essayists. 4 vols
WORTH and Wealth, and other Tales
WRIGHT, Elizabeth C. Lichen Tufts from the Alleghanies

CLASS VIII.

MISCELLANEOUS WORKS OF AUTHORS COLLECTED INTO VOLUMES AND SETS.

SECTION I.

WORKS.

ADAMS, John. Works. 9 vols
ADDISON, J. Works. 6 vols
AMES, Fisher. Works. 2 vols

BACON, Sir F. Works. 3 vols
BERKLEY, Bishop. Works. 2 vols
BRANTOME, P. Œuvres de. 8 vols
BROWNE, Sir T. Works. 3 vols
BURKE, E. Works. 9 vols
— Works. 3 vols

CALHOUN, J. C. Works. 6 vols
CHANNING, W. E. Works. 6 vols
COBBETT, W. Works. 12 vols
COLERIDGE, S. T. Works. 7 vols
COWPER's Works, edited by Grimshaw.
    8 vols

D'AVENANT, Sir W. Works. Folio
DICK, T. Works. 8 vols
DIDEROT. Œuvres de. 2 vols
DRYDEN, J. Works, edited by Sir W.
    Scott. 18 vols

FIELDING, H. Works
FRANKLIN, B. Works. 7 vols
— Works. 2 vols

GIBBONS, E. Miscellaneous Works
GOETHE's Works in German. 25 vols
GOLDSMITH, O. Miscellaneous Works.
    4 vols

HAMILTON, A. Works. 7 vols
HARPER, R. G. Select Works
HARRIS, James. Works
HOBBES, T. Works in English. 11 vols
HOGARTH, W. Works. 2 vols. Quarto
HONE, W. Works. 4 vols
HUME, D. Philosophical Works. 4 vols

IRVING, Washington. His Complete
    Works
    1. History of New York, etc., by
        Diedrich Knickerbocker. 1851

2. Sketch-Book of Geoffrey Crayon,
    Gent. 1852
3—5. Life and Voyages of Christopher Columbus, to which are
    added those of his Companions.
    3 vols. 1852
6. Bracebridge Hall, or the Humorists. A Medley. 1852
7. Tales of a Traveler, by Geoffrey
    Crayon, Gent. 1852
8. Astoria; or Anecdotes of an Enterprise beyond the Rocky
    Mountains. 1852.
9. Crayon Miscellany. 1853
10. Adventures of Capt. Bonneville
    in the Rocky Mountains and
    Far-West, etc. 1852
11. Oliver Goldsmith, a Biography.
    1852
12, 13. Mahomet and his Successors.
    2 vols. 1853
14. Chronicle of the Conquest of
    Granada, from the MSS. of Fray
    Antonio Agapida. 1852
15. Alhambra. 1853.
16. Wolfert's Roost

JEFFERSON, T. Writings. 9 vols
JENYNS, Soame. Works. 4 vols
JOHNSON, S. Works. 2 vols

LAMB, C. Works. 2 vols
LEIBNITZ, G. W. Œuvres. 2 vols
LOCKE, John. Works. 10 vols
— Philosophical Works. 2 vols

MICHELET, M. Miscellaneous Works
MILTON, J. Prose Works. 5 vols
MORE, Hannah. Works. 2 vols

OVERBURY, Sir T. Works

POE, Edgar. Works, edited by R. W.
    Griswold. 4 vols

RABELAIS, F. Works. 4 vols
REYNOLDS, Sir J. Works. 2 vols
ROBERTSON, W. Historical Works. 10
    vols

SANDS, R. C. Works. 2 vols
SIDNEY, Sir P. Miscellaneous Works
SMOLLETT, T. Miscellaneous Works
STERNE, L. Works
STORY, J. Miscellaneous Writings
SWIFT, DEAN. Works. 2 vols

TALFOURD, T. N. Miscellaneous Works
TOLAND, J. Collection of Pieces. 2 vols

WASHINGTON, George. Writings of. 12 vols
WEBSTER, D. Works. 6 vols

SECTION II,

ORATIONS AND SPEECHES.

ADAMS, J. Q. Jubilee of the Constitution, 1839

BROUGHAM, Lord. Dissertations and Addresses
— Speeches on Social and Political Subjects. 2 vols
— Discourses on the Objects of . Science and Literature
BURKE, E. Speeches and Correspondence. 2 vols

CHATHAM, Burke, and Erskine. Celebrated Speeches
CICERO. Orations. Translated
CLAY, H. Speeches. 2 vols
— Obituary Addresses on the Occasion of his Death
COX, J. The True American
CROMWELL, O. Speeches and Letters of, by T. Carlyle. 2 vols

DEMOSTHENES. Orations. Translated

EVERETT, E. Orations and Speeches. 3 vols

GOODRICH, C. A. Select British Eloquence

HARPER, R. G. Speeches on Political and Forensic Subjects

KING, W. R. Obituary Addresses on the Occasion of his Death
KOSSUTH'S Select Speeches

MOORE, Frank. American Eloquence. 2 vols

SERGEANT, J. Select Speeches
SHERIDAN, R. B. Speeches. 3 vols
SPEECHES. Miscellaneous Collection. 3 vols

STAUNTON, H. Chess Praxis
SUMNER, C. Recent Speeches and Addresses

WEBSTER, D. His Complete Works
— Obituary Addresses on the Occasion of his Death
WELLINGTON, Duke of. Speeches in Parliament. 2 vols
WINTHROP, R. C. Addresses and Speeches

SECTION III.

PROVERBS, EPITAPHS AND QUOTATIONS.

BOHN, H. G. Hand-Book of Proverbs
— Polyglot of Foreign Proverbs

DICTIONARY of Latin Quotations, Proverbs, Maxims, etc
— of Quotations from Greek, Latin and Modern Languages

EPITAPHS. A Collection of, by T. J. Pottigrew

FIELDING, T. Select Proverbs of all Nations
FROST, Annie. Parlor Charades and Proverbs

HALE, Mrs. S. J. Dictionary of Poetical Quotations

KELLY, J. Scottish Proverbs

MAGOON, E. L. Proverbs for the People

PETTIGREW, T. J. Chronicles of the Tombs; a Collection of Epitaphs
PROVERBS. Hand-Book of, by H. G. Bohn
— Foreign. Hand-Book of, by H. G. Bohn

TUPPER, M. F. Proverbial Philosophy

WATSON, J. F. Dictionary of Poetical Quotations

SECTION IV.

WIT, HUMOR AND ANECDOTES.

AMERICAN Wit and Humor

BALDWIN, J. G. Flush Times in Alabama
BURTON, W. E. Cyclopedia of Wit and Humor. 2 vols

DOWNING, Major J. My 30 Years of of the Senate

EULENSPIEGEL

GEORGIA'Scenes

HOOD's Own
— Up the Rhine. 2 vols

KEDDIE, W. Cyclopedia of Literary and Scientific Anecdotes
KENNEDY, J. P. Annals of Quodlibet

NEAL, J. C. Charcoal Sketches

OLDHAM, O. The Humorous Speaker

PERCY Anecdotes
PRENTICEANA; or Wit and Humor in Paragraphs

SCRAPES and Escapes, etc
STEPHENS, H. L. Comic Natural History of the Human Race

TERSAS, M. Odd Leaves from the Life of a Lousiana Swamp Doctor

SECTION V.

MESMERISM, ANIMAL MAGNETISM AND WITCHCRAFT.

ATKINSON, H. G., and Harriet Martineau. Laws of Man's Nature

BURNETT, C. M. The Philosophy of Spirits

CAHAGENET, L. A. The Celestial Telegraph
CROWE, Mrs. The Night Side of Nature. 2 vols

DELEUZE, J. P. F. Instruction in Animal Magnetism
DENDY, W. C. Philosophy of Mystery
DODS, J. B. Spirit Manifestations Examined and Explained
DUNLAP, S. F. Vestiges of the Spirit History of Man

EARLY Magnetism, in its higher relations to Humanity
ENNEMOSER, J. History of Magic. 2 vols
ESDAILE, J. Natural and Mesmeric Clairvoyance

GOETHE. Les Affinités Electives
GRISCOM, J. Animal Magnetism

LAZARUS, M. E. Passionul Hygiene

NEWNHAM, W. Human Magnetism.

OWEN, R. D. Footfalls on the Boundaries of another World

REICHENBACH, C. Phyico-Physiological Researches on Dynamics, etc

SALVERTE, E. Philosophy of Magic
SCHELLING. Idéalisme Transcendental
SCOTT, Sir W. Demonology and Witchcraft
STALLO, J. B. Philosophy of Nature
STILLING, J. Pneumatology

TOWNSHEND, C. H. Facts in Mesmerism and Magnetism

YOUNG, D. Wonderful History of the Morristown Ghost

SECTION VI.

ILLUSTRATED BOOKS.

ART Journal from 1849 to 1858. 8 vols. 4to

COOK's Illustrations of Shipping and Craft. 4to
CRYSTAL Palace. Illustrated Description of. 3 vols. 4to

FINDEN, E. The Beauties of Moore; a Series of Portraits. Folio

GEMS of European Art, edited by S. C. Hall. 2 vols. Folio

HOGARTH, W. Works, engraved by himself. Imp. Folio.
— The same. 2 vols. 4to

ILLUSTRATED Catalogue of the Great Exhibition
— of Art Industry in Paris
— of Art Industry in Dublin
IRVING, W. Vignette Illustrations from the Works of

KENDALL, G. W. Illustrations of Battles in Mexico. Folio
KUCHEL and Dresel's California Views. Oblong folio

LAVATER, G. L'Arte de Connaitre les Hommes par la Physiognomie. 10 vols. 8vo
MARTIN, M. Illustrated History of Australia

*7

PICTORIAL Gallery of English Race Horses

PORTRAIT Annual

PUGINET, W. Floriated Ornaments, illuminated. 4to

SOWERBY'S Conchological Illustrations, colored

TALLIS. History and Description of the Crystal Palace. 3 vols. Quarto

VIRGINIA Illustrated, by Porte Crayon

SECTION VII.

ENCYCLOPEDIAS, DICTIONARIES, CONCORD-
ANCES, AND OTHER BOOKS OF REFERENCE.

ALLEN, W. Cyclopedia of American Biography

ALEXANDER, J. H. Dictionary of Weights and Measures

ALIBONE, S. A. Critical Dictionary of English Literature, and British and American Authors. 2 vols

ANTHON, C. Dictionary of Greek and Roman Antiquities

— Classical Dictionary

ANTISELL, T. Handbook of the Useful Arts

— Handbook of Universal Biography

APPLETON's Dictionary of Machinery, Mechanics, etc

— Encyclopedia of Biography

— New American Encyclopedia. 16 vols

— Cyclopedia of Drawing

ADLER, G. J. German and English Dictionary

ASH, J. Dictionary of the English Language. 2 vols. 1775

BAILEY, N. Universal Etymological Dictionary. 2 vols

BARETTI's Italian and English Dictionary. 2 vols

BARTLETT, J. R. Dictionary of Americanisms

BAYLE, P. Historical and Critical Dictionary

BESCHERELLE, M. Dictionnaire de la Langue Française. 2 vols

BIOGRAPHY. Knight's English Cyclopedia. 7 vols

BOOTH, J. C. Encyclopedia of Chemistry

BOYERS' French Dictionary

BRANDE, W. T. Encyclopedia of Science, Literature and Art

BRYAN, M. Dictionary of Painters and Engravers

CALLICOT, T. C. Handbook of Geography

CHAMBERS' Cyclopedia of English Literature

— Information for the People. 2 vols

CLARKE, B. British Gazetteer. 3 vols

CLARK, Mrs. M. C. Concordance to Shakspeare

COMELATI, G. Dictionary of the Italian and English Languages. 2 vols

COPELAND, J. Medical Dictionary. 5 vols

CROOKS, G. R., and A. J. Schem. New Latin Dictionary

CROSBY, M. Annual Obituary Notices. for 185. 2 vols

CRÜDEN, A. Concordance of the Old and New Testaments

CYCLOPEDIA Britannica. 2 vols. 4to

DAVENPORT, R. New Dictionary, Italian and English. 2 vols

DICTIONNAIRE de l'Academie Française, Sixieme Ed. 3 vols. 4to

DODDRIDGE, P. Family Expositor

DUNGLISON, R. Dictionary of Medical Science

DUYCHINCK, E. A. and G. L. Cyclopedia of American Literature. 2 vols

EBERT, F. A. Bibliographical Dictionary 4 vols

EMERSON, A. G. American Farmer's Encyclopedia

ENCYCLOPEDIA Americana. 13 vols

— of Religious Knowledge

ENCYCLOPEDIÆ des Jeunes Etudiants. 2 vols

ENGLISH Cyclopedia. 20 vols. Quarto

ERNESTI, I. C. C. Lateinische Synonimik

FACCIOLATI et Forcellini. Totius Latinitatis Lexicon. 2 vols. 4to

FINDLEY, A. G. Directory of Pacific Ocean. 2 vols

GARDNER, C. J. Dictionary of the Officers of the Army of the U. S.

GEOGRAPHY. Knight's English Cyclopedia. 4 vols

— Murray's Encyclopedia. 3 vols

GODWIN, P. Handbook of Biography

GORTON, J. Biographical Dictionary

GREEN's Concordance to the Book of Common Prayer

GRAGLIA, C. Italian Pocket Dictionary

GWILT, J. Encyclopedia of Architecture

HAYDN's Dictionary of Dates. New edition. 1859

HAMILTON, A. G. New Key to unlock every Kingdom

HEEK. Iconographic Encyclopedia. 6 vols

HERBERT, L. Engineers' and Mechanics' Encyclopedia. 2 vols

HONAN, J. S. Cyclopedia of Commerce. 2 vols

HILPERT, J. L. German and English Dictionary. 2 vols

ICONOGRAPHIC Encyclopedia. 6 vols

INFORMATION for the People, by R. Chanbers. 2 vols

JAMIESON, A. Dictionary of Mechanical Science. 2 vols. 4to

JOHNSON, S. Dictionary of the English Language

JOURDAN, A. J. L. Dictionnaire des Termes dans les Sciences Naturelles. 2 vols

KELLY, P. Universal Cambist

KITTO, J. Cyclopedia of Biblical Literature. 2 vols

KNIGHT's English Cyclopedia. 20 vols. Quarto
— Biography. 7 vols
— Geography. 5 vols
— Natural History. 4 vols
— Arts and Sciences. 4 vols

KNIGHT, C. Cyclopedia of the Industry of all Nations
— Cyclopedia of London

LANGLEY, H. G. California Register, 1857 and 1859. 2 vols

LANMAN, C. Dictionary of Congress

LEVERETT, F. P. Lexicon of the Latin Language

LIDDELL, H. G. Greek-English Lexicon

MACGREGOR, J. Commercial Statistics. 5 vols

MAUNDER, S. Scientific and Literary Treasury
— Treasury of History
— Biographical Treasury
— Treasury of Natural History
— Treasury of Knowledge

McCULLOCH, J. R. Commercial Dictionary. 2 vols
— Geographical Dictionary. 2 vols

MUNSELL, J. Every Day Book of History and Chronology

MURRAY, H. Encyclopedia of Geography 3 vols

NATIONAL Encyclopedia of Useful Knowledge. 13 vols

NEUMANN and Baretti. Spanish Dictionary. 2 vols

— Pocket Dictionary, Spanish and English

NICHOL, J. P. Cyclopedia of Physical Sciences

NICOLSON, W. British Encyclopedia

PARKHURST, J. Hebrew and English Lexicon. 4to

POOLE, W. F. Index to Periodical Literature

PUGHE, W. O. Dictionary of the Welsh Language. 2 vols

RAMBACH, C. Theosaurus Eroticus Linguæ Latinæ

REES, A. Cyclopedia, or Universal Dictionary of Arts, Sciences and Literature. 46 vols

REID, A. Dictionary of the English Language

RICHARDSON, C. Dictionary of the English Language. 2 vols

RIPLEY, G. Handbook of Literature and the Fine Arts

ROSE, H. J. New General Biographical Dictionary. 12 vols

SCOTT, R. Greek-English Lexicon

SMITH, J. Panorama of Science and Art. 2 vols

SMITH, W. Dictionary of Greek and Roman Antiquities
— Dictionary of Greek and Roman Geography. 2 vols

SPIERS and Surenne's French Pronouncing Dictionary

STUART, R. Dictionary of Architecture. 2 vols

STRAUSE, J. Polyglot Pocket-Book, English, German, French, etc

TAHITIAN and English Dictionary

THOMSON, J. New Universal Gazetteer

TIMPERLEY, H. Dictionary of Printers, Printing, etc

TOMLINSON, C. Cyclopedia of Useful Arts. 2 vols

UNITED STATES Official Register. 3 vols

URE, A. Dictionary of Arts, Manufactures and Mines

VOCABULARY of the English and Malay Languages

WADE, J. British History Chronologically Arranged

WALKER, J. Pronouncing Dictionary

WATERSTON, W. Cyclopedia of Commerce

WEBSTER, N. American Dictionary of the English Language

WILSON, J. French and English Dictionary
WILLAUMEZ, Admiral. Dictionnaire de Marine
WORCESTER, J. E. Dictionary of the English Language. Quarto
WRIGHT, T. Universal Pronouncing Dictionary; a complete Literary Biographical and Technological Standard. 5 vols

SECTION VIII.

PERIODICALS, NEWSPAPERS AND MAGAZINES, BOUND AND ON FILES.

ALBION
—— ALMANAC, American
ALTA California, Daily
AMERICAN Register, 1817. 2 vols
—— Almanac from vol. 1, 1830, to vol. 32, 1860. 31 vols
—— Journal of Science and Art
—— Farmer's Magazine
—— Mechanics
—— Publishers' Circular
—— Stock Journal
ANNUAL of Scientific Discovery, from 1850 to 1860. 11 vols
—— Portrait
—— Scientific
ARTIZAN, The, from 1842 to 1860. 17 vols. Quarto. London
ART Journal, from 1849 to 1858. 9 vols. 4to
ART Union, Monthly Journal
ATLANTIC Monthly

BANKERS' Magazine, from July, 1847, to July, 1852. 5 vols
—— from 1857 to 1860
BELL'S Life in London
BENTLEY'S Miscellany
BLACKWOOD'S Magazine to 1861. 90 vols
BOOKSELLER. London
—— New York
—— San Francisco
BOOKSELLERS' Medium. New York
BRITISH and Foreign Medico-Chirurgical Review
BRONSON'S Quarterly Review
BUILDER, The, from 1843 to 1859. 16 vols. Folio

CALDAS, F. J. Semanario de la Neuva Granada
CALIFORNIA Newspapers
—— Chronicle, Daily
—— Courier, Daily
—— Culturist
—— Farmer
CENTURY

CHAMBERS' Journal
CHESS Monthly
CHINESE Repository, from 1832 to 1851. 19 vols
CHRISTIAN Library
CHRONICLE, Royal Military
CINCINNATUS
COLBURN'S United Service Magazine
COLONIAL Intelligencer; or Aborigines' Friend, for 1850-1
CONGRESSIONAL Globe, from 1834 to '60. 71 vols. 4to
CORNHILL Magazine
COSMOPOLITAN Art Journal
COTTAGE Magazine for 1812
COURIER and Enquirer
COUNTRY Gentleman

DE Bow's Review
DIAL, The. 4 vols
DUBLIN University Magazine

EDINBURGH Review to 1869. 59 vols
—— Selections from. 6 vols
ECLECTIC Magazine. 18 vols
EVENING Picayune, San Francisco

FARMERS' Magazine. 13 vols. Jan., 1840 to 1845
FILES of English Newspapers
—— Eastern Newspapers
FRANK Leslie's Illustrated Newspaper
FRANKLIN Journal. 1826—1828. 5 vols
—— from 1857 to 1860
FRIEND, The. A Monthly Journal. Vols. 8, 9, 10, 11. Honolulu

GENTLEMAN'S Magazine, from 1732 to 1840. 114 vols
GLEASON'S Pictorial Drawing Room Companion

HARPER'S Weekly
HESPERIAN
HISTORICAL Magazine
HOGG'S Weekly Instructor. New Series to 1853. 9 vols
HOME Journal
HOUSEHOLD Words. 17 vols., to 1859
HOVEY'S Magazine of Horticulture
HUNT'S Merchants' Magazine
HUNT, F. The Library of Commerce. Vol. 1
HUTCHINGS' Magazine. 4 vols., to 1861

ILLUSTRATED London News
INTERNATIONAL Magazine. 4 vols

JOURNAL des Mines. 19 vols
—— of Commerce
—— of the Houses of Lords and Commons
—— of the Franklin Institute

— of Medical Sciences
KNICKERBOCKER. The. 30 vols

LADIES' Home Magazine
LADY'S Book. Godey's
LE MONDE Illustrô
LITERARY World. A Journal of Popular Information, etc
LITERARY Letter. New York
LITTELL'S Living Age. New Series, to 1861
— Museum, to 1845. 37 vols
LONDON Athenæum
— Journal for 1845. Quarto
— Times, Tri-Weekly
— Dispatch

MATHEMATICAL Monthly Metropolitan Magazine for 1837
MECHANICS' Magazine
MEDICAL News and Library
MESSENGER. Southern Literary
MINING Magazine
MISSIONARY Herald
MORNING Post. San Francisco
MUSEUM. Littell's
— of Foreign Literature and Science

NEW Englander
NILES' Weekly Register. 50 vols., to 1836
NORTH American Review, from vol 4 to 44. 1861
NORTH British Review. 26 vols
NOTES and Queries

ONCE a Week
OREGON Newspapers
ORIENTAL Magazine for 1825

PACIFIC Medical and Surgical Journal, from 1858 to 1860
PACIFIC, The. San Francisco
— Star. San Francisco
PHILADELPHIA Monthly. 1827–28
PIONEER Magazine. 4 vols
PLACER Times
PUBLISHERS' Circular
PUNCH

QUARTERLY Review to 1860. 108 vols

REGISTER, Niles' Weekly
REPERTORY of Arts. Vol. 1
-- Stryker's American
RETROSPECTIVE Review. 16 vols
REVIEW, Edinburgh
— Selections from
— Foreign Quarterly
ROYAL American Magazine. 1774

SANDWICH Island Newspapers

SAN FRANCISCO Alta California
— Evening News, daily
— Herald, daily
— Journal of Commerce, daily
— Evening Bulletin
— Daily Times
— Prices Current to 1860
— Oriental
— Daily Whig from June 1852 to 1853. 2 vols
— Evening Mirror
— Medical Press
SCIENTIFIC American
— and Mining Press
SILLIMANS' Journal from the commencement in 1819 to 1860. 80 vols
SLOAT, L. W. San .Francisco Price Current and Shipping List, 1850 to 1852
SMITHSONIAN Contributions to Knowledge. 10 vols. 4to
SPIRIT of the Times
SOUTHERN Literary Messenger from August 1834 to 1861. 3 vols

TAIT'S Edinburgh Magazine
TRANSACTIONS and Collections of the American Antiquarian Society. 3 vols

VALENTINE, D. T. Manual of the Corporation of New York for 1853 and 1860
VANITY Fair

WESTMINSTER Review. 41 vols. Vols. 20–60
WHIG, The San Francisco Daily, from June 5 .
WILLIAMS, E. New York Annual Register for 1836.
WOOL Grower
WORKING Farmer

YOUNG Men's Magazine

SECTION IX.

GOVERNMENT AND OTHER REPORTS.

BACHE, Prof. A. D. United States Coast Survey. 8 vols. 4to. From 1847 to 1859
BLODGET'S Report on the Climatology of the United States

CALIFORNIA. Pamphlets Relating to, collected by A. S. Taylor, M. D.
— Specimens of the Press of, collected and arranged by A. S. Taylor, M. D. Folio

— Annual Reports of the Officers of the State, to 1859. 3 vols
— State Register for 1857 and 1859. 2 vols

COAST Survey Reports of the Superintendent. 6 vols

COMMON Schools of Cincinnati, Report from 1833 to 1848

ESPY, J. P. Meteorological Reports for 1850 and '57. 2 vols. 4to

GIBBON, Lieut., and Herrdon. Exploration of the Amazon

HARVARD. Catalogus Senatus Academici, etc. 1854

LIMANTOUR. Photographic Illustrations of the Documents of. Folio

MACKAY, A. Report on Western India
MACKAY, Capt. J., and Lieut. Blake. Report and Map of the Seat of War in Florida
MASONIC Grand Lodge of Iowa. Proceedings of, from 1844 to 1858. 2 vols
MESSAGES and Documents of the Presidents of the United States
MEXICAN Claims. Report of a Committee, 1854
MUNICIPAL Reports of San Francisco for 1859–60

PATENT Office Reports, from 1847 to 1859, on Mechanics and Agriculture
POST Offices in the United States in 1859

REPORT of the General Land Office Commissioner for 1851
— of the Secretary of the Treasury on Commerce and Navigation, to 1860. 7 vols
— on the Commercial Relations of the United States. 3 vols. 4to
— of Surveys and Explorations for Pacific Railroad Route. 10 vols. 4to
— of the Superintendent of Public Instruction in California, for 1855, '57 and '59
— of the California State Hospital Committee, for 1855
— of the State Land Sales in San Francisco in 1855
— on Sickness and Mortality on Emigrant Ships
— of the Census for 1852
— of the Exhibition of the Industry of all Nations. London, 1851

— of the Officers of the United States from the Seat of War in the Crimea
— of Superintendent of Common Schools of Pennsylvania. 1856
— of the Regents of the Smithsonian Institution, from 1853 to '59. 7 vols
— of the Presidents of the Mercantile Library of San Francisco, from 1853 to 1860
— of the California State Agricultural Society for 1856–7–8 and 9. 4 vols
— of the Horticultural Society for 1856–8–9
— of the Fair of the Mechanics' Institute for 1857 and '59. 2 vols

SECTION X.

BIBLIOGRAPHICAL WORKS, AND LIBRARY AND BOOKSELLERS' CATALOGUE.

ALBERT, J. F. M. Recherches sur Classification Bibliographique
ALIBONE, S. A. Dictionary of British and American Authors. 2 vols. 1859 and '60

BOSSANGE, H. Catalogue de Livres Française. 1853–7
BRUNET, J. C. Manuel du Libraire. 5 vols. 1842–44

CATALOGUE of Books published in Great Britain from 1831 to 1855
— of the Library of the Antiquarian Society, Worcester. 1837
— of the Library of the Salem Atheneum. 1858
— of the New York Apprentice's Library. 1860
— of the Loganian Library of Philadelphia. 1837
— of the Library Company of Philadelphia. 1835 and '56. 2 vols
— of the New York Society Library. 1850
— of the New York Mercantile Library. 1850
— of the New York State Library. 3 vols. 1855 and 56
— of the St. Louis Mercantile Library
— of the Baltimore Mercantile Library
— of the Books in the Lower Hall of the Public Library of Boston. 1858
— of the Boston Mercantile Library
— of the California State Library, Sacramento. 1855

— The same. 1860
— of the Mercantile Library of San Francisco. 1854
— The same. Manuscript. 1858
— The same. Classified, with an Index. 1861
— of Books for sale by B. Quatrich. 1860
— of Books for sale by H. G. Bohn. 1841. (The Guinea Catalogue.)
— of Books for sale by Appleton & Co. 1856
— of Books on the Masonic Institution in the Public Libraries'of the United States
— of the Lyceum and Library of the First District of New Orleans. 1858

CHAMBERS, R. W. W. Cyclopedia of English Literature. 2 vols

DUYCHENCK, E. and G. Cyclopedia of American Literature

EBERT, Fred. A. General Biographical Dictionary. Translated. 4 vols. Oxford, 1837

EDWARDS, E. Memoirs of Libraries. 2 vols. London, 1859

FOURNIER, F. J. Dictionaire des Livres Rares, Curieux, etc. 1805

GUILD, R. A. The Librarian's Manual. 1858

LUDEWIG, H. E. The Literature of the American Aboriginal Languages. 1858

LONDON Catalogue of Books published from 1831 to 1855

POOLE, W. F.. Index to Periodical Literature. 1853

PUTNAM, G. P. The Book Buyers' Manual. 1852

RHEES, W. J. Manual of the Public Libraries of the U. S. 1859

RICH, O. Catalogue of Books relating to America. 1493 to 1844. 3 vols

RICHARDERIE, G. B. Bibliothèque Universelle des Voyages. 6 vols. 1808

ROORBACH, O. A. Catalugue of American Books, from 1820 to 1857. 3 vols

SIMS, R. Handbook to the British Museum

TERNAUX, H. Bibliothèque Americaine ou Catalogue des Ouvrages relatifs a l'Amérique a l'an 1700. Paris, 1837

TRUBNER, N. Bibliographical Guide to American Literature. London, 1859

WATTS, R. Bibliotheca Britannica. 4 vols. 4to

ADDENDA.

SECTION I.

NOVELS AND ROMANCES.

ADDISON'S Stories of Indian Life
ANDERSON, H. The Improvisatore
ARNOLD, A. C. L. The Signet of King Solomon

CROWE, Mrs. C. Ghost Stories

EASTMAN, Mary. Dacotah ; or Life and Legends of the Sioux Indians
ENGLISH Hearts and English Hands

GULLIVER's Travels, by Dean Swift

GWINNE's School for Fathers

JULIA, The. Yacht Voyage

KATHIE Brande

MARTINEAU, Harriet. Deerbrook
MILLER, S. F. Wylkins Wylder, the Successful Man
Miss Gilbert's Career
MULOCH, Miss. Domestic Stories

ORTON, H. S. Camp Fires of the Red Men
OVER the Cliff
OWEN, A. A Lost Love

RASSELAS, by Dr. Johnson
ROWCROFT's Tales of the Colonies

SUE, E. Mysteries of Paris. 3 vols

TROLLOPE, A. Barchester Towers

SECTION II.

MISCELLANEOUS.

ABBOTT, J. S. C. The Mother at Home
ADAMS, C. B. Zoölogy

BIBLIOTHEQUE Illustrée des Classes Ouviers
BOHN, H. G. The Young Lady's Book
BROOKE, R. Visits to Fields of Battle in England

CANADA. Salmon Fishing in
CHAMBERS, W. Miscellany of Useful and Entertaining Knowledge. 10 vols
COLE's Life of Charles Kean. 2 vols
CRICKET Field, The

DANA, D. D. The Fireman
DAVY, Sir H. Consolations in Travel
DOUGLAS, Gen. Sir H. Fortifications
DUNLAP's Hymalaya Mountains

FISKE, D. W. Book of the first American Chess Congress
FELTON, J. H. The Decimal System for Scales and Measures

GOSS, P. H. Life in its Lower, Intermediate and Higher Forms
GRADUS ad Parnassum. Latin-Français

HAWKINS. The Human and Animal Frame

HEROES of Europe
HORNE, T. H. Essay of Privateers, Captures, etc
HUMBOLDT A. Von. Letters to Varnhagen von Ense

KENNY, C. The Manual of Chess
KINGSLEY, C. New Miscellanies

LAYCOCK, Dr. The Mind and Brain
LEE, Lieut. H. The War in the Southern Department

MANUAL of Natural History
McCOMBER's Institutes of the Mind
MISCELLANY of Useful and Entertaining Knowledge, by W. C. Chambers. 10 vols

OERSTED, H. C. The Soul in Nature

POPE or President. Disclosures of Romanism
POWELL on the Order of Nature

QUATREFAGES' Rambles of a Naturalist

SILLOWAY, T. W. Text Book of Modern Carpentry
STEPHENS, Sir G. Adventures of a Gentleman in Search of a Horse

THOM's Early English Romances. 3 vols
TODD's Young Farmer's Manual

VAUGHAN, R. Revolutions in English History. Vol. 1

WALKER, G. Chess Studies of Games actually Played
WASHINGTON. Accounts with the United States, 1775–83
WILFRED's Lectures on the Rifle
WRAXALL's Life in the Sea

ALPHABETICAL

General Index to the Catalogue.

A

Absor, by Scott, 14
Abott, J. Romulus. 73
King Charles I 73
Hannibal 73
King Alfred 73
Nero 73
Darius the Great 73
Xerxes 73
Cyrus 73
Mary, Queen of Scots 73
Pyrrhus 73
William the Conqueror 73
Cleopatra 73
Julius Cæsar 73
Alexander the Great 73
Madame Roland 73
Josephine 63
Marie Antoinette 73
Peter the Great 73
Henry 4th, King of France 73
Abbott, J. S. C. Napoleon Bonaparte 73
Napoleon at St. Helena 73
Kings and Queens 73
The Empire of Austria 63
The Empire of Russia 63
The French Revolution of 1789 63
The Mother at Home 103
South and North 50
Abednego, the Money Lender 14
Abelard and Heloise 73
Abercrombie, J. On the Intellectual Powers 34
Philosophy of the Moral Feeling 36
Abert, Lieut. J. W. Report on New Mexico in 1846 50
About, E. Greece and the Greeks 33
The Roman Question 33
Germaine 1
Ackerman, J. Y. Numismatic Manual 94
Actress in High Life 14
Adair, J. The American Indians 67
Adalbert, Prince. Travels 50
Adam Bede, by G. Elliott 14
Adam Blair and Mathew Wald 14
Adam Græme of Mossgray 14
Adams, John. Works 99
Adams, Mrs. John. Letters 94
Adams, J. Q. Jubilee of the Constitution, 1839 100
The Masonic Institution 94
Memoir of 73
Adams, Miss Hannah. Memoir of 73
Adams, R. and J. On Architecture 47

Adams, C. B. Zoology 108
Adams, N. A South-side View of Slavery 33
Adams, J. C. Adventures of 50
The Lost Hunter 50
Addison's Stories of Indian Life 107
Addison, J. Remarks on Italy 54
Works 99
Life of, by L. Aikin 73
Addresses and Messages of the Presidents of the United States 33
Adela the Octoroon 14
Adele 14
Adler, G. J. German and English Dictionary 102
Adventurer, The 94
Adventuress 14
Adventures of a Chaperon 14
Adventures of Sir Frizzle Pumpkin 14
Adventures of a Marquis 14
Adventures 50, 60
Afloat and Ashore 14
Afrija 14
Africa. Discovery and Adventure in 57
Africa. Travels in 57, 60
African History 67
After Dark 14
Afternoon of Unmarried Life 94
Against Wind and Tide 14
Agassiz, L. Classification of Insects 42
and A. A. Gould. Principles of Zoology 42
Contributions to Natural History of the United States 42
Agatha's Husband 14
Agathonia 14
Age of Chivalry 14
Agincourt 14
Agnel, H. H. Book of Chess 45
Agnes 14
Agnes Serle 14
Agnes Gray 14
Agnes de Mansfelt 14
A Good Fight 14
Agrippa, H. C. Of Occult Philosophy 49
Agriculture 41, 42
Aguecheek 94
Aguilar, Grace. Essays and Miscellanies 94
Women of Israel 73
Home Scenes 1
Mother's Recompense 1
Vale of Cedars 1
Woman's Friendship 1
Home Influence 1
Days of Bruce 1
A Hero 14

Ainsworth, W. H. The Miser's Daughter 1
Rookwood 1
The Star Chamber 1
Lancashire Witches 1
Aikin, Lucy. Court of Charles I 73
Aikin, J. Select British Poets 89
Ainslie, H. Scottish Songs 89
Akenside, M. Poems 89
Ballads 89
Albion 104
Almunac, American 104
Albert, J. F. M. Classification Bibliographique 106
Albemarle, Earl of. Memoirs of the Marquis of Rockingham 73
Alchemy, Magic, etc 49, 60
Alciphron 14
Alcott, Dr. W. A. Wilderness of Pills and Powders 73
Aldrich, T. B. Ballad of Babie Bell 89
The Course of True Love, etc 89
Alexander the Great. Life of 73
Alexander, D. A. The Israelitish Nation 67
Alexander, A. Authenticity of the Scriptures 26
Alexander, Col. Sir J. E. Life of a Soldier 73
Travels in Africa 67
Transatlantic Sketches 50
Alexander, J. H. Weights and Measures 102
Alexander, A. The Beauties of Chess 45
Alger, W. R. The Poetry of the East 89
Alfred the Great. Life of, by J. Abbott 73
Life of, by Asser 73
Life of, by Dr. R. Pauli 73
Alibone, S. A. Dictionary of English Literature, etc 102
Alice Arran 14
Alice, by Bulwer 14
Alice Learmont 14
Alice Sherwin 14
Alison, A. History of Europe 102
Life of Marlborough 73
Miscellaneous Essays 74
Essays on Taste 36
Allen and Lewis. Rural Architecture 47
Allen, C. B. Cottage Building 47
Allen, J. Battles of the British Navy 67
Allen, E. Life of 73
Allen, J. F. On the Grape Vine 41

Allen, P. The Expedition of Lewis and Clarke 50
Allen, R. L. The Domestic Animal 42
The American Farm 41
Allen, T. London and Westminster 63
Allen, W. Cyclopedia of American Biography 102
Allen, Capt. W. Expedition to the Niger 57
All in the Wrong 14
All's not Gold that Glitters 14
Allston, W. Poems 89
Lectures on Art 45
Almanac, National de la Republic Francaise 61
Almeida, T. Recreation Filosophica 40
Almost a Heroine 14
Alone 14
Alonzo and Melissa 14
Alton Locke 14
Alpha 36
Alpha and Omega 94
Alta California, Daily 104
Amabel 14
America and the West Indies, Geographically Described 61
America. Travels in 50, 54
American Adventures by Land and Sea 50
History 64, 71
Almanac 104
Anglers' Guide 45
Archives 68
Biography, by J. Belknap 73
Ethnological Society's Transactions 61
Farmers' Magazine 104
Journal of Science and Art 104
Mechanics' Magazine 104
Publishers' Circular 104
Register 104
State Papers 50
Stock Journal 104
Wit and Humor 100
Americans' Guide. The Constitution, etc 33
Ames, Fisher. Works 99
Amy Lawrence 14
Amy Lee 14
Amyas Leigh 14
Anastasius 14
Ancelot, Mme. Les Salons de Paris 63
Ancient Literature 87, 88
Andersen, Hans C. The Sand Hills of Jutland 1
Story Book 1
To be, or not to be 1
The Improvisatore 107
Anderson, A. British Embassy to China 57
Anderson, D. History of Commerce 34
Anderson, Florence. Zenaida 1
Anderson, J. Lake Ngami 57
Bible Lights, etc 54
Anderson, J. D. Report 34
Anderson, W. Mercantile Letter Writer 41
Andrews, A. British Journalism 71
Andrews, S. P. Discoveries in Chinese 93
Andrews, G. H. Agricultural Engineering 41
Anecdotes 103
Angela 14
Angell, Dr. D. M. Mirror of Fortune 46
Animal Magnetism 101
Annals of British Legislation 63
of the Parish 14

Anne of Geierstein 14
Annual of Scientific Discovery, etc 40
Portrait 104
Scientific 104
Anquetil, M. Histoire de France 63
Anson, Admiral. Voyage 69
Anspach, Rev. F. R. The Two Pilgrims 26
Anthon, J. American Precedents 31
Anthon, C. Dictionary of Greek and Roman Antiquities 102
Classical Dictionary 102
Antiquities 87, 88
Antiquary 14
Antisell, Dr. T. Hydro-Carbon Oils 47
Handbook of the Useful Arts 102
Handbook of Universal Biography 102
Antoninus, A. V. Meditations 87
Anthropology 43, 44
Apeleutherus. Intellectual Freedom 26
Apology for Religion of Nature 26
Appleton. Travelers' Guide 61
Illustrated Handbook 61
Dictionary of Machinery, etc 102
Encyclopedia of Biography 102
New American Encyclopedia 102
Cyclopedia of Drawing 102
Apuleius. Works 37
Aquinas, T. Life of 73
Arabella Stuart 14
Arabian Nights 14
Days 14
Arago M. The Comet 38
Arago, F. Biographies 73
Arbatel. Of Magic 49
Arbouville, Countess. Christine Van Amburg, etc 73
Archæology, Northern. Guide to 8, 17
Architecture 47, 48
Arculf, Bishop. Travels 54
Ardeche, M. History of Napoleon 73
Ariosto, L. Orlando Furioso 89
Aristinetus. Love Epistles 87
Aristophanes. Comedies 87
Aristotle. Metaphysics 87
Nicomachean Ethics 87
Politics 87
Organon and Social Treatises 87
Rhetoric and Poetic 87
Armstrong, F. C. The Young Middy 2
Armstrong, J. Life of General Richard Montgomery 73
Armstrong, Gen. J. The War of 1812 68
Army Regulations 31
Arnold, A. C. L. The Signet of King Solomon 107
Arnold, Benedict. Life of 73
Arnold J. Law of Marine Insurance 31
Arnold, T. Poems 89
Modern History 72
History of Rome 63
The Later Roman Commonwealth 63
Life and Correspondence of 73
Life of Hannibal 73
Arnott, N. Elements of Physics 40
Chimney Valves and Ventilation 47
Arrah Neil 14
Arthur Carryl 89
Arthur O'Leary 14
Arthur, T. S. Advice to Young Men 26
Twenty Years Ago, and Now 2
Heart Histories and Life Pictures 2

Arthur, T. S. Tales from Real Life 2
The Good Time Coming 2
What Can Woman Do 2
The Successful Merchant 2
The Hand but not the Heart 2
Temperance Tales 2
The Angel and Demon 2
Three Eras in a Woman's Life 2
Lizzie Glenn 2
King and the Knights of the Round Table 2
Arthur, W. Italy in Transition 63
Artist's Married Life of A. Durer 73
Artisan, The 47
Artisan Club Illustrations 34
Art Journal from 1849 to 1858 104
Art Union, Monthly Journal 104
Arts 36, 49
Arts, Fine 45, 46
Arts, Useful 47, 48
Arts nd aSciences. Knight's English Cyclopedia 47
Ash, J. Dictionary of the English Language 102
Ashe, T. Travels 50
Asiatic History 64, 67
Asia, Travels in 57, 59
Astronomy 38
Aspen Court 14
Aspenwald 2
Atar Gull, by Sue 14
Athanasia, by E. H. Seares 14
Athelings, by Mrs. Oliphant 14
Athenæus. Deipnosophists 87
Athens, its Grandeur and Decay 63
Atherton and other Tales 14
Atkinson, H. G., and Harriet Martineau. Laws of Man's Nature 101
Atkinson, T. W. Oriental and Western Siberia 57
Atlantic Monthly 104
Atlas to Australia 61
to Battles of American Revolution 61
Butler's Ancient 61
of Central America 62
Colton's, of the World 61
Gell, Sir W., of Rome 61
National, of the World 61
of Physical Geography 61
Lavoigne's Historical 72
of the Seat of War in Florida 62
to Alison's Europe 62
Ringgold's of San Francisco Bay 62
of State of New York 62
of U. S. Coast Surveys 62
Attaché in Madrid 54
Attic Philosopher 14
Attorney 14
Auber, P. British Power in India 66
Audubon, J. J. The Birds of America 42
Ornithological Biography 42
and J. Bachman. The Quadrupeds of America 42
Auldjo, J. Visit to Constantinople 54
Aunt Margaret's Mirror 14
Aurelian 14
Austen, Miss. Sense and Sensibility 2
Pride and Prejudice 2
Emma 2
Persuasion 2
Mansfield Park 2
Northanger Abbey 2
Memoirs of the Duchess of Orleans 73
of Sidney Smith 84
Austin, J. T. Life of Elbridge Gerry 73

Australia. Travels in 57, 59
Australian Crusoes, by Rowcroft 14
Autobiography, a Collection of Lives
by the parties themselves 73
Autocrat of the Breakfast Table 94
Avenger, The 14
Avillion 14
Ayesha 14
Aylmers 14
Ayola, J. Historia de Gibraltar 63
Ayrshire Legends 14
Ayton, W. E. Lays of the Scottish
Cavaliers 80
Azeglio. Italy and France in 16th
Century 63
The Challenge of Barletta 2
Nicolo dei Lapi 2

B

BABBAGE, C. Bridgewater Treatise 26
Economy of Machinery 38
Bache, Prof. A. D. United States
Coast Survey 103
and McCulloch's Reports in Re-
lation to Sugar, etc 47
Bachelor of the Albany 14
Bachelor of Salamanca 14
Bachelor's Story. O. A. Bunce 14
Bacon, Sir F. Works 99
Bacon, Francis Lord. Essays 94
On the Human Understanding 94
Bacon, Delia. Philosophy of Shaks-
pear's Plays 94
Badeau, A. The Vagabond 94
Bagster, —. The Word of God 26
Baily, J. Festus; a Poem 89
The Mystic, and other Poems 89
The Age 89
Bailey, Rev. J. Life Studies 95
Bailey, Joanna. Dramatic Works 92
Bailey, J. W. Microscopic Obser-
vations 44
Microscopic Observations in
South Carolina 44
Bailey, N. Dictionary 102
Bailey, S. Essays 36
Theory of Reasoning 37
Bain, A. Elements of Chemistry 38
Baird, H. M. Modern Greece 54
Baird, R. The West Indies 61
Baird, S. F., Cassin and Lawrence.
Birds 42
Baker, G. E. Life of William H.
Seward 74
Bakewell, F. C. Great Facts 47
Manual of Electricity 39
Bakewell, R. Geology 40
Baldwin, J. G. Flush Times of
Alabama 2
Party Leaders 73
Baldwin, T., and J. Thomas' Gazet-
teer of the United States 61
Ball, B. L. Rambles in Eastern
Asia, etc 57
Ballads, Old 89
and Songs 89
Ancient Spanish 89
Ballantyne, R. M. The Coral Island
Ungava 2
Snowflakes and Snubeams 2
Ballenline's Hudson's Bay; or
Every Day Life in the Wilds
of North America 50
Ballantyne, J. Hundreth Birthday
of Robert Burns 73
Balloon Travels of Robert Merry 54

Ballou, Rev. M. The Di●● Char-
acter 26
Ballyahan Castle 14
Balzac, H. Veronique 2
Bancroft, A. Life of Washington 73
Bancroft, G. History of the U. S. 68
Literary and Historical Miscel-
lanies 94
Banin, J. The Smuggler 2
Banished Son, by Caroline Lee
Hentz 14
Bankers' Magazine 104
Banks, History of 34
Bano, P. de. Magical Elements 49
Banquet des Sept Gourmands, par
P. Vincard 14
Barber of Bantry 6
Barber, J. W. Historical Collec-
tions of Massachusetts 68
Barclay, John. Argenis 2
Barclay, J. T. The City of the
Great King 67
Barclay, S. Recollections 68
Barclays of Boston 74
Barclay, R. Apology 26
Catechism and Confession of
Faith 26
Bard, S. Waikna 50
Baretti's Italian and English Dic-
tionary 102
Barham, Rev. H. Ingoldsby Le-
gends 2
Barington, A. Physical Geography 61
Barker, E. H. Literary Anecdotes 94
Barker, Jacob. Incidents in the
Life of 73
Barker, W. B. Lares and Penates 63
Barlow, Juel. The Vision of Co-
lumbus 89
Barlow, P. Treatise on the Strength
of Timber 38
Materials and Construction 47
Barnaby Rudge, by Dickens 14
Barnes, J. The Old Inn; or Travel-
ers' Entertainment 2
Barney O'Rierdon 14
Barnum, P. T. Life, by himself 73
Baron Trenck 2
Barrell, G. The Pedestrian in
France 54
Barrett, B. F. Life of Swedenborg 74
The New Dispensation 26
The Golden Reed 26
New Jerusalem Church 26
Barrington, A. Introduction to
Heraldry 93
Barrington, Sir J. Sketches 74
Barrow, J. Travels in China 57
Arctic Voyages 50
Of Contentment. Resignation.
etc 26
Barrow, Sir J. Memoirs of Naval
Worthies of Queen Eliza-
beth's Reign 74
Life of Peter the Great 74
Life of Lord George Anson 74
Life of Admiral Howe 74
Barry, P. The Fruit Garden 41
Barth, H. Travels in North and
Central Africa 57
Bartlett, D. W. The Heroes of
the Indian Rebellion 74
Presidential Candidates for 1860 74
Life of Joan of Arc 74
Life of Lady Jane Grey 74
Modern Agitators 74
Paris with Pen and Pencil 74
Bartlett, J. Collection of Familiar
Quotations 94

Bartlett, J. R. Dictionary of Amer-
icanisms 102
Personal Narrative in Texas and
New Mexico 50
Bartlett, Washington. Manuscript
Journal of Cruises 50
Bartlett, W. H. The Nile Boat 54
Forty Days in the Desert 54
Bartlett, W. H. C. Elements of
Analytical Mechanics 47
Elements of Mechanics 47
Bartol, C. A. Pictures of Europe 54
Barton, R. Poems 89
Bartram, J., and H. Marshall's Me-
moirs 74
Bartram, W. Travels, etc 50
Bascom, J. Political Economy 54
Bashforth, F. Treatise on the Con-
struction of Oblique Bridges 47
Basnage. History of the Jews 67
Bastile. Chronicles of 2
Dates, Mrs. D. B. Four Years on
the Pacific Coast 50
Bates, E. Doctrines of the Friends 26
Bauer, J. Lives of Alex. and Wm.
Humboldt 74
Bautin, M. Art of Extempore
Speaking 37
Bayle P. Historical and Critical
Dictionary 102
Historical Dictionary 73
Bayne, P. Essays 94
Bay Path, by Dr. J. G. Holland 14
Beamish, N. L. Northmen in Amer-
ica 68, 87
Beatrice 14
Beatrice Cenci 14
Beattie, J. Poetical Works 89
Beattie, W. Life and Letters of
Thomas Campbell 74
The Waldenses, Illustrated 61
Beaty's Illustrations of Hanoverian
Scenery 54
Beauchampe, by Simms 14
Beauchampe, by James 14
Beaumarchais, P. Theatre de 92
Beaumont and Fletcher. Works 92
Beauties, by Leigh Hunt 94
Beaumont. W. Physiology of Di-
gestion 45
Beccaria, C. B. Crimes and Pun-
ishments 33
Bechstein, J. M. Cage and Cham-
ber Birds 42
Beck T. R. and J. R. Medical Ju-
risprudence 31
Becket. T. A. Life of, by Robert-
son 14
Life of, by H. H. Milman 14
Beckford, W. Memoirs of 74
Beckmann, J. History of Inven-
tions 47
Beckwourth. J. Life and Adven-
tures of 74
Bede's Ecclesiastical History 26
Bede, C. Adventures of Mr. Ver-
dant Green 2
Bedford, H. Life of St. Vincent de
Paul 74
Beale, L. S. How to Work with a
Microscope 47
Beechcroft, by Catharine Yonge 14
Beecher, Miss. Appeal to the Peo-
ple 26
Common Sense Applied to Re-
ligion 26
Domestic Economy 44
Domestic Receipt Book 44
Beecher, E. Conflict of Ages 26

Beecher, Miss C. E. Letters to the People 45
Beecher, Henry Ward. Star Papers 94
New Star Papers 94
Life Thoughts 94
Fruit, Flowers and Farming 41
Beechey, Capt. F. W. Voyage to the Pacific 59
Beeson, J. A Plea for the Indians 33
Behind the Scenes, by Lady Bulwer 14
Behind the Scenes in Paris 14
Bohman, J. Aurora 25
Election of Grace 26
His Epistles 26
Teutonic Philosophy 26
Theosophic Philosophy 26
His Third Book 26
Memoirs of 74
Life of, by F. Okely 74
Being Rich, by H. Consience 14
Belcher, Capt. Sir E. Voyage round the World 59
Voyage of the Samarang 59
Arctic Voyage in Search of Sir John Franklin 50
Belcher, J. The Clergy of America 71
Belden, E. D. The City of New York 61
Belford Regis 15
Belinda 15
Belisarius. A Fable 2
Belisle, D. W. History of Independence Hall 68, 71
Belknap, J. American Biography 74
Bell, Sir C. Anatomy of Expression 46
Bell, H. C. Life of Mary Queen of Scots 74
Bell, J. D. A Man 37
Bell, R. Lives of the English Poets 74
Life of George Canning 74
History of Russia 63
Bell, T. History of British Quadrupeds 42
Natural History of British Reptiles 42
British Stalk Eyed Crustacea 42
Bell, W. E. Carpentry made Easy 59
Bell's Life in London 104
Belle Brittan on a Tour to Newport etc 50
Belle of Washington 15
Belle Smith Abroad 54
Belleville, J. H. Manual of the Barometer 40
Belsham, W. Essays 94
Bement, C. N. Poulterer's Companion 42
Benedict, E. C. American Admiralty Jurisdiction, etc 31
Run through Europe 54
Bennett, J. C. History of the Saints 68
Bennett, J. Gordon. Memoirs of his Life and Times 74
Bennett, E. Clara Moreland 2
Wild Scenes on the Frontiers 2
Ben Sylvester's Word 2
Bentham, J. The Book of Fallacies 33
Tratados de Legislation 33
Bentley's Miscellany 104
Benton, J. A. The California Pilgrim 26
Benton, T. H. Abridgement of Debates in Congress 33
Thirty Years' View 33
The Dred Scott Decision Examined 33
Beranger, P. J. De. Œuvres Completes 101

200 of Lyrical Poems, translated 89
Dernier Chanson 89
Berber 15
Berenice 15
Berger, E. Charles Auchester 2
Berkeley, H. Memoirs of Madame d'Arblay 74
Berkley, Bishop. Works 40
Bermuda, a Colony, a Fortress, and a Prison 50
Bernal Diaz. Memoirs, by himself 74
Bernard, C. Gerfaut 2
Le Gentilhomme Campagnard 2
Bernard, H. National Education in Europe 92
Bernard the Wise. Voyage to Palatine 54
Bernard, W. D. Voyage of the Nemesis 54
Berni, F. Orlando Inamorato 89
Bertha, by W. B. McCabe 15
Bertha Percy, by Margaret Field 15
Bertrams, by A. Trollope 15
Bertrand, C. F. Le Parfumeur 46
Beryman, Capt. W. M. The Militinman's Manual 49
Bescherelle, M. Dictionnaire Française 102
Betrothed, by Scott 15
Betrothed, by A. Manzoni, 15
Beulah, by Augusta J. Evans 15
Beverley's History of Virginia. 68
Bewick, T. History of Quadrupeds 42
Bibel, Die 26
Bible 26
with References 26
with the Apocrypha 26
Biblical Legends, by G. Weil 15
Bibliographical Works 106, 107
Bibliotheque Illustree des Classes Ouviers. 108 108
Bibliotheque Portative 94
Biddle, H. P. Poems 89
Biernatyki. The Hallig 2
Bigelow, J. The Useful Arts 67
Bigelow Papers 89
Bigelow, J. R. State Constitutions 31
Binder, W. E. Viola 2
Madelon Hawley 2
Bingham, H. The Sandwich Islands 92
Binney, A. Terrestrial Mollusks 42
Binney, H. Eulogy on John Marshall 74
Binns, E. Anatomy of Sleep 45
Binns, J. 29 Years in Europe, etc 54
Biographie Nouvelle des contemporains 74
Universelle des contemporains 74
Biography. Knight's English Cyclopedia 102
Biography 73
Bird, Dr. R. M. Calavar 2
Nick of the Woods 2
Birds of America, by J. J. Audubon 42
Natural History of 42
Birthday Present 15
Bischoff, G. The Woolen Trade, etc 34
Chemistry, Physiology and Geology 40
Bishop, H. E. Floral Home 50
Bittersweet 15
Bivouac 15
Bjornstjerna. British Empire in the East 67
Black Diamonds from Darkey Homes 15
Black Dwarf 15

Black Gauntlet 15
Black Mantle 15
Black Warrior. Case of the 33
Black, W. On Brewing 47
Blackshear's Memoirs of S. F. Miller 74
Blackstone, W. Commentaries 31
Blackwell, E. Laws of Life 45
Blackwood's Magazine to 1861 104
Blaine, D. P. Encyclopedia of Rural Sports 46
Blair, H. Chronological Tables 72
Blakesley, Rev. J. W. Four Months in Algeria 87
Blakey, R. Political Literature 33
Blanc, Louis. Ten Years 63, 72
Bland, W. On the Forms of Ships, etc 49
Bleak House 15
Bledsoe, A. T. Theodicy 26
Blessed Family 15
Blessington, Lady. Conversations with Byron 94
Life and Correspondence 74
Blind Rosa, by H. Consience 15
Blithedale Romance 15
Blodget, L. Climatology of the U. S. 40
Blonde and Brunette 2
Blunt, J. The Formation of the Confederacy of the U. S. 33, 68
Shipmaster's Assistant 49
Bocacio, G. Decameron 2
Bocalini, T. Advertisements of Parnassus 89
Boetius, A. M. S. Consolations of Philosophy 87
Bogart, W. H. Daniel Boone 74
Bohn, H. G. Classical Library 87
The Young Lady's Book 108
Handbook of Proverbs 100
Foreign Proverbs 100
Pottery, Porcelain, etc 47
Bonaparte, N. Life of, by J. S. C. Abbott 47
at St. Helena, by J. S. C. Abbott 47
by L'Ardeche 74
Captivity at St. Helena 74
Napoleon Code 74
Confidential Correspondence with Josephine 94
Correspondence with his brother Joseph 94
Court and Camp of 94
Dictated to his Generals 94
France during the Reign of 63
Napoleon Dynasty 63
Gallery 63
Life of, by W. Grimshaw 63
and his Marshals, by J. T. Headley 63
Life, by Hazlitt 63
by Count Lebedoyere 63
Life of, by J. G. Lockhart 63
Maitland's Narrative of his Surrender 74
in Exile, by O'Meara 74
Life of, by W. Scott 74
Bonaparte, Prince Napoleon. Napoleonic Ideas 33
Bond, Dr. H. Genealogies of Watertown, Waltham and Weston, Mass 93
Genealogies and History of Watertown, etc 68
Bond, J. W. Minnesota 50
Bon Gaultiers' Ballads 89
Bonner, T. D. Life and Adventures of J. Beckwourth 74
Bonneville, Capt. Adventures of 50

Bonnechose, E. D. Conquettes d' l'Angleterre 63
Bonomi, J. Nineveh 67
Book of Common Prayer 26
of Costume 46
of Costume; or The Annals of Fashion 94
Colored 94
for a Corner 15
of 1,000 Comical Stories 15
of Mormon 26
of Snobs 15
Books of Reference 102, 104
Bookseller. London 104
New York 104
San Francisco 104
Booksellers' Medium. New York 104
Boone, D. Life of 74
and the Hunters of Kentucky 74
Booth and Morfits. Encyclopedia of Chemistry 39
Border Beagles 15
Border War 15
Borrow, G. The Bible in Spain 54
Lavengro 2
The Romany Rye 2
Borthwick, J. D. Three Years in California 50
Bossange, H. Catalogue de Livres Francaise 104
Bossuet, J. B. Sur l'Histoire Universelle 71
Sermons Choisies 26
Boston Municipal Register 61
Directory 61
Boswell, J. Life of Sam'l Johnson 74
Botany 41, 42
Both, M. L. Clock and Watch Makers' Manual 47
Botta, C. The War of Independence of the United States 68
Bougainville, L. Voyage round the World 50
Boulton, J. Illustrations of British Song Birds 42
Bourne, B. F. Captive in Patagonia 50
Bourne, J. Catechism of the Steam Engine 38
Treatise on the Steam Engine 38
Treatise on the Screw Propeller 38
Bourne, V. Poetical Works 80
Bourne, W. O. Gems from Fable Land 2
Boussingault, J. B. Rural Economy 41
Bouvier, J. Law Dictionary 31
Bovee, C. N. Thoughts, etc 95
Bowditch, N. American Navigator 49
Suffolk Surnames 93
Bowen, A. The Naval Monument 68
Bowen, F. Critical Essays 95
Life of B. Lincoln 74
Life of J. Otis 74
Life of Baron Steuben 74
Bowring, J. The Polish Poets 89
The Language and Literature of Holland 93
Bowring, Sir J. Siam 57
Bowman, A. The Castaway 2
The Kangaroo Hunters 2
Boyd, W. C. Guide through Italy 61
Boyer's French Dictionary 102
Boy's Adventures in Australia 15
Boy Hunters 15
Brace, C. L. Hungary 54
Home Life in Germany 54
The Norse Folk 54
Brack, F. Tactique 40
Advance Posts, etc 89
Brackinridge, H. Modern Chivalry 2

Braddock, Gen. The expedition of, in 1775 68
Bradford, A. C. Nellie Bracken 2
Bradley, Mary E. Douglas Farm 2
Dragelone 15
Brainerd, D. Life of, by W. B. O. Peabody 74
Brand, J. Antiquities 87
Brande, W. T. Manual of Chemistry 39
Encyclopedia of Science, etc 105
Brandon 12
Brant, Thayendanegea. Life of, by L. W. Stone 74
Brantome, P. Œuvres de 99
Bravo, The, by Cooper 15
Bray, C. The Philosophy of Necessity 35
Bray, Mrs. Courtenay of Walreddin 2
De Foix 2
Fitz of Fitz-Ford 2
Henry de Pomeroy 2
The Protestant 2
The Talba 2
Trelawney of Trelawne 2
Trials of the Heart 2
Warleigh 2
White Hoods 2
Bread upon the Waters 15
Breakfast, Dinner and Tea 48
Breck, J. The Flower Garden 41
Brees, S. C. Railway Practice 38
Bremer, Frederika. The Home 2
Strife and Peace 2
A Diary; H. Family and other Tales 2
The Neighbors, etc 2
The Presidents Daughters and Nina 2
Hertha 2
New Sketches of Every Day Life 2
Brothers and Sisters 2
Father and Daughter 2
Brewster, Anne. Compensation 2
Brewster, Sir D. Optics 49
Natural Magic 49
More Worlds than One 38
Life, etc., of Sir J. Newton 74
Martyrs of Science 74
Brewster, W. Life and Time, by A. Steele 74
Brialmont, M., and G. R. Gleig. Life of Wellington 74
Bride of Lammermoor 15
Bridgman, T. Young Gardeners' Assistant 41
Brington, D. G. The Florida Peninsula 61
Brinley, T. The Life of Wm. T. Porter 74
Bristed, C. A. Five Years in an English University 74
Sword and Gown 2
Buy Livingstone 2
British and Foreign Medico-Chirurgical Review 104
British Expedition to the Crimea 68
British Essayists 95
British India, Historical Account of 67
British Poets 89
Broadhead, J. R. History of the State of New York to 1601 68
Brock, Mrs. C. Home Memories 2
Brock, Rev. W. Sketch of Sir H. Havelock 74
Broderip's Zoological Recreations 42
Brockedon, W. Passes of the Alps 51

Brodie, G. The British Empire 63
Broken Hyacinth 15
Bronson, O. A. Christianity, etc 26
The Convent 74
Quarterly Review 104
Bronte, Miss. Villette 2
Shirley 2
The Professor 2
Wuthering Heights 2
Jane Eyre 2
Tenant of Wildfell Hall 2
Life of 2
Brooke, H. The Fool of Quality 2
Brooke, R. Fields of Battle in England 103
Brooke, W. Eastford 2
Brooke, Rajah. Events in Borneo, etc 67
Brooks, C. T. Songs and Ballads 2
Brooks, Shirley. Aspen Court 2
Broquieres, B. Travels in Palestine 54
Brothers Clerks 15
Brothers and Sisters 15
Brough, J. C. Fairy Tales of Science 2
Brough, R. B. Sir John Falstaff 74
Brougham, J. Basket of Chips 95
Brougham, Lord. Political Philosophy 73
Statesmen 74
Philosophers 74
Men of Letters 74
Dissertations, etc 100
Speeches 100
Discourses 100
Natural Theology 26
Broughton, Lord. Visits to Italy 54
Brown. The Fudges of England 2
The Younger 2
Brown, A. M. Wreath around the Cross 26
Browne, C. B. Life of 74
Arthur Mervin 2
Wieland 2
Edgar Huntley 2
Jane Talbot 2
Brown, G. Grammar 92
Brown J. Sixty Year's Gleanings 74
Highland Clans of Scotland 63
Brown, J. J. The American Angler's Guide 46
Brown, R. Domestic Architecture 47
Brown, T. N. Life of Hugh Miller 74
Brown, Capt. T. Taxidermist's Manual 42
Brown, T. Fudges in England 89
Philosophy of the Human Mind 36
Brown, T. W. Minnie Hermon 2
Browne, D. J. The Trees of America 41
Modern Farming 41
American Poultry Yard 42
Browne, J. Ross. Etchings of a Whaling Cruise 50
Yusef 54
Browne, T. Pseudoxia Epidemica 26
Religio Medici 26
Brown, Sir. T. Works 99
Brownie of Bodsbeck 15
Browning, Elizabeth B. Napoleon III 89
Poems 89
Aurora Leigh 89
Men and Women 89
Prometheus Bound 89
Browning, H. C. Life of Goethe 73
Browning, M. Life of a Hunter 75

Browning, R. Poems 89
Brownlow and Pryne. Ought Slavery to be Perpetuated 33
Brown's Letters to Man about Town 15
Bruce, J. Life of, by F. B. Head 75
Travels 57
Brunet, J. C. Manuel du Libraire 106
Brunton, Mrs. Self-Control 2
Discipline 2
Bryan, M. Dictionary of Painters and Engravers 102
Bryant, E. What I saw in California 50
Bryant, J. D. Pauline Seward 3
Bryant, W. C. Poems 89
Selections from American Poets 89
Discourse on Irving 75
Letters from Spain 54
Brynshock, C. Law of War 32
Buchanan, G. History of Scotland 63
Buchanan, R. The Grape, etc 41
Holy Land 54
Bucke, C. Beauties of Nature, etc 57
Ruins of Ancient Cities 72
Buckle, H. T. History of Civilization 63
Buckingham, Duke of. The Court of George IV 75
Buckingham, J. S. America 59
Canada, Nova Scotia, etc 59
Autobiography 75
Buckingham, J. T. Newspaper Literature, etc 95
Buckland, F. T. Curiosities of Natural History 44
Buckland, W. Geology and Mineralogy 40
Buckmaster, J. C. Inorganic Chemistry 39
Budge, J. The Miner's Guide 40
Buffon, G. L. I. Natural History 42
Buffum, E. G. Gold Mines of California 50
Bug Jargal 15
Builder, The 104
Bulfinch, T. The Age of Chivalry 3
Bullard, Mrs. Sights and Scenes in Europe 54
Bulwer, Lady. Behind the Scenes 3
Bulwer, Sir E. L. England and the English 54
The Siamese Twins and other Poems 89
Athens 3
Devereux 3
Pelham 3
Night and Morning 3
The Caxtons 3
My Novel 3
Eugene Aram 3
Godolphin 3
Leila, and Calderon the Courtier 3
Rienzi 3
The Disowned 3
Zanoni 3
Last Days of Pompeii 3
Lucretia 3
Ernest Maltravers 3
Alice 3
Paul Clifford 3
Pilgrims of the Rhine 3
Harold 3
The Pelham Novels etc 3
What Will He do with It 3
Bunbury, Selina. Summer in Northern Europe 54
Bunce, A. Bachelor's Story 36
Bungay, G. W. Offhand Takings 95

Bungener, L. F. Trois Sermons 2
Dunner, History of Louisiana 68
Bonsen, C. C. Religious Liberty 26
Bunyan, J. Grace Abounding 26
Pilgrim's Progress 26
Burkhardt, J. L. Egypt and Nubia 54
Travels in Arabia 75
Burdett, C. Margaret Moncrieffe 3
Burgess, N. G. The Photograph and Ambrotype 46
Burgess, Tristam. Memoir and Speeches 75
Battle of Lake Erie 68
Burgh, J. Dignity of Human Nature 37
Political Disquisition 33
Burgoyne's Campaign and the Battle of Bemis Heights 3
Burke, E. Life of, by M. Prior 75
On the French Revolution 33
Speeches and Correspondence 100
Works 99
Burke, J. B. British Peerage and Baronetage 94
General Armory 94
The Landed Gentry 93
Burke, J. and J. B. The Royal Families 94
Burkhardt, C. B. Fairy Tales 3
Burlamaqui, J. Natural and Politic Law 31
Burnap, G. W. Doctrine of the Trinity 26
Life of L. Calvert 75
Burnet, G. Four Discourses 26
Life of God in the Soul of Man 26
Burnett, Bishop. The Reformation in England 63
History of his own time 63
Burnett, C. M. Philosophy of Spirits 37
Burnett, F. Doctrina Antiqua 37
Archæologiæ Philosophicæ 37
Barnett, J. Notes on the Northwest 68
Burney, J. Buccaneers in America 50
Barney, Miss. Evelina 3
The Secret 3
Burnham, G. P. The Hen Fever 71
Burns, J. Mothers of the Wise and Good 75
Burns, Robert. Life of, by J. G. Lockhart 75
by T. Carlyle 75
and Works, by Chambers 89
Works, edited by A. Cunningham 89
Poetical Works 89
Burns and Clarinda. Correspondence 95
Burr, Aaron. Memoirs of, by M. L. Davis 76
Private Journal 75
Life of, by J. Parton 82
Report of his Trial 31
Burritt, Elihu. Thoughts on Things, etc 54
Burrowes, Rev. G. The Song of Solomon 26
Burrowes, T. H. Pennsylvania School Architecture 47
Burton, J. H. Criminal Trials in Scotland 32
Burton, R. Anatomy of Melancholy 3
Burton, Capt. R. F. Travels in Africa 57
Pilgrimage to Mecca 57
Bush, G. Mahomet 75

Burton, W. E. Cyclopedia of Wit and Humor 100
Anastasis 26
Bush Boys, by Mayne Reid 15
Bushnell, C. J. Tradesmen's Cards, etc 94
Bushnell, H. God in Christ 26
Nature and the Supernatural 95
Busk, M. History of Spain and Portugal 63
Busoni, M. P. Memoirs de la Duchesse d'Orleans 75
Butler, H. D. The Family Aquarium 44
Butler, S. Poetical Works 89
Hudibras 89
Atlas of Ancient Geography 61
Butler, T. P. The Philosophy of the Weather 49
Butler, W. A. Ancient Philosophy 37
Butterfly 16
Buttmann, A. I. Poeti Italiani 89
Buxton, Sir F. Memoirs of 73
Byrdsall, F. The Locofoco Party 33
Byers and Kellom's Nebraska and Kansas Gold Fields 61
Byrn, M. L. Artist and Tradesman's Companion 46
Byron, Lord. Life of, by J. Galt 76
Works 89

C

Cabell, S. L. The Unity of Mankind 43
Cabin Boy's Story 16
Cabin and Parlor 15
Cabin Book 15
Cabinet Album 95
Cabot, J. E. Tour to Lake Superior 50
Cabot, S. Life of, by C. Hayward 75
Caddell, C. M. Jesuits' Missions 50
Cæsar. Commentaries 87
Life of, by J. Abbott 75
Cæsar Biroteau 3
Cahagnet, L. A. Celestial Telegraph 26
Caird, J. Prairie Farming in America 41
Cakes and Ale 15
Calavar 15
Caldas, F. J. Semanario de la Nueva Granada 104
Caldwell, C. M. C. Autobiography of 75
Caleb Williams 15
Calderon de la Barca, Mme. Life in Mexico 50
Calderon the Courtier 15
Calhoun, J. C. Works 99
Calidas. Sacontala 92
California Newspapers 104
Chronicle, Daily 104
Courier, Daily 104
Culturist 104
Farmer 104
Register 61
Pamphlets Relating to 105
Specimens of the Press of 105
Annual Reports of 106
State Register 106
Callery and Ivan. The Insurrection in China 67
Callicot, T. C. Handbook of Geography 102
Callimachus. Works 87
Calvert, J. Gold Rocks of Great Britain 40
Calvert, L. Life of, by G. W. Burnap 75

Camels. Reports upon 34
Camile 3
Camoens. Les Lusiadas 89
Camp, G. S. Democracy 73
Campan, Mad. Court of Marie Antoinette 75
Campbell, F. Frederick the Great 78
Campbell, J. The Lords Chancellors 75
The Chief Justices 75
Shakspeare's Legal Acquirements 95
Campbell, J. L. Agriculture 41
Campbell, J. W. History of Virginia 68
Campbell, Major. The Old Forest Ranger 3
Campbell, T. Poetical Works 89
Life and Letters of · 75
Campbell, W. Life of DeWitt Clinton 75
Campbell, W. W Border Warfare 68
Canada Directory 61
Salmon Fishing in 108
The Backwoods of 50
Canning, G. Life of, by R. Bell 75
Canot, Captain 57
Canterbury Tales 15
Capacity and Genius 36
Capper. South Australia 57
Capron, E. S. History of California 68
Cap Sheaf 95
Captain Blake 15
Captain Molly 15
Captain O'Sullivan 15
Captain Singleton and Col. Jack 15
Captains of the Old World 75
Carbonari. Memoirs of 33
Card Drawing 15
Carey, H. C. Letters to the President 34
Social Science 36
The Slave Trade 33
Carey, M. The Fever in Philadelphia 45
Carlen, Emilie. Home in the Valley 3
Woman's Life 3
Carleton, J. H. Battle of Buena Vista 68
Carleton, R. The New Purchase 3
Carleton, W. Traits and Stories 3
The Black Baronet 3
Carlyle, T. Frederick II 75
Life of John Sterling 76
Life of Robert Burns 75
Life of Schiller 75
Essays 95
Heroes and Hero Worship 35
Past and Present 95
Sartor Resartus 95
Letters and Speeches of Cromwell 95
French Revolution 63
Latter Day Pamphlets 33
German Romance
Caroline Mordaunt 15
Carolina Sports 15
Carpenter, W. B. Human Physiology 45
Comparative Physiology 45
The Microscope 47
Carrell, A. Counter Revolution in England 63
Carroll, Anna E. Star of the West 96
Carruthers, R. Life of Pope 75
Carson, Kit. Life and Adventures 75
Cary, Alice. Poems 89
Married, not Mated

Cary, H. F. Early French Poets 89
Cary, Phœbe. Poems 89
Case of the Black Warrior 32
Cassin, J. The Birds of California, etc 42
Cass, Louis. France 63
Cassiodorus. Historia Ecclesiastica 26
Cassique of Kiawah 15
Castaways 15
Caste 15
Castellao, A. L. Turkey 54
Castle Builders 15
Castle Dangerous 15
Castle Ehrenstein 15
Castle of Otranto 15
Castle Richmond 15
Castle Rackrent 15
Castlenau, M. de. Reigns of Francis II., etc 63
Catalogues 106, 107
Catalogue of Books on Masonry 94
Books published in Great Britain 106
Antiquarian Society, Worcester 106
Salem Athenæum 106
New York Apprentice's Library 106
Loganian Library 106
Library Company, Philadelphia 106
New York Society Library 106
New York Mercantile Library 106
New York State Library 106
St. Louis Mercantile Library 106
Baltimore Mercantile Library 106
The Public Library of Boston 106
Boston Mercantile Library 106
California State Library 106, 107
Mercantile Library, San Fran'co 107
The same. Manuscript. 1858 107
The same. Classified, with an Index. 1861 107
Books for sale by B. Quatrich 107
Books for sale by H. G. Bohn.
1841. (The Guinea Catalogue.) 107
Books for sale by Appleton & Co. 1856 107
Books on the Masonic Institution, in the Public Libraries of the United States · 107
of the Lyceum, New Orleans 107
Cathara Clyde 15
Catharine Ashton 15
Catharine de Medicis 15
Catharine Walton 15
Catharine II. Memoirs of, by herself 75
Court and Reign of, by S. M. Smucker 75
Catcott on the Deluge 40
Catlin, G. The American Indians 68
Catlow, A. Drops of Water 44
Catullus and Tibullus 87
Caudle Curtain Lectures 15
Cavalier 15
Cavalry Tactics 49
Cave, E. Lives and Acts of Apostles 26
Cavendish, G. Life of Cardinal Wolsey 76
Caves. French in Algeria 57
Caxtons 15
Cecil 15
Celebrated Men, Lives and Trials of 75
Cellini, B. Memoirs, by himself 75
Census of the United States 81
Census of the State of New York for 1845 and 1855 34
Century 101
Cervantes, S. M. Don Quixote 3
Persiles y Sigismunda 3
Persiles and Sigismunda 3

Chadwick, W. Life of Daniel De Foe 75
Chain Bearers 15
Chalo Noir 15
Challenge of Barletta 15
Chalmers, G. Revolt of the Colonies 68
Chalmers' T. Miscellanies 26
Memoirs of 15
Chambers, R. Traditions of Edinburgh 61
Annals of Scotland 61
Life and Works of Burns 76
Chambers, W. Things in America 50
Miscellany 108
Chambers, W. and R. The Russian War 63
Chamber's Cyclopedia of English Literature 102
Information for the People 102
Chamich, M. History of Armenia 67
Chamier, Capt. The Life of a Sailor 3
Tom Bowling 3
Champolion, Figeac. Egypte 67
Chancery Law 31, 32, 33
Chandler, Ellen. This, That and the Other 3
Chandler, Maria F. The Spirit Harp 89
Chandler, Mary. The Elements of Character 36
Channing, E. T. Life of W. Ellery 75
Channing, W. E. Memoir of 75
Discourses 94
Works 26
Channing, W. A Physician's Vocation 54
Chapin, E. H. Humanity in the City 95
Discourses 26
Chapones, Mrs. Letters 36
Chapter on Wives 15
Charcoal Sketches 15
Charity Green 15
Charlemagne. History of 75
Charlemont 15
Charles Auchester 15
Charles I. Court of, by Lucy Aiken 75
Life of, by Abbott 75
Charles II. Beauties of the Court of, by Mrs. Jameson 75
Charles V. Life of, by W. Robertson 75
Cloister Life of 75
Charles IX, and His Times 75
Charles X and Louis Phillippe 63
Charles Mandel 15
Charles O'Malley 15
Charles Vavasseur 15
Charlevoix, F. X. Histoire du Japon 67
Charles, P. Notabilities 75
Etudes sur Anglo-Americaines 64
Anglo-American Literature 96
Chastellux, M. Travels in America 50
Chatham, Burke and Erskine. Speeches 100
Chateaubriand, F. A. Autobiography 75
Melange 95
Analyse de l'Histoire de France 71
Chateaubriand, M. Itineraire 54
Chateau de Pyrenees 15
Chatfield, P. The Tin Trumpet 95
Chatterton, T. Life of, by J. Dix 75
Poems 89
Chaucer, G. Works 89
Poetical Works 89
Riches of 89
Chaudet, M. L'Art de l'Essayeur 54
Cheever, G. A Reel in the Bottle 3

Cheever, Rev. N. T. Voices of
Nature 28
Life in the Sandwich Islands 50
Chelsea Pensioners 15
Cheltenham, Guide to 61
Chemistry 39, 40
Chesney, Col. Russo-Turkish Campaigns 63
Chess 45, 46
Chess Handbook 46
Monthly 104
Chestnutwood 15
Chesterfield, Lord. Letters 92
Chesterfield, Lady. Letters 92
Chesterton, G. I.. Adventures 54
Chevalier, M. On the Value of Gold 34
Child, L. M. Isaac T. Hopper 75
Philothea 3
Letters from New York 95
Religious Ideas 28
Child Wife 15
Children of the Abbey 15
Chillingworth, W. Religion of the
Protestants 26
China Manufactory 15
China Pictorial, etc 57
Chinese Novels 15
Chinese Repository 104
Chinese Works on Surgery, etc 45
Chitty, J. On Commerce 32
Chitty and Hulme, J. W. On Bills
of Exchange 32
Chitty, Jun. On Contracts 32
Choate, Rufus. Reminiscences of 75
Chopin, M. Russie 54
Chorley, H. F. Life of Mrs. Hemans 75
Choules, J. O. Cruise of the North
Star 3
Christian Advices 27
Christian Library 104
Christie Johnstone 15
Christmas Stories 15
Christine Van Amburg 15
Christine 15
Chronicle, Royal Military 104
Chronicle of the Crusades 67
Chronicles of the Bastile 15
Chronicles of Clovernook 15
Chronicles, Six Old English 63
Chroniques de l'œil de Bœuf 15
Chroniques Populaires de Berry 15
Chronology 72, 73
Chubb, T. Tracts 21
Churchill, C. Poems 89
Churchill's Collection of Voyages
and Travels 59
Churton, E. The Railroad Book of
England 61
Cibber, C. Life, by himself 75
Cicero. Life of, by C. Middleton 75
Five Books. De Finibus 87
Oratory and Orators 87
Academics 87
Laelius 87
Immortality of the Soul 87
Tusculan Disputations 87
Tusculan Questions 87
Nature of the Gods 87
Orations, Offices, and Laelius 87
Letters to his Friends 87
Offices 36
On the Laws 32
Political Works 87
Cincinnati 61
Cincinnatus 104
Circumnavigation of the Globe 59
Civil Engineering 47, 48
Clacy, Mrs. C. Lady's Visit to Australia 47

Lights and Shadows of Australian Life 57
Claiborne, J. F. H. Life of Gen.
Sam. Dale 75
Clara Moreland 15
Clara Stephens 15
Clarence 15
Clarissa Harlowe 15
Clarendon, Earl. View of Hobbes'
Leviathan 27
Clark, B. British Gazetteer 61
Clark, Mrs. Charlotte. Life 75
Clark, Dr. J. H. Sight and Hearing 45
Clark, I. G. Knick-knacks 95
Clark, Mrs. M. C. The Iron Cousin 3
Concordance to Shakspeare 102
Clark, W. G. Literary Remains 95
Clarke, Dr. S. Of the Attributes of
God 27
Clarkson, T. The African Slave
Trade 71
Sketch of, by T. Taylor 75
Classic Tales 3
Claxton, T. Autobiography 75
Clay, H. Life of, by E. Sargent 75
Private Correspondence 95
Speeches 100
Obituary Addresses on 100
Clayton, J. W. Memoirs of Charles
II 75
Cluskey, M. W. Political Text Book 3
Cleaveland, J. Banking System 34
Cleaveland, H. R. Life of Hendrick
Hudson 75
Cleaveland, H. W., and Backus.
Cottages 47
Clemens, Hon. Jere. The Rivals 3
Mustang Gray 3
Clement Lorimer 16
Cleopatra. Life of, by Abbott 75
Clermont 16
Cleve Hall 16
Cleveland, R. J. Voyages 59
Clinton, DeWitt. Life of, by J. Renwick 75
by W. Campbell 75
Clinton, Sir H. Campaign in America 68
Clive, Lord. Life of 75
Cloquet, J. Recollections of Lafayette 75
Clowes, J. Dialogues 27
Coale, G. B. Manual of Photography 46
Coast Survey of U. S. 61, 106
Sketches 61
Cobbett, W. Porcupines' Works 34
Protestant Reformation 63
Le Maitre d'Anglais 92
Life of Andrew Jackson 75
Works 99
Cobbold, R. H. Pictures of the
Chinese 57
Cobden, J. C. White Slaves of England 3
Cockburn, H. Memorials of his Time 75
Cocke, W. A. Constitutional History 33
Cocks, C. Bordeaux 54
Cockton, H. Valentine Vox 3
The Love Match 3
The Steward 3
Code de Napoleon 32
Code of Procedure in the State of
New York 32
Coe, J. The True American 100
Cœur, Jacques. Life of 75
Coffin, E. S. Marine Traverse Tables 49
Coffin, N. W. America, etc 80
Coggeshall, G. Voyages 59
American Privateers, etc 68

Coggeshall, W. T. Easy Warren 3
Home Hits and Hints 3
Coiner, The, by Gerald Griffin 16
Coit, Rev. T. Puritanism 27
Coke, Hon. H. J. Ride to Oregon
and California 50
Colburn, Z., and A. L. Holley. Locomotive Boilers 38
Colburn's United Service Magazine 104
Colden, C. D. Life of Robt. Fulton 75
Cole, S. W. American Fruit Book 41
American Veterinarian 41
Cole's Life of Charles Kean 108
Coleman, L. The Apostolic Church 27
Coleridge, H. Northern Worthies 75
Coleridge, S. T. Biographia Literaria 75
Reminiscences of, by J. Cottle 75
Dramas 92
Poetical Works 89
Church and State; and Sermons 27
Confessions of an Enquiring
Spirit 27
Hints 27
Works 99
Colletta, P. History of Naples 63
Collibor, S. Nature and Existence
of God 27
Collingwood, Admiral. Correspondence 95
Collins, L. Kentucky 68
Collins, P. McD. Voyage 57
Collins, S. Miscellanies 95
Collins, T. W. Humanics 36
Collins, W. Poetical Works 89
The Dead Secret 3
After Dark 3
Hide and Seek 3
The Queen of Hearts 3
Woman in White 25
Colman, H. European Life 54
European Agriculture 41
Colnett, Capt. J. Voyage 59
Colon, F. Juzgados Militaires 49
Colonial Intelligence 104
Colton. Atlas of the World 61
Colton, C. Life and speeches of
Henry Clay 75
Colton, Rev. C. C. Lacon 95
Colton, Rev. W. Land and Sea 54
Ship and Shore 54
The Sea and the Sailor 50
Three Years in California 50
Columbia, British. Report on 50
Columbia. Descriptive of the District of 61
Columbus, C. Life and Voyages, by
W. Irving 75
Colwell, S. Ways and Means of
Payment 34
Combe, G. Constitution of Man 45
Physiology 43
Notes on the United States 50
Comedati, G. Italian and English
Dictionary 102
Comical Romance, by Scarron 16
Comines, P. Memoirs 75
Commerce 34, 35
Commerce and Navigation Reports 34
Commerce of British America 34
Commercial Relations of the U. S. 34
Common Errors 16
Common Schools of Cincinnati 106
Compensation 15
Compton, B. Life of R. C. Trench 75
Comstock, J. C. Natural Philosophy 46
Comte, A. Republique Occidentale 33
Ensemble du Positivisme 37
Philosophie Positive 37

Concordances 102, 104
Concordance to the Book of Common Prayer 103
To Shakspeare 102
To the Bible 102
Con Cregan 7
Conde, J. A. Arabs in Spain 63
Confessions of a Blind Heart 16
Congress. Debates and Proceedings of 33
Register of Debates in 33
Cases of Contested Elections 33
Congressional Globe 33
Conklin, M. C. The Mother and Wife of Washington 76
Connoisseur, The 95
Conrad, R. T. Aylmere 89
Conscience, H. Vera 3
The Conscript 3
The Curse of the Village, etc 3
The Demon of Gold 3
The Miser of Ricketicketack 3
The Lion of Flanders 3
Conscript, by A. Dumas 16
Constitution of the United States 31
Constitution and Laws of California 31
Contarini Fleming 16
Contes ; Cheykh Mohdy 16
Contes et Romans, par Voltaire 16
Contributions to History of Pennsylvania 3
Convent of St. Clair 16
Conversations of Goethe 95
Convict 16
Cook. Eliza. Poems 89
Cook, J. Voyages round the world 59
Cooke, E. W. Plates of Shipping and Craft 49
Cooke, G. W. China 57
Cooke, J. E. Henry St. John, Gentleman 3
Virginia Comedians 25
Cooke, J. P. Jr. Chemical Physics 39
Cooke, Lieut. Col. Report of His March to San Diego 50
Cookery and Domestic Economy 48, 49
Cook's Guide, by a Lady 48
Cooley, A. J. Cyclopedia of Receipts 48
Coolidge, R. H. Report on Sickness in the Army 34
Cooper, J. F. Novels 3
Afloat and Ashore 3
Bravo ; a Tale 3
Chain-Bearer 3
The Crater 3
Deer Slayer 3
The Headsman 3
Heidenmauer 3
Homeward Bound 3
Home as Found 3
Jack Tier 3
The Last of the Mohicans 3
Lionel Lincoln 3
Mercedes of Castile 3
The Monikins 3
Ned Myers 3
Notions of the Americans 3
Oak Openings 3
The Pathfinder 3
The Pilot 3
The Pioneers 3
The Prairie 3
The Red-Skins 3
Satanstoe 3
The Sea Lions 3
The Spy 3
Two Admirals 3
The Water Witch 3

Cooper, J. F.
Wept of the Wish-ton-Wish 3
Wing and Wing 4
Wyandotte 4
History of the Navy 68
Lives of Naval Officers 76
Cooper, Miss. Country Life 80
Cooper, Capt. S. Instruction for Militia and Volunteers 40
Coopers, The 16
Copeland, R. M. Country Life 45
Copeland, J. Medical Dictionary 102
Copway, G. Forest Life 76
Coquette, by Mrs. Foster 16
Cora and the Doctor 16
Coral Island 16
Cordova, J. de. Texas 34
Corinne 16
Cormenin, Viscount de. Orators of France 76
Cormere, M. Sur les Finances 34
Cornano, L. On Health and Long Life 45
Corne, H. Le Cardinal de Richelieu 76
Corneille and his Times, by F. Guizot 76
Corneille, Pierre et Thomas. Theatre de 92
Corner Cupboard 48
Cornhill Magazine 104
Cornwallis, K. British Columbia 61
Corpus Juris Civilis 31
Correspondence Relative to Expedition to Japan 33
Cortes, H. Dispatches 68
Cory, I. Fragments of Ancient Authors 67
Cosas de Espana 54
Cosmopolitan Art Journal 104
Costello, L. S. Early Poetry of France 4
Catharine de Medicis 4
Life of Jacques Cœur 76
Costumes 94
Cottage Magazine 104
Cottage on the Cliff 16
Cottle, J. Reminiscences of S. T. Coleridge 16
Coughlan, Mrs. Memoirs 76
Coulter, John. Adventures 60
Adventures in the Pacific 60
Count of Arensberg 16
Count of Monte Cristo 16
Count Robert of Paris 16
Counterparts 16
Countess of St. Albans 16
Country Curate 16
Country Gentleman 104
Courcillon, E. Le Cure Manque 16
Couret, L. du. Life in the Desert 57
Courier and Enquirer 109
Courtenay, E. 38
Courtenay, T. P. Memoirs of Sir William Temple 76
Courtenay of Walreddin 16
Courtship and Marriage 16
Courtship and Matrimony 16
Cousin, V. La Societe Française 76
History of Philosophy 71
Cousin Cicily 16
Cousin Maude and Rosamond 16
Cousin William 16
Cowell, B. Spirit of '76 in R. Island 68
Cowper, W. Poems 89
Life and Works, by Southey 76
Cowper's Works 99
Cox, Ross. Adventures 50
Cox, W. The House of Austria 63
The Duke of Marlborough 76

Cox, W. Russian Discoveries 59
Coxe, A. C. Impressions of England 54
Coxens, F. S. Acadia 60
Sparrowgrass Papers 95
Crabbe, G. Synonyms 93
Craik, G. L. British Commerce 34
The Literature of England 95
Cranston House 16
Cranmer, T. Life and Times of 76
Crater ; or Vulcan's Peak 16
Craven's Walker's Manly Exercises 46
Recreations in Shooting 46
Crawford, J. Embassy to Siam 57
Indian Archipelago 67
Crawford, Mabel. Life in Tuscany 54
Creasy, E. S. Eminent Etonians 76
Creichton, Capt. J. Memoirs of 76
Creole Orphans 16
Cricket Field, The 108
Crighton, A. History of Arabia 67
and Wheaton, H. Scandinavia 67
Criana, the Queen of Danube 4
Crittenden, S. W. and S. H. Book Keeping 47
Crock of Gold 16
Crocket, Col. David. Life, by himself 76
Croker, T. C. Killarny Legends 4
Croly, G. Beauties of the British Poets 89
Life and Times of George IV 76
Cromwell, O. Letters and Speeches 76
Life of, by J. T. Headley 76
Life of, by M. Russell 76
A Vindication, by D'Aubigne 76
and the English Crown, by F. Guizot 63
Crooks, G. R., and A. J. Schem. Latin Dictionary 102
Crosby, F. Everybody's Lawyer 32
Crosby, Hon. N. Obituaries 67
Crosland, Mrs. Lydia. A Woman's Book 4
Crotchet Castle 4
Crowe, E. C. History of France 63
Crowe, Mrs. C. Ghost Stories 107
The Night Side of Nature 101
Crowen, T. J. Cookery 49
Cruden, A. Concordance 102
Cruikshank, G. Three Courses, etc 4
Cruise of the Midge 4
Crystal Palace 101
Cudworth, R. Intellectual System 36
Culbertson, M. S. Darkness in the Flowery Land 69
Culpepper, N. British Herbal 41
Cummings, J. Apocalyptic Sketches 27
Cummings, Maria. The Lamplighter 4
El Fureides 4
Cumming, R. C. Five Years in South Africa 67
Cunningham, Allan. Painters of Great Britain 76
Life and Works of Burns 76
Cunningham, P. Handbook of London 54
Cupples, G. The Green Hand 4
Cure Manque 16
Curse of Clifton 16
Curse of the Village 16
Curtis, G. T. History of the Constitution of the United States 68
Curtis, G. W. Notes of a Howadji 54
Potiphar Papers 4
Curtis, Joseph. Memoirs of 76
Curtis, Laura J. Christine 4
Now-a-Days 4
Curwen, S. Journal and Letters 76
Curzon, R. Monasteries of the Levant 54

Curson, R. Armenia 54
Cushing, L. S. Of Legislative Assemblies 32
Manual 32
Custis, Geo. W. P. Recollections 76
Cutts, J. M. Conquest of California and New Mexico 68
Cuvier, G. L. Animal Kingdom 43
Cyclopedias 102, 104
Cyclopedia Britannica 102
Cyclopedia of Political and Constitutional Knowledge 33
Cyril Thornton 16
Cyrilla 16
Cyrus the Great, by Abbott 76

D

Dacre, Lady. Tales 4
Adventures of a Chaperon 4
Dadd, G. H. Cattle Doctor 41
Diseases of Cattle 41
Daisy Burns 16
Daisy Chain 16
Dalrio, E. The Game of Chess 46
Daltons 16
Dana, C. A. Household Book of Poetry 89
Dana, D. D. The Fireman 108
Dana, J. D. Mineralogy 40
Custraces 43
Zoophytes 43
Dana, M. S. B. Letters 27
Dana, R. H. Two Years before the Mast 50
To Cuba and Back 50
The Seaman's Friend 49
Dancing Feather 16
Dante 89
D'Arblay, Mme. Memoir of 76
D'Argens, M. Chinese Letters 95
Jewish Spy 95
Darien 16
Darius the Great. Life of 46
Darlington, W. Memoirs of J. Bartram and H. Marshall 76
Darnley 16
Darwin, C. Voyage of a Naturalist 44
The Origin of Species 44
Dassens, G. W. Tales 4
D'Aubigne, J. H. M. History of the Reformation 63
D'Aubigne, T. Life of Cromwell 76
Davenant, W. Works 92
Davenport, R. Italian Dictionary 102
Davenport, R. A. Perilous Adventures 69
David Copperfield 16
Davidson, L. M. Memoir of 76
Poetical Remains 89
Davidson, M. M. Biography of 76
Poetical Remains 89
Davie, W. R. Life of 76
Davies, C. Logic of Mathematics 38
Shades and Shadows 38
Algebra 38
Surveying and Navigation 38
Descriptive Geometry 38
Geometry and Trigonometry 38
Differential and Integral Calculus 38
Analytical Geometry 38
Arithmetic 38
and W. G. Peck. Mathematical Dictionary 38
Davies, C. M. History of Holland 63
Davies, T. A. Answer to Hugh Miller, etc 40

Davis, A. J. Divine Revelations 27
Principles of Nature 36
Davis, C. H. Deposit of Flood Tide 44
Davis, Elizabeth. Autobiography 76
Davis, J. F. China 67
The Chinese 67
Davis, M. L. Memoirs of Aaron Burr 76
Davis, W. H. El Gringo 51
Davy, Sir H. Consolations in Travel 108
Davy, J. Life of Sir Humphrey Davy 76
Day, T. Sandford and Merton 4
Days of Bruce 16
Days of my Life 16
D'Axeglio. Challenge of Barletta 4
Dead Secret 16
Dear Experience 16
Debit and Credit 16
De Bow, G. D. B. Statistical View of the U. S. 34
De Bow's Review 104
Decameron 16
Decatur, S. Life of 76
Decker. Tactique 49
De Custine, M. Russia 54
Deer Slayer 16
Defoe, D. Robinson Crusoe 4
Captain Singleton, etc 4
Memoirs of a Cavalier, etc 4
Moll Flanders, etc 4
Roxana, etc 4
The Great Plague, etc 4
Life of Duncan Campbell, etc 4
De Foix 16
De Forest, J. W. European Acquaintance 54
Indians of Connecticut 68
Seacliff 4
Degerando, M. Self-Education 92
De La Beche, Sir H. Geological Observer 40
De Lagny, G. The Knout, etc 54
De Lalande, L. J. L. Physiology Vegetale 39
De La Motte, F. Ornamental Alphabets 46
Delano, A. A Life on the Plains, etc 61
Delessert, E. Voyage 4
Deleuze, J. P. F. Animal Magnetism 39
De Lolme, J. L. The English Constitution 32
D'l'Orme 16
Demon of Gold 16
Demophilus. Pythagorean Sentences 87
De Morgan, A. Probabilities 38
Demosthenes. Orations on the Crown, etc 87
The Olinthiac, etc 87
Dendy, W. L. Philosophy of Mystery 39
Dendy's Wild Hebrides 54
Denison, Mrs. C. W. Gracie Amber 4
Old Hepsey 4
Denny, Major E. Upland Co., Pa 68
De Pauw. Egyptians and Chinese 87
De Porte's Poets of Germany 89
De Quincey, T. Autobiographical Sketches 76
The Cæsars 95
Opium Eater 95
Essays 95
Theological Essays 95
Klosterheim 95
Miscellanies 95
Letters to a Young Man 95
Political Economy 34
Historical Essays 95

De Quincey, T. The Avenger, etc 4
Derby, G. H. Phœnixiana 4
Des Cartes· Life of 76
Descartes, R. Meditations Metaphysiques, etc 36
Desert Home 16
Deserted Wife 16
Designs for Furniture, etc 47
De Stael, Madame. Alemagne Germany 54
Corinne 11
Des Voeux: Lettres 27
De Tocqueville, A. Democracy in America 33
De Veaux. Falls of Niagara 51
Deverwau 16
De Vries, D. P. Voyages 61
D'Ewes, J. China, etc 67
De Wette. Human Life 27
Theodore 27
Introduction to the Old Testament 27
Dewey, O. Discourses 27
De Witt, C. D. Histoire de Washington 76
Dexter, S. Reminiscences 76
Dexter, Timothy. Life of 76
Dhu, Helen. Stanhope Burleigh 4
Diable Boiteaux 16
Translated 16
Dial, The 104
Diary of a Physician 16
Diary of an Old Doctor 16
Diary of the Howard Association of New Orleans 76
Diary, in MSS., of a Whaling Voyage 89
Dibdin, C. Sea Songs 89
Dibdin, Dr. T. F. Tour in France, etc 54
Dick, T. Works 99
On Society 37
Astronomer 38
Celestial Scenery 38
Sidereal Heavens 38
Dickeson, M. W. Numismatic Manual 94
Dick Markham 16
Dick Tarlton 16
Dickens, C. Memoirs of Grimaldi 76
Pictures from Italy 54
World Here and There 89
David Copperfield 4
Pickwick Club 4
Sketches 4
Barnaby Rudge 4
Christmas Stories 4
Home Narratives 4
Home and Social Philosophy 4
Bleak House 4
Hard Times 4
Little Dorrit 4
Tale of Two Cities 4
New Stories 4
Short Stories 4
Dombey and Son 4
Old Curiosity Shop 4
Oliver Twist 4
The Same 4
Martin Chuzzlewit 4
Nicholas Nickleby 4
Dictionaries 102, 104
Dictionnaire de l'Academic Francaise 102
Historique 72
Technologique 9
Dictionary of Latin Quotations 100
of Quotations from Greek 100
of Love 93
of Modern Slang, Cant, etc 93
Diderot. Œuvres de 99

Didron, M. Christian Iconography 27
Diodorus Siculus. Historical Library 72
Dionysius Halicarnassus. Roman
  Antiquities 63
Diplomacy 31
Directories. San Francisco 61
  New York 61
  Sacramento 61
  Marysville 61
  Boston 61
Discarded Daughter 16
Discipline 16
Discoveries and ·Adventures in
  Africa 67
Disowned
Disraeli, B. Vivian Grey 4
  The Young Duke 4
  Contarini Fleming 4
  Miriam Alroy 4
  Henrietta Temple 4
  Venetia 4
D'Israeli, Isaac. Amenities of Lit-
  erature 95
  Miscellanies of Literature 95
  Curiosities of Literature 95
Distinguished Men 76
Disturnell's N. Y. Register 61
Ditson, G. L. Circassia 67
  Crescent, etc 63
  France, Egypt and Ethiopia 64
  Para Papers 95
Divine Songs 89
Dix, J. A. A Winter in Madeira 54
Dix, W. G. The Unholy Alliance 63
Dixon, E. H. Scenes of a New York
  Surgeon 76
Dixon, Rev. E. S. The Dovecote
  and Aviary 43
  Poultry 43
Dixon, Capt. G. Voyage 69
Dixon, W. H. William Penn 76
Doctor Antonio 16
Doctor Oldham 16
Doctor Thorne 16
Documents of the State of New
  York 68
Documents of Central American
  Affairs 33
Dodd, C. R. Manual of Dignities 94
Dodd's Curiosities of Industry 47
Doddington, G. B. Diary of, Auto-
  biography 76
Doddridge, P. Family Expositor 102
Dodds, J. B. Spirit Manifestations 101
Dudsley, R. Old Plays 92
Doesticks. What He Says 4
  Pluribustah 4
  The Elephant Club 4
Dollars and Cents 16
Dombey and Son 16
Domestic Economy 48, 49
Donaldson, S. J. Lyrics and Poems 86
Doniphan, Capt. Expedition 51
Donovan, E. The Insects of China 43
Donovan, M. Domestic Economy 48
  Chemistry 34
Donna Bianca of Navarre 16
Donne, J. Poetical Works 89
Don Quixote 16
Doomed Chief 4
Dora Deane 16
Doran, Dr. Queens of England 76
  Monarchs Retired from Business 76
  New Pictures and old Panels 76
Dore, by a Stroller in Europe 64
Dorr, B. Churchman's Manual 27
Dorr, Julia. C. Lanmere 4
Doubleday, T. Life of Sir R. Peel 76
Douglas Farm 16

Douglas, Gen. Sir H. Military
  Bridges 38
  Naval Warfare 49
  Fortifications 107
Douglas, Stephen A. Life and
  Speeches of 76
Douglas, W. British Settlements
  in America 68
Dover, Lord. Life of Frederick II 76
Dow, Lorenzo. Writings 97
Downing, A. J. Country Houses 47
  Landscape Gardening 47
  Rural Essays 41
  Fruit and Fruit Trees 41
Downing, C. T. Stranger in China 67
Downing, Major J. My 30 Years
  out of the Senate 101
Downing, S. Hydraulics 38
Dragoon Campaigns 51
Drake, Cavendish and Dampier 61
Drake, J. R. Culprit Fay 89
Drake, S. G. History of Boston 68
  Indian Captivities 61
  Tragedies of the Wilderness 61
Drama, The 92
Draper, J. W. Human Physiology 45
Drayson, Capt. The Earth, etc 44
Dream Life, by Ik. Marvel 95
Dred, by Mrs. Stowe 16
Drelincourt, C. Death 27
Dresses and Costumes 95
Drew, T. R. The Restrictive System 34
Drummond, W. Origines 73
Drury, Anna. Misrepresentation 4
Drury, R. Adventures 67
Dryden, J. Works 92
  Poems 89
Dublin University Magazine 104
Dubois, Abbe. The People of India 67
Duchene, P. Letters 95
Dudley Castle, by Mrs. Sherwood 1
Duer, J. Marine Insurance 32
Duer, W. A. Jurisprudence 33
Dufferin, Lord. A Yacht Voyage,
  etc 59
  Letters from High Latitudes 64
Duggan on Bridge Building 38
Duke, The 16
Duke of Monmouth 16
Dumas, A. The Count of Monte
  Cristo 4
  Edmond Dantes 4
  The Three Guardsmen 4
  The Forty-five Guardsmen 4
  Twenty Years After 4
  Bragelonne 4
  The Iron Mask 4
  The Queen's Necklace 4
  Isabel of Bavaria 4
  Adventures of a Marquis 4
  Emanuel Philibert 4
  Ingenue 4
  The Conscript 4
  The Mohicans of Paris 4
  Royalists and Republicans 92
Dumas, A. Jr. The Demi Monde 92
Dunallan, by Grace Kennedy 16
Duncan Campbell, by D. De Foe 16
Dundonald, Admiral Earl. Services,
  etc 64
Dunglison, R. Medical Dictionary 102
Dunham, S. A. Spain and Portugal 64
  Denmark, Sweden and Norway 64
  Poland 64
  The Germanic Empire 64
  The Middle Ages 64
Duniway, Mrs. Crossing the Plains,
  etc 4
Dunlap's Hymalaya Mountains 103
Dunlap, F. S. Spirit History of Man 101

Dunn Brown in Foreign Parts 64
Dunn, J. Oregon Territory 68
Dunsford, H. Homœopathy 45
Duppa, R., and T. De Quincey.
  Lives of Angelo and Raphael 76
Du Prats, M. History of Louisiana 68
Dupuy, E. A. The Planter's Daugh-
  ter 4
Durer, A. Artist's Married Life 76
Duvallou, B. Vue de la Espanole 54
Duychinck, E. A. and G. L. Cyclo-
  pedia 102
Dwight, B. W. Modern Philology 93
Dwight, H. E. Travels in Germany 55
Dwight, M. A. Mythology 87
Dwight, T. History of Connecticut 68
  The Hartford Convention 68
  The Father's Book 27
  Travels 61
  Character of Jefferson 76
  Life of Gen. Garibaldi 76
  Life of, by W. B. Sprague 76
  The Roman Republic 64
Dymond, J. Inquiry into War 34
Dynevor Terrace 16

E

Eagle Pass, by Cora Montgomery 16
Earl, G. W. Native Races, etc 67
  The Eastern Seas 67
Early Magnetism 101
Eastford 16
Eastlake, C. L. Oil Painting 47
Eastman, Mary. Dacotah 107
Easton, A. Horse-power Railways 38
Easy Nat 16
Easy Warren 16
Eaton, C. Rome 64
Eaton, Gen. W. Life of 76
Ebert, Fred. A. Bibliographical
  Dictionary 107
Ebony Idol 16
Echoes of a Belle 16
Eccleston, J. English Antiquities 64
Eckfeldt and Dubois. Gold and
  Silver Coin 94
  Manual of Coins 94
Eclectic Magazine 104
Economy, Domestic 48, 49
Economy, Political 34
Economy of Human Life 97
Economy 16
Eddies Round the Rectory 16
Eden, R. H. Law of Injunctions 32
Edgar Huntley, by C. B. Brown 16
Edinburgh Review 104
  Selections from 104
Edith Hall
Edith Hale 16
Edith 16
Edmond Dantes 16
Education and Elementary Works 92, 93
Edward Evelyn, by Miss Strickland 16
Edward Mansfield, 16
Edward the Black Prince 76
Edwards, A. M. Life beneath the
  Waters 44
Edwards, C. Finger Rings 89
  The Juryman's Guide ·32
Edwards, E. Memoirs of Libraries 107
Edwards, F. S. Campaign in New
  Mexico 51
Edwards, J. On the Will 97
  Life of, by S. Miller 76
Edwards, Rev. J. E. European
  Life 65
Edgeworth, Miss. Novels 4
Egan, P. The Flower of the Flock 6

Effingham, C. The Virginia Comedians 4
Egypt. Travels in 54, 67
Elder Sister, by Marian James 16
Elder, W. Periscopics 95
  Life of Dr. Kane 76
Eldon, Lord. Life of, by H. Twiss 78
Electricity 39, 40
Elementary Works 92, 93
Elephant. Natural History of 43
Elephant Club 16
El Furiedes 16
Elgin, Earl of. Mission to China 67
Elicabide, M. C. Proce de Fastes Criminels 32
Eliot, G. T. Mill on the Floss 5
  Adam Bede 5
  Scenes from Clerical Life 5
Eliot, J. Life of 76
Elizabeth; or Exiles to Siberia 16
Elizabeth, C. English Martyrology 27
  Siege of Derry 5
Elizabeth, Queen. Life of 76
Ellen de Vere 16
Ellen Middleton 16
Ellery, W. Life of 76
Ellet, C. Physical Geography 61
Ellet, Mrs. Characters of Schiller 95
  Domestic History of the Revolution 68
  Women Artists 76
  Women of the Revolution 76
Elliot, C. W. New England 68
Elliot, J. Life of 76
  Debates in Conventions 33
Elliott, F. R. Fruit Growers' Guide 41
Elliott, S. H. A Look at Home 5
Elliott, W. Carolina Sports 5
Ellis, G. Metrical Romances 89
Ellis, G. E. Life of A. Hutchinson 76
  Life of William Penn 76
  Life of John Mason 77
Ellis, H. T. Hongkong to Manilla 5
Ellis, Mrs. Chapters on Wives 5
  Look to the End 5
  The Mother's Mistake 5
Ellis, Rev. W. Three Visits to Madagascar 57
  Polynesian Researches 69
Elm Tree Tales 16
Elphinstonii, J. Poetæ Sententiosi 89
Elton, R. Memoir of Jonathan Macy 77
Elwood, T. Life 77
Elwyn, A. L. Glossary of Americanisms 93
Emancipation 17
Emanuel Philibert 17
Embury, Mrs. The Waldorf Family 17
Emeline 17
Emerson, A. G. Farmers' Encyclopedia 102
Emerson, R. W. Essays 95
  Nature 95
  Representative Men 95
  English Traits 95
  Poems 89
Emigrant Ships. Report on 34
Emilia Wyndham 5
Emily and her Brothers 17
Emma 17
Emory, Major. Report of Mexican Boundary Commission 61
Encyclopedias, Dictionaries, Concordances and other Books of Reference 102, 104
Encyclopedia Americana 102
  Britannica 102
  of Religious Knowledge 102
Encyclopedie des Jeunes Etudiants 102

Engel, M. Memoirs, etc 61
Engineering, Civil 47, 48
English and Scottish Ballads 89
English Cyclopedia 102
English Cyclopedia of Biography 77
English Hearts and English Hands 107
English Mary 17
Enlistments. Messages in regard to 34
Enneomoser, J. History of Magic 49
Entail 17
Enthusiasm. Natural History of 27
Entz, J. F. Exchange and Cotton Trade 35
Eoline 17
Eothen 55
Ephemeris; or Nautical Almanac 44
Epictetus. Works 87
Epicurean 17
Episodes of Insect Life 44
Epitaphs 100
Epitaphs. A Collection of, by T. J. Pettigrew 100
Eric 17
Erman, A. Siberia 58
Ermina 17
Ernesti, I. C. C. Lateinisch Synonimik 102
Ernest Linwood 17
Ernest Maltravers 17
Ernestin 5
Eros and Anteros 5
Errand Boy 17
Erskine, J. E. Cruise in the Pacific 59
Erskine, Lord. On Revealed Religion 27
Eschylus 87
Esdaile, J. Clairvoyance 39
Esop's Fables 87
Espy, J. P. Meteorological Reports 106
Essays and Reviews 95
Essays on Education 93
Estelle 17
Estelle Grant 5
Ethel 17
Ethel's Love Life 17
Ethelwerd's Old English Chronicle 61
Ethical Philosophy 36, 37
Ethnological Transactions 44
Ethnology 43, 44
Eugene Aram 17
Eugene, Prince. Memoir 77
Eulenspiegel 101
Euler. Natural Philosophy 40
Euripides. Translated 92
Europe. Travels in 54, 57
Europe and the Allies 71
Europe. History of 64
Europe. Reminiscences of 55
European History 63, 66
European Life, Legend, etc 55
Eusebius. Ecclesiastical History 64
Eutaw, by Simms 17
Evans, Augusta J. Beulah 5
Evans, F. W. The Shakers 71
Evans, G. The Dairyman's Manual 41
Evans, S. Youthful Piety 27
  The Society of Friends 27
Evans, T. Old Ballads 89
Evelina, by Miss Burney 17
Evelyn, J. Philosophic Discourse 41
  History of Religion 27
Evening Bulletin 104
Evening Picayune 104
Evenings at Haddon Hall 5
Evenings at Donaldson Manor 17
Everett, A. H. Essays 95
  Life of Patrick Henry 77
  Life of Gen. Warren 77
Everett, E. Life of Washington 77

Everett, E. Life of John Stark 77
  Mount Vernon Papers
  Orations and Speeches 100
Every Woman her own Lawyer 32
Ewbank, T. Machines for Raising Water, etc 38
  Matter and Force 38
  Life in Brazil 51
Executive Papers of the Congress of the United States 33
Exiles of Florida 17
Exmouth, Admiral. Life of 77
Experiences of a Gaol Chaplain 5

F

Faass, Rev. F. W. All for Jesus 27
Faber, G. S. Napoleon 77
Facciolati et Forcellini. Latinitatis Lexicon 102
Fairbanks, G. R. History of St. Augustine 68
Fairburn, W. Information for Engineers 47
Fairchild Family 17
Fairchild, S. L. Last Night of Pompeii 90
Fairfax Correspondence 64
Fairholt, F. W. Tobacco 41
Fairy Tales 17
Fairy Tales of Science 17
Falconer, T. The Discovery of the Mississippi, etc 51
Falconer, W. Poetical Works 90
False Heir, by James 17
Famin, C. Chile, Paraguay, etc 51
Fanaticism 27
Farmer, J. Genealogical Register of New England 94
Farmer of Inglewood Forest 17
Farmers' Magazine 104
Farnham, Eliza W. My Early Days 51
  Prairie Land 51
  California 51
Farnham, J. T. Travels in California 51
Farraday, M. Chemistry and Physics 39
  Chemical Manipulations 39
  Forces of Matter 40
Farrar, F. W. Eric 5
  Julian Home 5
Farrar, Mrs. Life of John Howard 77
Fashion and Famine 17
Father and Daughter 17
Father Clement 17
Father Henson's Story 17
Father's Eye 17
Fathers, Apostolic 27
Faulkland 17
Featherstonhaugh, G. W. Excursions 51
Federalist, The 33
Felt, J. B. Annals of Salem 68
Felton, C. C. Life of W. Eaton 77
Felton, J. H. The Decimal System 108
Female Biography, by M. Hays 17
Female Life among the Mormons 51
Fenelon, F. Telamacus 5
  Lives of Ancient Philosophers 77
Fenn, J. The Paston Letters 95
Ferdinand and Isabella 77
Ferguson, A. The Roman Republic 64
Ferguson, H. English Surnames 93
Ferguson, J. Life of 77
Ferguson, W. Notes of a Professional Life 77
Fern, Fanny. Life and Beauties of 77
  Rose Clark 5
  Ruth Hall 5

Fern, Fanny.
 Leaves from Fanny's Portfolio 6
 Fresh Leaves 5
 Little Ferns 5
Ferrier, J. F. Metaphysics 36
Ferris, B. G. Utah and the Mormons 51
Ferry, G. Vagabond Life in Mexico 51
Fessenden, T. American Gardener 41
Fonchtwanger, L. On Gems 40
 On Fermented Liquors 39
Feuerbach, A. R. Criminal Trials 32
Feuillet, C. The Romance of a
 Poor Young Man 5
Fichte, J. G. Destination of Man 27
 Memoir of, by W. Smith 77
 Nature of the Scholar 95
Field, G. Colors and Pigments 46
Field, H. M. Summer Pictures 65
Field, J. M. Maj. Thorpe's Scenes 5
Field, Margaret. Bertha Percy 5
Field, T. W. Of the Pear Tree 41
Field, Rev. W. Life of Dr. S. Parr 77
Fielding, H. Works 99
 Joseph Andrews 5
 Tom Jones 5
 Works 5
Fielding, T. Select Proverbs 100
Fielding, T. H. Practical Perspec-
 tive 46
 Painting and Lithography 46
Filangieri, C. Ciencia de la Legis-
 lacion 36
Files of English Newspapers 104
 Eastern Newspapers 104
Finance 34, 35
Finances. Reports of 35
Finden, E. The Beauties of Moore 101
Findeu's Views of the Ports and
 Harbors 61
Fine Arts 45, 46
Findlay, A. G. Directory of the
 Pacific 61
Fisher's Daughter 17
Fisher's River Scenes 17
Finke, D. W. First American Chess
 Congress 46
Fiske, J. Grape Culture 41
Fitch, J. Life of 77
Fitz Boodle's Confessions 17
Fitz, of Fitz Ford 17
Fitzgerald, J. E. The Charter, etc.,
 of the Hudson's Bay Co. 68
Flagg, E. Report 36
 Venice 64
Flanders, H. Constitution of the U. S. 33
 Chief Justices of the U. S. 77
Fleetwood 17
Fletcher, J. History of Poland 64
Flint, C. L. Milch Cows 41
Flint, T. Indian Wars 68
 The Last Ten Years 77
Flora Columbiana 41
Florain, M. Nama Pompilius 5
 Gonzalve de Cordove 5
Florence of Worcester's History 64
Florence Dombey 17
Florence De Lacey 17
Florence Macarthy 17
Florence Sackville 17
Florian. Estelle 90
 Moors of Spain 64
Florida. War Documents 35
 The War in 68
Florus, Sallust, etc 87
Flower of the Flock 17
Flower of the Forest 17
Flush Times in Alabama 17
Folger, R. M. British Sterling and
 U. S. Currency 35

Fonblanque, A., Jr. How we are
 Governed 35
Fontevelle. Plurality of Worlds 38
Fool of Quality 17
Foote, A. H. Africa and the Amer-
 ican Flag 58
Foote, Rev. H. W. Virginia 68
Forayers 17
Forbes, A. History of California 68
Forbes, Prof. E. The European
 Seas 43
Forbes, F. E. Five Years in China 68
Forbes, J. Residence in India 68
 Eleven Years in Ceylon 58
 Oriental Memoirs 58
 Norway and its Glaciers 65
Ford, Mrs. Gracie Truman 5
 Mary Bunyan 5
Ford, R. Handbook for Spain 61
 The Spaniards 65
 Gatherings from Spain 65
Forest Days 17
Forest Tragedy 17
Forester, T. Norway 65
 Mesopotamia and Assyria 65
 Paris and its Environs 61
Foresters 17
Forest, R. Military Engineering 49
Forrent, W. S. Sketch of Norfolk,
 Va., etc 68
Forster, J. Essays 64
 Life and Adventures of Oliver
 Goldsmith 77
 Statesmen of the Common-
 wealth of England 77
Forsyth, W. The Captivity of Na-
 poleon 77
Fortune Hunter 17
Fortunes of Glencore 17
Fortunes of Nigel 17
Forty-five Guardsmen 17
Foster and Whitney. Geology of
 Lake Superior 40
Foster, Mrs. Handbook of Litera-
 ture 95
Foster, L. Wayside Glimpses 51
Foster, J. Life and Correspondence 27
 Natural Religion 27
 Essays 95
 Popular Ignorance 95
 Critical Essays 95
 Lectures 95
Fosteriana 95
Four Books. Chinese Novels 17
Four Old Plays 92
Fournier, F. J. Dictionaire des
 Livres 107
Fowler, O. S. Memory, etc 36
Fowler, W. C. English Grammar 93
Fox, C. J. The Reign of James II 64
 Memoirs of, by Lord J. Russell 77
 Memoirs of, by J. Trotter 77
Fox, John. Arts and Monuments 77
Fox, Maria. Memoirs of 77
Fox, W. J. Lectures 95
 Religious Ideas 27
Fragments, Political, of Archytas,
 etc 87
France and England, by de Loisne 77
Francis II. and Charles IX 77
Francis, C. Life of S. Rale 77
 Life of John Eliot 77
Francis, C. S. Handbook of New
 York 61
Francis, G. H. Orators of the Age 77
Francis, J. B. Hydraulic Experi-
 ments 38
Francis, Dr. J. W. Old New York 68
Franche, H. New Theory of Disease 43

Frank Fairlegh 17
Frank Freeman's Barber Shop 17
Frank, Harry and Lucy 17
Frank Leslie's Illustrated News-
 paper 104
Frank Mildmay 17
Frankenstein 17
Franklin, B. Autobiography 77
 Life of, by J. Sparks 77
 Works 99
 Letters to 95
Franklin Journal 104
Franklin, Sir John. The Arctic Re-
 gions 69
Frazer, J. B. Historic Account of
 Persia 67
 Mesopotamia and Assyria 67
Freaks of Fortune 17
Fred Arden 17
Fred Graham 17
Fred Markham 17
Frederick II. History of, by T.
 Carlyle 77
 His Court and Times 77
 by Lord Dover 77
 by T. B. Macaulay 77
Free Masonry 94
Freedley, E. T. The Legal Adviser 35
 On Practical Business, etc 35
Freer's Life of Henry IV 77
Free-Thinker 95
Fremont, J. C. Expedition 51
 Life and Explorations, by C. W.
 Upham 51
 Life, by J. C. Smucker 51
French, B. F. Historical Collections
 of Louisiana 68
 The Iron Trade 71
Fresenius, C. R. Chemical Analysis 39
Fresh Hearts, by the Author of New
 Priest 90
Freytag, G. Debit and Credit 5
Friarswood Post Office 17
Friend, The. A Monthly Journal 104
Friends in Council 95
Frithiof's Saga 90
Froebel, J. Travel in Central Amer-
 ica 51
Froissart, Sir J. Chronicles 64
Frontier Lands of the Christian and
 Turk 55
Frost, Annie. Parlor Charades, etc 100
Frost, J. Incidents of Travel 59
 Wild Scenes in a Hunter's Life 59
 Great Cities of the World 61
 Life of Andrew Jackson 77
 Life of Gen. Taylor 77
Frothingham, R. The Siege of
 Boston 68
Fry, Elizabeth. Memoirs of 77
Fudges in England, by Brown the
 Younger 17
Fuller, Rev. Andrew. Works 27
 Works and Remains 27
Fuller, Frances and Meta. Poems 90
Fuller, Margaret. Life Without and
 Life Within 95
Fuller, Dr. T. History of the
 Worthies of England 77
Fullerton, Lady. Ellen Middleton 5
 Grantley Manor 5
 The Lady Bird 5
Fullom, S. W. The History of
 Woman 71
Fulton, Robt. Life, by C. D. Colden 77
 by J. F. Reigart 77
 by J. Renwick 77
Furness, W. H. History of Jesus 27

Furniss, W. Views across the Sea 55
Future Life, by G. Wood 17

G

Gaarisa Vane, by J. Loud 17
Galignani's New Paris Guide 61
Gallois, M. L. Histoire de la Revolution de 1848 64
Galt, J. Life of Cardinal Wolsey 77
   Life of Lord Byron 77
   Sir Andrew Wylie of that Ilk 5
   The Provost, and other Tales 5
   The Annals of the Parish, and Ayrshire Legatee 5
   The Entail 5
   Laurie Todd 5
Galt, J. M. Of Insanity
Galton, F. The Art of Travel 47
Galvanism 39, 40
Gambos, F. X. Mining Ordinances of Spain 39
Ganoell, W. Life of Roger Williams 77
   Life of S. Ward 77
Garde. Meuble Ancien et Moderne 47
Garden. Manual of the 5
Garibaldi. Life of 77
Gardiner, Wm. The Music of Nature 44
Garland, H. Life of John Randolph 77
Garlick, T. Artificial Propagation of Fish 44
Gardner, A. K. The French Metropolis 55
   Old Wine in New Bottles 55
Gardner, C. K. Dictionary of Officers of the U. S. Army 77
Garnet, J. M. Female Education 93
Gaskell, E. O. Life of Charlotte Bronte 77
Gaskell, Mrs. E. Right at Last 5
   Mary Barton 5
   Lizzie Leigh 5
   Ruth 5
   The Moorland Cottage 5
   North and South 5
   Agnes Gray 5
   My Lady Ludlow 5
Gass, P. Lewis and Clark's Journal 51
Gauss. Theoria Motus 40
Gaut Gurley 17
Gavard, M. Les Rois de France 77
Gay, J. Poetical Works 90
Gay, Madame. Celebrated Saloons 64
Ghost Seer, by Schiller 17
Geiger, E. G. History of the Swedes 64
Geikie, A. Story of a Boulder 40
Geldart, Mrs. T. History of England 64
Gell, Sir W. Topography of Rome 61
Gell and Gandy's Pompeiana 55
Gems from Fable Land 101
Gems of European Art 101
Gems of Spanish Poetry 90
Genealogy 93, 94
Genevieve 17
Gentilhomme Campagnard 17
Gentleman's Magazine 104
Geoffrey of Monmouth's History 64
George, A. Queens of Spain 64
George II. Memoirs of, by Lord Hervey 77
George IV. Life and Times, by G. Croly 77
George Mason 17
George Melville 17

Georges, The. Four Kings of England 77
Georgi, A. My Life and Acts 77
Georgia Scenes 101
Georgian Era 77
Geographical Works 61, 62
Geography. Knight's English Cyclopedia 102
   Murray's Encyclopedia 102
Geography. New English Encyclopedia 61
Geology 40, 41
Gerald Fitzgerald 17
Gerfant 17
Germaine
German Fairy Tales 17
German Popular Tales 17
German Romance 17
Gerbart, E. V. Philosophy and Logic 37
Gerrald, J. Trial for Sedition 32
Gerry, E. Life of, by J. T. Austin 77
Gerstaecker, F. Each for Himself 5
   Wild Sports in the Far West 5
   Journey round the World 59
Gervase Skinner 17
Gervinus, G. G. Shakspeare 95
Gesner, M. Œuvres Choises 90
Getz, G. Precedents in Conveyancing 32
Gibbes, R. W. South Carolina 68
   Mœasaurus, etc 4
   Cuba for Invalids 51
Gibbon, Lieut., and Herndon. Exploration 106
Gibbon, E. Works 95
   The Roman Empire 64
   Life of Mahomet 77
   Memoir of 77
Gibbons, J. S. Banks of New York 71
Gibbs, G. Administrations of Washington and Adams 68
Gibson, W. M. The Prisoner of Weltevreden 55
Giddings, J. R. The Exiles of Florida 51
Gilbert Gurney 17
Gil Blas 17
Gildas' Old English Chronicle 64
Giles, H. Lectures and Essays 95
Gilfillan, G. Literature, etc 95
   Bards of the Bible 77
Gilford, W. Memoir 78
Gillespie, W. M. Of Road-making 38
Gilley's Narrative 55
Gillis, Lieut. J. M. Astronomical Expedition 51
Gilman, C. Southern Matron 5
Gilpin, W. S. Landscape Gardening 41
Girard, C. Fishes 43
Girardin, E. Stories of an Old Maid 5
Giraud, J. P., Jr. Birds 43
Gironiere, P. Phillipine Islands 58
Gisborne, L. Darien 51
Gladstone, T. H. Englishman in Kansas 51
Glannil, J. Disconrses, etc 27
   On Preaching 27
   Modern Sadducism 27
Gleason's Pictorial 104
Gleig, G. R. Chelsea Pensioners 5
   The Country Curate 5
   Warren Hastings 77
   Military Commanders 77
   History of the Bible 71
   The Campaigns at Washington 68
Gleize, J. A. Thalysie 5
   Selena 5
Glenwood, or the Parish Boy 17

Glimpses of Europe
Gobineau, Count. Races of Mankind 44
Godfrey Malvern 17
Godman, J. D. Natural History 43
Godolphin 17
Godwin, P. Handbook of Biography 102
   History of France 64
Godwin, W. Commonwealth of England 64
   Fleetwood 5
   Caleb Williams 5
Goethe's Poems and Ballads 90
Goethe, J. W. Novels and Tales 5
   Wilhelm Meister 5
   Autobiography 77
   Life of, by H. C. Browning 77
   Life of, by G. H. Lewes 77
   Faust 92
   Herman and Dorothea 92
   Iphigenia in Tauris 92
   Dramatic Works 92
   Conversations 95
   Correspondence 95
   Essays on Art 95
   Theory of Colors 46
   Les Affinites Electives 101
   Works in German 90
Gold Fields of St. Domingo 51
Gold Fields of Australia and California 40
Golden Clew 17
Golden Dagon; or the Irawaddi 58
Golden Legacy 17
Goldoni, F. D. Memoirs 77
Goldsmith, Rev. J. View of the World 61
Goldsmith, O. History of England 64
   Animated Nature 43
   Miscellaneous Works 99
   by W. Irving 77
   by J. Forster 77
   Poems 90
   Beattie and Campbell's Poems 90
   Vicar of Wakefield 5
   Deserted Village 5
Gonzalve de Cordove; par Florian 17
Good, J. M. The Book of Nature 43
Goodrich, C. A. British Eloquence 100
Goodrich, F. B. Man upon the Sea 69
Goodrich, S. G. Recollections of a Lifetime 77
   History of all Nations 72
   Parley's Stories 5
Goodwin, E. Lily White
Gordon and Glendenning. The Pinetum 41
Gordon, P. Geography Anatomized 51
Gordon, T. The Greek Revolution 64
Gordon, W. The American Revolution 68
Gore, Mrs. Progress and Prejudice 5
   Cecil 5
   The Hamiltons 5
   Mrs. Armytage 5
   Mothers and Daughters 5
   Abednego the Money Lender 5
Gorrie, P. D. Churches and Sects 27
Gorton, J. Biographical Dictionary 102
Gorton, S. Life of 78
Gosse, P. H. Life 106
   The Aquarium 43
   Naturalist in Jamaica 51
   The Microscope 44
Gouge, W. M. Fiscal History of Texas 85
Gould, A. A. Molusca and Shells 43
Gould, Hannah. Poems
Gourdone. Congress de Paris 64

Government 31, 35
Government and other Reports 105, 106
Grace Lee 17
Gracie Amber 17
Gracie Truman 17
Gradus ad Parnassum 108
Grafton, H. D. On Camp and March 49
Graglia, C. Italian Dictionary 102
Graham, J. History of the U. S. 69
    Life of Geo. Morgan 78
Graham, J. D. Report 51
Graham, T. Chemistry 39
Grammaire Anglaise 93
Grammont's Court of Charles II 64
Granby 17
Grant, Mrs. Memoirs 78
Grant, J. Random Recollections 78
    The British Senate 78
    Life of Mary of Lorraine 78
    Jane Seaton 5
Grant, R. Physical Astronomy 38
Grant, Dr., and the Nestorians 58
Grantley Manor 17
Grattan, T. C. The Netherlands 64
    Agnes de Mansfelt 5
    Jacqueline of Holland 5
    Legends of the Rhine 5
    The Heiress of Bruges 5
Graves, Mrs. Woman in America 51
Gray, A. Botanical Text Book 41
    Plants of the U. S. 41
    Plantæ Wrightianæ 41
Gray, T. Poetical Works 90
    Letters 95
Graydon, A. Memoirs of his own
    Time 76
Grayson, E. Standish the Puritan 5
Greek Anthology 87
Greek Literature. History of 96
Greek Romances of Heliodorus, etc 87
Greek and Roman Antiquities 64
Gregg, J. Commerce of the Prairies 51
Gregg, W. Creed of Christendom 27
Gregororius, F. Corsica 55
Gregory, O. Christian Religion 27
    Letters on Christian Religion 27
Greely, H. Overland Journey 51
    Glances at Europe 55
    Life of 78
Green, C., and S. Y. Wells. The
    Shakers 69
Green, Rev. G. Concordance 27
Green, G. W. Biographical Studies 78
Greene, G. W. Historic Studies 72
Greene, N. Life, by G. W. Greene 78
    by W. G. Simms 78
Green, N. W. The Mormons 51
Green, T. J. Texian Expedition 51
Greenhalgh, T. Lancashire Life 5
Green Hand 17
Greenhow, Horatio. Memorial of 78
Greenhow, R. Oregon and California 69
Greener, W. Science of Gunnery 46
Greenleaf, S. The Four Evangelists 27
Green's Concordances to the Book
    of Common Prayer 102
Greenwood, Grace. A Tour in
    Europe 55
    A Forest Tragedy 5
Grenville Papers 64
Gresham, T. Life of 78
Gretton's Vicisitudes of Italy 64
Grey, Lady J. Life of 78
Grey, Mrs. The Duke 5
    The Little Beauty 5
Greyslaer 17
Griffin, F. W. Qualitative Analysis 39
Griffin, Gerald. Card Drawing 5

Griffin, Gerald. The Half-Sir 5
    The Coiner 5
    The Rival 5
    Tracy's Ambition 5
    Duke of Monmouth 6
    Tales of the Jury Room 5
    Holland Tide—The Aylmers— 5
    The Handy Word—Barber of
    Bantry 5
    Poems and Plays 90
Griffin, J. Chemistry 39
    Chemical Recreations 39
Griffith, W. Marine Architecture 47
Grimaldi, J. Life of 78
Grimm. Popular Tales 5
Grimshaw, W. Life of Napoleon 78
Gringo, Harry. Tales of the Marines 5
Griscom, J. Animal Magnetism 101
Griswold, R. W. Poets of America 78
    Prose Writers of America 78
    Female Poets of America 78
    Poets of England 78
    The Republican Court 78
Grote, E. History of Greece 64
Grove, W. R. Physical Forces 40
Grumbler, A. Miscellaneous Tho'ts 96
Grund, F. J. Aristocracy in America 51
Gwilt, J. Encyclopedia of Archi
    tecture 102
Gwinne's School for Fathers 107
Guardian, The. British Essayists 96
Guarini, B. Il Pastore Fido 90
Guays, L. D. Religious Philosophy 41
Guenon, M. F. Milch Cows 41
Guerrazzi, F. D. Beatrice Cenci 5
    Isabella Orsini 5
Guide Books 61, 62
Guide of Rome 61
Guild, R. A. The Librarian's Manual 107
Guillemard, R. Adventures 55
Guizot, F. Oliver Cromwell 78
    Corneille and his Times 78
    History of Civilization 64
    Revolution of 1640 64
    Representative Government 33
Gullich, T. J., and J. Timbs. Paint
    ing 41
Gulliver's Travels 107
Gunn, T. B. Boarding Houses 96
Gurney, J. J. Evidences of Chris
    tianity 27
    Habit and Discipline 37
Gurowski. Russia as it is 55
    America and Europe 69
Gus Howard, by J. F. Smith 18
Gutzlaff, C. Sketch of Chinese His
    tory 67
    Three Voyages 58
Guy Carlton 18
Guy Livingstone 18
Guy Mannering 18
Guy Rivers 18
Guyot, A. Earth and Man 44
    Physical Geography 61
Guzman D'Alfarache 18
Gypsey Babes 17
Gypsey Chief 17
Gypsey Mother 17

H

HANNUNNAM, Lieut. My Last Cruise 51
Habits of Good Society 93
Hacklander. Countess of St. Albans 18
Hadji Baba 18
Hagar the Martyr 18
Hai Evn Yockdan 5

Hair, T. H. Collieries of Northum-
    berland 40
Hakluyt, R. Navigations, etc 60
Haldane, R. and J. Memoirs of 78
Hale, C. E. Kansas and Nebraska 51
Hale, D. Memoir of 78
Hale, H. Ethnography 44
Hale, S. History of United States 69
Hale, Mrs. S. J. Woman's Record 78
    Poetical Quotations 100
Half-Sir 18
Haliburton, T. C. Rule and Misrule 69
Haliburton, Judge. Sam Slick 6
    Nature and Human Nature 6
Hall, A. O. Old Whitney's Christ-
    mas Trot 6
Hall, B. F. Opinions of Attorney
    Generals 32
Hall, D. R. Teaching a Science 93
    Frank Freeman's Shop 6
Hall, E. The Puritans 71
Hall, J. Life of T. Posey 78
    Legends of the West 6
Hall, Miss. American Cookery 48
Hall, Mrs. New Book of Cookery 48
Hall, Mrs. M. Queens of England 78
Hall, Rev. R. Works 27
Hall, R. D. Eastern Vermont 69
Hall, S. C. Book of Gems 90
    British Ballads 90
    Midsummer Eve 6
    The Outlaw 6
Hall, Mrs. Ireland 55
Hall, Mr. and Mrs. Handbook of
    Dublin 61
Hall, H. W. Voyage of the Nemesis 60
Hallam, H. Constitutional History 64
    Middle Ages 64
    Literature of Europe 71
Halleck, F. Poetical Works 90
    Selections from the British Poets 90
Halleck, W. H. Military Art and
    Science 49
Hallig, by Biernatzki 18
Halliwell, J. O. Archaic Words 93
Hallock, W. A. Life of Justin Ed-
    wards 78
Hamilton, A. The Federalist 33
    Works 33
    Life of, by J. Renwick 78
    by his son, J. C. Hamilton 78
Hamilton, A. G. New Key 103
Hamilton, G. Physiology 43
Hamilton, J. Sinai, the Hedjaz, etc 55
Hamilton, J. C. History of the U. S. 69
Hamilton, R. Merchandise 47
Hamilton, Sir W. Philosophy 36
    Lectures on Metaphysics 36
    Logic 37
Hamiltons 18
Hammond, J. Life of Silas Wright 78
Hammond, J. D. Political History
    of New York 71
Hammond, J. H. Architect 47
Hammond, Capt. M. Memoir of 78
Hammond, S. H. Wild Northern
    Scenes 51
    and L. Mansfield. Country
    Margins 96
Hampden, A. Hartley Norman 6
Hampden, John. Memorials of 78
Hampden, R. D. Life of Aquinas 36
Hampton Heights 18
Hancock, T. The Friends in Ireland 64
Handbooks for Home Improvement 48
Handbook of Games 46
Hand and Word 18
Handel. Life of 78
Handy Andy 18

Hanger, C. H. Thoughts 90
Hanna, Rev. W. Life and Writings of Chalmers 27
Hannay, J. Satire and Satirists 96
Hannibal. Life of, by T. Arnold 78
by Abbott 78
Hans of Iceland 18
Happy Grandmother 18
Happy Home 18
Harbaugh, Rev. H. The True Glory of Woman 96
Harcourt's Algeria 68
Hard Times 6
Hardee, Col. W. J. Tactics 49
Hardy, Lieut. Travels in Mexico 51
Hare and Wallace. Decisions 32
Hare, J. Guesses at Truth 27
Hare, R. Explosiveness of Nitre 40
Hargraves, E. H. Australia 61
Hurlan, R. Fauna Americana 43
Harland, Marion. The Hidden Path 6
Moss Side 6
Alone 6
Nemesis 6
Harold, by Bulwer 18
Harold Tracy 18
Harp of a Thousand Strings, etc 18
Harper, R. G. Select Works 99
Speeches 100
Harper's Gazetteer of the World 61
Harper's Weekly 104
Harrington 18
Harrington's Sermons 27
Harris, J. The Great Commission 27
The Great Teacher 27
Works 99
Harris, Capt. W. C. Wild Sports in Africa 68
Harry Ashton 18
Harry Coverdale's Courtship 18
Harry Harson 18
Harry Lee 18
Harry Lorrequer 18
Harry Muir 18
Hart, J. D. Practice of Courts of California 32
Harte, W. Gustavus Adolphus 78
Hartley, D. On Man 37
Hartley Norman 18
Hartman, T. Charity Green 6
Harvard. Catalogus, etc 106
Harvey, W. H. Nereis Doreali-Americana 41
Hasheesh Eater 96
Hastings, Sybil. Harvestings, etc 90
Hastings, Warren. State of the East Indies 64
by G. R. Gleig 78
Hatch, Cora. Discourses on Religion 27
Hatfield, R. G. House Carpenter 47
Hau Kiou Choan 18
Haunted Homestead 18
Haussey, Baron D. Great Britain 65
Havelock, Gen. Life of, by J. T. Headley 78
by Rev. W. Brock 78
Haven, Alice B. The Coopers 6
Loss and Gain 6
Haven, J. Mental Philosophy 36
Hawker, Col. P. Guns and Shooting 46
Hawkes, Rev. F. L. Church in Virginia 69
in Maryland 69
History of North Carolina 69
Monuments of Egypt 67
Com. Perry's Expedition to Japan 68
Hawkins, J. W. Life of 78

Hawkins. The Human and Animal Frame 108
Hawks, F. L. Cyclopedia of Biography 78
Hawks of Hawks-Hollow 18
Hawksworth, J. Voyages in the Southern Hemisphere 60
Hawthorne, N. Life of Franklin Pierce 78
The Marble Faun 6
The Snow Image, and other Twice-told Tales 6
Twice-told Tales 6
The Blithedale Romance 6
The Scarlet Letter 6
House of the Seven Gables 6
Mosses from an Old Manse 6
Hayden, W. B. Modern Spiritualism 27
Haydon, B. R. Autobiography 18
Haydn, J. Dictionary of Dates 72
Hayes, Dr. J. J. Arctic Boat Journey 51
Hayling Island. Topographical, etc 51
Hays, M. Female Biography 78
Hayward's Gazetteer of Massachusetts 61
Hayward, C. Life of John Cabot 78
Hazard, S. Pennsylvania Archives 69
Hazen, E. Technology 93
Hazlitt, Helen. The Heights of Eidelberg 6
Heart's Ease 6
Hazlitt, W. Life of Napoleon 78
The Plain Speaker 96
Table Talk 96
The Round Table 96
Criticisms on Art 96
Of Shakspeare's Plays 96
Lectures on the English Poets 96
On English Comic Writers 96
The Dramatic Literature 96
Head, F. R. Life of Bruce 55
Head, G. Forest Scenes 61
Headley, J. T. The Adirondack 61
Life of Washington 78
Washington and his Generals 78
Napoleon and his Marshals 78
General Havelock 78
General Scott 78
Life of Cromwell 78
Life of Andrew Jackson 78
Letter from Italy 55
The Alps and the Rhine 55
Rambles and Sketches 65
Imperial Guard 64
The Last War with England 69
Sacred Mountains 27
Sacred Scenes and Characters 27
Headley, P. C. Life of Lafayette 78
Josephine the Empress 78
Mary, Queen of Scots 78
Headlong Hall 18
Head of the Family 18
Headsman 18
Heart, by Tupper 18
Heart Histories, etc 18
Heart of Midlothian 18
Heartsense 18
Hearts Unveiled 18
Heber, R. Life of 78
Poetical Works 90
Journey through India 58
Hecker, J. G. The Soul 27
Hector O'Halloran 18
Hedge of Thorns 18
Heek. Iconographic Encyclopedia 103
Heeren, A. H. L. Manual of Ancient History 72
Ancient Greece 64

Heidelberg 18
Heidenmauer 18
Heights of Eidelberg 18
Heine, H. Fammtlichte Werke 90
Heir of Redcliffe 18
Heiress of Greenhurst 18
Heiress of Bruges 18
Helen 18
Helen and Arthur 18
Heliodorus, Longus, etc 87
Hell, X. Steppes of the Caspian 68
Helme, Mrs. Farmer of Inglewood Forest 6
Heloise 6
Helper, H. R. The Impending Crisis 33
Helps, A. The Spanish Conquest 69
Helvetius. On Man 36
Hemans, Felicia. Poetical Works 90
Memorials of 78
Henderson, A. History of Wines 48
Henderson, W. A., and D. Hughson. Cookery 48
Henfrey, A. Botany 41
Hennell, C. C. Origin of Christianity 28
Hennings' Statutes of Virginia 31
Henrietta Temple 18
Henry IV. of France 78
Henry, C. S. History of Philosophy 37
Henry de Pomeroy 18
Henri de la Tour 18
Henry Esmond 18
Henry, J. Moravian Life 51
Henry Milner 18
Henry of Ofterdingen 18
Henry, Patrick. Life of, by Everett 78
by Wm. Wirt 78
Henry St. John, Gentleman 18
Henry, W. S. Campaign Sketches 69
Henslow, Rev. J. S. Botany 41
Hentz, Caroline Lee. The Lost Daughter 6
Rena; or The Snow Bird 6
Love and Marriage 6
The Banished Son 6
Eolina 6
The Planter's Northern Bride 6
Helen and Arthur 6
Marcus Warland 6
Linda 6
Robert Graham 6
Courtship and Marriage 6
Ernest Linwood 6
Heptameron de la Reine de Navarre 18
Her Age 18
Herbert, Edward Lord. Life 78
Herbert, G. Poetical Works 90
Herbert, H. W. Frank Forester's Field Sports 46
Fish and Fishing in the U. S. 46
American Game in its Seasons 46
Frank Forester's Sporting Scenes 46
Frank Forester's Horse 46
Hints to Horse-keepers 44
The Horse of America 44
Captains of the Old World 78
Persons and Pictures 18
Captains of the Roman Republic 78
Henry VIII. and his Six Wives 78
Herbert, L. Engineers' Encyclopedia 103
Herbert, W. London Livery Companies 71
Herder, J. G. Philosophy of History 79
Hermits' Dell 18
Herndon, W. D. The Amazon 51
Herodotus 87
Heroes of Europe 108
Herrick, R. Hesperides 90
Herring, R. Samples of Paper 47

Herschel, Sir J. Scientific Inquiry 44
Treatise on Astronomy 38
Herschel, R. H. Journey to Syria 55
Herschel, Sir W. Of Natural History 44
Hertha 18
Hervey, Lord. Memoirs of George II 78
Hervey, T. K. Book of Christmas 90
Hervey, G. W. The Rhetoric of
Conversation 93
Hesiod. Calimachus and Theogenes 87
Hesperian 104
H. Family 18
Hewitt, M. E. Poems 90
Hickok, L. P. Moral Science
Rational Cosmology
Hide and Seek 18
Hidden Path 18
Higgins, G. Celtic Druids 71
Higgins, W. M. The Earth 44
High Life in New York 18
Highland Widow 18
Hildreth, P. Banks 35
Hildreth, R. Lives of Infamous
Judges 78
Japan 58
Theory of Morals 77
Theory of Politics 33
History of the United States 69
Hildreth, S. P. The Northwest
Territory 69
Hilpert, J. L. German and Eng
lish Dictionary 103
Hill, G. C. Capt. John Smith 78
Life of Gen. Putnam 78
Hill, Rev. Rowland. Life 78
Hill, T. Geometry and Faith 28
Hillard, G. S. Six Months in Italy 55
Life of Capt. John Smith 78
Hills of Shatamuc 18
Hind, J. Farriery 41
Hind, J. R. The Solar System 38
Hines, G. Oregon 69
Hinman, R. Letters 64
Histoire, etc., la Revolution de
Russie 72
Historic Doubts of Napoleon 72
Historical Magazine 69
Historical Collections of Louisiana 69
of South Carolina 69
of Pennsylvania 69
of New York 69
of Florida 69
History 61, 73
General 72, 73
Special 71, 72
of Education 93
of Silk, Cotton, etc 47
of the Devil, by D. De Foe 18
of the Protestant Church in
Hungary 64
of the United States 69
Hitchcock, Prof. E. Geology of the
Globe 40
Elementary Geology 40
Hitchcock, E. A. Alchemists 49
Hittell, T. S. Adventures of J. C.
Adams 78
Hittell, J. S. Evidences against
Christianity 28
Phrenology 45
Hive of the Bee Hunters 18
Hobart, N. Life of Swedenborg 78
Hobbes, T. Works 28
Ecclesiastical History 28
Hobson, B. Works in Chinese 45
Hodson, Major. Twelve Years in
India 58
Hoffman, C. F. A Winter in the
West 51

Hoffman, C. F. Jacob Leisler 78
Greyslaer 6
Hoffman, D. Legal Study 34
Rogarth, W. Works 101
Hogg, James. Brownie of Bodsbeck 6
Hogg's Weekly Instructor 104
Holbach, Baron. Good Sense 28
Holbein, H. The Dance of Death 28
Holberg, Lewis. Memoir 78
Holbrook, J. The Mail Bags 78
Holbrook, J. E. Herpetology 43
Holbrook, S. F. Three-score Years 78
Holcombe, J. P. The Merchants'
Book of Reference 35
American Cases 33
The Law of Debtor and Creditor 33
Holgate, J. B. Genealogy 94
Holland, J. Poems 90
Bitter Sweet 90
Holland, J. G. The Bay Path 6
Miss Gilbert's Career
Holland, Lady. Memoir of Rev.
Sidney Smith 78
Holland, Lord. Foreign Reminis-
cences 55
Holland Tide 18
Hollande et la Belgique 61
Holliday, J. Life of Earl of Mans-
field 78
Holmes, A. Annals of America 69
Holmes, E. Life of Mozart 78
Holmes, Mrs. Meadow Brook 6
Tempest and Sunshine 6
Lena Rivers 6
Homestead on the Hillside 6
Cousin Maude and Rosamond 6
Dora Deane 6
Maggie Miller, etc 6
Holmes, O. W. Poems 90
Holmsby House 18
Holthouse, H. J. Law Dictionary 32
Holton, P. F. New Granada in the
Andes 51
Home, by Anna A. Leland 18
Home, by Miss Bremer 18
Home and Social Philosophy 18
Home and World 18
Home as Found, by Cooper 18
Home Comforts 18
Home, H. Elements of Criticism 96
History of Man 73
Home Hits and Hints 18
Home Influence, by Grace Aguilar 18
Home in the Valley, by Emilie
Carlen 18
Home is Home 18
Home Journal 104
Home Memories, by Mrs. C. Brock 18
Home Narratives, by Dickens 18
Home Scenes, etc., by Grace Aguilar 18
Homer's Iliad and Odyssey 87
Iliad, literally translated 87
Odyssey. Translated 87
Translated 87
Homes of American Authors 95
Homestead on the Hillside 18
Homeward Bound 18
Honn, J. S. Cyclopedia of Com-
merce 103
Honan, M. B. Personal Adventures
in Italy 55
Hone, W. Works 99
The Every-Day Book 96
The Year Book 96
Ancient Mysteries and Plays 96
Hood, E. P. John Milton 78
Hood, G. History of Music in New
England 73
Hood, T. Poems

Hood, T. Memoirs of, by his
Daughter and Son 78
Hood's Own 18
Prose and Verse 96
Tylney Hall 6
Up the Rhine 55
Whims and Waifs 90
Hooke, N. History of Rome 64
Hook, T. Jack Brag 6
Gilbert Gurney 6
The Widow and the Marquis 6
All in the Wrong 6
The Parson's Daughter 6
Maxwell 6
Gervase Skinner 6
Cousin William 6
Hooker, W. Medical Delusions 45
Physician and Patient 45
Hope Leslie, by Mrs. Sedgwick 18
Hope, T. Anastasius 6
Costume of the Ancients 94
Origin and Prospects of Man 49
Hopkins, E. Geology and Magnetism 40
Hopkins, S. The Puritans 64
Hopper, I. Life of 78
Hoppin, J. M. Notes of 55
Horace. Works of, translated 87, 90
Horatius. Opera 87
Hornby, Mrs. E. Stamboul 55
Horne, T. H. Privateers, Cap-
tures, etc 108
Horse-Shoe Robinson 18
Hortensius. Reason and Elegance 96
Horticulture 41, 42
Horwitz, O. Brushwood 55
Hosmer, H. L. Adela, the Octoroon 6
Hosmer, W. H. C. Poems 90
Hotchkin, J. H. Western New
York 69
Hot Corn 18
Houdin, R. Memoirs of 78
Hough, Major. British Exploits in
India 67
Hours of Infancy 18
House of Seven Gables 18
Household of Bouverie 6
Household of Sir Thomas More 18
Household Words 104
Novels and Tales 6
Housman, R. F. English Sonnets 90
Houssaye, A. Le Roi Voltaire 78
Men and Women 78
Philosophers and Actresses 78
Houston, Mrs. Texas, etc 51
Houston, S. Life of 79
Hovedem, Roger de. Annals 64
Hovey's Magazine of Horticulture 104
Howard, B. C. The Dred Scott
Case 33
Howard, H. Poetical Works 90
Howard, J. Life of, by Mrs. Farrar 79
Howard, L. Ecclesiastes and Wis-
dom 28
How Could He Help It 18
Howe, Admiral. Life of 19
Howe, Julia W. The World's Own 90
A Trip to Cuba 51
Howe, H. Virginia Collections 69
Howe, Gen. Sir W. His Conduct in
America 64
Howell, J. Dodona's Grove 90
Howland, Jno. Life of, by E. M.
Stone 79
Howitt, Anna M. Art Student 55
Howitt, Mary. History of the U. S. 61
Calendar of the Seasons 90
Howitt, R. Australia 58
Howitt, W. A Boy's Adventure 6
Tallengetta 6

Howitt, W.
  Students' Life in Germany 55
  German Experiences 55
  Australia 58
  Rural Life in England 55
Howitt, Wm. and Mary. Stories 6
Hoyle's Games 46
Hoyt, E. Military Art 49
Hubbard, F. M. Life of W. R.
  Davie 79
Hubbard, J. N. Life of Maj. Van
  Campan 79
Hubback, Mrs. May and December 6
  The Three Marriages 6
Huber. V. A. English Universities 64
Huc, M. Journey through Tartary,
  Thibet 58
  The Chinese Empire 58
  Christianity in China, etc 58
Hudson, H. N. Lectures on Shaks-
  peare 96
Hudson, H. Life of 79
Hughes, J. T. Doniphan's Epedition 61
Hughes, T. M. Journey to Lisbon 55
Hugo, V. Bug-Jargal 6
  Hans of Iceland 6
  Hunchback of Notre Dame 6
Huish, R. Of Bees 43
  Memoirs of O'Connell 79
Human Nature 28
Human Progression. Theory of 28
Human Soul 28
Humboldt, A. Cosmos 60
  La Nueva Espana 35
  Views of Nature 44
  Letters to Varnhagen von Ense 108
  Travels in America 81
  The same, abridged 51
  The Island of Cuba 51
  Life, Travels and Books
    and William. Lives of, by
    Klencke 79
  Lives of, by J. Bauer 79
Hume, D. Life of 79
  History of England 64
  Philosophical Works 90
Humor 100, 101
Humphrey's and Westwood's Moths 43
Humphreys, H. N. The Coin Col-
  lector 94
  The Coinage 94
  Of Writing 46
Hunchback of Notre Dame 18
Hungarian Brothers 18
Hundley, D. R. Social Relations 51
Hundred Boston Orators 79
Hungarian Castle 18
Hungerford, J. The old Plantation 6
Hunt, F. .The Library of Commerce 104
  Lives of American Merchants 79
Hunt's Merchants' Magazine 104
Hunt, F. K. The Rhine and its
  Scenery 55
  The Rhine Book 61
Hunt, G. H. Outram and Have-
  lock's Campaign 67
Hunt, Leigh. A Book for a Corner 6
  Poetical Works 90
  Selections from Beaumont and
    Fletcher 92
  Autobiography 79
  Indicator 96
  Stories from the Italian Poets 96
  The Town 96
  Selections from English Authors 96
  Imagination and Fancy 96
  Essays and Miscellanies 96
  Men, Women and Books 96
  The Palfrey 96

Hunt, Leigh. Worth and Wealth 96
Hunt, R. The Poetry of Science 40
  Manufactures in Metals 47
Hunt, T. F. Parsonages, Alms
  Houses, etc 47
  Architettura Campestre 47
  Tudor Architecture 47
Hunt, V. D. The Horse and his
  Master 43
Hunter, J. Captivity among the
  Indians 51
  The Founders of New Plymouth 69
  The Separatists of the time of
    James I 79
Huntingdon, Henry of. Chronicle 64
  Husband and Wife 90
Hussar, The 55
Hutchings' Magazine 104
Hutchinson, A. Life of 79
Hutchinson, Col. Memoirs of 79
Hutchinson, F. The Passions and
  Affections 37
  On Witchcraft 28
  Moral Philosophy 28
Hutchinson, T. History of Massa-
  chusetts 69
Hutton, W. Life 79
Hyde, J. F. The Chinese Sugar Cane 41

I

Iamblicus. Mysteries 87
Iceland, Greenland, etc 69
Iconographic Encyclopedia 103
Ida May 18
Ida Norman 18
Idler 18
Idler, The. British Essayists 96
Illumines, Essai sur la Secte de 72
Illustrated Books 101
Illustrated Catalogue of the Great
  Exhibition 101
  of Art Industry in Paris 101
  of Art Industry in Dublin 101
Illustrated London News 99
Illustrated Register of Rural Affairs 41
Impey, Sir J. E. Memoir of 79
Inchbald, Mrs. The Simple Story
  Nature and Art 6
India. Pictorial, Descriptive, etc 58
India, by Mrs. Southworth 18
Indian Biography, by B. B. Thacher 79
Indian Fairy Book 6
Indian Pilgrims 19
Indiana. Laws of 31
Inebriate's Hut 19
Infant's Grave 19
Infirmary 19
Information for the People 103
Ingenue 19
Ingersoll, J. History of the late
  War . 19
Ingoldsby, G. My Cousin Nicholas 6
Ingoldsby Legends 19
Ingraham. Rev. J. H. The Pillar
  of Fire 55
  Prince of the House of David 28
  Throne of David 28
  The Sunny South 51
Ingulph. Chronicle of Croyland 64
Initials 19
Ink. History of 41
Inquire Within 48
Insects. Natural History of 43
International Magazine 104
Intimate Friends 19
Ireland, J. B. Wall-Street to Cash-
  mere 58

Ireland, W. H. History of Kent 64
Irish, The, at Home and Abroad 85
Iron Cage 19
Iron Cousin 19
Iron Mask 19
Irving, J. T. Indian Sketches 61
  The Attorney 6
Irving, L. Cookery 48
Irving, T. Conquest of Florida 69
Irving, Washington. Works 99
  History of New York 99
  Sketch Book 99
  Life of Columbus and his Com-
    panions 99
  Bracebridge Hall 99
  Tales of a Traveler 99
  Astoria 99
  Crayon Miscellany 99
  Oliver Goldsmith 99
  Mahomet and his Successors 99
  Conquest of Granada 99
  Alhambra 99
  Wolfert's Roost 99
  Washington 79
  Vignette Illustrations of 101
  Biography of Margaret M. Da-
    vidson 79
Irvingiana 79
Isabel 19
Isabel of Bavaria 19
Isabella Orsini · 19
Island Home 19
Israel Potter 19
Italie, Nouveau Guide 61
Iturbide, A. Memoirs 79
Ivanhoe 19
Ivors 19
Izard, Ralph. Correspondence 69

J

Jack Brag 19
Jack Hinton 19
Jack Hopeton 19
Jack Tier 19
Jacob Faithful 19
Jacqueline 19
Jacqueline of Holland 6
Jackson, Andrew. Life of, by J.
  Parton 79
  Pictorial Life of, by J. Frost 79
  Life of, by W. Cobbett 79
  Life of, by J. Jenkins 79
  Life of, by J. T. Headley 79
Jackson, D. Alonzo and Melissa 6
Jackson, J. R. What to Observe 44
Jacobs, W. The Precious Metals 40
Jaeger, B. Insects 47
Jaenisch, C. F. Chess Preceptor 46
James II. The Reign of 79
James, G. P. R. Eminent Foreign
  Statesmen 79
  Charlemagne 79
  Louis XIV 79
  Richard Cœur-de-Lion 79
  Edward, the Black Prince 79
  History of Chivalry 64
  Leonora D'Orco 7
  Lord Montague's Page 7
  Darnley 7
  Forest Days 7
  Rose D'Albret 7
  The Convict 7
  Arrah Neil 7
  Arabella Stuart 7
  Heidelberg 7
  Russell 7
  The Smuggler 7

James, G. P. R.
　Morley Ernstein 7
　Agincourt 7
　The False Heir 7
　Castle Ehrenstein 7
　The Step-Mother 7
　Sir Theodore Broughton 7
　Man at Arms 7
　Beauchampe 7
　Philip Augustus 7
　D' l'Orme 7
　The Cavalier 6
James, J. A. Young Man's Friend 96
James, Marion. The Elder Sister 7
　Ethel 7
James, W. Military Occurrences 69
　Naval Occurrences 69
Jameson, Mrs. Sacred and Legend-
　ary Art 96
　Sketches 96
　Celebrated Female Sovereigns 79
　Stories and Memoirs 79
　Characteristics of Women 79
　Beauties of Charles II 79
　Early Italian Painters 79
Jamieson, A. Dictionary of Science 38
Jane Eyre 19
Jane Seton 19
Jane Talbot 19
Japan. Report of the Expedition to 35
Japanese Manners and Customs 58
Japhet in Search of a Father 7
Jardine, Sir W. Naturalists' Library 43
Jarves, J. J. Sandwich Islands 60
　Italian Sights 55
　Parisian Sights 55
　Art Hints 46
　Kiana 7
Jaufrey the Knight 19
Jay, John. Life of, by Wm. Jay 79
　Life of, by J. Renwick 79
Jeaffreson, J. C. Isabel 7
　Novels, etc 96
Jeanie's Diary 19
Jefferson, T. The Youth of 79
　Life of, by H. S. Randall 79
　Writings 99
　The Writings of, by H. Lee 96
Jeffrey, F. Contributions 96
Jenks, J. W. Rural Poetry 90
Jenkins, J. Life of Jackson 79
Jenkins, J. S. Political Parties 33
Jenny Lind. By N. P. Willis 79
Jenyns, Soame. Works 99
Jerrold, B. Jerrold's Wit 96
Jerrold, D. Cakes and Ale 7
　Mrs. Caudle 7
　Punch's Letter Writer 7
　Sketches of the English 7
　Punch's Letters 7
　Men of Character 7
　A Man Made of Money 7
　Chronicles of Clovernook 7
　Comedies and Dramas 92
　Life, by his Son 79
Jesse, E. Natural History 43
　Anecdotes of Dogs 43
Jesse, J. H. Memorials of London 64
　England under the Stuarts 64
　The Pretenders 64
Jewett, J. R. Captivity 52
Jewitt, E. Missal Painting 46
Job Abbot 28
John Halifax 19
Johnson, Anna. Peasant Life 55
　Cottages of the Alps 55
Johnson, A. B. Our Union 33
Johnson, C. Highwaymen and
　Pirates 79

Johnson, C.
　History of the Pyrates 69
　Travels in Abyssinia 58
Johnson, E. Nuces Philosophicæ 37
　Hydropathy 45
Johnson, G. W. John Selden 79
Johnson, J. Typographia 47
Johnson, S. Dictionary 103
　English Poets 79
　Life of, by Boswell 79
　Works 99
Johnson, Mrs. S. B. Hadji in Syria 55
Johnsoniana 79
Johnston, G. Zoophytes 43
　Introduction to Conchology 43
Johnston, Capt. A. R. New Mexico 52
Johnston, J. F. Chemistry of Com-
　mon Life 48
Johnston, A. K. Atlas to Alison's
　Eu ope 64
　Atlas 61
　of Physical Geography 61
Johnston, J. W. F. Agriculture 42
Joly, J. C. Compania de Jesus 64
Jomini. De la Guerre 49
　Tableau de la Guerre 49
　Atlas pour les Dernieres Guerres 49
　Guerres de Frederic II 49
Jones. Life of Rowland Hill 79
Jones, E. The Emperor's Vigil, etc 90
Jones, H. Maria. Pride of the Village 7
　The Gipsey Mother 7
　Rosaline Woodbridge 7
　The Gipsey Chief 7
Jones, Rev. G. The Zodiacal Light 38
Jones, J. Ecclesiastical Researches 28
Jones, J. B. Border War 7
　Freaks of Fortune 7
Jones, J. M. Naturalist in Bermuda 58
Jones, J. Paul. Life of 79
Jones, Rev. T. G. Recreations 96
Jones, T. K. The Animal Kingdom 43
Jones, T. W. Sight and Hearing 45
Jones, Sir W. Life of 79
Jonson, Ben. Works 92
Jopling, J. Perspective 46
Joseph Andrews 7
Joseph. Story of 79
Josephine, the Empress. Life of, by
　J. S. Memes 79
　by Abbott 79
　by P. C. Headley 79
Josephus, F. History of 72
Jouffroy, T. S. Ethics 37
Jourdan, A. J. L. Dictionnaire des
　Termes 103
Journal of Medical Sciences 105
　of the Embassy to China 58
　des Mines 104
　of Commerce 104
　Houses of Lords and Commons 104
　Franklin Institute 104
Judd, S. Margaret 7
Judson, Rev. A. Life, by F. Way-
　land 79
Judson, Emily C. Life and Letters 79
Julia, The. Yacht Voyage 107
Julian, by Wm. Ware 19
Julian the Emperor 28
Julian Home 19
Juliana Oakley 19
Julian Percival 19
Jane Clifford 19
Junot, Mad. Memoirs of 79
Jurisprudence 31, 35
Justin Cornelius 87
Justin Martyr 28
Justinian. Corpus Juris Civilis 32
Juvenal. Persius Sulpicia 98

K

Kaempfer, E. L'Empire du Japon 67
Kaloolah 19
Kane, Dr. E. K. Expedition 52
　Second Expedition 58
　Life of 79
Kane, R. Chemistry 39
Kangaroo Hunters 19
Kant, E. Pure Reason 36
　Metaphysics 36
Kate Aylesford 19
Katherine Ashton 19
Katherine Seward 19
Kathie Braude 107
Katie Stewart 19
Kavanagh, by Longfellow 19
Kavanagh, Julia. Women of France 79
　The Two Sicilies 55
　Daisy Burns 7
　Adele 7
　St. Gildas 7
　Grace Lee 7
　Nathalie 7
　Rachael Gray 7
　Seven Years 7
Keating. H. H. Expedition 52
Keats, J. Poetical Works 90
　Life, Letters, etc 79
Keddie, W. Anecdotes 101
Keightley, T. History of England 64
　Outlines of History 72
　Mythology 88
　Fairy Mythology 88
Kelly and O'Kelley's 19
Kelly, J. Scottish Proverbs 100
Kelly, J. W. Excursions 52
Kelly, P. Universal Cambist 103
Kelly, W. Victoria 58
Kelly, W. K. History of Russia 58
Kelt, T. Mechanics' Text Book 39
Kemble, Frances A. Poems 90
Kemp, E. How to lay out a Gar-
　den, etc 43
Kempis, T. A. Imitation of Christ 28
Kendall, G. W. Expedition 52
　War with Mexico 69
Kenilworth 19
Kennedy, Grace. Dunallan 7
　Father Clement 7
Kennedy, J. P. Rob of the Bowl 7
　Swallow Barn 7
　Horse-Shoe Robinson 7
　The Hawks of Hawk's Hollow 7
　Annals of Quodlibet 16
　Life of Wm. Wirt 79
Kenneth 19
Kenny, C. Chess 108
Kenrick, J. Ancient Egypt 67
　Primitive History 67
Kent, J. Commentaries 32
Keppel, H. Borneo 34
Kerr, J. Poultry 43
Kettrell, T. P. Southern Wealth, etc 35
Kewen, E. J. C. Poems 90
Keyser, R. Religion of the North-
　men 64
Khartoon and the Nile 58
Kiana, by J. J. Jarves 19
Kidd, S. China 58
Kidder, D. P. Brazil 52
Kidder, K. P. Apiarian Science 44
Killarney Legends 19
King, C. Croton Aqueduct 39
King, Lord. Life of John Locke 79
King, Rev. T. Starr. The White Hills 52
King, Vice President. Obituary 79
King, W. H. The Steam Engine 39

Kings and Queens 79
Kingsbury, C. P. Artillery and Infantry 49
Kingsley, C. Amyas Leigh 7
  Fool of Quality 7
  Hypatia 7
  Alton Locke 7
  Two Years Ago 7
  Yeast 7
  Glaucus 44
  New Miscellanies 108
  Poems 90
  Andromeda 90
  Sir W. Raleigh 79
Kingsley, J. L. Life of Ezra Stiles 79
King's Own 19
Kingston, W. H. G. Old Jack 7
  Old Jack, a Man-of-Wars' Man 7
  Salt Water 7
  Fred Markham 7
Kinne, A. Kent's Commentaries 32
Kip, L. Army Life on the Pacific 52
Kip, Rev. W. J. Catacombs of Rome 28
Kirk, C. D. Wooing and Warring 7
Kirkes, W. and J. Paget's Physiology 45
Kirkland, Mrs. Holidays Abroad 55
  Memoir of Washington 79
Kirkland, S. Life of 79
Kirwan. Men and Things 55
  The Happy Home 7
Kit Kelvin's Kernels 7
Kitto, J. Cyclopedia 28
  Scripture Lands 28
Klencke. Lives of Alex. and W. Humboldt 79
Kling, J. The Chess Euclid 46
Klippart, J. H. The Wheat Plant 42
Knapp, Dr. Chemistry 39
Knapp, F. Life of Gen. Steuben 79
Knapp, S. L. Timothy Dexter 79
Knickerbocker, The 105
Knight, C. Cyclopedia of Political Knowledge 33
  Cyclopedia of Industry 103
  Cyclopedia of London 103
Knight, Helen C. Life of Montgomery 79
Knight of Gwynne 19
Knight's English Cyclopedia 103
  Biography 103
  Geography 103
  Natural History 103
  Arts and Sciences 103
Knox, John. Life of 79
Knox, J. P. St. Thomas, etc 69
Knox, R. Races of Men 44
Know-Nothing, The 7
K. N. Pepper Papers 19
Koch, C. W. The Revolutions 65
Koeppen, A. L. The Middle Ages 7
Kohl, J. G. Travels in England 55
  Austria 55
  Russia 55
Kohlrausch, F. History of Germany 65
Koran, The 28
Kossuth's Select Speeches 100
Kotzebue, A. Von. Life 80
Kraister, C. Glossology 93
Krapf, J. L. Travels in Eastern Africa 55
Krummacher, F. A. Parables 28
Krusenstern, L'Admiral. Voyage 60
Kuchel and Dressel's California Views 101
Kurtz, J. H. Bible and Astronomy 28

L

Labat, R. P. Voyage aux l'Amerique 52
Labatt, H. J. Practice Act 31
Labaume, E. Campaign in Russia 65
Lackington, J. Memoirs 89
Lacroix, F. Patagonie 52
Ladies' Home Magazine 105
Lady Angeline 19
Lady Bird 19
Lady's Book 105
Lady of the Isles 19
Lady of the Manor 19
Laertius, Diogenes 80
Lafayette in America 52
Lafayette. Life of, by J. Cloquet 80
  Life of, by P. C. Headley 80
Lafever, M. Architectural Instructor 47
Lafitte 13
Lafosse, G. T. L'œil de Bœuf 7
Laharpe, M. De. Cours de Literature 96
Laing, Caroline H. Old Farm House 7
Laing, S. Sea Kings 65
Laird of Norlaw 19
Lake of Killarney 19
Lamartine, A. Mary, Queen of Scots 80
  Celebrated Characters 80
  Revolution of 1848 65
  The Restoration 65
  History of Turkey 65
  The Girondists 65
  Trois mois ou Pouvoir 34
  Genevieve 7
  Visit to the Holy Land 55
Lamb, C. Life and Works 96
  Essays of Elia 96
  Rosamund Gray 7
  The Dramatic Poets 92
  Works 99
Lamb, Gen. J. Memoirs of 80
Lambert, A. B. Genus Pinus 42
Lambrequer, L. Tapisserie 47
Lamennais, F. Le Societe Premier 96
Lamplighter 19
Lancashire Life 19
Lancashire Witches 19
Lancelott, F. Queens of England 80
Lances of Lynwood 19
Lander, R. and J. The Niger 58
Landon, Miss. Works 90
  Romance and Reality 7
Landor, W. S. Pericles and Aspasia 96
  Selections from 96
Langley, H. G. California Register 103
Langdon, M. Ida May 17
Langstroth, L. The Hive and Bee 47
Lanman, C. Dictionary of Congress 103
  Essays for Summer Hours 19
  The Wilds of America 52
Lanman, J. H. History of Michigan 69
Lanmere 19
Lanzi, L. History of Painting 46
Laou-Seng Urh. A Chinese Drama 92
La Perouse. La Recherche de 60
La Place, D. M. Voyage 60
La Place, P. S. System of the World 38
Lardner, D. Lectures 47
  Manufacture of Porcelain and Glass 47
  Railway Economy 47
  Arithmetic 38
  Mechanics 39
  The Steam Engine 39
  Animal Physics 45
  Geometry 49
  On Heat 39

Lardner and Walker. Of Electricity 39
Lasalle, R. C. de. Life of 80
Lascasas, Count. Memoirs of Napoleon 80
Lasselle, Mrs. N. P. Belle of Washington 7
Last Days of Pompeii 19
Last of his Name 19
Last of the Mohicans 19
Latham, J. H. Iron Bridges 39
Latham, R. G. Varieties of Man 44
  Man and his Migration 44
  Races of the Russian Empire 44
  The English Language 93
Lathrop, J. C. Life of Kirkland 80
Latrobe, C. J. Rambler in Mexico 52
Latter Days 19
Lauquier et Carpentier. Vie de Louis Philippe 80
Laurence, A. Diary and Correspondence 80
Laurence, W. R. Visitation and Search
Laurens, H. Narrative 80
Laurie's History of Free Masonry 72
Laurie, Rev. T. Dr. Grant and the Nestorians 58
Laurie Todd, by John Galt 19
Lavater, C. G. Physiognomy 45
  L'Art de Connaitre les Hommes 45
L'Avengro 19
Lavoisne, M. Historical Atlas 72
Law 31, 32, 33
Law of Nations 31
Law, H. On Roads 47
Law, J. Life of 80
Lawrence, E. British Historians 80
Lawrence, W. Physiology, etc 45
  Lectures on Man 44
Lawson. Episcopal Church of Scotland 65
Lawson, T. Meteorological Registers 44
Lawson, W. J. History of Banking 72
Lawyer's Story 19
Lay, G. T. Chinese as they are 58
Layard, A. H. Nineveh and Babylon 58
  Nineveh and its Remains 58
Laycock, Dr. The Mind and Brain 108
Lazarus, M. E. Passional Hygiene 45
Lead Pipe. Reports of the use of 45
Leaf and Flower Pictures 46
Leake, J. Q. Life of Gen. J. Lamb 80
Leather Stocking and Silk 7
Leaves from a Family Journal 19
Leaves from the Tree of Jadrasyl 19
Lebedoyere, Count. Memoirs of Napoleon 80
Le Courtisan Desabuse 7
Ledbury, Mr. Adventures 19
Lederhose, C. F. Life of Melancthon 80
Ledyard, J. Life of 80
Lee, Arthur. Life of 80
Lee, C. Life of 80
Lee, C. A. Elements of Geology 40
Lee, Eliza. Parthenia 7
  Canterbury Tales 7
Lee, Holme. Sylvan Holt's Daughter 7
  Against Wind and Tide 7
  Hawksview 7
Lee, H. The Campaign of 1781 69
  War in Southern Department 69
Lee, R. H. Memoir and Correspondence 80
Lee, Lieut. S. P. Cruise of the Dolphin 60
Legend of Montrose 19
Legend of the Rhine 19
Legends and Record 19

Legends of the Rhine 19
Legends of the West 19
Leibnitz and Clarke. Philosophy and Religion 28
Leibnitz. Œuvres 36
Leibnitz, G. W, von. Life of 80
Leighton, A. Poems 90
Leidy, J. Flora and Fauna 43
Fossil Ox 43
Leila 19
Leisler, J. Administration of 80
Leland, Anna A. Home 7
Leland, C. G. Of Dreams 90
Le Monde Illustre 105
Lempriere's Classical Dictionary 88
Lena Rivers 19
L'Enclos, Ninon de. Memoirs 80
Leo X. Life of 80
Leonora D'Orco 19
Lepeo, A. F. E. De Tout in Peu 7
Lepsius, Dr. R. Egypt and Ethiopia 67
Le Sage, A. Rene, Bachelor of Salamanca 7
The Devil on Two Sticks 7
Le Diable Boiteaux 7
Gil Blas 7
Histoire de Gil Blas 7
Life of Gusman D'Alfarache 7
Lesley, J. P. Iron Manufacturers' Guide 40
Manual of Coal and its Topography 40
Leslie, C. R. Recollections 80
Leslie, Miss. More Receipts 48
Pencil Sketches 7
Lette, J. M. California Illustrated 52
Letters from Three Continents 60
Leuchars, R. B. The Construction of Hot Houses 48
Levant. Travels in 54, 57
Levasseur, A. Lafayette in America 52
Lever, C. Arthur O'Leary 7
The O'Donohue 7
Harry Lorrequer 7
Tom Burke of Ours 7
The Knight of Gwinne 7
The Daltons 7
The Fortunes of Glencore 7
Roland Cashel 7
The Martins of Cro Martin 7
Gerald Fitzgerald 7
Maurice Tiernay, the Soldier of Fortune 7
Jack Hinton 7
Leverett, F. P. Latin Lexicon 103
Levi, L. Annals of British Legislation 72
Levin, W. Legal Common-place Book 32
Lewes, G. H. History of Philosophy 69
Life of Goethe 80
Sea Side Studies 44
Studies in Animal Life 43
Lewis and Clarke's Expedition 52
Lewis Arundel 19
Lewis, E. J. The American Sportsman 46
Lewis, J. Protestantism 28
Lewis, Lady T. Semi-Detached House 7
Lewis, W. The Chess-Board Companion 46
Games of Chess 46
Leycester. The 7
Leyes de California 31
Leyes del Territoria de Nuevo Mexico 31
Liancourt, R. Travels 62
Liddell, H. G. Greek-English Lexicon 102

Liddell, H. G. History of Rome 65
Liebig, Baron. Modern Agriculture 42
Lieber, F. Manual of Political Ethics 34
Civil Liberty 34
Property and Labor 25
The Penitentiary System 35
Life of G. B. Niebuhr 80
Hermeneutics 33
Laura Bridgeman 49
Lieber, O. M. Survey of South Carolina 62
Liebig, J. Animal Chemistry 39
Agricultural Chemistry 39
Complete Works and Chemistry 39
Familiar Letters on Chemistry 39
Life of a Sailor 19
Life for a Life 19
Life Struggle 19
Light and Darkness 7
Lights and Shadows of Scottish Life 8
Lilly, Sir W. Life of 80
Lily and Totem 19
Lily White 19
Limantour. Photographic Illustrations 105
Lincoln, B. Life of 80
Lincoln, Mrs. Lectures on Botany 42
Lincoln, R. W. Lives of the Presidents 80
Lind, Jenny. Life of 80
Linda 19
Lindeo, Liele. Chestnutwood 8
Lindsay, Lord. Letters on Egypt etc 65
Linen, James. Poems 90
Lingard, Dr. J. England 65
Linn, Dr. L. F. Life of 80
Linwoods 19
Lion of Flanders 19
Lionel Lincoln 19
Lippincott's Gazetteer 61
Lisianski, W. Voyage 60
Lister, T. H. Granby 8
Listner in Oxford 28
Literary World. The 105
Literary Letter 19
Literature, Ancient 87, 88
Littell's Living Age 105
Museum 105
Little Beauty 19
Little Beggars 19
Little Dorrit 19
Little Female Academy 19
Little, G. Life on the Ocean 60
Little Henry and his Beaver 19
Little Mornere 19
Little Pedlington 19
Little Woodman 19
Livermore, A. A. War with Mexico 69
Lives of Eminent Men of France 80
Eminent British Statesmen 80
Eminent Men of Italy 80
of Great Britain 80
British Physicians 80
Living and Loving 19
Living in the Country 96
Livingston, Rev. D. Travels 58
Livingston, J. Law Register 32
Eminent Americans 80
Livy's History of Rome 88
Lizzie Leigh 19
Llewellyn, E. L. Title Hunting 7
Locke, J. Terrestrial Magnetism 39
Human Understanding 36
Thoughts on Education 93
Works 99
Philosophical Works 99
Life and Letters of 80

Lockhart, J. G. Life of Sir Walter Scott 80
Life of Napoleon 80
Life of Robert Burns 80
Spanish Ballads 70
Lockman, J. Travels of the Jesuits 60
Lodge, E. Portraits 80
Illustrations of History 64
Loftus, W. K. Travels in Chaldea, etc
Lofty and the Lowly 19
Logan. The Master's House 8
Logic 37
London Athenæum 105
London Catalogue 107
London Dispatch 105
London Journal 105
London Times, tri-weekly 105
Lonsdale, Lord. Reign of James II 80
Long, J. Voyages and Travels 52
Long, Major. Expedition 52
Longfellow, H. W. Poems 90
Miles Standish 90
Ballads and other Poems 90
Poets and Poetry of Europe 90
Voices of the Night 90
Hiawatha 90
Spanish Student 92
Kavanagh 8
Hyperion 8
Long Look Ahead 19
Lonz Powers 19
Look at Home 20
Look to the End 20
Looker-on, The 96
Lord and Lady Harcourt 20
Lord, D. N. Figurative Language 93
Lord, E. The Epoch of Creation 44
Lord Montague's Page 20
Lorenzo Benoni 20
Lorenzo de Medici 80
Loring, J. S. Boston Orators 80
Loss and Gain 20
Loss and Gain 20
Lossing, B. J. Field Book of the Revolution 69
Mount Vernon 69
History of the United States 69
History of the Arts, etc 46
Signers of the Declaration 86
Lost Daughter 20
Lost Heiress 20
Lothrop, S. K. Life of S. Kirkland 80
Loud, J. Gabriel Vane 8
London, J. C. Aboretum et Fruticetom 43
The Villa Gardener 43
Loudon, Mrs. Gardening for Ladies 42
Louisiana, Civil Code of 32
Louisiana Historical Collections 69
Louis Phillipe. Mon Journal 65
Louis XIV. Memoirs by the Duke de St. Simon 65
Life of, by G. P. R. James 80
Louis XVI. Life of, by A. Renee 80
Lounger, The 96
Love and Marriage 20
Love after Marriage 20
Love Match 20
Love Me Little, Love Me Long 20
Love of Country 20
Loviott, Fanny. Lady's Captivity 58
Lover, S. Handy Andy 8
Rory O'More 8
Barney O'Rierdon 8
Treasure Trove 8
Lover's Stratagem 20
Low, D. Domestic Animals 42

Low, H. Sarawak 58
Lowe, Sir H. The Captivity of Napoleon 80
Lowell, J. R. Poems 90
The Bigelow Papers 90
Lower, M. English Surnames 93
Lowig, Dr. C. Chemistry 39
Lucan's Pharsalia 88
Lucian of Samosata 88
Lucknow, Defence of 67
Luck of Barry Lyndon 20
Luck of Ladysmede 20
Lucretia 20
Lucretius. De Rerum Natura 88
Lucretius. Nature of Things 88
Lucy Crofton 20
Lucy Howard's Journal 20
Lucy and her Dhaye 20
Ludewig, H. E. The Aboriginal Languages 107
Lunt, G. Poems 90
Three Eras of New England 69
Luther, M. Life of 80
Table Talk 90
Lycesters, The 20
Lyde, A. F. Buds of Spring 90
Lydia, a Woman's Book 20
Lyell, Sir C. Elementary Geology 41
Principles of Geology 41
Wonders of Geology 41
Geological Excursions 47
Petrifactions 41
The Medals of Creation 41
Travels in North America 52
Second Visit to America 52
Lyman, S. P. Life of Daniel Webster 20
Lyman, T. Diplomacy 31
Lynch, W. F. The Dead Sea 66
Lyon, Capt. G. F. Tour in Mexico 20
Lyxars, J. Tobacco 45

M

M. Letters from Three Continents 65
Mabel 20
Mabel Vaughan 8
MacCabe, W. B. Bertha 8
Macartney, W. Of the United States 69
Macaulay, J. I. Field Fortifications 49
Macaulay, T. B. History of England 96
Essays 96
Essays and Poems 96
Life of Frederick II 80
Life of William Pitt 80
Biographical Sketches 80
New Biography 80
Lays of Ancient Rome 90
Macfarlane, C. British India 67
Japan 68
Macfarlane, J. The Night Lamp, etc 90
MacGavock, R. W. Tennessean Abroad 65
MacGeoeghegan. History of Ireland 65
Macgillvray, W. Travels of Humboldt 60
Macgregor, J. Commercial Statistics 35
Machinvelli, N. History of Florence 65
Macilwain, G. Memoirs of Abernethy 60
Mackay, A. Western India 58
Mackay, Capt. J., and Lieut. Blake. War in Florida 105
Mackay, C. Life and Liberty in America 52
English Songs 90
Voices from the Mountains, etc 90
Mackay, R. W. On the Intellect 28

Mackay, R. W. S. Canada Directory 62
Mackenzie, A. Voyages 52
Mackenzie, A. S. A Year in Spain 55
Life of Decatur 80
Life of Perry 80
Life of Paul Jones 80
Court Martial of 32
Mackenzie, Mrs. C. Life in the Mission 58
Mackenzie, Sir G. S. Travels in Iceland 55
Mackenzie, R. S. Tressilian 8
Mackie, J. M. Life of S. Gorton 80
Life of Wang 80
Life of Leibnitz 80
Mackintosh, Sir Jas. Memoirs of 80
History of England 65
Miscellaneous Works 96
MacLeod, D. Pynnshurst 65
Maclise, J. Comparative Osteology 44
MacPherson's Poems of Ossian 90
Mademoiselle Mori 6
Maddex, R. R. Life of the Countess of Blessington 80
The Infirmities of Genius 80
Madison, James. On the Federal Constitution 34
Life and Times 80
Madrid in 1835 55
Magazines 104, 105
Magdalen the Enchantress 20
Magdalen Hepburn 20
Maggie Miller 20
Magic 49, 50
Magne, J. H. Milch Cows 42
Magnetism, Animal 101
Magoon, E. L. Living Orators of America 81
Orators of the Revolution 81
Orators of France 81
Orators of the Age 81
Proverbs for the People 100
Republican Christianity 98
Mahawanso, The 72
Mahomet. Life of, by Edward Gibbon 81
Life of, by G. Bush 81
and his Successors, by Irving 81
Mahon, D. H. Civil Engineering 39
Industrial Drawing, etc 46
Mahon, Lord. History of England 65
Mahony, Rev. F. Father Prout 96
Maiden Aunt 20
Maid Marian 20
Mail Coach 20
Maillard, A. M. Miles Tremenhere 8
Maitland. The Surrender of Napoleon 81
Maitland, J. A. Sartaroe 8
The Lawyer's Story 8
Diary of an Old Doctor 8
Major Thorpe's Scenes in Arkansaw 80
Malcolm, H. Travels 58
Malcolm, H. F. India and the Mutineers 67
Malcolm, Sir J. Central India 58
Malebranche, N. Search after Truth 28
Malibran, Madame. Memoirs of 81
Mallet, P. H. Northern Antiquities 88
Malmesbury, Wm. of. Chronicle 65
Malone, E. Authenticity of the Shakspeare Papers 96
Malte Brun, C. Geography 62
Tableau de la Pologne 62
and Balbi's System of Geography 62
Man and Money 90
Man at Arms 20
Mandeville, J. W. Report for 1859 62
Marlette, Report for 1865 62

Man. Ideal 28
Manilius, M. Five Books 38
Mann, E. J. Deaf and Dumb 90
Mann, Mrs. H. Christianity in the Kitchen 48
Man of Business 36
Man Made of Money 20
Manon Lescaut 20
Mansfield, Earl. Life of 81
Mansfield, E. D. Life of Gen. Scott 81
Legal Rights of Women 32
American Education 93
Statistics of Ohio 35
Mansfield Park 20
Mant, R. Horæ Liturgicæ 28
Manual of Domestic Economy 48
Manual of Natural History 108
Manufacturing 47, 48
Mantonia, A. The Betrothed 8
Mapes, J. J. American Repository 48
Maps and Views to President's Messages 34
Map of Central America 62
Map of the Seat of War in Florida 62
Maps of the Coast Survey 62
Maps to Alison's Europe 69
Maritime and Inland Discoveries 60
Marble Faun 20
March, C. W. Daniel Webster 81
Marchioness of Brinvilliers 20
Marcou, J. Geology of America 41
Marcus Warland 20
Marcy, Capt. E. B. The Red River 52
Mardi 20
Margaret 20
Margaret Moncrieffe 20
Marguerite 20
Mariana, J. P. Turkish Spy 98
Marian Elwood 8
Marian Wallace 20
Marie Antoinette. Life of, by Abbott 81
by Madame Campan 81
Marigny, T. Voyages in the Black Sea 55
Marion Barnard 20
Marlborough, Duke of. Memoirs, by W. Coxe 81
The same, by Sir A. Alison 81
Marlborough, Duchess of. Memoirs, Private Correspondence 81
Marles, M. Histoire de l'Inde 67
Marmontel. Memoirs, by himself 81
Maroon, by Simms 20
Marquette, Father. Life of 81
Married or Single 20
Married not Mated 20
Marryat, Frank. Mountains and Molehills 52
Marryat, F. S. Borneo 58
Marryat, Capt. Diary in America 52
Masterman Ready 8
Poor Jack 8
The Settlers in Canada 8
The King's Own 8
Pacha of Many Tales 8
Peter Simple 8
Percival Keene 8
Rattlin, the Reefer 8
Frank Mildmay 8
Japhet in Search of a Father 8
Newton Forster 8
Midshipman Easy 8
Snarleyow 8
Jacob Faithful 8
The Poacher 8
The Phantom Ship 8
The Privateersman 8
The Pirate and Three Cutters 8
The Mission 8

Marryat, Miss. Temper 8
Marsh, G. P. The English Language 93
Marsh, Mrs. G. P. Poems 90
Marshall, C. Remembrancer 69
Marshall, J. Federal Constitution 32
Life of Washington 81
Eulogy on 81
Martell, Martha. Second Love 8
Marthe; a Memorial 81
Martin Chuzzlewit 90
Martin Merivale 90
Martins of Cro' Martin 90
Martin, C. Civil Costumes of England 94
Martin, M. Australia 62
Martin, R. M. History of Australia 101
British Possessions in the Mediterranean 65
British Colonial Library 65
History of South Africa 67
History of Canada 69
History of Nova Scotia 69
The West India Islands 69
The Indian Empire 67
History of the Possessions of the East India Company 67
Martineau, Harriet. British Rule in India 67
Deerbrook 107
Society in America 62
Feats on the Fiord 65
Martineau, Rev. J. Miscellanies 96
Martyrs of Science 81
Marvell, A. Poetical Works 90
Mary Anne 20
Mary Barton 90
Mary Bunyan 90
Mary Darwent 90
Mary Lindon 20
Mary of Lorraine 81
Mary, Queen of Scots. Life of, by H. G. Bell 81
by P. C. Headley 81
by A. Lamartine 81
by D. McLeod 81
by Abbott 81
Mary Staunton 20
Mason, G. C. Art and Manufactures 48
Mason, J. Life of 81
The Laws of Wealth 35
Masonic Grand Lodge of Iowa 106
Massey, G. Poems and Ballads 90
Massinger and Ford. Dramatic Works 92
Masson, D. British Novelists 96
Masson, M. Celebrated Children 81
Life of Milton 81
Masterman Ready 20
Masters and Workmen 20
Master's House 20
Match Girl 20
Maternus, J. T. Translated 88
Mathematics 38
Mathematical Monthly 105
Mather, C. Life of 81
Mather, J. Remarkable Providences 81
Mathilde 90
Matrimonial Brokerage 20
Matrimonial Misfortunes 20
Matthew Carraby 20
Matthew of Westminster 65
Matthew Paris' English History 65
Matthew, P. Emigration Fields 62
Matthias and his Impostures 81
Maunder, S. Scientific and Literary Treasury 103
Treasury of History 103
Biographical Treasury 103
Treasury of Natural History 103

Maunder, S.
Treasury of Knowledge 103
Maunderell, H. Journey to Jerusalem 65
Maundeville, Sir J. Travels in Palestine 65
Maurice, F. D. Ancient Philosophy 37
Theological Essays 28
Maurice, J. K. N. Pepper Papers 8
Maurice Tiernay 90
Maury, A. Principles of Eloquence 96
Maury, M. F. Directions to Wind and Current Charts 44
The Physical Geography 44
Sailing Directions 49
Maximus Tyrius. Dissertations 88
Maxwell 90
Maxwell, J. S. The Czar 65
Maxwell, W. H. Life of Wellington 81
Victories of Wellington 81
The Irish Rebellion of 1798 65
The Bivouac 8
Stories of Waterloo 8
Captain Blake 8
Hector O'Halloran 8
Captain O'Sullivan 8
Peter Clancey 8
May and December 20
May Flower 20
Mayo, A. D. Symbols of the Capital 96
Mayo, S. The Berber 8
Kaloolah 8
McClellan, Capt. G. B. Report from Seat of War 66
McClintock, Capt. The Fate of Sir J. Franklin 60
McCamber's Institutes of the Mind 108
McCormick, R. C. St. Paula to St. Sophia 55
McCrie, T. Life of John Knox 81
McCulloch, Prof. Reports on Sugar Cane 42
McCulloch, J. R. Commercial Dictionary 103
Geographical Dictionary 103
McDougal, G. F. Voyage of the Resolute 62
McGee, T. D'A. Irish Settlers in North America 69
McGowan, E. Adventures 62
McHarg, C. K. Life of Talleyrand 81
McHenry, J. O'Halloran 8
McIlvaine, C. P. Evidences 28
McIntosh, J. American Indians 88
McIntosh, Maria J. The Lofty and the Lowly 8
Donaldson Manor 8
Violet 8
Meta Gray 8
McKenney, T. L. Tour to the Lakes 62
McLean, J. Service in Hudson Bay 62
McLeod, D. Life of Sir W. Scott 81
Mary, Queen of Scots 81
Pynnshurst 8
McPherson, D. Antiquities of Kertch 88
McSherry, J. History of Maryland 69
Meade, Bishop. Old Churches 69
Meadow Brook 20
Mears, J. Voyages 62
Mechanics' Register 48
Mechanism 29, 40
Mechanics 38, 39
Mechanics' Magazine 105
Mechi, J. How to Farm Profitably 42
Medical News and Library 105
Medicine 45
Meek, A. B. Songs and Poems 90
Southwestern History 69
Melancthon, P. Life of 81

M'Elheran, J. The Condition of Women of the Gothic and Celtic Races 65
Mellichampe, by Simms 90
Melsheimer, Dr. F. E. Coleoptera 43
Melville, G. J. W. Holmby House 8
Melville, H. Piazzi Tales 8
Israel Potter 8
Mardi 8
Omoo 8
Typee 8
White Jacket 8
Moby Dick, the Whale 8
Memes, J. S. Life of the Empress Josephine 81
Memorial 81
Memoirs of a Cavalier 20
Memoirs of Capt. Crouke 20
Memoirs of Celebrated Characters 81
Memoirs of Sergeant Dale 20
Memorable Year 67
Men and Women, by A. Houssaye 81
Mendelssohn, M. Jerusalem 67
Men of Character 20
Men of the Time 81
Men's Wives 20
Menu. Ordinances of 39
Menzel, W. History of Germany 65
Mercedes of Castile 90
Merchants' and Bankers' Register 35
Meredith, Mrs. C. Tasmania 68
Meredith, O. Lucile 90
Poems 90
Merkland 20
Merlin, Countess. Memoirs of Malibran 81
Mesmerism 101
Messages and Documents 106
Messenger. Southern Literary 105
Meta Gray 20
Metallurgy 40, 41
Metaphysics 36
Metaphysical Essays 28
Metcalfe, S. J. Caloric 39
Methodist. The 81
Mexican Claims 106
Mexican War, its Heroes, etc 70
Mezzofanti, Cardinal. Life of 81
Miall, J. G. Our Forefathers 70
Michaud, J. F. History of the Crusades 65
Michaux, F. A. Travels 62
Michelet, M. Life of Luther 81
Miscellaneous Works 99
Modern History 73
History of France 66
The People 34
Love 96
Woman 96
Middleton, C. Powers of the Christian Church 28
Popery and Paganism 28
Life of Cicero 81
Midnight, and other Poems 90
Midshipman Easy 20
Midsummer Eve 90
Miguet, F. A. French Revolution 65
Miles, P. Rambles in Iceland 66
Miles Tremenhere, by A. Maillard 90
Military and Naval Works 48, 49
Military Maxims of Napoleon 49
Mill, J. S. Political Economy 35
On Liberty 36
System of Logic 37
Milledulcia 96
Miller, Hugh. Life and Times of 81
Impressions of England 66
Cruise of the Betsy 66
Popular Geology 43

Miller, Hugh.
Testimony of the Rocks 41
Footprints of the Creator 41
Old Red Sand-stone 41
Scenes and Legends 8
My Schools and Schoolmasters 81
Miller, S. Life of Jonathan Edwards 81
Eighteenth Century 73
Miller, S. F. Bench and Bar 81
Memoirs of Gen. D. Blackshear 81
Wylkina Wylder 107
Miller, T. Godfrey Malvern 8
History of the Anglo-Saxons 65
Miller, W. A. Elements of Chemistry 39
Millingen, J. G. Duelling 72
Mill on the Floss 20
Milman, H. M. History of the Jews 67
Life of T. A'Beckett 81
Nala, and other Poems 90
Milne, W. C. Life in China 58
Milner, J. Russia 56
Milton, J. His Prose Works 99
Paradise Lost 90
Poetical Works 90
On Education 93
Patriot and Poet 81
Life of, by D. Masson 81
Mineralogy 40, 41
Mining 40, 41
Mining Magazine 105
Minnie Grey 20
Minnie Hermon 20
Minister's Wooing 20
Minot, G. R. Massachusetts 70
Minturn, R. B., Jr. New York to
Delhi 58
Minucius, Felix. Octavius 28
Miranda, F. Revolution in S. America 70
Miriam Alroy 29
Miscellanea Sacra 28
Miscellaneous Works of Authors 99, 100
Miscellanies, by S. Warren 20
Miscellany, by W. C. Chambers 108
Miser's Daughter 20
Miser of Ricketstack 20
Miseries of Human Life 20
Mishna, The. Eighteen Treatises 28
Misrepresentation, by Anna Drury 20
Miss Gilbert's Career 107
Miss Slimmen's Window 20
Missing Bride 20
Mission, or Scenes in Africa 20
Missionary Herald 105
Mitchell, Col. J. Life of Wallenstein 81
Mitchell, D. G. Battle Summer 56
Fresh Gleanings 56
Mitchell, O. M. Planetary Worlds 38
Popular Astronomy 38
Mitford, M. Lay. Our Village 8
Belford Regis 8
Atherton and other Tales 8
Mitford, Miss. Recollections 81
Moby Dick 20
Modern Accomplishments 20
Modern British Plutarch 81
Modern Chivalry 20
Modern Flirtations 20
Modern Pilgrims 20
Modern Society 20
Modern Standard Drama 102
Mofras, Duflot. Exploration de
Oregon, etc 60
Mohdly, Cheykh. Contes 8
Mohicans of Paris 20
Moir, D. M. Poetical Literature 105
Moliere, J. B. P. Œuvres 102
Molina, J. History of Chili 20
Moll Flanders 20
Molthausen, B. Journey 60

Monastery 20
Money 34, 35
Money Maker 20
Monikins, The 21
Monk of Cimies 21
Monro, V. Syria, etc 56
Monroe, J. Of Chess 46
Monroe, Jas. Conduct of the Exe-
cutive 34
Monstrelet, E. Chronicles 65
Montague, Lady M. W. Letters 96
Montaigne, M. Essays 96
Montez, Lola. The Arts of Beauty 46
Lectures and Autobiography of 81
Montgomery, Cora. Eagle Pass 52
Montgomery, Gen. R. Life of 81
Montgomery, H. Life of Gen. Z.
Taylor 81
Montgomery, Jas. Poetical Works 90
Literature, etc 90
Letters 90
Memoirs of 81
Life of, by Helen C. Knight 81
Monumens des Grands-Maitres 65
Moodie, Mrs. Roughing it in the
Bush 52
Life in the Clearings 52
Moody, C. P. The Moody Family 87
Moore, F. American Eloquence 100
Diary of the Revolution 70
Songs and Ballads 90
Moore, G. Health and Disease 45
The Soul and the Body 45
The Body and the Mind 45
Man and his Motives 36
Moore, G. H. The Treason of Maj.
Lee 70
Moore, N. F. Ancient Mineralogy 41
Moore, T. Memoirs and Journal 81
Life and Letters of Byron 81
Letters of Lord Byron 81
Life of Sheridan 81
Poetical Works 90
Lalla Rookh 90
The Epicurean 8
History of Ireland 65
Orchidaceous Plants 42
Moorland Cottage 2
Moral Philosophy 36, 37
Moral Tales 21
Moran, B. Footpath and Highway 56
More, H. Apocalypse Apocalypseos 28
Conjectura Cabalistica 28
Of Godliness 28
Mystery of Iniquity 28
Life of, by H. Thompson 81
Life of, by R. Ward 81
Sacred Dramas 28
Practical Piety 28
The Spirit of Prayer 28
Essay on St. Paul 28
Moral Sketches 96
Works 99
More, Margarita. Household of Sir
T. More 8
More, Sir Thomas. Utopia 8
Morrell, J. D. Philosophy of Reli-
gion 28
Moreri, L. Dictionaire Historique 81
Morford, H. Rhymes 90
Morgan, —. The Moral Philosopher 28
Morgan, Gen. D. Life of, by J.
Graham 81
Morgan, Lady. Life of Salvator
Rosa 81
Passages from my Autobiogra-
phy 81
O'Donnell 8
Florence McCarthy 8

Morgan, Lady. The Wild Irish Girl 8
Dramatic Scenes 92
Morgan, L. H. League of the Iro-
quois 70
Morine' Mechanic 39
Morley Ernstein 21
Mormoniad 90
Mormons ; or Latter-Day Saints 28
Morning Post, San Francisco 105
Morphy, P. Triumphs of 46
Games of Chess 46
Morrell, Capt. B. Four Voyages 60
Morris, E. Joy. Life and Love in
Norway 56
Corsica 56
Morris, Gov. L. Papers of 96
Morris, Gouverneur. Life 8
Morris, R. Courtship and Matri-
mony 8
Morrison and Himmaleh. Voyage 60
Morse, J. Report on Indian Affairs 52
Morton, N. New England's Memo-
rial 20
Mosaica 96
Moses, M. Revolution in France 65
Mosheim, J. L. Ecclesiastical His-
tory 73
Moslem and Christian 56
Mosses from an old Manse 21
Moss Side 21
Mother-in-Law 96
Mothers and Daughters 21
Mother's Mistake 21
Mothers of the Wise and Good 81
Mother's Recompense 21
Mother Ross 21
Mother's Trials 21
Motherwell, W. Poems 90
Minstrelsy 90
Motley, J. L. Dutch Republic 65
Moulton, Louise. My Third Book 8
Moulton, R. K. Constitutional
Guide 31
Moultrie, W. The Revolution 70
Mountford, W. Euthanasy 78
Mourning Queen 21
Movier, D. R. Hajji Baba 8
Zoreb 8
Ayesha 8
Mowatt, Anna Cora' Autobiogra-
phy 81
Mimic Life 81
The Fortune Hunter 8
Twin Roses 8
Mozart. Life of
Mrs. Catharine Crawley 21
Mudie, R. Observation of Nature 44
Man, Moral 28
Man Physical 45
Man Intellectual 36
Man in his Relations 37
Feathered Tribes 43
Mugge, T. Afraja 8
Mulenberg, Major-Gen. Life 82
Muirhead, J. P. Life of James
Watt 82
Mulaney, J. Trip to Newfoundland 52
The Laying of the Ocean Tele-
graph 46
Muller, C. O. Scientific Mythology 88
Ancient Art 46
Muller, F. Characteristics of Go-
ethe 96
Muller, J. Physics and Meteorolo-
gy 40
Muloch, Miss. John Halifax 8
Nothing New 8
Agatha's Husband 8
Avillion 8
Olive 8

Muloch, Miss. The Ogilvies 8
  A Life for a Life 8
  A Hero 8
  Bread upon the Waters 8
  Alice Learmont 8
  Domestic Stories 107
  Poems 90
Munchausen, Baron. Adventures 9
Munday, Capt. R. Borneo 67
Mundy, Major-General. Life of Admiral Rodney 82
Municipal Reports of San Francisco 106
Municipalist, The 94
Munn, D. The Land Drainer 42
Munsell, J. Paper making History and Chronology 73
Murphy, Rev. R. Electricity, Heat, etc 30
Murray, Miss A. Letters 62
Murray, C. A. The Prairie Bird 9
Murray, Hon. C. A. Travels 62
Murray, H. Geography 62
  British India 67
  Travels of Marco Polo 60
  British America 70
Murray, J. Hand-book for London 62
  Hand-book for Southern Germany 62
  Hand-book for Northern Italy 67
  Hand-book for Greece, Turkey, etc 62
  Hand-book for the Continent 62
  Hand-book for France 62
  Hand-book for London 62
  Hand-book for Spain 62
  Hand-book for Syria 62
  Hand-book for India 62
Murray, L. The Power of Religion 28
Museum. Littell's 105
Muspratt, Dr. S. Chemistry 39
Mustang Gray, by Hon. Jer. Clemens 21
Mustee, by B. F. Presbury 21
Mutiny in India 67
My Aunt Kate 21
My Cousin Nicholas 21
My Early Days, by Eliza Farnham 21
Myers, P. H. Prisoner of the Border 9
My Godmother 21
My Lady Ludlow 21
Myles, W. History of the Methodists 73
My Novel 21
Myrtle, Minnie 9
Mythology 87, 88
My Third Book 21
My Three Uncles 21
Mysteries of Udolpho 21
Mysterious Marriage 21
My Uncle Timothy 21

N

Nack J. Romance of the Ring 90
Names 93
Napier, Sir C. William the Conqueror 9
Napier, W. P. F. Peninsular War 85
Napoleon's Historical Miscellanies 65
  Memoirs 82
  Court and Camp 82
  Life of, by J. S. C. Abbott 82
  At St. Helena, by J. S. C. Abbott 82
  Life of, by Ardeche 82
  In exile, by B. E. O'Meara 82
  Correspondence with Joseph 82

Napoleon
  Life of, by J. G. Lockhart 82
  Captivity at St. Helena 82
  His Surrender, etc 82
  Life of, by W. Hazlitt 82
  Life of, by W. Grimshaw 82
  Memoirs of, by Lascases 82
  By Lebedoyera 82
  And his Marshals, by Headley 82
  Napoleon Dynasty, by the Berkley Men 82
  By Madame Junot 82
  Napoleon Code 82
  Gallery, of his Life, etc 82
Napoleon III. Life of, by Smucker 82
Napoleon, Louis. Le Proce de 32
Nash, J. A. The Farmer 42
Nathalie 21
National Encyclopedia 103
Natural History 40, 45
Natural History. Knight's English Cyclopedia 43
Natural History. Reports of the Regents of New York 44
Nature and Art 21
Nature Delineated 44
Nature and Human Nature 21
Naval Works 48, 49
Navarre. Reine de L'Heptameron 9
Neal J. True Womanhood 9
Neal, J. C. Charcoal Sketches 9
Neale, E. The Closing Scene 28
Neale, Flora. Thine and Mine 9
Neander, A. Planting of Christianity 72
Neander, Dr. A. Christian Religion 28
  History of Christian Dogmas 28
  Christian Life 28
  History of the Christian Church 28
  The Emperor Julian 28
Ned Myers 21
Neeles, H. Literary Remains 41
Neighbor Jackwood 21
Neighbors 21
Neill, E. D. History of Minnesota 70
Neligan, Rev. W. H. Rome 56
Nellie of Truro 21
Nelly Bracken 21
Nelson. Life of 82
Nelsonian Reminiscences 82
Nemesis 31
Nennius' Chronicle 65
Nero. Life of 82
Neumann and Barretti. Dictionary 103
Never too Late to Mend 21
Neville. Hydraulic Tables 39
Newcomb, H. Christianity 20
Newcomes 21
New Englander 105
New England Tale 21
New England's Chattels 21
New Ipswich, History of 70
Newman, F. W. The Soul 29
  English Universities 72
Newman, J. H. Loss and Gain 21
Newman, T. W. Regal Rome 65
Newnman, W. Human Magnetism 45
New Priest in Conception Bay 21
New Purchase 21
Newsboy 21
New South Wales Almanac 62
Newspapers 104, 106
New Stories 21
Newton Forster 21
Newton, Sir J. Life, Writings 82
New York State Documents 70
New York Historical Society Collections 70

New York State Register 34
Nick of the Woods 91
Nicholas, N. H. The Royal Navy 65
Nicholas Nickleby 21
Nicolini, G. B. History of the Jesuits 65
Nicollet, J. N. The Mississippi River 35
Nichols, J. P. Architecture of the Heavens 38
  Cyclopedia 40
Nichols, P. The Mechanic's Companion 30
Nicholson, J. B. Art of Book Binding 48
Nicholson, W. British Encyclopedia 49
Niebuhr. Reminiscences of 82
Niebuhr, B. G. Lectures 65
  History of Rome 65
Night and Morning 21
Nightingale, Florence. On Nursing 45
Nightmare Abbey 21
Niles, H. Acts of the American Revolution 70
  Weekly Register 106
Noble, L. L. The Lady Angeline, etc 91
Noble, Rev. S. The New Church 29
Noir, M. L'A. Lamps of the Temple 29
Nolte, V. Fifty Years 82
Nordhoff, C. Whaling and Fishing 60
Norman, B. M. Travels in Yucatan 52
Normanby, Marquis. Year of Revolution 65
North American Review 105
North and South 21
North British Review 105
Northcote, W. The Slave of the Lamp 9
Northcote, J. Life of Reynolds 82
Northern Regions 60
Norton, A. Statement of Reasons 29
  Translation of the Gospels 29
Norton, C. E. Travel in Italy 56
Norton, Mrs. Other Poems 91
Notes and Queries 98
Notes of Travel in Zanzibar, etc 58
Nothing New 21
Nothing to Wear 91
Nothing to Say 91
Nothing to Do 91
Nothing to Eat 91
Nothing to You 91
Notions of the American s 21
Nott, E. Lectures on Temperance 90
Nott and Gliddon. Types of Mankind 44
  Races of the Earth 44
Nour Mahal 96
Novels and Romances 1, 25, 107
Novels and Tales, by Goethe 21
Novels, Chinese 9
Novels, Select 9
Novels and Tales from Household Worlds 9
Now-a-Days 21
Now and Then 21
Noyes, J. O. Roumania 56
Noyes, R. G. Translation of Job 99
  Of the Proverbs, Ecclesiastes and the Canticles 99
  Of the Hebrew Prophets 99
  Of the Book of Psalms 99
Nugent, Lord. Memorials of Hampden 82
Numa Pompilius 21
Numismatics 94
Nun 21

11

O

Oak Openings 21
Oatman Girls. Captivity of 82
Obedience 21
Observer, The 46
O'Callaghan, E. B. History of New
   York 70
Oceanica. Travels in 57, 59
Ocellus 88
Ockley, S. History of the Saracens 67
O'Connell. Memoirs of 82
Odd Fellows. Laws of the Order 32
Odericus Vitalis' History 65
O'Donnell 21
O'Donohue 21
Oersted, H. C. The Soul in Nature 108
O'Flanagan, J. R. The Blackwater 62
Ogilvie, G. The Master Builder's
   Plan 44
Ogilvies 21
Oglethorpe, Jas. Life of 82
O'Halloran 21
Ohio. Statistics 34
Okely, F. Life of Jacob Behman 82
Olcott, H. S. Sugar Canes 42
Old Brewery and New Mission 21
Old Curiosity Shop 21
Old Doctor 21
Old England's Worthies 82
Old Farm House 21
Old Forest Ranger 21
Oldham, O. The Humorous Speaker 101
Old Haun 21
Old Hepsy 21
Old House by the River 21
Old Inn 21
Old Jack 21
Old Lady's Complaint 21
Old Mortality 21
Old Mackinaw 21
Old Neighborhoods 21
Old Plantation 21
Old Stone Mansion 21
Old Things and New Things 21
Old Whitney's Christmas Trot 21
Oliphant, L. Earl of Elgin's Mis-
   sion to China and Japan 58
Oliphant, Mrs. The Athelings
   Adam Græme 9
Olive 21
Olive and the Pine 91
Olive Branch 9
Oliver and the Jew Fagin 21
Oliver, B. L. Forms of Practice 32
   Practical Conveyancing 32
Oliver Twist 21
Olivia; or the Maid of Honor 21
Olmstead, F. A. A Whaling Voy-
   age 60
Olmsted, F. L. Journey through
   Texas 52
   Journey to the Slave States 52
   Journey through the Back
   Country 52
O'Meara, B. E. Napoleon in Exile 82
Omoo 21
Once a Week 105
Onderdonk, H. Revolutionary In-
   cidents 70
O'Neal's Beach and Bar 82
Onward 21
Opera Dancer 21
Orations and Speeches 100
Orators, Living, of America 82
   Of the Revolution 82
   Of France 82
   Of the Age 82

Oratory 37
Ordenanza Militar 49
Oregon Newspapers 105
Oriental Magazine 105
Ormond 21
Ormsby, R. McK. The Whig Party 72
Orosius' History 65
Orphan Boy 21
Orphans of Normandy 21
Orpheus. Mystical Hymns of 91
Orton, H. S. Camp Fires 107
Osborn, H. S. Palestine 56
Osborn, Lieut. S. Arctic Journal 52
Oscanyan, C. Sultan and his Peo-
   ple 56
Osceola, the Seminole 21
Osgood, Frances S. Poems 91
Osgood, S. Mile-Stones 96
   The Hearthstone 96
Ossian's Poems 91
Ossoli, Margaret. At Home and
   Abroad 56
Ostler, E. Life of Admiral Ex-
   mouth 82
Oswald, J. Dictionary 93
Otis, Mrs. H. Gray. The Barclays 9
Otis, Jas. Life 82
Otto, Dr. F. J. Detection of Pois-
   ons 45
Ought American Slavery to be Per-
   petuated 97
Our Farm of Four Acres 42
Our First Families 21
Our Globe 62
Our Village 21
Outlaw 21
Out of the Depths 21
Overman, F. Metallurgy 41
Over the Cliff 107
Ovid. Metamorphoses 88
   The Fasti, Tristia, Epistles 88
Owen, A. A Lost Love 107
Owen, D. D. Geology of Wiscon-
   sin 41
Owen, R. The Classification 43
   Paleontology 44
Owen, R. Dale. Footfalls 97
Oxberry's Dramatic Biography 82
Oxford Chronological Tables 73

P

Pacha of Many Tales 21
Pacific Medical and Surgical Journal 105
Pacific Railroad Reports 21
Pacific Star. San Francisco 5 35
Pacific, The. San Francisco 105
Packard, F. A. Of Convicts in
   Prisons 35
Page, D. Geology 41
Page, D. P. Of Teaching 93
Page, T. G. La Plata, etc 52
Paget, J. Hungary and Transylvania 56
Paine, Caroline. The Tent and
   Harem 58
Paine, M. Institutes of Medicine 45
   Materia Medica 45
   Commentaries 45
   On the Soul 23
Paine, R. T. Memoir of 82
Paine, T. Theological Works 29
Painters and Sculptors. Lives of 82
Palestine. Early Travels in 56
Paley, W. Natural Theology 29
Palfrey, J. G. Jewish Scriptures 29
   Evidences of Christianity 29
   New England 70
Palfrey, W. Life of 82

Palgrave, Sir F. Normandy and
   England 65
   The Anglo Saxons 65
Palmer, J. W. California and India 58
Pamela 21
Paragreens in Paris 21
Pardee, R. G. The Strawberry 42
Pardoe, Miss. A Life Struggle 9
   The Hungarian Castle 9
   Episodes 65
   Francis I. of France 65
   Louis XIV. of France 65
Parent's Assistants 22
Parenty, Abbe. Life of St. Angela 82
Paris tel qu'il est, etc 62
Paris, Versailles 62
Paris, J. A. Treatise on Diet 45
Paris Sketch Book 22
Park, Mungo. Life and Travels of 82
Parker, E. G. Rufus Choate 82
   American Orators 82
Parker, S. Tour 52
Parker, T. Discourse on Religion 29
Parkhurst, J. Hebrew Lexicon 103
Parkman, F. Prairie Life 52
   Vassall Morton 9
   The Conspiracy of Pontiac 70
Parkyns, M. Life in Abyssinia 58
Parnell, E. A. Chemical Analysis 39
Parnell T. Poetical Works 91
Parr S. Metaphysical Tracts 36
   Life, Writings 82
Parrott, F. Journey to Ararat 58
Parry, W. E. Arctic Voyages 62
Parsons, C. G. Tour among the
   Planters 52
   View of Slavery, etc 34
Parsons, Chief Justice. Memoirs
   of 82
Parsons, G. S. Nelsonian Reminis-
   cences 82
Parson's Daughter 22
Parsons, T. Essays 97
Parthenia 23
Partisan 22
Parton, J. Life of Aaron Burr 82
   Life of Horace Greeley 82
   Life of Jackson 82
   The Humorous Poetry 91
Parvin, T. The Proceedings of the
   Grand Lodge of Iowa 94
Pascal, B. Jacqueline 9
   Penace 29
   Thoughts and Letters 97
   Provincial Letters 97
Pasha Papers 97
Passions, The 31
Paston Letters 97
Pastor's Fireside 22
Patent Office Reports 42
Pathfinder 22
Patriot Preachers 82
Patronage 22
Patterson, S. E. B. Masters and
   Workmen 9
Patton, J. H. History of the Uni-
   ted States 70
Paul and Virginia 22
Paul Clifford 22
Paul Fane 22
Paul Ferroll 22
Paulding, J. K. Puritan and his
   Daughter 9
   Life of Washington 82
Pauli, Dr. R. Life of Alfred the
   Great 82
Pauline Seward 22
Peabody, Mrs. Miss Slimmen's
   Window 9

Payson, G. Totemwell 9
Peabody, W. B. O. Life of Cotton
  Mather 82
  Life of Alexander Wilson 82
  Life of L Putnam 82
  Life of D. Brainerd 82
  Life of J. Sullivan 88
  Life of General Oglethorpe 82
Peace 22
Peacocke, G. Headlong Hall 9
  Nightmare Abbey 9
  Maid Marian 9
  Crotchet Castle 9
Peacocke, Dr. J. S. Creole Or-
  phans 9
Peaks and Passes 62
Pearce, R. Memoirs of Marquis
  Wellesley 82
Pearce, S. Annals of Luzerne Coun-
  ty 76
Pearl Fishing, etc 22
Peck, Rev. G. Wyoming 76
Peck, G. W. Melbourne, etc 68
Peck, J. M. Life of Daniel Boone 82
Peck, Rev. J. T. The True Woman 82
  Christianity 29
Peeps from a Belfry 21
Peg Woffington 22
Pegge, S. The English Language 93
Peirce, B. Mechanics 39
Pelham 22
Pelham Novels 23
Pellico, Silvio. Mie Prigioni 82
Pencil Sketches 22
Pendennis 22
Peninsular Scenes and Sketches 22
Penn, W. Life of, by D. E. Ellis 82
  Life of, by W. H. Dixon 93
  No Cross No Crown 29
Pennsylvania Records 70
Pennsylvania Archives 70
Penny Tract 22
Pentamerone 22
Pen Owen 22
Pepys, S. Diary 83
Perce, E. The Battle Roll 73
  The Last of his Name 9
Percival, J. G. Poetical Works 91
  Clio. No. 3 91
  The Dream of a Day 91
Percival Keene 22
Percy Anecdotes 101
Percy, T. Reliques 22
Pere la Chaise 22
Periodicals, Newspapers, and Maga-
  zines 104, 105
Perkins, E. T. Na Mota 52
Perry, Com. M. Expedition to Ja-
  pan 58
Perry, O. H. Life of 82
Persecutions of the Protestants 65
Persile y Sigismunda 22
  Translated 22
Persons' Satires. Translated 88
Persian Letters 97
Perthes, F. Memoirs of 82
Peschel, C. F. Physics 40
Pestalozzi, J. H. Educational
  Principles 82
Peterman and Milner's Physical At-
  las 44
Peter Schlemil in America 22
Peter Simple 22
Peter Wilkins 22
Peters, R. United States Digest 32
Peters, W. Poets and Poetry of
  Greece 88
Peterson, C. J. Old Stone Mansion 9
  Kate Aylesford 9

Peterson, G. History of Rhode
  Island 76
Peterson, R. E. Familiar Science 40
Peter the Great. Life of 88
Petrarch. One Hundred Sonnets 91
  Sonnets and Odes 91
  Triumphs of 91
  Poems 91
Petronius Arbiter. The Satyricon 88
Pettigrew, T. J. Collection of Epi-
  taphs 100
Peveril of the Peak 22
Pfeiffer, Ida. Lady's Second Jour-
  ney 60
  Journey to Iceland 56
Phædrus 88
Phædrus and Terrence 88
Phantom Ship 22
Phelps, Mrs. L. Ida Norman 9
  Hours with my Pupils 93
Phelps, S. D. Sunlight and Hearth-
  light 9
Philadelphia in 1852 82
Philadelphia Monthly 105
Philibert 22
Philidor, A. D. Studies of Chess 46
Philip, A. P. W. Preserving of
  Health 45
Philip Augustus 22
Philips, Gov. Voyage to Botany
  Bay, etc 58
Philips, J. A. Manual of Metallur-
  gy 41
  Mining and Metallurgy 41
Philips, W. Protection and Free
  Trade 35
Philip II. Reign of, by W H. Pres-
  cott 82
Phillippo, J. United States and
  Cuba 34
Phillips, G. J. System of Mining 41
Phillips, G. Geology 41
Phillips, S. Three Plain Discourses 99
Phillips, W. On Marine Insurance 32
Philology, Technology and Names 93
Philosophers. Lives of, by Laertius 82
  Lives of, by Fenelon 82
Philosophical Transactions 40
Philosophy 36, 37
Philosophy, Science and Arts 36, 49
Philostratus 88
Philothea, by L. Maria Child 22
Phipps, J. The State of Man 97
Phœnixiana 22
Phrenology 45
Physics 38, 40
Physiognomy 45
Physiology 45
Piazza Tales 22
Picciola 22
Pickering, C. The Races of Man 44
Pickering, E. Agnes Serle 9
Pickwick Club, by Dickens 22
Pictorial Gallery of Race Horses 102
Pictures from Battle Fields 72
Pierce B. Treatise on Sound 40
Pierce, Franklin. Life of, by Haw-
  thorne 82
Piggott, A. S. Of Copper 41
Pigott, G. Scandinavian Mythology 88
Pike, B. Jr. Catalogue of Instru-
  ments 40
Pike, Z. M. Life of 82
Pilgrims of the Rhine 22
Pilgrims of Walsingham 22
Pilot 22
Pindar's Odes. Translated 88
Piney Wood Tavern 22
Pinkerton J. Voyages and Travels 56

Pinkney, W. Life of 82
Pioneer Magazine 105
Pioneer Women of the West 88
Pioneers 22
Pirate 22
Pirate and Three Cutters 22
Pitcairn's Island [60
Pitkin, T. History of the United
  States 70
  Statistical View of the United
  States 82
Pitt, Wm. Life of 82
Placer Times 105
Plans of the Battles of the Revolu-
  tion 70
Planter's Daughter 22
Planter's Northern Bride 22
Plant Hunters 22
Plato's Works. Literally translated 88
  Against the Atheists 88
  Apology of Socrates, etc 88
Platt, J. Manners and Customs 62
Plautus. Comediæ Tres 88
  Comedies. Literally translated 88
Pletterhaus, Louisa. Poor Young
  Lady 88
Plinius, C., Secundus. Natural His-
  tory 88
Plotinus. Five Books. Translated 88
  Select Works. Translated 88
Pluribustah 22
Plutarch's Lives. Translated 88
  Morals. Translated 88
Poacher 22
Pococke, E. India in Greece 67
Poco Mas. Adventures in Spain 56
Poe, Edgar. Works 99
  Eureka, a Prose Poem 91
Poems, by the author of John Hali-
  fax 91
Poeti Italiani, Dantes, Petrarca, etc 91
Poetry 89, 92
Poetry of the Passions 91
Poets, English. Lives of 83
  Female, of America 83
  and Poetry of America 83
  of England 83
  of Europe 83
Polar Seas and Regions 60
Political economy 34, 35
Politics 33, 34
Pollard, E. Black Diamonds 9
Polo, Marco. Travels 68
Polybius. General History 88
Poole, J. Little Pedlington 9
Poole, S. Englishwoman in Egypt 56
Poole, W. F. Index to Periodicals 103
Poor Boy and Merchant Prince 22
Poor Cousin 22
Poor Fellow 22
Poor Jack 22
Pope, A. Poetical Works, by Ca-
  ruthers 91
  by Cary 91
  Life of 83
Pope or President 106
Popular Tales, by Miss Edgeworth 22
Popular Tales, by Griffam 22
Popular Tales from the Norse 22
Porcelain and Glass Manufactures 48
Porphyry. Select Works 88
Porter, Jane. Hungarian Brothers 9
  The Recluse of Norway 9
  Scottish Chiefs 9
  Thaddeus of Warsaw 9
  Pastor's Fireside 9
  Lakes of Killarney 9
  Angela 9
Porter, Rev. J. L. Damascus 56

Porter's Common 92
Portrait Annual 102
Portrait Gallery 83
Portraits, with Memoirs 83
Portraits of my Married Friends 22
Posche and Goepp. New Rome 34
Posey, T. Life of 83
Post, H. N. V. Visit to Greece, etc 56
Post-Offices in the United States 106
Potiphar Papers, by G. W. Curtis 22
Potter, A. Handbook for Readers 93
Potter, Major Roger Sherman. 83
Powell, B. Natural Philosophy 56
Powell, J. J. Laws of Contracts 32
Powell on the Order of Nature 108
Practice of Surveying and Leveling 39
Praed, W. M. Poetical Works 91
Prairie 22
Prairie Bird 22
Prayer, Common 29
Preacher and King 22
Preble, E. Life of 83
Precaution 22
Prenticeana 101
Prentiss, S. S. Memoir of 83
Presburg, B. F. The Mustee 9
Prescott, G. B. Electro-Telegraph 39
Prescott, H. P. Tobacco 42
Prescott, W. H. Miscellanies 97
Life of C. B. Brown 83
Ferdinand and Isabella 83
Reign of Phillip II. 83
Conquest of Mexico 70
Conquest of Peru 70
President's Daughter 22
Presidents of the United States 83
President's Messages and Documents 34
Preston, J. A Liveless Life 29
Pretenders, The, by J. H. Jesse 83
Prevost, Abbe. Manon Lescaut 9
Priaulx, O. Questionless Mosaicæ 29
National Education 93
Pride and Prejudice 22
Pride of Life 26
Pride of the Village 22
Priestly, J. Christian Truth 22
Prime, S. I. Travels in Europe, etc 56
The Bible in the Levant 83
Prime, W. C. Boat Life in Egypt 56
Tent Life in the Holy Land 56
Prinsep, H. T. Thibet, Tartary, etc 58
Prior, J. Life of Burke 83
Life of Goldsmith 83
Prior, M. Poetical Works 83
Prison Discipline Society Reports 35
Prison Life of Silvio Pellico, etc 83
Prisoner of the Border 22
Pritchard, J. C. History of Man 44
Privateersman 22
Proceedings of the Court Martial of
A. S. McKenzie 32
Proclus. Commentaries on the
Timæus 32
Fragments of his Lost Writings 32
The Theology of Plato 32
Elements of Theology 29
Procrastination 22
Proctor, Anne. Legends and Lyrics 9
Professor 22
Progress and Prejudice 22
Propertius' Elegies 86
Prose Writers of America 83
Protestant, The 22
Prout, Father. Reliques of 97
Proverbs, Epitaphs and Quotations 100
Proverbs. Hand-book of 100
Foreign. Hand-book of 100
Provost and other Tales 22

Publisher's Circular 105
Puddleford and its People 22
Puddleford Papers 22
Puffendorf's Laws of Nature, etc 31
Pugh, W. O. Dictionary, Welsh 103
Pugin, A. W. Floriated Ornaments 46
Pulaski, Count. Life of, by Sparks 83
Pulsky, F. The tri-color on the Atlas 58
Pulsky, Theresa. Tales and Traditions 9
Punch 105
Punch's Letter Writer 22
Punch's Letters to his Son 22
Punch's Prize Novelists 22
Puritan and his Daughter 22
Pursh, F. Plants of North America 42
Pursuit of Knowledge 97
Putnam, G. P. Book-buyer's Manual 107
Putnam, I. Life of, by F. Bowen 83
Life of, by W. B. O. Peabody 83
A Biography, by G. C. Hill 83
Putnam, J. D. R. The Rower's Manual 46
Putnam's Hand-book 97
Pynshurst 22
Pyrrhus 83

Q

Quackenbos, G. P. Natural Philosophy 40
Quain and Wilson's Anatomical Plates 45
Quaker Soldier 9
Quarantine and Sanitary Convention 35
Quadrupeds, Natural History of 43
Quarterly Review 105
Quartrefage's Rambles of a Naturalist 108
Queechy 22
Queen of Hearts 22
Queen's Necklace 22
Quentin Durward 22
Queens of England, by Mrs. M. Hall 83
by A. Strickland 83
by F. Lancelot 83
of France, by Mrs. F. Bush 83
of Spain, by A. George 83
Quevedo, Francisco de. Visions 9
Quincy, J. Jr. Memoir of 83
Quincy, J. Memoir of 83
Quits 22
Quinctillian. Institutes 88
Quod, John. The Attorney 9
Quotations 100

R

Rabelais, F. Works 9
Œuvres de 9
Rachael Gray 22
Rachel. Memoirs 83
Racine, J. Theatre Complete 22
Œuvres de 22
Radcliffe, Ann. Mysteries of Udolpho 9
Romance of the Forest 9
Raffles, Sir S. History of Java 67
Rainey, T. Ocean Steam and Post 35
Rale, S. Life of 83
Raleigh, Sir Walter. By C. Kingsley 83
Life of, by Mrs. Thompson 83

Rambach, C. Theosaurus Eroticus 103
Rambler, The 97
Ramsay, A. C. The Mexican War 70
Ramsay, Chevalier. On Religion 29
Ran Away to Sea 22
Randall, H. S. Jefferson 83
Sheep Husbandry 42
Randolph, J. Life of 83
Randolph, J. T. Cabin and Parlor 9
Ranke, L. History of the Popes 65
History of Servia 65
Civil Wars in France 65
Rasselas 108
Ratlin the Reefer 22
Rauch, F. A. On the Human Soul 29
Raumer, K. German Universities 65
Rawlinson, R. Historic Evidences 73
Rawson the Renegade 22
Ray, J. Medical Jurisprudence 32
Reach, A. B. Claret and Olives 56
Clement Lorimer 9
Read, T. B. Poems 91
Reade, C. Love Me Little 9
Peg Woffington 9
Christie Johnstone 9
Never Too Late to Mend 9
White Lies 9
A Good Fight, etc 10
The Eighth Commandment 97
Readings for the Young 97
Reason Why 97
Reality 22
Recaptured Negro 22
Recluse of Norway 22
Recollections of a Southern Matron 22
Recopilacion de Ranas Militaires 32
Records of Rhode Island 70
Rectory of Moreland 22
Red Book 22
Redding C. Modern Wines 48
Redfield, J. W. Physiognomy 45
Redgauntlet 22
Red Jacket 83
Red Rover 22
Redskins 22
Redwood 22
Reed, A. Martha 29
Reed, H. On English History 97
On English Literature 97
Reed, J. Life of, by J. Renwick 83
Life of, by H. Reed 83
History of Rutland, Mass 70
Reel in a Bottle 29
Remelin, C. Vine Dresser's Manual 42
Rees, A. Cyclopedia 103
Reeves, J. Law of Shipping 32
Reginald Dalton 22
Register, Niles' Weekly 105
Register of Army and Navy Officers 83
Reglamento para la Infanteria 49
mandato en la Mexicana 49
Reichenbach, C. Magnetic Letters 39
Dynamics of Magnetism 39
Reid, A. Dictionary 103
Reid, Mayne. Wild Life 53
The Wood Rangers 53
Odd People 60
The White Chief 10
The Boy Hunters 10
Young Voyagers 10
Young Yagers 10
Desert Home 10
Rifle Rangers 10
Scalp Hunters 10
Bush Boys 10
War Trail 10
Plant Hunters 10
Ran Away to Sea 10
Osceola, the Semicolv 10

Reigart, J. F. Life of Robert Fulton 83
Reine Canziani 96
Religion 26, 30
Religious Society of Friends 73
Reminiscences of the Zouaves 83
Rene ; or the Snow Bird 22
Renaudot, E. Ancient India and China 58
Renee, A. Louis XVI. et sa Cour 83
Rennell, J. Western Asia 62
System of Herodotus 58
Rennie, J. Bird Architecture 44
Renwick, J. Life of D. Rittenhouse 83
Life of Count Rumford 83
Life of J. Reed 83
Life of John Jay 83
Life of Hamilton 83
Life of De Witt Clinton 83
Repertory of Arts 105
Stryker's American 105
Reports 105, 106
of the General Land Office 106
of the Secretary of the Treasury 106
on the Commercial Relations 106
of Pacific Railroad Route 106
Instruction in California 106
State Hospital Committee 106
of the State Land Sales 106
on Sickness and Mortality 106
of the Census for 1858 106
Industry of all Nations 106
from the Seat of War 106
Schools of Pennsylvania 106
Smithsonian Institution 106
Mercantile Library of San Francisco 106
State Agricultural Society 106
Horticultural Society 106
Mechanic's Institute 106
Harper's Ferry Invasion 34
on Small Arms 49
of Mutual Life Insurance Company 36
of the Prison Society 35
of Commerce and Navigation 35
Repton, H. Landscape Gardening 42
Resignation 22
Retribution 22
Retrospective Review 105
Raumont, A. de. The Carafas 66
Reuss, W. F. Trade 35
Revere, Lieut. Tour in California 53
Reveries of a Bachelor 10
Reviews. British, Medico-Chirurgical 104
Brownson's Quarterly 104
Edinburgh 105
Selections from 105
Foreign Quarterly 105
North American 105
North British 105
Quarterly 105
Revue de deux Mondes 105
Reynard the Fox 91
Reynolds, G. W. M. Opera Dancer 10
Olivia 10
Reynolds, Sir J. Life of 83
On Pictures 46
Works 46
Rhees, W. J. Manual of the Public Libraries of the United States 1859 107
Rhode Island Colonial Records 70
Rhodius Apollonius. Argonautics 88
Ribault, J. Life of 83
Ricauti, J. A. Rustic Work 46
Rice, N. P. Discovery of Etherization 43

Rice, Rosella. Mabel 10
Rich, O. Catalogue of Books 107
Richard Cœur de Lion. Life of 83
Richard Hurdis 23
Richard of Cirencester's Chronicle 66
Richard Savage 23
Richard the Fearless 10
Richardiere, B. de la. Bibliotheque 90
Richards, T. A. Appleton's Hand-Book 62
Richards, W. E. Electron 91
Richardson and Gray's Zoology 43
Richardson, C. Dictionary 103
Richardson, J. Arctic Expedition 63
Journal of a Boat Voyage 53
To Central Africa 58
Richardson, S. Pamela 10
Clarissa Harlowe 10
Sir Charles Grandison 10
Richter, J. Paul. Extracts from 97
Richmond in by-gone Days 97
Ridge, B. Health and Disease 45
Ridgeley, D. Annals of Annapolis 70
Rienzi 23
Rifle Rangers 23
Right at Last 23
Rigsby, J. The Shoe and Canoe 53
Riley, H. H. Puddleford 10
Puddleford Papers 10
Riley, J. Narrative of his Shipwreck 58
Sequel to 58
Rinaldo Rinaldini 23
Ringgold, C. Charts 62
Riplet's Strength of Nations 34
Ripley, J. Hand-book 103
Ripley, H. J. The Gospels 99
Acts of the Apostles 99
Ripley, R. S. War with Mexico 70
Rita 10
Ritchie, J. S. Wisconsin 62
Ritchie, L. Schunderbannes 10
Robert Oakland 10
Ritchie, Mrs. Twin Roses 10
Mimic Life 83
Autobiography of an Actress 83
Ritson, J. Ancient Songs and Ballads 91
Rittenhouse, D. Life of 83
Ritter, H. History of Philosophy 73
Rivals, by Clemens 23
Rivals, by Gerald Griffin 23
Rivero, M. Peruvian Antiquities 88
Rivers, W. J. History of South Carolina 70
Rives, W. C. Life of James Madison 83
Rob of the Bowl 23
Rob Roy 23
Robbins, A. Loss of the Commerce 60
Robbins, C. Old North Church 72
Robert Graham 23
Robert Oaklands 23
Roberts, W. Conveyances 39
Robertson, Rev. F. W. Sermons 97
Lectures and Addresses 97
Robertson, W. Charles V. by Prescott 83
Life of T. A'Becket 83
Ancient India 87
Historical Works 99
History of Scotland 66
History of America 70
Robin Hood. Ballads and Songs 91
Robinson, A. Life in California 53
Robinson, C. Voyages 53
Robinson Crusoe 23
Robinson, Dr. E. Biblical Researches 86

Robinson, Mrs. Kansas 53
Robinson, Mrs. Mary. Memoirs of 83
Robinson, P. F. Rural Architecture 48
Farm Buildings 48
Robinson, Rev. S. The Church of God 99
Robinson, Solon. Hot Corn 10
Roche, R. M. Children of the Abbey 10
Rochefoucauld. Maxims et Pensees 97
Moral Reflections and Maxims 97
Rochester 23
Rockingham, Marquis. Memoirs of 83
Albermarle 83
Rockwell's Report of Routes 35
Roderick Random 23
Rodney, Admiral. Life of 83
Roe, A. S. Time and Tide 10
The Star and Cloud 10
A Long Look Ahead 10
True to the Last 10
How Could He Help It 10
Rogers, C. Scottish Minstrel 91
Rogers, H. The Greyson Letters 97
Eclipse of Faith 97
Reason and Faith 97
Rogers, H. J. Code of Signals 35
Marine Telegraphic List 35
Roger of Wendover's History 66
Rogers, S. Table Talk 97
Poetical Works 91
Rogers, Woodes C. Voyage 66
Roget, P. M. Thesaurus 93
Rohault us, J. Tractatus Physicus 40
Rojoux. Histoire de Angleterre 66
Roland Cashel 23
Roland, Madame. Life of 84
Rollin, C. Ancient History 73
Rollin, L. La Decadence 66
Romaic Beauties and Trojan Humbugs 86
Roman Baths 23
Romance and Reality 23
Romance and its Hero 23
Romance of a Poor Young Man 23
Romance of Forest 23
Romany Rye 23
Romaunt. Island Home 10
Rome 66
Rome, History of 66
Rome, Topographical Map of 62
Romilly, Sir S. Life of 83
Romulus. Life of 83
Ronald and Richardson's Chemical Technology 48
Rondelet, A. Le Pont de Rialto 65
Rookwood 23
Roorbach, O. A. Catalogue 107
Roper, W. Life of Sir Thomas More 83
Ropes, H. Cranston House 10
Rory O'More 23
Rosa, Salvator. Life of 83
Rosa, the Parisian Girl 23
Rosaline Woodbridge 23
Rosamond Gray 23
Rosamund 23
Rosary 23
Roscoe H. Lives of Eminent Lawyers 83
Digest of the Law of Evidence 39
Roscoe, W. Life of Leo X. 83
Lorenzo de Medici 83
Rose Clark 23
Rosa D'Albert 23
Rose Douglas 23
Rose, H. J. Biographical Dictionary 103

Ross, A. Adventures in Oregon 53
   Rocky Mountains 53
   Fur Traders in the Far West 53
   View of Religions 29
Roth, E. Life of Napoleon III. 84
Rousseau, J. J. Confessions de 84
Roving in the Pacific 59
Rowcroft's Tales of the Colonies 108
Rowland, H. A. Maxims of Infidelity 99
Roxana 23
Royal American Magazine, 1774 105
Royal Military Chronicle, 1811 49
Ruffini, Doctor Antonio 10
   Lorenzo Benoni 10
   Dear Experience 10
   Lavinia 10
Rumford, Count. Life of 84
Rundell, Mrs., and Birch. Cookery 48
Rupert, Prince, and the Cavaliers 84
Rupp, J. D. Lancaster County 23
   Religious Denominations 72
Rural Hours 97
Ruschenberger, W. S. W. Voyage 60
   Three Years in the Pacific 60
   Natural History 43
Rush, J. The Human Voice 45
Rush, R. Occasional Productions, etc 97
   Memoranda 66
Ruskin, J. Modern Painters 46
   Architecture and Painting 46
   The Seven Lamps 46
   The Stones of Venice 46
   Pre-Raphaelitism 46
   The Political Economy of Art 46
   The Elements of Drawing 46
   The True and Beautiful 45
   Beauties of 46
Russell 23
Russell, C. W. Life of Mezzofanti 84
Russell, Lady Rachael. Letters 84
Russell, Lord John. Memoirs of Fox 84
   Memoirs of Thomas Moore 84
Russell, Martha. The Tree of Idrasyl 10
Russell, Rev. M. Egypt, etc 67
   Nubia and Abyssinia 67
   Barbary States 67
   Polynesia 59
   Palestine 72
   Life of Cromwell 84
Russell, W. Extraordinary Men 84
   Extraordinary Women 84
Russell, W. H. India 59
   Expedition to the Crimea 66
   The War 66
Rustic Rhymes 91
Ruth 23
Ruth. Hall 23
Rutledge 23
Ruxton, G. F. Adventures in Mexico 53
   Life in the Far West 53
Ryan, J. R. Adventures in California 53
Ryland, J. E. Life of John Foster 84

S

Sabine, L. Life of Preble 84
   Loyalists of the Revolution 84
   Duels and Dueling 72
Sacred Edict of Kang-He 29
Sewulf's Travels in Palestine 56
Saffell, W. T. R. Revolutionary War 70

Saga of Frithiof 91
Saint Augustine's Confessions 29
Saint Gildas 23
Saint Giles and St. James 23
Saint Hospice 23
Saint Pierre. Paul et Virginie 10
Saint Ronan's Well 23
Saint Valentine's Day 23
Saintine, X. B. Piccio'a 10
Sala, G. A. Journey due North 53
   The Adventures 10
Sale, George. See Koran 29
Salle, R. de la. Life of 84
Sallust. Florus and Paterculus 88
   Gods and the World 88
   Histories 88
Salt Water 23
Salvation, Philosophy of 29
Salverte, E. Philosophy of Magic 101
Sampson, M. B. Rationale of Crime 55
Sampson, W. Life, by himself 84
Sam Slick, the Clock Maker 23
Sand, Mad. Geo. Teverino 10
Sanderson, J. Signers of the Declaration 84
Sand Hills of Jutland 23
Sands, R. C. Works 100
Sandwich Island Newspapers 105
Sanford and Merton 10
San Francisco Alta California 105
   Evening News, daily 105
   Herald, daily 105
   Journal of Commerce, daily 107
   Evening Bulletin 105
   Daily Times 105
   Ordinances, etc., 1854 31
   Prices Current to 1860 105
   Oriental 105
   Daily Whig from June, 1852, to 1853 105
   Evening Mirror 105
   Medical Press 105
   Pacific Expositor
Sanitary Economy, etc 45
Santaren, V. Americus Vespucius 60
Santo Sebastiano 23
Sargent, W. Expedition of Braddock 70
Sarratt, J. H. Game of Chess 46
   New Treatise 46
Sartaroe 23
Sartorius, C. Mexico 53
Satanstoe 23
Savage, J. Our Representative Men 84
Savage, W. Art of Printing 48
Savarin, B. Physiologie du Gout 97
Savigny, C. Von. Roman Law 72
Saxe, J. G. Poems 91
   The Money King 91
Saxton, L. C. Fall of Poland 66
Say and Seal 23
Say, J. B. Political Economy 35
Say, T. Conchology, etc 43
Saymore, Sarah E. Hearts Unveiled 10
Scalp Hunters 23
Scarlett, Sir J. C. South America 60
Scarlet Letter 23
Scarron, Paul. Comical Romance 10
   Comical Works 10
Scattergood Family 23
Scenes and Legends of Scotland 23
Scenes from Clerical Life 23
Scenes in the Rocky Mountains 53
Scenes of the Holy Land 56
Schelling. Idealisme Transcendentale 36
Schiller, F. Don Carlos 92

Schiller, F.
   Mary Stuart, Bride of Messina 92
   The Ghost Seer 92
   Wallenstein 92
   Early Dramas 92
   Letters. Translated 97
   Correspondence with Goethe 97
   Thirty Years' War 66
   Revolt of the Netherlands 66
   Minor Poems 41
   Poems and Ballads 41
   Life of, by T. Carlyle 84
   Life of 84
Schimmelpininck, Mary A. Autobiography 84
Schlegel, A. W. Dramatic Art 97
   Esthetic and Miscellaneous Works 97
Schlegel, F. Philosophy of History 73
   Lectures on Modern History 73
   Philosophy of Life 39
   History of Literature 73
Schleiermacher. Dialogues of Plato 97
Schlosser, F. C. The 18th Century 73
Schmidt, H. I. Education 93
Schmitz, L. The Middle Ages 66
Schmucker, S. S. Mental Philosophy 39
Scholfield, N. Geometry and Mensuration 38
   Trigonometry 38
Schoelcher, V. Life of Handel 84
School and Holiday 96
Schoolcraft, H. R. American Indians 70
   The Indian Tribes 70
   Journal through the Northwest 53
   Expedition to Itasca Lake 53
   Travels in the Mississippi Valley 53
Schoolcraft, Mrs. Black Gauntlet 10
School Days at Rugby 23
Schouw, J. F. The Earth and Man 44
Schubert, G. H. Mirror of Nature 44
Schunderhannes, the Robber 23
Science 36, 49
Scientific American 105
   And Mining Press 105
Scientific and Literary Treasury 48
Scoffern, J. Resources of Warfare 49
Scoresby, W. Records of his Life 84
Scott, M. Tom Cringle's Log 11
Scott, R. Greek-English Lexicon 103
Scott, Rosa. Marian Wallace 11
Scott, Sir Walter. Waverly Novels 10
   Waverly Novels and Waverly Tales 10
   Waverly 10
   Guy Mannering 10
   The Antiquary 10
   Rob Roy 10
   Black Dwarf, and old Mortality 10
   Heart of Mid-Lothian 10
   Bride of Lammermoor, and Legend of Montrose 10
   Ivanhoe 10
   The Monastery 10
   The Abbot 10
   Kenilworth 10
   The Pirate 10
   The Fortunes of Nigel 10
   Peveril of the Peak 10
   Quentin Durward 10
   St. Ronan's Well 10
   Redgauntlet 10
   The Betrothed 10
   The Talisman 10
   Woodstock 10
   The Highland Widow, and the Two Drovers

Scott, Sir Walter
  The Sergeant's Daughter, Aunt
    Margaret's Mirror, and the
    Tapestried Chamber, etc 10
  Saint Valentine's Day 10
  Anne of Geierstein 10
  Count Robert of Paris 10
  Castle Dangerous 10
  Tales of a Grandfather, from
    Scottish History 10
  The same, from History of
    France 11
  Poetical Works 91
  Lady of the Lake 91
  History of Scotland 66
  Demonology, etc 101
  Life, by McLeod 84
  Memoirs, by Lockhart 84
  Life of Napoleon 84
Scott, Rev. W. A. The Bible and
  Politics 29
  Daniel, a Model for Young Men 29
  The Giant Judge 29
  Queen Esther 29
  Trade and Letters 97
  The Wedge of Gold 97
  Samson 29
Scott. Gen. W. Infantry Tactics 49
  Life and Services, by Mansfield 84
  Life of, by Headley 84
Scottish Chiefs 97
Scottish Songs and Ballads 9
Scouring of the White Horse 11
Scout 23
Scrapes and Escapes, etc 101
Scriver, C. Cotswold's Emblems 29
Scrope, W. Days of Deer Stalking 46
Sancliff 33
Sea Lions 23
Sealsfield, C. The Cabin Book 11
Seaman, E. C. The Progress of Na-
  tions 73
S. E. O. Hungary and its Revolu-
  tions 66
Sears, E. H. Athanasia 11
  The Olden Time, etc 10
  Regeneration 97
Sears. Classical Studies 97
Sea Stories 11
Secchi, A. Electrical Rheometry 39
Second Love 23
Secret, The 23
  Convention of 1787 34
  Societies of the Middle Ages 66
Secundus, J. The Kisses 9
Sedgwick, C. Life of L. M. Davidson 84
Sedgwick, M. Memoir of Curtis 84
Sedgwick, Miss. C. M. New En-
  gland Tale and other Miscel-
  lanies 11
  Redwood 11
  Clarence 11
  Hope Leslie 11
  Married or Single 11
Sedgwick, T. Of Damages 32
Seaman, B. Voyage of the Herald 60
Segur, Count P. Expedition to Rus-
  sia 66
Selden, J. Memoirs of 84
  Table Talk 97
Selena 23
Self-Control 23
Selwyn, W. Law of Nisi Prius 23
Semi-Detached House, 23
Sentimental Journey 23
Seneca, L. A. Works 88
Sense and Sensibility 91
Sergeant, J. Select Speeches 100
Sermons, Unitarian 29

Settlers in Canada 23
Seven Years 63
Sewall, T. Phrenology 45
Seward, W. H. Life, by G. E. Bar-
  ker 84
  Life and Public Services of 84
  Life of John Quincy Adams 84
Sewell, E. Katherine Ashton 11
  Cleve Hall 11
  Ursula 11
Sewell, Miss. A Summer Tour 66
Sewell, W. Dialogues of Plato 97
Seyd, E. California and its Resour-
  ces 52
Seymour, C. B. Self-Made Men 84
Sforzosi. History of Italy 66
Shabby Genteel Story 23
Shaffner, T. P. The Telegraph Man-
  ual 39
Shahmah in Pursuit of Freedom 97
Shakspeare, H. Wild Sports of In-
  dia 50
Shakespeare, W. Plays, edited by
  Johnson, Stevens, etc. 92
  Dramatic Works 92
  Complete Works 92
  Dramatic and Poetical Works 92
  Supplement to his Plays 92
  By W. Hazlitt 92
  Poems 91
Shakspeare. His Times, by Tweddell 84
  By F. Guizot 84
Sharpe, S. History of Egypt 67
Sharswood G. Commercial Law 32
Shaw, H. Dresses and Decorations
Shaw, S. His Journal 84
Shea, J. G. The Mississippi Valley 63
Sheahan, J. W. Life of Stephen A.
  Douglas 84
Shearer, L. Decisions of the Su-
  preme Court of California 31
Shelley and Byron. Last Days of 84
Shelley, Mrs. Rambles in Germany
  and Italy 11
  Frankenstein 11
Shelley, Lady. Shelley Memorials 84
Shelley, P. B. Essays and Letters 97
  Poetical Works 91
  Works 91
Shelton, F. W. Peeps from a Bel-
  fry 11
Shenstone, W. Poetical Works 91
Shepard, C. U. Mineralogy 41
Shepherd's Fountain, by Mrs. Sher-
  wood 23
Sheridan, R. B. Dramatic Works 92
  Speeches 100
  Memoirs, by T. Moore 84
  Life of, by J. Watkins 84
Sherlock, Bishop T. His Works 29
Sherman, U. Governmental His-
  tory 70
Sherman, Mrs. Memoir of 84
Sherwood, Mrs. Works 11
Shiel, R. L. Sketches of the British
  Bar 84
Shirley 23
Short Stories, by C. Dickens 23
Siborne, Capt. W. Battle of Wa-
  terloo 66
Sidney, A. Government 34
  Life of 84
Sidney, Sir P. Works 100
  Life and Times 84
Sidney, S. Australia 89
Siege of Derry 23
Sigourney, Mrs. L. H. Poems 91
  Lucy Howard's Journal 11
  Past Meridian 97

Sigurd, the Crusader 64
Silk Manufactures 48
Silliman, B. Jr. Of Physics 40
Silliman, Prof. B. Visit to Europe 50
Silliman's Journal 105
Silloway, W. Text Book of Car-
  pentry 48
Simcoe, Col. J. G. The Queen's
  Rangers 70
Simon, Duke de Saint. Memoirs of 84
Simmonds, P. L. Curiosities of
  Food 48
Simms, W. G. Life of Captain
  J. Smith 84
  Life of Gen. N. Greene 84
  History of South Carolina 70
  Egeria 91
  The Lily and Totem 11
  The Foragers 11
  Catharine Walton 11
  Guy Rivers 11
  Richard Hurdis 11
  Border Beagles 11
  The Partisan 11
  Beauchampe 11
  The Yemassee 11
  Mellichampe 11
  Eutaw 11
  Blind Heart 11
  The Maroon 11
  Southward Ho 11
  Charlemont 11
  The Wigwam and Cabin 11
  The Cassique of Kiawah 11
Simple Story 23
Simpson, Sir G. Journey 63
Simkson, J. H. The Navajo. Coun-
  try 63
Simpson, J. F. Hand-book of Din-
  ing 48
Sims, R. The British Museum 107
Sinclair, C. Lord and Lady Har-
  court 11
  Modern Accomplishment 11
  Modern Society 11
  Modern Flirtations 11
  Beatrice 11
Sinding, Rev. P. C. Scandinavia 66
Siogvolk, P. Walter Ashwood 11
Sir Andrew Wylie 23
Sir Charles Grandison 23
Sir Frizzle Pumpkin 23
Sir Ralph Esher 23
Sir Rohan's Ghost 23
Sir Theodore Broughton 23
Sismondi, J. C. L. Literature 97
  The Italian Republic 66
  Fall of the Roman Empire 66
Sister Agnes 11
Sisters of Soleure 11
Sitgreave, Capt. L. Zuni and Colo-
  rado River 63
Six Nights with the Washingtonians 23
Six Years' Travel in Russia 63
Skearington, G. System of Far-
  riery 42
Skelton, J. Poems 91
Sketches, by Dickens 23
Sketches of Every Day Life 23
Sketches of Switzerland 66
Sketches of the English 23
Slade, A. Turkey and the Turks 66
Slaveholder Abroad 63
Slave of the Lamp 23
Slick, Jonathan. High Life in New
  York 11
Sloan, S. The Model Architecture 48
  Constructive Architecture 48
Sloat, L. W. Price Current 105

Smedley, E. Venetian History ... 84
Smedley, F. E. Lewis Arundel ... 11
Frank Fairleigh ... 11
Harry Coverdale's Courtship ... 11
Smee, A. Electro-Metallurgy ... 41
Smellie, W. Natural History ... 44
Smibert, T. Clans of Scotland ... 94
Smike, by Dickens ... 23
Smiles, S. Life of George Stephen-
son ... 84
Self-Help ... 84
Biographies ... 84
Smiles and Frowns ... 23
Smith, Adam. Moral Sentiments ... 37
Wealth of Nations ... 35
Smith, Alex. Poems ... 91
City Poems ... 91
Story of Mont Blanc ... 56
The Marchioness of Brinvillers ... 11
Adventures of Mr. Ledbury ... 11
The Scattergood Family ... 11
Smith, D. Italian Irrigation ... 39
Smith, C. B. Christian Metaphysics ... 29
Smith, C. H. The Human Species ... 44
Smith, Mrs. E. O. Newsboy ... 11
Smith, E. P. Political Economy ... 35
Smith, E. R. The Araucanian In-
dians ... 53
Smith, G. Consular Cities of China ... 59
Smith, H. Festivals, Games ... 46
Zillah ... 11
Smith, H. and J. Poetical Works ... 91
Smith, Irene D. The Elm Tree
Tales ... 11
Smith J. Science ... 103
Smith, J. The Book of Mormon ... 29
Smith, Capt. J. History of Virginia ... 57
A Biography ... 84
Life of, by G. S. Hillard ... 84
by W. G. Simms ... 84
Smith, J. C. Gazetteer of the
World ... 62
Smith, Sir J. E. English Flora ... 42
Smith, J. F. Alice Arran ... 11
Dick Marbank ... 11
Temptation ... 11
Rochester ... 11
Gus Howard ... 11
Stanfield Hall ... 11
Amy Lawrence ... 11
Fred Graham ... 11
Henri de la Tour ... 11
Charles Vavasseur ... 11
Marion Bernard ... 11
Dick Tarleton ... 11
Harold Tracy ... 11
Harry Ashton ... 11
Woman and her Master ... 11
The Virgin Queen ... 11
Minnie Grey ... 11
Fred Arden ... 11
Ellen de Vere ... 11
Smith, J. P. Queens of England ... 84
Smith, J. Jay. American Histori-
cal and Literary Curiosities ... 70
Smith, J. P. Scripture and Geology ... 29
Smith, J. T. Comparative History ... 73
Smith, J. V. C. Pilgrimage to
Egypt ... 56
Fishes of Massachusetts ... 43
Smith, J. W. Mercantile Law ... 32
Smith, M. G. Treatise on Teeth ... 45
Smith, Sidney. His Works ... 29
Sermons ... 29
Miscellanies ... 97
Life and Letters ... 84
Smith, S. C. Chile con Carne ... 53
Smith, T. Asheton. Reminiscences ... 84

Smith, W. Life of Fichte ... 84
History of New York ... 70
Dictionary of Antiquities ... 108
Dictionary of Geography ... 102
Thorndale, or the Conflict ... 11
Smithsonian Contributions ... 49
Smollett, Tobias. Works ... 11
Roderick Random ... 11
Smucker, S. The Four Georges ... 97
Arctic Explorations ... 53
The Four Georges ... 84
History of Napoleon III. ... 84
Of Catharine II ... 84
Of J. C. Fremont ... 84
Smuggler, by J. Banin ... 23
Smuggler, by James ... 23
Smyth, C. P. Teneriffe ... 36
Smythe, W. French Revolution ... 68
Lectures on Modern History ... 73
Snarleyow ... 23
Snow-flakes and Sunbeams ... 24
Snow Image ... 23
Soane, G. Curiosities of Literature ... 97
Sociable, or 1001 Amusements ... 46
Social Philosophy ... 36, 7
Socrates. Life, Teachings and Death ... 84
Solis, A. de. Conquesta de Mejico ... 70
Somerville, M. Physical Geography ... 62
Physical Sciences ... 40
Songs and Ballads from the German ... 91
Songs and Ballads of the Revolution ... 91
Songs of England and Scotland ... 91
Sophocles. Tragedies ... 92
Souvenir, Dramatic ... 92
Sorrows of Werter ... 11
Sortain, J. Count Arensberg ... 11
Soto, De. Life of ... 84
Soule, F. Annals of San Francisco ... 70
Soulie, F. La Chateau de Pyrenees ... 11
Marguerite ... 11
South Carolina, History ... 70
Southern Literary Messenger ... 105
Southey R. Complete Poetical
Works ... 91
Chronicles of the Cid ... 66
His Letters ... 97
Common Place Book ... 97
Life of Nelson ... 84
Life and Works of W. Cowper ... 84
British Admirals ... 84
Southey Caroline. Solitary Hours ... 91
Southgate, H. Travels ... 86
Southword Ho. ... 23
Southwold ... 23
Southworth, Emma D. E. N. The
Discarded Daughter ... 11
The Missing Bride ... 11
The Deserted Wife ... 11
The Curse of Clifton ... 11
Retribution ... 11
India ... 11
The Wife's Victory, etc. ... 11
The Lost Heiress ... 11
The Inebriate's Hut ... 11
The Three Beauties ... 11
The Lady of the Isles ... 11
The Two Sisters ... 11
Vivia ... 11
Old Neighborhoods, etc ... 11
The Haunted Homestead ... 11
Souvestre, E. Man and Money ... 11
Leaves from a family Journal ... 11
The Attic Philosopher ... 11
Sovereigns, Female Lives of ... 84
Sowerby, G. B. Conchological
Manual ... 43
Conchological Illustrations ... 43
Sowerby, J. E. Ferns of Great Bri-
tain ... 42

Soyer, A. The Pantropheon ... 45
Culinary Campaign ... 45
Spain. A year in ... 56
Spalding, W. English Literature ... 97
Italy ... 56
Spanish and English Testament ... 20
Sparks J. Life of Franklin ... 84
Life of Washington ... 84
Life and Writings of Washington ... 84
Life and Writings of Franklin ... 84
Life of J. Ribault ... 84
Life of Ledyard ... 84
Life of Pulaski ... 84
Life of La Salle ... 84
Life of Father Marquette ... 84
Life of C. Lee ... 84
Life of Gouverneur Morris ... 84
Correspondence of the Revolu-
tion ... 70
Spectator, The ... 97
British Essayists ... 97
Selections from ... 97
Speeches ... 100
Speeches. Collections ... 100
Speed, J. Historie of Britaine ... 66
Spence, Rev. J. Anecdotes ... 97
Spencer, H. Social Statistics ... 37
Spenser, E. Political Works ... 91
Spier, Mrs. Life in Ancient India ... 59
Spiers, A. Commercial Terms ... 93
Spiers and Surenne's French Dic-
tionary ... 103
Spinoza, Essai Metaphysique sur ... 36
Spirit Harp ... 91
Spirit of the Times ... 105
Spiritual Despotism ... 29
Spofford, P. Pagano-Papisms ... 29
Sports ... 45, 46
Spotiswoode, W. Russia ... 56
Sprague, J. T. The Florida War ... 70
Sprague, W. B. Life of T. Dwight ... 85
Spring, G. Power of the Pulpit ... 29
Spry, H. H. Modern India ... 59
Spurgeon, Rev. C. H. Sermons ... 29
Gems ... 29
Spurzheim, J. G. Phrenology ... 45
Phrenology and Physiology ... 45
Education ... 90
Spy ... 27
Squier, E. G. The Serpent Symbol,
etc ... 70
The States of Central America ... 70
Aboriginal Monuments ... 70
Nicaragua ... 70
and Davis, E. H. Monuments
of the Mississippi Valley ... 70
Notes on Central America ... 83
Stael. Corinne; or Italy ... 11
Alemagne ... 11
Translated ... 11
Stallo, J. B. Philosophy of Nature ... 37
Standish, the Puritan ... 23
Stanfield Hall ... 23
St. Angela Merici. Life of ... 85
Stanhope, Lady H. Memoirs of ... 85
Travels ... 56
Stanhope Burleigh ... 23
Stanley, Rev. A. P. Life ... 85
Stansbury, H. Great Salt Lake ... 53
Stanton, H. B. Reforms and Re-
formers ... 72
Stapleton's Canning and his Times ... 86
Star and Cloud ... 23
Starbuck, C. Hampton Heights ... 11
Star Chamber ... 23
Stark, J. Life of, by E. Everett ... 85
Starling, E. Noble Deeds of Wo-
man ... 85
Stars and Angels ... 26

Statesmen of the Commonwealth 85
State Trials 31, 32, 33
Statistics 61, 62
Statute Law 31
Statutes of California 31
Staunton, H. Chess Praxis 100
　The Chess Tournament 46
　The Chess Player's Hand-book 46
　The Chess Player's Companion 46
Steadman, E. C. Poems 91
Stebbings, Rev. H. The Christian Church 29
　Reformation .
Steele, A. Life of W. Brewster 85
Steinmetz, A. Japan and her People 59
Stephens, A. Memoirs of Tooke 85
Stephens, A. J. English Constitution 66
Stephens, Anna S. Heiress of Greenhurst 11
Stephens, Sir G. Of a Horse 108
Stephens, H. The Farmer's Guide 42
Stephens, Mrs. H. Magrur, the Martyr 11
　Mary Derwent 11
Stephens, H. I. Comic History 72
Stephens, J. Essays 97
Stephens, J. L. Travels in Greece 56
　Travels in Egypt and Arabia 56
　Central America 53
　In Yucatan 53
Stephenson, G. Life of 85
Step-Mother 23
Sterling, J. Life of 83
Sterne, Laurence. Works. 11
　Tristam Shandy 11
　Sentimental Journey 11
Steuben, Baron. Life of, by Bowen 85
Steuben, Gen. Life of, by Knapp 85
Stevenson, D. Canal Engineering 39
Stevenson, W. B. South America 53
Steward 23
Stewart, C. S. Brazil and La Plata 53
Stewart, W. C. Practical Angler 46
Stiles, E. Life of 83
Stilling, J. Pneumatology 101
　Autobiography of 85
Stinson, A. L. Easy Nat 11
Stirling, W. Charles V 85
Stirling, W. A., Earl of. Life of, by W. A. Dner 85
St. John, C. Sports of the Highlands 56
St. John, B. Purple Tints of Paris 56
　Village Life in Egypt 56
St. John, J. A. Egypt and Nubia 56
　Celebrated Travelers 85
St. Leonard, Lord. Book of Property 35
Stockhardt, J. A. Chemistry 39
Stoequeler. Life of Wellington 85
Stockton, Com. R. F. Life, etc 85
Stokes, J. Cabinet Maker 48
Stone, E. M. Life of John Howland 85
Stone, W. L. Border Warfare 70
　Life of Brant 83
　Life and Times of Red Jacket 85
　Matthias and his Impostures 85
Stories for the Home Circle 24
　From Blackwood 24
　From the Italian Poets 24
　Of an Old Maid 24
　Of English and Foreign Life 24
　Of Waterloo 24
Storrow, C. S. On Water Works 39
Story Book, by Hans Andersen 24
　Of a Feather 24
　Of a Pocket Bible 11

Story, J. Life and Letters 85
　Miscellaneous Writings 100
　Equity Jurisprudence 32
　Equity Pleadings 32
　Conflict of Laws 32
　Law of Agency 32
　Law of Bailments 32
　Bills of Exchange 32
　Law of Partnership 32
　Promissory Notes 32
Story, S. A. Caste 11
Story, W. W. On Contracts 32
　On Sales 32
Stout, F. B. Nicaragua 62
Stowe, Mrs. H. B. Sunny Memories 56
　Father Henson's Story 12
　The May Flower 12
　Dred 12
　Uncle Tom's Cabin 12
　The Minister's Wooing 12
Strabo. Geography 48
Strahlenberg's Europe and Asia 62
Strain, J. G. Journey to Chili, etc 53
Smith, Major H. Fortification, etc 49
Stranger at Home 24
Stratton, R. B. The Oatman Girls 85
Strauss, J. Polyglot Pocket-Book 103
Strauss, D. F. Life of Christ 29
Street, A. B. Woods and Waters 53
　Poems 91
Stretch, L. M. Beauties of History 73
Strickland, Agnes. Queens of England 85
　Queens of Scotland 85
　Pilgrims of Walsingham 12
　Edward Evelyn 12
Strickland, W. P. Old Mackinaw 62
Strife and Peace 24
Stuart and Revett. Athens 66
Stuart, C. Naval Dry Docks 49
Stuart, J. W. Life of Trumbull 85
Stuart, R. Dictionary of Architecture 95
Student 24
Storm, C. C. Morning Communings 30
Subaltern, The 12
　In America 53
Successful Merchant 24
Sue, E. Mysteries of Paris 106
　The Wandering Jew 12
　Atar Gull 12
　Mathilde 12
Suetonius. The Twelve Cæsars, etc 85
Sullivan, J. Life of 85
Sullivan, W. Men of the Revolution 85
Sully, Duke of. Memoirs 85
Sumner, C. Speeches and Addresses 100
Sunlight and Heartblight 24
Surgeon's Daughter 24
Susan Gray 24
Susannah 24
Swainson, W. Natural History 44
　Taxidermy, etc 44
　Instincts of Animals 44
　Animals in Menageries 44
　Classification of Animals 43
　Natural History of Quadrupeds 43
　Natural History of Birds 43
　Natural History of Fishes 43
　Shells and Shellfish 43
　And Shuckhard's, of Insects 43
　New Zealand 80
Swallow, G. C. Geology of Missouri 41
Swallow Barn 24
Swan, J. G. Northwest Coast of America 60
Sweat, J. Highways of Travel 56

Sweat, Mrs. Ethel's Love Life 12
Swedenborg, E. Animal Kingdom 41
　Economy of the Animal King dom 41
　Principles of Chemistry 30
　The Physical Sciences 40
　Principia 77
　Divine Love and Wisdom 29
　Divine Providence 29
　Conjugial Love 29
　Four Leading Doctrines 29
　Heaven and Hell 29
　Heavenly Arcana 29
　Four Treatises 29
　Spiritual Diary 29
　True Christian Religion 29
　Dictionary of Correspondences 29
　Life of, by B. F. Barrett 85
　Life of, by N. Hobart 85
Swell Life at Sea 12
Swift, Dean. Works 100
Swift, J. Poems 91
　Tale of a Tub 12
　Gulliver's Travels 12
Swinton, W. Rambles among Words 97
Swiss Cottage 24
Switzerland, History of 66
Sword and Gown 24
Sylvan Holt's Daughter 24
Sylvia's World 24
Symbols, Book of 29
Synesius on Providence. See Plotinus 29

T

Tableau de l'Histoire de Europe 66
Tacitus 88
Tahitan and English Dictionary 103
Tait, J. R. Dolce far Niente 91
Tait, T. The Strength of Materials 39
Tait, W. Magdalenism in Edinburgh 97
Tait's Edinburgh Magazine 104
Talba 24
Tale of a Tub 24
Tale of Two Cities 24
Tales from Household Words 24
Tales and Takings 24
Tales and Traditions of Hungary 24
Tales, by Countess D'Arbouville 24
Tales for the Marines 24
Tales from Real Life 24
Tales from the German 12
Tales of a Grandfather 24
Tales of Fashionable Life 24
Tales of the Genii 24
Tales of the Jury Room 24
Tales of the Peerage and Peasantry 24
Talfourd, T. N. Miscellaneous Works 104
　Writings 97
Talisman 24
Tallagetta; The Squatter's Home 24
Talleyrand, Prince. Life of 85
Tallis, Crystal Palace 10
Talmon, Thrace. Edith Hale 12
　Captain Molly 12
Tapestried Chamber 24
Tappan, W. B. Poems 91
Tarleton, Col. Campaign in 1781 70
Tasso, T. Godfrey of Boulogne 91
　Jerusalem Delivered 91
Tattler, The 97
Tattler and Guardian 24
Ta tsing-leu lee, Code, etc., of China 31
Tattersall, G. Gallery of Race Horses 11

Tautphœus, Baroness. The Initials 12
Quita 12
Cyrilla 12
Taylor, A. J. Medical Jurisprudence 33
Taylor, A. S. Poisons 45
Taylor, Bayard. Travels in Greece 56
Northern Travel 56
Landscapes from Egypt 56
The Lands of the Saracen 56
At Home and Abroad 56
Views Afoot 56
India, China and Japan 56
Journey through Central Africa 50
Cyclopedia of Travels 60
ElDorado 33
Poems of the Orient 91
Taylor, C. Five Years in China 59
Taylor, C. B. Legends and Records 12
Taylor, H. Notes from Life; in seven Essays 97
Taylor, Isaac. The World of Mind 36
Taylor, Jeremy. Holy Living, etc 29
Taylor, R. On Christianity 29
Taylor, R. C. Statistics of Coal 62
Taylor, T. Sketch of Clarkson 85
Taylor, W. California Life Illustrated 53
Street Preaching 29
Taylor, W. C. British Plutarch 85
Ancient History 70
History of Ireland 66
Taylor, W. B. S. University of Dublin 72
Taylor, Gen. Z. Life of, by H. Montgomery 85
Life of, by J. Frost 85
Technology 93
Tefft, B. F. Webster 85
Hungary and Kossuth 66
Tegners' Saga of Frithiof 91
Teignmouth, Lord. Life of Sir W. Jones 85
Telegraph. Story of 97
Telamacus 24
Temper, by Miss Marryat 24
Temper and Temperament 24
Tempest and Sunshine 24
Temple, E. Christian's Treasure Of Truth 30
Temple, Sir W. Memoirs of 85
Temptation 24
Tenant House 24
Tennant of Wildfell Hall 24
Ten Months in Mexico 53
Tennemann. History of Philosophy 72
Tennyson, A. Poems 91
In Memoriam 91
Maud, and other Poems 91
Idyls of the King 91
Tensas, M. D. Odd Leaves 97
Ten Thousand a Year 24
Terence. Comedies 88
Terentius, Afer. Comediæ 92
Ternaux, H. Bibliothequé Americaine 107
Voyages de l'Amerique 53
Essai sur l'Ancien Gundinamares 53
Histoire de Mexique, par Tezo 53
Tertullian's Apology 30
Testamentum Novum Græcum 30
Teverino 24
Thackeray, W. M. Book of Snobs 12
Pendennis 12
Jeames' Diary, etc 12
Luck of Barry Lyndon 12
Mr. Brown's Letters 12
Paris Sketch Book 12
Punch's Prize Novelists 12

Shabby Genteel Story 12
Yellow-Plush Papers 12
Henry Esmond 12
The Virginians 12
The Newcomes 12
Men's Wives and Fitz Boodle 12
Ballads 91
English Humorists 97
The Four Georges 97
Thacher, J. Military Journal 70
Biography 85
Thaddeus of Warsaw 24
Thalysie 24
Thatcher, B. B. Indian Biography 85
Thayer, W. M. Amos Lawrence 85
Theism, Christian 3
Theocritus. Bion, Moschus, etc 88
Theodore 24
Theodosius and Constantia 12
Theognis. Works 88
Theology 36, 30
Theophilus and Sophia 24
Thierry, A. The Conquest of England 66
History of the Tiers Etat 66
Thiers, A. The Mississippi Bubble; a Memoir of John Law 85
Consulate and Empire 66
French Revolution 66
Thine and Mine 24
Thinks I to Myself 24
Thirlwall, C. History of Greece 66
This, That and the Other 24
Thomas and Baldwin, Gazetteer 62
Thomas, Rev. C. W. West Coast of Africa 59
Thomas, F. S. The Psychologist 30
Thomas, G. Account of Pennsylvania 53
Thomas, I. Printing in America 72
Thomas, J. J. Farm Implements 73
Thomason, Rev. D. R 97
Thompson, A. S. New Zealand 59
Thompson, B. F. Long Island 70
Thompson, D. P. Gaunt Gurley 12
Thompson, H. Life of Hannah More 85
Thompson, J. Gazetteer 62
Thompson, J. P. Memoirs of D. Hale 85
Thompson's Life of G. Villars 85
Thom's Early English Romances 12
Thomson, Mrs. A. T. Life of Italeigh 85
Duchess of Marlborough 85
Thompson, J. New Universal Gazetteer 103
Thomson, T. Mineralogy and Geology 41
Thomson, W. Laws of Thought 97
Thompson, W. M. Land and Book 56
Thoreau, H. Life in the Woods 85
Thornbury, W. Life in Spain 56
Thorndale 24
Thornton, J. Landing at Cape Ann 70
Thornton, J. Q. Oregon 53
Thornton, R. J. Botany 42
Thorp, W. The British Empire 66
Thorpe, T. B. The Bee Hunters 24
Thoresby, R. Diary and Letters 85
Thousand and One Stories 24
Three Beauties 24
Three Clerks 24
Three Courses and a Dessert 24
Three Guardsmen 24
Three Marriages 24
Three Spaniards 24
Thucydides. History 66
Thunberg, C. P. Voyages au Japon 59

Thnos Mathos. Early Magnetism 30
Thurber, Prof. American Weeds 42
Tibullus. Poems, translated 88
Ticknor, C. Philosophy of Living 45
Ticknor, G. Spanish Literature
Tiffany, O. Brandon 12
The Canton Chinese 59
Tighe Lifford 12
Tilberghier, G. Essai 36
Tillotson, J. His Works 30
Timbs, J. School-Days of Eminent Men 85
Inventors and Discoveries 85
Year Book of Facts for 1859 40
Time and Tide 24
Timperley, C. H. Printers and Printing 40
Titcomb, Timothy. Letters 97
Gold Foil, etc 97
Title Hunting 24
To Be, or Not To Be 24
Todd, Rev. J. Memoirs of H. K. White 82
Todd, J. Hints to Young Men 97
Todd's Young Farmer's Manual 108
Toland, J. Christianity not Mysterious 30
Collection of pieces from his MSS 30
Letters to Serena 30
Tedradymus 30
Collection of Pieces 100
Tom Dowling 24
Tom Brown at Oxford 97
School Days at Rugby 97
Tom Burke of Ours 24
Tom Cringle's Log 24
Tomes, R. The Americans in Japan 59
Panama in 1855 53
Tom Jones 24
Tomlinson, C. Amusements in Chess 46
Useful Arts 48
Tomlinson, W. P. Kansas in 1858 53
Tone, Theobold W. Life 85
Tooke, J. Horne. Memoirs of 85
Diversions of Purley 93
Topographical Map of the Road from Missouri to Oregon 53
Topographical Works 61, 62
Lorabia, P. P. T. Ejercicios Espirituales 30
Totemwell 24
Touchard, Lafosse. Histoire de Paris 66
Toulotte, M. A. C. T. De la Barbarie 77
Tout en Peu 24
Townsend, C. H. Facts in Mesmerism 101
Townsend, Virginia. While it was Morning 12
Living and Loving 12
Townsend, W. C. Modern State Trials 33
Tracts 30
Tracy's Ambition 24
Train, G. F. Young America in Wall Street 63
The American Merchant 60
Spread Eagleism 60
Traits and Stories of the Irish 24
Thrall, R. T. Hydropathic Encyclopedia 45
Transactions of the American Antiquarian Society 106
Transactions of the California State Agricultural Society 42
Horticultural Society 42

Transcendentalism 9L
Travels 50, 58
Travels, by Baron Munchausen 24
Travels to the Cordilleras 53
Travis, G. Letters 30
Treasury of History 73
Treasury of Natural History 43
Treatise 31
Tredgold, T. On the Steam Engine 30
Warming and Ventilating 39
Trelawney, Capt. The Younger
Son 12
The Last Days of Shelley and
Byron 85
Trelawney of Trelawne 24
Tremaine 04
Tremenheere, H. S. Constitution
of the United States 34
Trench, R. C. Life of Compton 85
The Study of Words 93
Glossary of English Words 93
Sermons 30
Trescott, W. H. Diplomatic His-
tory 31
Tresaillian and his Friends 24
Trevelyan 24
Trials of Jessie Loring 24
Trials of Margaret Lindsay 24
Trials, State 31, 32, 33
Trials of the Heart 24
Tri-colored Sketches of Paris 56
Trimmer, J. Practical Geology 41
Tristam Shandy 24
Trollope, A. Barchester Towers 108
The Kellys and O'Kellys 12
The Bertrams 12
Castle Richmond 12
Doctor Thorne 12
The Three Clerks 12
Italian Women 85
West Indies 53
Trollope, Mrs. Belgium 56
Domestic Manners 53
Trotter, J. Memoirs of Chas. Jas.
Fox 85
Tronin, M. Memoirs de 85
Trubner, N. American Literature 107
True to the Last 24
True Womanhood 24
Trumbull, H. Discovery of America 71
Trumbull, Jonathan. Life of 85
Autobiography, Letters, etc 85
Tucker, A. Light of Nature 30
Tucker, G. History of the United
States 71
Tucker, J. S. Memoir of Earl St.
Vincent 85
Tuckerman, H. T. Italian Sketch
Book 56
Sicily 56
A month in England 56
The Optimist 97
Characteristics of Literature 97
Rambles and Reveries 97
American Painters 85
Horatio Greenough 85
Essays 85
Thoughts on the Poets 85
Tudela, Benjamin of. Travels 85
Tudor, W. The Life of Jas. Otis 85
Tuel, J. E. War in Italy 85
Twomey, M. Geology of South Car-
olina 41
Tupper, M. F. Proverbial Philoso-
phy 100
Poetical Works 91
Mr. Esop Smith 97
Crock of Gold 17
Turnbull, B. Cuba 53

Turnbull, W. The Strength of Tim-
ber 40
Turner, E. Chemistry 40
Turner, G. A. Poems 91
Turner, J. Pallas Armata 49
Turner, S. Sacred History 86
Turner, W. R. Charges against 33
Turner, Jack Hopeton 12
Tuthill, Mrs. L. C. Reality 12
Tweddle, G. Shakspeare 85
Tweedie, Rev. Dr. Ruined Cities
of the East 57
Twelfth Night at the Century Club 97
Twelve Years in China 89
Twenty Years After 24
Twice Told Tales 34
Twins and Heart 24
Twin Roses 24
Twiss, H. Life of Lord Eldon 85
Two Admirals 24
Two Drovers 24
Two Millions 91
Two Sisters 24
Two Sisters 24
Two Years Ago 24
Tyle, S. Baconian Philosophy 24
Tylney Hall 24
Tyndall, the Glaciers of the Alps 56
Types 24
Typhon, War with the Gods 91
Tyson, P. T. Geology of California 41
Tytler, A. F. Universal History 73
Tytler, P. F. History of Scotland 66
North Coast of America 53

U

Uhlemann, M. Three Days in Mem-
phis 57
Ullman, C. Worship of Genius 30
Umsted, Mrs. Southwold 12
Uncle Ralph 24
Uncle Tom's Cabin 24
Undivided Household 24
Ungava 33
Ungewitter, F. H. Europe 66
United States. Acts and Resolu-
tions 31
Astronomical Expedition 38
Digest of the Decisions 33
Diplomatic Correspondence 33
Official Register 103
Public and General Statutes 31
Statutes at Large 31
versus Limantour 33
Universal Biography. Hand-book
of 85
Upham, C. W. Life of Sir Henry
Vane 85
Life of J. C. Fremont 85
Upham, T. C. On the Will 36
Mental Action 45
Ups and Downs 25
Upton, R. A. Home Studies 95
The Housekeeper, etc 42
Ure, A. Dictionary of Arts, etc 104
Ursula 25
Useful Arts 47, 48
Useful Little Girl 85
Utopia 25

V

Vara-Macus of the East Indies 62
Vaughan, H. Sacred Poetry 92
Vaughan, R. Revolutions 108
Vale of Cedars 85

Valentine, T. D. History of New
York 71
Corporation Manual 105
Valentine Vox 85
Valerius. Paterculus, Florus, etc 85
Valerius 12
Valledo, J. De Matematicas 58
Valoo, A. Le Chale Noir 12
Van Campen, Major. Life of 85
Vancouver, G. Voyage 60
Vandenhoff, G. Actor's Note Book 85
Van Doren, H. Mercantile Morals 27
Vane, H. Life of 85
Vanity Fair 25
Van Schaack, P. Life 85
Van Stanwood, G. Lives of Chief
Justices 85
Life of Algernon Sydney 85
Varu; or the Child of Adoption 12
Varro, O. Eddies round the Rec-
tory 12
Vasari, G. Lives of Eminent Paint-
ers 85
Vassall Morton 25
Vattel, E. Laws of Nations 31
Vaux, J. H. Memoirs 85
Vegetable Substances for Food 45
Veile, Mrs. Following the Drum 85
Venegas, M. History of California 71
Noticia de la California 53
Venetia 85
Veon, H. Duty of Man 30
Vera, by H. Conscience 25
Verdant Green, Adventures of 25
Veritas; a Poem 93
Vermond, P. Chronique Populaires 12
Vernon Grove 12
Vernon, Dr. L. Memoirs d'un
Bourgeois 85
Veronique 85
Verplanck, G. C. Discourses 97
Vert, Mad. le. Souvenirs of Travel 57
Vespucius. Researches concerning 85
Vestiges of Creation 44
Venillot, L. Les Français en Alge
ria 59
Vicar of Wakefield 25
Vicar of Wrexhill 25
Vicat, L. J. Treatise on Cement 40
Victoria 25
Vidocq. Memoirs of 85
Vigny, A. Servitude et Grandeur 37
Village Doctor 25
Villary, Geo. Life of 85
Vilette 25
Villoelada, F. N. Donna Blanca 12
Vinca d, P. Banquet Gourmands 12
Vincent, Earl St. Life of 85
Viola 25
Violet 25
Violet; or The Times we Live In 25
Virgil 33
Virgin Queen 25
Virginia Comedians 85
Virginia Illustrated, by Porte Cray-
on 102
Journal of the House 34
Documents of the House 34
Proceedings in the Convention 34
Journal of Convention in 1776 34
Journal of the Senate in 1775-6 34
Virginians 25
Vision of Rubeta 92
Visions of Francis Quevedo 25
Vivia 25
Vivian Grey 85
Vocabulary, English and Malay 100
Volney, C. F. C. View of the Uni
ted States 44

Voices of Nature 30
Voltaire, F. M. M. Theatre de 92
Contes et Romans 12
Memoirs, by himself 86
Siecle de Louis XIV 66
Louis XIV 86
Louis XV 86
Voltaire, le Roy 86
Von Raumer, F. England in 1841 57
Vose, G. L. Railroad Construction 39
Voyages around the World 59, 60
Voyages, Collections of 59, 60
Voyages and Travels 60, 58
Voyages of the Adventure and Bea-
gle 60
Vues de la Hollande 51

W

W, The Owl Creek Letters 97
Waddington, A. Frazer River
Mines 71
Wade, J. British History 103
Wafer, L. Voyage to America 53
Wablen, A. Moeurs et Costumes 94
Wakefield, E. G. England and
America 67
Waldeness, The, by W. Beattie 66
Waldor, M. Chas. Mandel 12
Waldor f Family 25
Walker, G. Chess and Chess-Play-
ers 46
Chess Studies 108
The Three Spaniards 12
Walker, J. Pronouncing Diction-
ary 103
Rhyming Dictionary 92
Walker, S. C. Planet Neptune 30
Walker's Manly Exercises 46
Wallenstein: Life of 86
Wallis, S. T. Spain 57
Walpole, H. Castle of Otranto 12
Anecdotes of Painting 46
Reign of George III 66
Private Correspondence 97
Royal and Noble Authors 66
Walsh, J. H. Domestic Economy 49
Walsh, R. Didactics 98
Walter Ashwood 25
Walton, J. and C. Cotton. Angler 46
Walter Thornley 25
Wanderings of a Pen and Pencil 57
Wandering Jew 25
Warburton, E. Darien 12
Prince Rupert 86
Conquest of Canada 71
Crescent and the Cross 57
Ward, C. G. Cottage on the Cliff 12
The Fisher's Daughter 12
Mysterious Marriage 12
Ward, H. The Cape and the Kaffirs 59
Ward, H. G. Mexico in 1829 53
Ward, J. Mathematician's Guide 38
Ward, J. H. Manual of Naval Tac-
tics 49
Ward, M. F. English Items 57
Ward, R. Life of Hannah More 86
Ward, R. P. Tremaine 12
Ward, S. Life of 86
Ward, W. India and Hindoos 86
Warden, J. A. Cultivation of
Hedges 42
Warden, R. B. View of Man and
Law 34
Ware, W. Zenobia 12
Julian 12
Aurelian 12
Warleigh 25

Warner, Misses. Say and Seal 12
Dollars and Cents 12
Wide, Wide World 12
Queechy 12
The Hills of Shatemuc 12
Warren, Joseph. Life of 86
Warren, Gen. Inauguration of the
Statue 96
Warren, J. C. Life of 86
Warren, J. E. Vagamundo 57
Warren, S. Ten Thousand a Year 12
Diary of a Physician 12
Miscellanies 12
Now and Then 12
Warren, T. R. Dust and Foam 53
War Trail 25
Washington, George. Revolution-
ary Orders 71
Writings of 100
Accounts with the United States 108
Maxims of 98
Political Legacies 98
Life of, by Irving 86
by John Marshall 86
by M. L. Weems 86
by J. K. Paulding 76
by A. Bancroft 86
by J. T. Headley 86
by Harriet Kirkland 86
by E. Everett 86
by J. Sparks 86
and his Generals, by Headley 86
in Domestic Life 86
Recollections and Memoirs of,
by G. Washington Parke Cur-
tis 86
by M. L. Weems 86
Waterhouse, G. R. Natural Histo-
ry of Mammalia 43
Waterton, C. Wanderings 51
Waterston, W. Cyclopedia of
Commerce 76
Water Witch 25
Watkins, J. Memoirs of Sheridan 86
Watson, A. Home Garden 42
Watson, J. F. Poetical Quotations 100
Annals of Philadelphia 71
Tales and Takings 12
Watt, J. Life of, by J. Muirhead 86
Watts, J. Flora Lyrica and Di-
vine Songs 92
Watts, R. Bibliotheca Brittanica 107
Waverley 25
Wayland, F. Memoirs of A. Jud-
son 86
Political Economy 86
Moral Science 39
Wayne, Gen. Anthony. Life of 86
Weale, J. Railway Making 39
Webb, J. Antiquity of China 67
Webb, T. S. Free Mason's Monitor 94
Webster, D, Life of, by P. Lyman 86
by R. F. Teft 86
by C. W. March 86
Life and Memorials of 86
Works 100
Obituary Addresses on 100
Webster, F. Phonographic Teacher 48
Webster, J. Works 92
Webster, N. Dictionary 103
Weems, M. L. Life of Washington 86
Weights and Measures. Report of 35
Weil, G. Biblical Legends 12
Weir, J. Lone Powers 12
Weisbach, J. Mechanics 39
Welby, Miss A. Poems 92
Weld, C. R. The Pyrenees 57
Wellesley, Marquis. Memoirs 86
Wells, D. A. Common Things 48

Wells, D. A. Familiar Science 48
Things not Generally Known 48
Year Book of Agriculture 42
Scientific Discovery 40
Wellington, Duke of. Speeches 100
Life of, by an Old Soldier 86
by M. Brialmont & R. G. Gleig 86
by J. H. Stocqueler 86
Life of, by Yonge 86
Memoirs of, by W. H. Maxwell 86
Victories of, by W. H. Maxwell 86
Welsford, H. English Language 93
Wentz, Sara A. Smiles and Frowns 12
Wept of Wish-ton-Wish 25
Westgarth, W. Australia, etc 59
Westminster Review 105
Weston, G. Progress of Slavery 72
Westwood. British Moths 43
Wetherill, C. M. Vinegar 48
Wetmore, A. Gazetteer of Missouri 62
Wharton. Queens of Society 86
What can Woman do 25
Whately, R. Logic 37
Wheat and Tares 20
Wheaton, H. International Law 31
History of the Northmen 66
Life of W. Pinckney 86
Wheeler, D. Gospel Labors 10
Wheeler, H. G. History of Con-
gress 34
Wheeler, G. Rural Homes 48
Homes for the People 48
Whewell, W. Philosophy of the
Inductive Sciences 37
History of the Inductive Sci-
ences 72
Elements of Morality 37
Philosophy of Discovery 98
Plurality of Worlds 38
Which; The Right or the Left 12
Whig. San Francisco Daily 105
While it was Morning 25
Whipple, E. P. Essays and Reviews 98
Lectures 98
Whist, Laws and Practice of 46
Whiston, W. Astronomical Prin-
ciples 38
White Acre v. Black Acre 12
White, C. Constantinople 57
White Chief, by Mayne Reid 25
White, Gilbert. Selborne 44
Whitehall 25
White Hoods 25
White, H. K. Life of 85
Poetical Remains 92
Poetical Works 92
White, J. History of France 66
White, Rev. J. Christian Centuries 30
White Jacket 25
White Lies 25
White, R. G. Shakspeare's Scholar 98
White Slave 25
White Slaves of England 25
Whitear, W. B. A Whale Ship 60
Whitefield, G. Voyage 53
Whitehall 12
Whitehead, C. E. Wild Sports 13
White Slave 13
Whiting, H. M. Life of Z. M. Pike 86
Whiting, W. Sermons and Memoirs 30
Whitman, Sarah H. Edgar Poe 86
Whitman, W. Leaves of Grass 92
Whitney, Anne. Poems 92
Whitney, J. D. Metallic Wealth 41
Whittier. J. G. Old Portraits 98
Literary Recreations 98
Whittlesey, C. Ancient Works 84
Life of John Fitch 86

Whyte, J. C. The British Turf 46
Widdupp, J. Of Celestial Bodies 40
Wide, Wide World 25
Widow and Marquis 35
Widow Barnaby 25
Wieber, F. M. The Widow Bedott Papers 13
Wieland. Oberon 92
Winland, by C. B. Brown 25
Wierzbicki, F. P. California 54
Wife's Sister 25
Wife's Trials and Triumphs 25
Wife's Victory. 25
Wigan, A. L. Duality of the Mind 36
Wight, W. O. Abelard and Heloise 86
Wigwam and Cabin 25
Wilberforce, S. Church 30
Wilcox, C. M. Rifles 48
Wild Flower 13
Wild Irish Girl 25
Wild Nell 25
Wild Scenes in a Hunter's Life 25
Wild Scenes on the Frontier 25
Wild Sports in the Far West 25
Wild Sports in the South 25
Wilfred's Lectures on the Rifle 108
Wilhelm Meister 25
Wilkes, C. U. S. Exploring Expedition 60
Wilkes, G. Europe in a Hurry 57
Wilkie, G. Manufacture of Iron 48
Wilkinson, Eliza. Letters 71
Wilkinson, G. Ancient Egyptians 88
Wilkinson on Color 47
Wilkins Wilder 25
Willaumez, Admiral. Dictionaire 104
Willett, W. M. Col. Marious Willet 71
William the Conqueror. Life 86
Williams, F. Annual Register 105
Williams, Rev. J. Life of Alexander 86
Williams, J. J. Tehuantepec 54
Williams, J. S. Invasion of Washington 71
Williams, Roger. Life of 86
Williams, S. W. Middle Kingdom 67
Williams, T., and Calvert, J. Fiji 60
Williams, W. R. The Lord's Prayer 30
Religious Progress 30
Williamson, H. North Carolina 71
Williard, Emma. Historia 71
Willibalds' Travels in Palestine 87
Willis, N. P. Here and There 57
Fun Jottings 57
Summer Cruise 57
Famous Persons and Places 57
Pencillings by the Way 87
Jenny Lind 86
The Convalescent 86
Health Trip 54
The Rag Bag 98
Out-Doors at Idlewild 98
Rural Letters 98
People I have met 98
Paul Fane 13
Willis the Pilot 13
Willmott, R. A. Literature 96
Wills, W. H. Old Leaves 98
Wilson, M. American History 71
Wilmer, C. A. Our Press-Gang 98
Wilmer, L. A. Life of de Soto 86
Wilson, A. Life of 86
Wilson, D. Life of Henrietta Robinson 85
Mexico 71

Wilson, H. H. and J. Mill. India 67
Wilson, J. On Punctuation 48
French Dictionary 104
Wilson, Prof. J. Noctes Ambrosianae 98
Recreations of Christopher North 98
Wilson, Rev J. L. Western Africa 69
Wilson, R. A. Mexico 54
Wing and Wing 25
Wingate's Maryland Register 62
Winnie and I 13
Winscom, Jane A. Onward 13
Winslow, C. F. Preparation of the Earth 44
Winter Lodge 13
Winterbotham, W. Of America 54
Chine 54
Winthrop, J. History of New England 71
Winthrop, R. C. Speeches 100
Wirt, W. Letters of the British Spy 54
Memoirs of 86
Life of Patrick Henry 86
Wise, J. Æronautics 30
Wise, Lieut. Los Gringos 54
Scampavias 54
Witchcraft 101
Witches of New York 13
Wit, Humor and Anecdotes 100, 101
Wither, O. Fair Virtue 92
Wolfden 25
Wollaston, W. Religion of Nature 30
Wolsey, Cardinal. Life of, by J. Galt 86
Life of, by G. Cavendish 86
Woman and her Master 25
Woman in White 26
Woman's Faith 25
Woman's Friendship 25
Woman's Life 25
Woman's Thoughts about Woman 98
Women of Israel 86
Of the Revolution 86
Of France 86
Wond, G. Future Life 13
Wood, J. Administration of Adams 34
Wood, W. Recollections of the Stage 86
Wood, W. H. H. Digest 31
Wood, W. M. Fankwei 59
Woodbury, Capt. D. P. On the Arch 40
Woodcraft 25
Woodhill 25
Woodstock 25
Woodward, R. B. History of Wales 60
Wooing and Warring 25
Wool Grower 105
Wo cester, J. E. Dictionary 104
Worcester, Florence of. Chronicles 66
Worcester, N. Last Thoughts 30
Wordsworth, W. Poetical Works 92
Yarrow Revisited 92
Working Farmer 105
World Here and There 25
World, The 98
Wormley, E. Amabel 13
Worth and Wealth 98
Worthea, W. E. Encyclopedia of Drawing 47
Wortley, Lady E. Travels 54
Wrangel, Admiral. Polar Sea 60
Wraxall, L. Armies of the Great Powers 86
Wraxall, N. W. Historical Memoirs 66
Posthumous Memoirs 66

Wraxall's Life in the Sea 108
Wright, Elizabeth C. Lichen Tufts 98
Wright, H. Missionary Discourses 30
Wright, Silas. Life and Times of 86
Wright, T. Biographia Britannica 86
Early Political Songs 92
History of Scotland 66
History of Essex 66
Dictionary 104
Wuthering Heights 13
Wyandotte 25
Wyatt, Sir T. Poetical Works 92
Wyatt, T. Memoirs of Generals, &c 86
Wycherley, Congreve, Vanbrugh 92

X

Xenophon's Anabasis 88
Cyropedia and Hellenics 88
Xerxes. Life of 86

Y

Year Book of Facts 40
Yeast, a Problem 25
Yeddo, Japanese Map of 62
Yellowplush Papers 95
Yemassee 25
Yoakum, H. History of Texas 71
Yonge, Catherine. Daisy Chain 13
The Castle Builders 13
Friarswood Post-Office 13
Beechcroft 13
The Heir of Redcliffe 13
Richard the Fearless 13
Heartsease 13
Yonge, C. D. Parallel Lives 86
Life of Wellington 86
Youatt, W. Sheep 43
Cattle 43
The Dog 43
The Horse 43
The Pig 43
Youman, E. L. Chemistry 40
Youmans, E. L. Household Science 49
Young, A. Chronicles 71
Young Americans Abroad 57
Young, D. Morristown Ghost 101
Young Duke 25
Young, E. Poetical Works 92
Night Thoughts 92
Young Foresters 25
Young Fur Traders 25
Young Men's Magazine 105
Young Middy 25
Young Student's Library 98
Young Voyagers 25
Young Yagers 25
Younger Son 25
Youthful Pilgrims 30
Yule-Tide Stories 13

Z

Zauesios, J. Predestination 30
Zanoni 25
Zarate, A. de. Histoire de Peru 71
Zenobia 25
Zilla 25
Zillah, The Child Medium 25
Zohrab 25
Zoology 42, 9
Zschokke, H. History of Switzerland 66

www.ingramcontent.com/pod-product-compliance
Lightning Source LLC
Chambersburg PA
CBHW030553270326
41927CB00007B/905